BLOOD SPORT

BLOOD SPORT

HUNTING IN BRITAIN SINCE 1066

EMMA GRIFFIN

YALE UNIVERSITY PRESS
NEW HAVEN AND LONDON

For information about this and other Yale University Press publications, please contact:

U.S. Office: sales.press@yale.edu   www.yalebooks.com
Europe Office: sales @yaleup.co.uk   www.yaleup.co.uk

Set in Perpetua by Carnegie Book Production, Lancaster
Printed in Great Britain by St Edmundsbury Press, Bury St Edmunds

Library of Congress Cataloging-in-Publication Data

Griffin, Emma.
    Blood sport: hunting in Britain since 1066 / Emma Griffin.
      p. cm.
    Includes bibliographical references.
    ISBN 978–0–300–11628–1 (alk. paper)
    1. Hunting—Great Britain—History.   I. Title.
    SK185.G66 2007
    799.2941—dc22

                                                                      2006039461

A catalogue record for this book is available from the British Library

10 9 8 7 6 5 4 3 2 1

For David and Benedict

Contents

List of Illustrations   viii

Acknowledgements   x

Prologue: 'How topping to be alive and well up in the hunt'   xi

Introduction   1

  1   A New Sport is Born   11

  2   A Royal Affair   25

  3   The Forest Charter   36

  4   Hunting Goes Tame   49

  5   The Tudors   67

  6   Elizabeth and the Puritans   77

  7   Two Sporting Monarchs   88

  8   Civil Wars and the Decline of the Deer   97

  9   A New Era Dawns   110

 10 Hunting the Fox: 'fascinating and soul stirring sport' 124

 11 'A busy and anxious disposition to legislate'   141

 12 Game Laws in the Nineteenth Century   152

 13 Hunting Attacked   163

 14 A New Jerusalem?   183

 15 A Last Reprieve   201

 16 The End of the Road   219

 17 Conclusion   235

Notes   240

Bibliography   264

Index   277

Illustrations

1. Excerpt from the margins of the third scene of the Bayeux Tapestry. *Bayeux Tapestry. A Comprehensive Survey.* Ed. Frank Stenton *et al.* London, 1957.   14

2. King John stag hunting. The British Library, Cotton MS Claudius, D II. f. 116. Reproduced by permission of the British Library, London.   30

3. A peasant netting a small bird using a net on a pole. *The Luttrell Psalter: Two Plates in Colour and One Hundred and Eighty-three in Monochrome from the Additional Manuscript 42130 in the British Museum.* Ed. Eric George Millar. London, 1932.   60

4. A peasant netting a covey of partridges. *Queen Mary's Psalter: Miniatures and Drawings by an English Artist of the Fourteenth Century, Reproduced from Royal Ms.2B.VII in the British Museum.* Ed. George Warner. London, 1912.   60

5. Women using nets and ferrets to catch rabbits. *Queen Mary's Psalter: Miniatures and Drawings by an English Artist of the Fourteenth Century, Reproduced from Royal Ms.2B.VII in the British Museum.* Ed. George Warner. London, 1912.   61

6. Queen Elizabeth poised to take the first cut of a stag. [George Gascoigne], *The Noble Arte of Venerie or Hunting.* London, 1575. Reproduced by permission of the Huntington Library, San Marino, California.   78

7. 'Unharbouring ye Stagg'. Richard Blome, *The Gentleman's Recreation.* London, 1686. Reproduced by permission of the Huntington Library, San Marino, California.   89

8. A tame deer being released from its cart for hunting. *Country Life* (1899).   107

9. Deer Park at Burley, Rutlandshire. The Stapleton Collection. Reproduced by permission of the Bridgeman Art Library.   108

10. Samuel Howitt, 'Partridge Shooting, 1'. *Orme's Collection of British Field Sports, Illustrated in 20 Beautifully Coloured Lithograph Plates from Designs by S. Howitt*. London, 1807. Reproduced by permission of Cambridge University Library.   120

11. Henry Alken, 'A Squire Trap, by Jove!' Nimrod [Charles James Apperley], *Life of John Mytton*. London, 1915.   132

12. 'A good day's work in the covers – counting the bag'. Reproduced by permission of the Mary Evans Picture Library, London.   155

13. An Edwardian lady mounting her horse *or* An Edwardian lady hunting side-saddle. *Country Life* (1901).   167

14. Followers of the Pytchley Hunt watching a fox escape from the hounds. Photo by John Chillingworth, 17 January 1953, Hulton Archive. Reproduced by permission of Getty Images.   190

15. The League Against Cruel Sports protest about a hunt, at The Swan in Amersham. Photo by Kent Gavin, 26 December 1963, Hulton Archive. Reproduced by permission of Getty Images.   191

16. Members of the Hunt Saboteurs Association using smoke bombs to stop huntsmen in Sussex. Photo by Loomis Dean, 1 February 1965, Time & Life Pictures. Reproduced by permission of Getty Images.   197

17. Hunting with the Quorn in the 1980s. Photo by Annie Baker. Reproduced by permission of Annie Baker.   206

18. The Countryside Alliance March, 1 March 1998. Photo by Mike Dodd. Reproduced by permission of Mike Dodd.   222

Acknowledgements

During the course of this project I have received financial support from a number of institutions, and encouragement and advice from colleagues, friends and family. The project was conceived and begun in the final year of my British Academy Postdoctoral Fellowship, and a semester at l'université de Paris VIII in 2004 provided the opportunity to start writing in earnest. The Gilder Lehrman Institute, Sidney Sussex College, Cambridge, and the UEA funded research trips which made completion of the book possible.

In a work of this nature, dealing with a long period and many themes, I have inevitably drawn upon the expertise of many colleagues and friends. I should like to express my especial thanks to the following. Ed Jaspers helped me to frame the original project and Robert Poole and an anonymous reader read the draft manuscript: the final version has been considerably strengthened by their comments and criticisms. Stephen Church, David D'Avray, John Griffin, Claire Griffiths, Tom Leng, Rob Liddiard, David Milne, Sarah Pearsall, and Andy Wood all read parts of the manuscript at various points, contributed useful suggestions, and saved me from error. Jane Bevan not only read the chapters on foxhunting, but also responded cheerfully to my questions about some of its finer points. In addition, I should like to thank Tim Blanning, Stephen Church and Diana Donald for allowing me to read their unpublished work. At Yale University Press, Heather McCallum has been an exemplary editor. Finally, my greatest debt of gratitude goes to my husband David Milne for encouragement throughout the project, for reading and commenting upon the entire text at several stages, and for providing such boundless love and support.

'How topping to be alive
and well up in the hunt'

I find it easy enough to recover a few minutes of that grey south-westerly morning, with its horsemen hustling on in scattered groups, the December air alive with the excitement of the chase, and the dull green landscape seeming to respond to the rousing cheer of the huntsman's voice when the hounds hit off the line again after a brief check. Away they stream, throwing up little splashes of water as they race across a half-flooded meadow. Cockbird flies a fence with a watery ditch on the take-off side. 'How topping,' I think, 'to be alive and well up in the hunt;' and I spurt along the sound turf of a green park and past the front of a square pink Queen Anne house with blank windows and smokeless chimneys, and a formal garden with lawns and clipped yew hedges sloping to a sunk fence. A stone statue stares at me, and I wonder who lived there when the house was first built. 'I am riding past the past,' I think, never dreaming that I shall one day write that moment down on paper; never dreaming that I shall be clarifying and condensing that chronicle of simple things through which I blundered so diffidently.

But the day's hunting is ended, and I must watch myself jogging back to the Kennels, soaked to the skin but quietly satisfied in my temporary embodiment with the Hunt establishment; beneath a clean-swept sky, too, for the rain-clouds have gone on with the wind behind them. Soon we are passing the village green; a quarter of a mile from the Kennels, Denis Milden blows a long wavering blast to warn the kennelman and the head-groom that we are almost home. When we turn in at a gate under some trees there are men waiting with swinging stable-lanterns, which flicker on their red jerseys, outside the long range of portable loose-boxes which Denis has put up. He and his whips are quickly off their horses and into the kennel-yard among the jostling hounds. He has told me to find my way indoors and get my tea and a bath. Cockbird is led into a loose-box under the superior eye of Meeston, the head-groom, a gruff, uncommunicative man in a long, dirty white kennel-coat. Cockbird gives his head a shake, glad to be rid of his bridle. Then he lowers it, and I pull his ears for a while — an operation which

most horses enjoy when they are tired. The place is pervaded by a smell
of oatmeal and boiled horse-flesh, and the vociferations of the hounds
accompany me as I tread stiffly through the darkness to a wicket-gate,
and so to the front door of the old wood-built huntsman's house ...[1]

These words, penned by the renowned First World War poet Siegfried
Sassoon, form a stark contrast to his earlier work. Sassoon's war poetry
cast an unsparing gaze on the horrors of trench warfare, unflinching in its
reflection of the appalling reality of life and death at the front. As the war
ended in 1918, Sassoon confirmed his alienation from the establishment
when he turned to the egalitarian promise of socialism. Having fought and
made friends with compatriots from the so-called 'working classes', Sassoon
became convinced that conservatism was morally bereft and that the stark
inequalities that existed in England required immediate attention.

As a man transformed by a hideous war, Sassoon nevertheless found that
some trappings of his previous life were harder to let go than others. Sassoon
was an avid huntsman and, through his eventful life, this love of the chase
never left him. Having branched into prose writing in the 1920s, Sassoon
published *Memoirs of a Fox-hunting Man* to critical and public acclaim in 1928.
In contrast to his bleak account of life in the trenches, *Memoirs* recounts the
idyllic life of a young man with a private income living the life of a rural
squire, immersed in cricket, writing and, above all, the pleasures of the hunt.
Sassoon's exceptional gifts as a writer were never more evident than when he
turned his attention to his favourite pastime.

Yet despite turning to a brighter subject matter in *Memoirs*, Sassoon's work
remained haunted by the spectre of the First World War. Sassoon was unable
to revisit the hunting world of his Edwardian youth without disclosing his
fears that the pleasures he recalled had been all but obliterated in the horrors
of war. However, while Sassoon was no doubt right that many of the trappings
of upper-class life had been lost forever, foxhunting was not amongst the
First World War's casualties. Most hunts scaled down their operations during
the war, but hunting never died. After 1918 it rose to ever greater levels of
popularity, giving pleasure to increasing numbers of people as each decade
passed. And the story of foxhunting in the twentieth century encapsulates
the history of hunting in England over the past millennium, with its endless
adaptations to a changing environment and ad hoc responses to the demands
of a growing population and a more complex society. Modernisation left its
mark on the world of hunting, but caused it to evolve rather than disappear.
The history of hunting is not a story of decline but of innovation and the
pages that follow shall trace this story.

Introduction

On 1 March 1998, a quarter of a million protesters took part in a peaceful march in central London – the largest public demonstration the country had seen since the anti-nuclear marches of the early 1980s. But these protesters were not the anti-establishment figures that have traditionally taken to the streets to rail against the ills of society. Instead, most of the people on the streets were right-wing voters, many participating in a public demonstration for the first time in their lives. They hardly fitted the archetype of your usual revolutionaries. In fact you might say that they were the 'establishment'.

Despite the organisers' claims that the march was an invitation to express concern about any aspect of country life, the protesters' banners and placards revealed a particular concern with one of the most conservative of rural issues: the future of foxhunting. The timing of the march (it was held just weeks before a strongly supported private member's bill designed to abolish hunting returned to the Commons) and its aftermath (the bill's failure) left little doubt about the true motivation of its organisers and participants. The largest and most politically significant demonstration of the decade was in reality a pro-hunting rally. It was a striking reminder of the depth and sincerity of feeling on the future of hunting within some sections of British society.

Unsurprisingly, the descent of the countryside upon Hyde Park aroused enormous political and social excitement, and for weeks beforehand heated discussion filled newspapers, radio and television broadcasts, and private homes. But in the midst of all this chatter some of the most remarkable aspects of the pro-hunting demonstration were missed. Hunting, after all, has held an unshakeable position in the upper reaches of English society for more than a thousand years. Through most of this time, the possibility that the hunters would be on the defensive was simply inconceivable. For centuries, hunting had been integral to elite life, the favoured pastime of many of Britain's most illustrious monarchs. William the Conqueror created fine forests, such as the New Forest in Hampshire, in order to indulge his passion for hunting, and his two eldest sons were killed during ill-fated hunting expeditions. Henry VIII enlivened his love letters to Anne Boleyn with dramatised accounts of his hunting exploits. James I drove his courtiers to distraction by neglecting business and whiling away his time on lengthy hunting expeditions. Such examples can be multiplied many times.

Indeed, certain members of the British monarchy continued to enjoy hunting's ruddy pleasures well into the twenty-first century. No less a personage than Prince Charles hunted with the country's most fashionable packs, and famously declared that he 'might as well leave this country and spend the rest of my life skiing' if the Labour government ever succeeded in making hunting illegal.[1] (With these comments, Charles mobilised Old Labour support for the bill more effectively than any government whip.) With patronage from such quarters, hunting's place in English society had appeared infallible.

Yet in 1998, Britain's hunters and their supporters were out on the streets, engaged in direct action of the kind that had traditionally been the preserve of the disenfranchised and the powerless. Nor do the surprises of the Countryside March stop here. Perhaps the most extraordinary aspect of the march was the indication it provided that hunting, in any form, still existed in late twentieth-century Britain. In the 1990s, hunting's continued popularity was too obvious to attract comment. But when one looks at it rationally, the fact that men and women continued to chase and kill wild animals in Britain on the eve of the twenty-first century, was the most curious aspect of this demonstration of all.

Hunting is an ancient activity that had been enjoyed in England long before the emergence of written records. But most prehistoric customs perished at some point on the journey to modernity, so why did hunting not share their fate? For most of the past millennium, Britain has been an agricultural society. Yet hunting and agriculture mix far less well than one might imagine. In a rural society where most people scratch out a living from the soil, nothing is more precious than land. The hunters need large reserves of land to protect and shelter the animals they wish to hunt, but if they take the finest land for their sport, where will their neighbours build their homes, grow their crops and raise their livestock? Occasionally hunting may have been the most productive way to exploit barren land, but many medieval forests were located on good-quality soils and their use as hunting grounds was a form of conspicuous consumption indicating a flagrant disregard for providing basic necessities for the people.[2] Most hunting harks backwards and stands bluntly opposed to the march of progress. Its survival from ancient to modern times could never be taken for granted.

Hunting comprises a blend of the traditional and the artificial – it is both naturalistic and highly contrived. Not only must land to hunt over be preserved, but so too must the wild animals themselves, as too much hunting will very quickly strip the land of anything left to chase. Few nations have been forced to confront the consequences of unchecked hunting more starkly than nineteenth-century America, where rapacious buffalo-hunting in the Great Plains reduced the bison population from an estimated 30 million in 1800 to a fraction of that – fewer than 1,000 – a century later.[3] Humans can kill wild animals far more quickly than the animals can reproduce themselves, and to avoid the decimation of animal stocks most hunting societies have developed more sustainable hunting practices. Hunters are usually the most diligent conservationists, managing the environment over which they hunt so as to conserve the animals' habitat, and restricting their hunting so as to preserve stocks. Hunting has always been a complex pastime; carefully managed, ever in conflict with other ways of exploiting the land, and often on the very brink of survival. It is not a timeless, peasant tradition, but an endless, and often artificial, attempt to protect huntable 'wild' animals in an ever more cultivated land.

In the thousand years that have elapsed between the Norman Invasion and the present, the precariousness of hunting has always been evident. The wild boar and the wolf, for example, both once native to Britain, were early victims of over-zealous hunting, disappearing at some point before the fifteenth century. Time and again, however, the greatest threat has come not from the hunters themselves but from the loss of the animals' natural habitat. At the time of William the Conqueror's invasion, no native animal was more highly revered than the wild deer. But a herd of wild deer requires a large and carefully protected woodland habitat if it is to thrive. As Britain's population steadily expanded, it became ever more difficult to justify preserving large expanses of the finest woodland for deer. Through the sixteenth and seventeenth centuries, landowners gradually chose to put their land to more lucrative uses, and during the Civil Wars, angry rebels massacred the nation's few remaining deer, not only for their flesh, but also, one suspects, in order to show their contempt for the privileged status that the deer had long enjoyed. Few landowners managed to replenish the deer on their estates with much success following the Restoration in May 1660, and by the eighteenth century, deer-hunting was largely confined to parks, and to a few rural outposts in Exmoor and Scotland. A sport that had lain at the heart of aristocratic life for centuries had moved to the periphery. It had become an expensive luxury that even the nation's wealthiest families were finding ever more difficult to pursue.

Not that this of course marked the end of hunting, for in its place more sustainable alternatives quickly sprang up. Hunting the fox had traditionally been held in very low esteem. Since the fox lacked the size, strength and physical beauty of a male deer, and was not even fit for the table, how could a true huntsman find sport in chasing it? But the qualities that had long made foxhunting a second-rate sport now offered the future of hunting a lifeline. The fox was vermin. There was no need to set aside valuable agricultural land as a breeding ground for foxes, as they managed to thrive in the most unfavourable of circumstances. The hunters simply needed land on which to hunt – and they did not even need to own it. Since foxes were pests and the hunters performed a useful function in killing them, it was not difficult to persuade landowners to grant the hunt access to their land. So as deer-hunting was squeezed out of existence, foxhunting took its place. A new national sport had emerged, enjoyed in all parts of the country, and not confined to the most remote and rural corners. Foxhunting positively thrived in some of the most densely populated parts of the south-east of England, on the outskirts of cities, and in suburban as well as rural areas. In the twentieth century there were several hunts in the Home Counties, some just a stone's throw from one of the world's largest cities, with many of their members no doubt exchanging the saddle for the commuter train on a Monday morning.

The rise of foxhunting from obscurity to respectability was quite remarkable, but establishing a new sport in a country in the throes of an industrial revolution was a delicate and uncertain operation. In the eighteenth century, the modern sport of foxhunting rapidly became so popular – and so effective – that the fox population teetered on the brink of extinction. It managed to survive only through the importation of thousands of fox cubs from Holland and France. The traffic in foxes and intensive breeding programmes gradually revived the fox population, but the future of foxhunting was still not assured. Keen hunters feared the enclosure of open fields would make the land they rode over inaccessible, but the new hedges that private landowners erected actually improved the sport by forcing the hunters to negotiate challenging jumps. In the nineteenth century, it was thought that the construction of the railways cutting through traditional hunting countries signalled the end of the hunt, yet the Victorian era became the heyday of foxhunting and the railways contributed to this growth by allowing hunters and their horses to travel to distant meets. In the twentieth century some feared that foxhunting would fail to survive the appearance of cars and motorways, yet once more the sport simply adapted to the changed circumstances: motorways were impassable, but the car extended the joys of the hunt to a wider audience by enabling people to follow on four wheels rather than on four legs.

Foxhunting had always been a minority sport, yet by the end of the twentieth century it was more popular than it ever had been. Doomsayers had often claimed that their beloved sport was knocking on heaven's door, but each time hunting had proved more adaptable than the pessimists had feared and swiftly evolved to fit new circumstances. And this, surely, was the most remarkable thing about the Countryside March. In the previous thousand years, English society had undergone a series of changes: modernising, urbanising, and industrialising. These combined forces had eventually put an end to forms of hunting that were wholly uneconomic. Yet in the face of these pressures, the hunters had nonetheless somehow managed to preserve their sport in a form that would be immediately recognisable to their medieval ancestors. Hunting's survival had been tortuous, but its roots in English history were deep indeed. No wonder an upstart politician's attempt to abolish hunting aroused the passions of those with the strongest links to Britain's rural past.

Hunting refers to the practice of chasing wild animals for the purpose of profit or sport. But despite endless variation in the details of hunting, there are certain common experiences integral to the art. At its heart, hunting involves an attempt to pit human wits against the wiles of the natural world. The hunters need an intimate knowledge of the animal kingdom; of the places animals lie, the hours they move, and the paths they take. They need to be able to read the ground, to understand animal behaviour, and to possess the skill and speed to react to an animal in flight. It is a challenge seductive in its simplicity, yet endlessly complex and unpredictable in execution. It has exercised and entertained men and women from all corners of the globe and in very diverse environments since the dawn of time.

At its simplest and most ancient, the hunt involves the pursuit of wildlife — perhaps for food, or to defend human settlements from dangerous predators. Either way, the hunters are driven by practical necessity, and this in turn determines the way they go about their task. Their goal will be to obtain a kill with the minimum of fuss, so they will probably use a combination of nets, traps and snares, as well as simple implements such as catapults or spears. The hunters may enjoy their work, but hunting for recreation is a privilege they cannot afford. They are hunting to acquire the valuable resources contained in an animal's carcass — its flesh, but also its bones for making tools, its hide for shelter and shoes, and its fur for clothing. Their aim is to expend as little energy as possible in acquiring these necessities. It is a form of subsistence characteristic of pastoral or hunter-gatherer societies, corresponding to a period in human history before the advent of agriculture and animal husbandry.

As societies turned from hunting and gathering to land cultivation, the symbolic and cultural dimension of the hunt assumed ever greater importance. The less any given society depended upon hunting for subsistence, the more potent a symbol of wealth and leisure it seemed to become. In ancient Egypt, for example, the cultivation of the valley of the Nile and the domestication of wild animals during the first three dynasties helped to diminish the importance of hunting as a source of nutrition. And at the same time, hunting found a new role as a form of recreation for those whose lives were uncomplicated by the daily grind of earning a living. In the Old Kingdom, the hunting of wild game became the privilege of the Pharaohs and noblemen, who employed professional huntsmen and beaters to assist with their sport. Kings and dignitaries hunted large animals for recreation: the peasants hunted smaller animals – geese, ducks and quails – to supplement their meagre diets. A class-based distinction had clearly emerged.[4] It was a pattern that would be repeated many times across the globe, as different parts of the world turned away from nomadic lifestyles to fixed agriculture.[5]

In ancient Greece, hunting became less important in providing basic sustenance for the people. As it lost its position as a necessary pursuit, so the symbolism and imagery of hunting became more pronounced. Mythology, art and literature from the time of Homer teem with hunting heroes, indicating the high regard in which the art of hunting was held.[6] Artemis, goddess of hunting, mountains and forests, was frequently illustrated in vase-painting and sculpture, armed with bow and arrow, pursuing wild animals.[7] Odysseus hunted with his dog Argos as a boy, even after a serious hunting accident at Parnassus, where he was gored by a great wild boar just above the knee.[8] The fourth of the labours of Heracles took him to Arcadia, where he was challenged to capture and bring back alive an Erymanthian boar. Other labours included slaying mythical creatures such as the Nemean lion, the many-headed Hydra, the Cerynitian hind, and the Cretan bull.[9] The Greek world was positively alive with hunting triumphs and terrors.

As in other early civilisations, it was the act of hunting, and not simply the flesh and bones which the hunter brought home, that mattered. Plato distinguished hunters who hunted for pleasure – the 'sacred hunters' – from those who hunted for food – 'idle men ... not worthy of praise'. The lazy hunter subdued his prey with traps and snares; he killed through deception 'instead of on the victory of a soul that likes struggle'. The sacred hunters went about their business in a far nobler way: they employed 'horses, dogs and [their own] bodies ... they use running, blows, and missiles thrown by their own hands to prevail over all their prey, and this is the type that should be practised by whoever cultivates the courage that is divine'.[10] The sacred hunters still expected to take home something for the pot, but displaying courage on the hunting field was more important than returning home with an overflowing game bag. For the ancient Greeks, hunting was about something more than the quest for food: it was an art, a skill, the ultimate symbol of a man's status and courage.

Egypt and Greece provide some of the earliest examples of societies where hunting developed as an elaborate, aristocratic ritual. Britain at this time was of course less advanced than these great civilisations, and there is little to suggest that hunting had assumed such mythic proportions here. In the first century BC, the Greek geographer Strabo observed that hunting dogs were exported from Britain to Rome. Perhaps these well-trained hounds were also used for hunting in Britain, but if they were, Strabo does not make this clear.[11] In the second century AD, Lucius Flavius Arrianus, a Greek historian born in Asia Minor, commented that 'Those Celts who do not make a living by hunting, dispense with the purse nets and hunt for the sheer pleasure of it ... You must be content if you kill even one hare in the season of winter. These hounds furnish great sport for you.'[12] Arrianus once again draws the crucial distinction between hunting for a living and hunting for 'the sheer pleasure of it'. It is not entirely certain, however, that he is speaking of the Celts in Britain.

It was not until the Romans left Britain in the fifth century AD that evidence of hunting's development becomes clear. The great Anglo-Saxon landowners possessed fine hunting grounds, and the occasional florid literary description indicates that they expected to acquit themselves in manly hunting expeditions within them. Their hunting took the form of a drive hunt. The hunters were divided into two teams – one waited silently, the other drove the herds of animals towards the hidden ambush. The result was comprehensive slaughter of wildlife. Dozens, hundreds even, of animals could be killed in a single day; the great drive hunts were efficient, but also, by necessity, occasional affairs.

The Norman Conquest marks a defining moment in the history of hunting in England. The Saxon overlords had certainly hunted for recreation, but the Normans imported new hunting techniques – the *par force* hunt – and their innovations were to alter hunting practices in Britain permanently. The *par force* hunt pitted a small band of hunters against one solitary wild animal. For the Normans, that solitary animal was usually a deer or a boar, though this of course changed in the centuries that followed. No matter what the quarry, the hunters' first task was to locate a suitable beast for that day's hunting. This was not a question of finding simply any animal to hunt, but rather of selecting a fine, strong animal – one likely to provide the hunting party with an exhilarating chase. At the appointed hour, dogs, horses and men set off in pursuit of their chosen prey. In contrast to the drive hunt, however, where the hunters drive their quarry to a fixed point, no one could know where a *par force* hunt would end, and the mounted huntsmen needed a firm seat and a steely nerve if they were to keep on terms with the hounds till the kill.

Most elements of the *par force* hunt have changed many times since the Norman Invasion of the eleventh century: the quarry, the hounds, the number of hunters, the way they select their quarry, and the way they kill it – all have changed countless times in the past one thousand years. But the essential form of the hunt – mounted riders, a trained pack of dogs, and a solitary focal point – has remained stubbornly constant. The pastime that grand landowners, pig-farmers, agricultural labourers and elderly ladies congregated in London to preserve in March 1998 may in fact be directly traced to the *par force* hunting introduced by the Norman nobility following the Conquest. The attacks on hunting challenged the value placed upon tradition in modern British society. Perhaps this is why a minority pursuit nonetheless polarised British society at virtually every level.

In common with much aristocratic hunting elsewhere in the world, the *par force* hunt was an ostentatious demonstration of wealth, power and prestige, not a utilitarian search for food. Picture the modern foxhunt: dozens of horses and riders, dozens of hounds at full pelt, maybe for several hours, before one fox is killed. Contrast the energy that the many riders, horses and hounds have spent with that contained in the one small fox they have killed. We might replace the fox with a larger edible animal – a deer, for instance – or even make it a good day's hunting, and replace the fox with two or three large, fat deer, but the essential problem with *par force* hunting – the fact that more energy is spent in killing the quarry than it contains – remains.[13]

In a well-fed society such as modern Britain no one needs to worry about the amount of energy used by horses, hounds and riders in pursuit of a fox. But turn the clock back a thousand years to a society in which famine occurred on a regular basis, and the problem becomes more apparent. Hunting may have been jolly good fun, but it was hardly a practical way of feeding a hungry population. In reality though, when one considers who actually hunted *par force*, this problem starts to recede. Those who adopted the fashionable new Norman hunting techniques were kings and magnates – the kind that did not need to worry about where their next meal would come from. The *par force* hunt might result in something good for the table, but it was the thrill of the chase that really mattered. It was a glorious visual display of a great landowner's many dogs, his fine steed and, of course, his own skill at remaining in the saddle. It provided him with the opportunity to demonstrate his wealth, status and skill in the way so prized by the medieval nobility.

Par force hunting has always been revered above all other forms of hunting. Its reputation, however, was built by the lucky few who rode to hounds, not by the many who were excluded. The great and the good scorn the traps and snares used by servants and the poor. But the majority of Britain's population could not afford to share this haughty view. We certainly should not forget that most lowly figure in hunting culture: the poacher. The poacher hunts contrary to the law. But whose laws have historically governed ownership of the wild animals and birds with which we share the land? In the late nineteenth century, the rural poor looked back nostalgically to an age when a wild animal was the property of whosoever had the wit and skill to catch it. Quite which era they were harking back to is not clear, however, as for a thousand years at least the law had been used to designate certain wild animals the exclusive property of the few, and anyone caught using his wit or his skills to catch them was branded a poacher and punished accordingly.

The perennial problem with hunting has been that each section of society has had its own ideas about who owns the wild animals that roam the countryside. The year 1066 introduced a new era in the history of hunting, but it also kicked off a fresh set of battles between all sections of society over who owned what. The records that enable us to sketch the history of hunting in England were not of course created with the needs of future generations of historians in mind. They are legal documents, recording the disagreements between landowners over who had the right to hunt where. They contain colourful incidents, such as the time when John Quennell, a sixteenth-century gentleman, caused chaos by encouraging drunken guests at a friend's christening party to indulge in a little post-dinner poaching and got so lost that he failed to reappear until the next morning. But history only tells us about Quennell's misadventure because he trespassed on another man's hunting in the process. Such anecdotes remind us of the conflicts that have long lain at the heart of hunting.

Hunting offers excitement, exhilaration and entertainment, but it brings in its wake complex social arguments, and the well-publicised battle over the future of hunting at the end of the twentieth century was simply the latest such skirmish in a very long line. From the time of the Norman Conquest, when William trampled over common law and landlords' crops alike by reclassifying wild animals as royal property, hunting of all kinds has been a source of social conflict. It is a driving concern in the medieval forest laws, in Magna Carta, in the Puritans' moral crusade, in Charles I's battles with his parliaments, as well as in the modern Labour Party. At every stage in Britain's history, the progress of hunting has reflected the power struggles, class divisions and social mores at the heart of our culture. The history of hunting is the story of a long struggle to gain mastery of the land and its resources. It is a story that affects all of us, whether we choose to hunt or not.

CHAPTER ONE

A New Sport is Born

[A hard man was the king ...]
He made great protection for the game
And imposed laws for the same
That who so slew hart or hind
Should be made blind
He preserved the harts and boars
And loved the stags
As if he were their father. (*Anglo-Saxon Chronicle*)[1]

At daybreak on Michaelmas Eve (28 September) 1066, the fleet of William, the ambitious Duke of Normandy, made landfall on the English coast near Pevensey, triggering a momentous and oft-recounted series of events. On his historic march to the town of Battle, six miles from Hastings, he glimpsed the rich and cultured land that was soon to be his. That land – woodlands, moorland, heaths, fenland, arable, grassland, marshes – all became William's following his slaying of the recently crowned Harold, just sixteen days later on 14 October. The new king lost no time in dividing up his spoils, keeping a quarter to himself and his half-brothers and granting a further quarter to his most trusted and loyal servants, numbering under a dozen in all. Though a few Anglo-Saxon tenants-in-chief successfully held on to their estates, much of what was left passed into the hands of immigrant lords.[2] This radical redistribution of the land took place on a scale never previously seen and was to shape the English landscape for centuries to come.

The illegitimate son of Robert I of Normandy and Herleva, a lowly tanner's daughter, William had become Duke of Normandy following his father's death in 1035. With many in the young duke's family hoping to benefit from his death, his childhood was dangerous: three of his guardians met untimely ends in suspicious circumstances, and his tutor was almost certainly murdered. In this world of bloodshed and violence, hunting wild animals was as natural as night following day, and the plains and forests of Norman France sheltered countless wildlife for the purpose. The wolves, bears, boars and many smaller animals (hares, rabbits, wildcats, foxes, martens, badgers, otters, squirrels and others) provided abundant quarry, but the animals prized most highly were the wild deer – the red, roe and fallow deer. The male red deer, or stag, was the largest and noblest of these. With a mature male measuring nearly four feet high, it outranked all others for the quality of its chase, and was even believed to possess a small bone in its heart which prevented it from dying from fear. And though the first years of William's reign afforded little time for hunting of any kind, as his rule became more secure in the 1070s William turned to his newly acquired English territories for the sport he had so enjoyed in Normandy earlier in life.

At the time of the Conquest, hunting was already firmly established amongst the great English landowners. A number of kings between the ninth and eleventh centuries were revered for their skill in the art of hunting. King Alfred, for example, was said by his biographer Asser to be an ardent hunter, toiling incessantly in every aspect of hunting and 'not in vain ... for no one else could compare with him in skill and success in that art'.[3] Edward the Confessor apparently indulged in hunting each day, heading to the glades and woods with huntsmen and dogs after his devotions were complete.[4] And Harold, before his early death, was regarded as a huntsman of particular skill: he is depicted in the second scene of the Bayeux Tapestry riding on horseback with hounds running ahead.[5] Skill at hunting was regarded as the mark of nobility: in the words of Eadmer of Canterbury, keeping horses and hunting with hounds was the mark of an earl.[6]

Yet our knowledge of hunting in England before the Conqueror's arrival is sketchy and, unusually, the only detailed account of English hunting practice concerns the sport not of royalty and nobility, but of their servants. It is contained in a dialogue to help boys with learning Latin written by the West Sussex monk Aelfric. This sole source, completed at the end of the tenth century, provides a unique insight into the world of early medieval hunting, and deserves to be quoted at length. According to the Dialogues of Aelfric, then:

MASTER:	Is this man one of your companions?
BOYS:	Yes, he is.
MASTER:	Do you know anything?
HUNTSMAN:	One craft only.

MASTER: What is that?

HUNTSMAN: I am a hunter.

MASTER: Whose?

HUNTSMAN: The king's.

MASTER: How do you practise your craft?

HUNTSMAN: I weave my nets and put them in the right place,
             and I train my dogs to chase wild animals, until they
             suddenly come to the nets and thus are trapped, and I
             cut their throats in the nets.

MASTER: Don't you know how to hunt without nets?

HUNTSMAN: I can also hunt without nets.

MASTER: How?

HUNTSMAN: I chase the wild animals with swift dogs.

MASTER: What kinds of animals do you usually catch?

HUNTSMAN: I catch stags and boars and deer and goats and
             sometimes hare.

MASTER: Did you go hunting today?

HUNTSMAN: No, because it is Sunday, but I went hunting yesterday.

MASTER: What did you catch?

HUNTSMAN: Two stags and one boar.

MASTER: How did you catch them?

HUNTSMAN: I caught the stags in nets, and I slew the boar.

MASTER: How did you dare to slay a boar?

HUNTSMAN: The dogs drove him toward me, and standing in front
             of him I suddenly cut his throat.

MASTER: That was very brave of you.

HUNTSMAN: A huntsman must not be fearful, because many kinds of
             beasts live in the woods.

MASTER: What do you do with your game?

HUNTSMAN: I give the king everything I catch, because I am his
             huntsman.

MASTER: What does he give you?

HUNTSMAN: He clothes me well and feeds me, sometimes he gives
             me a horse or an arm-ring, so that I will more willingly
             exercise my craft.[7]

That Aelfric's *Dialogues* is concerned with the king's huntsman and not with
the king needs to be stressed, for, as we shall see, hunting was an important
marker of status, and a king could hardly be expected to hunt in the same
way as his servants. Nonetheless the account details three basic hunting
techniques which, though reworked in many different contexts by hunters

1. Two men hunting on foot, armed with batons and dogs, seen here along the bottom of this excerpt from the margins of the third scene of the Bayeux Tapestry.

of different means and abilities, formed the backbone of hunting practice for several centuries. Firstly, the dialogue describes the use of nets – the most efficient and functional form of hunting wild animals practised in the Middle Ages. Nets, traps and snares were the tools of the huntsman when the primary purpose of the hunt was food rather than recreation, and this was consequently the technique employed by the lesser huntsman – the peasant hunting for his own needs or those of his master – rather than by the nobility. Secondly, the dialogue illustrates the simple chasing of wild animals with swift dogs, a technique familiar at all levels of society. Trained dogs were capable of killing all but the largest wild animals, though the huntsmen might also use bow and arrow to slow the animal's flight or a sword to kill it outright. The margins of the Bayeux Tapestry show two men hunting in this style, running after their dogs in pursuit of a wolf, armed with batons in both hands.[8] Another scene from the margins depicts two large hounds pulling down a stag while a dismounted huntsman looks on.[9] All, from the wealthy landowner to the peasantry, hunted with swift dogs, though those with the means hunted on horseback, rather than on foot, as befitted their superior station. Thirdly, in explaining the boar hunt, the *Dialogues* describes the use of a simple ambush. This, sometimes known as a 'drive hunt', involved dividing the hunters into two teams, one of which – the beaters – drove the hunted animal towards the other – the hidden huntsmen, commonly wielding a bow, though in this instance a sword.

An Anglo-Saxon charter from Worcestershire suggests that the third of these techniques – the drive hunt or ambush – occupied a place of particular importance in eleventh-century England. In a letter to King Edgar, Bishop Oswald set out the terms on which he leased his land: assistance with his deer hunt was a condition of tenure. Some of this assistance involved building and furnishing a hunting lodge and providing spears, but other duties – such as digging ditches, erecting fences and beating game – suggest that some form of drive hunting was being practised.[10] In Weardale, the inhabitants of Alcletshire were required to build a hunting lodge in the forest sixty feet long, with a buttery, larder, chamber and latrines, and to erect a hedge around the lodge for their landowner, the Bishop of Durham.[11] The frequent reference to deer-hedges in eleventh-century charters suggests that the deer were being driven or corralled into an enclosure, where the archers would shoot at them, presumably from some sort of standing.[12] The size of the lodges and the sheer number of men called upon to assist indicate that these Anglo-Saxon deer hunts are taking place on a large scale: they were grand and public affairs. Such deer hunts, therefore, not only resulted in venison for the table, they were also an overt display of wealth and power. The hunting techniques were fundamentally the same as those used by the servants in Aelfric's *Colloquy* when hunting boar, but they have been scaled up considerably to fit the needs, both practical and symbolic, of a great landowner.[13]

There are several unanswered questions concerning the hunting practices of pre-Conquest English lords, but we know even less of William the Conqueror's hunting, beyond the simple fact that he was a keen huntsman. The chronicler Ordericus Vitalis recalled William once enjoying 'one of his regular hunting expeditions in the Forest of Dean' and, the *Anglo-Saxon Chronicle* reminds us, he loved the red deer as much 'as if he were their father'.[14] What hunting techniques he used, however, and how, if at all, these differed from contemporary English practice is impossible to establish. We are on more certain ground in turning to consider the land policies that William introduced in pursuit of his sport. William developed a network of forests and forest laws, and his forest policies have left an indelible mark on the ecology of the English countryside.

If deer are to thrive, large tracts of quiet, protected woodland are needed. To enable the deer to graze, the vert – trees, grass and bushes – needs to be preserved, so other animals' grazing must be restricted. Woodland requires protection from wood-felling and from animals such as sheep and goats that destroy young trees. No less importantly, some form of control over hunting, particularly during the breeding season, is necessary so that a new generation of deer can take the place of those hunted. Maintaining a huntable population of wild deer requires a complex and protected habitat, and William introduced new policies to ensure that the finest English forests provided just the protection needed by wild deer.[15]

His policy is known by the name of 'afforestation', though it did not involve the homely planting of trees that the word implies. Afforestation involved not tree-planting, but the mere naming of large tracts of land as royal forest: in other words, land became forest by nothing more than royal diktat. Indeed, the land incorporated into the royal forests did not even need to be woodland: common land, arable land, heath and moor, were all incorporated into the 'royal forest'. The defining feature of a royal forest was simply that it had been decreed as such by the king. Of course, the idea underlying the creation of forest was the preservation of deer, and as these flourish in woodland, the nucleus of the royal forests consisted of wooded areas. But the match was not exact, and the forest could, and did, contain inhabited and cultivated areas.[16]

Once land had been classed as royal forest, it did not itself become the property of the Crown. Instead, following afforestation, the land and people within the royal forest became subject to a distinct code of law – the forest law – lying outside the common law of the realm. Forest law placed large tracts of land and their inhabitants under the personal rule of the king, governed by courts and officers of his own appointment.

Within the royal forests, new concepts of ownership regarding the wild animals were introduced. The Anglo-Saxons, following Roman jurists, had reasoned that until they were captured wild animals, no matter where they were found, were *res nullius*: property with no owner. Thus anyone could hunt the wild beasts on the land where they found them, so long as it did not lead them to trespass on another's land. William reversed this assumption. He argued that certain animals – the red deer, the fallow deer and the roe deer – within his forests were not ownerless: they belonged to him. When land was declared forest, the right to hunt wild deer was therefore removed from local landowners and inhabitants and vested in the king alone. Anyone caught killing deer was henceforth guilty of theft of the king's property. As deer tend to wander periodically out of wooded areas, the newly created 'forests' covered an area far beyond the woodland in which deer normally reside; hence medieval 'forests' that extended beyond the woodland with which we now associate the term.

How far the Norman kings built upon Anglo-Saxon traditions in the construction of their network of forests is difficult to establish. English hunting grounds had been confined to land in and around the royal palaces; it was only on the king's own lands that his hunting was protected. Norman forests, by contrast, covered large swathes of land belonging to others. The true origins of William the Conqueror's royal forests are most likely to be found not in Anglo-Saxon England but in Norman France. Post-Conquest charters reveal a similar set of assumptions regarding the protection of deer and their habitat on both sides of the Channel, and these charters undoubtedly drew upon older Norman traditions. The principle of royal forests is evident in ninth-century charters of Charlemagne in which he granted land to his subjects but reserved the rights over 'vert and venison' for himself, and although many of the institutions of Charlemagne's empire were dismantled in the years following its collapse, the protection of vert and venison remained intact. Indeed, as Duke of Normandy, William himself granted woods to the abbey of Caen in which he reserved 'in his lordship' the stags, roe and wild boar in the woods, and forbade the cutting of woods and clearing of the land. When he introduced forest law to his new kingdom, therefore, he was building upon the Norman principle of splitting ownership of animals from ownership of the land. English forests were the application of a long-established Norman tradition to a newly acquired territory.[17]

For those who found themselves living on land that the king had incorporated into his forests, life changed dramatically. In extreme cases, the local people were expected to quit their homes in the forest. During the creation of Hampshire's 'New Forest' in 1079, for example, 'so great was [the king's] love of hunting ... that he laid waste more than sixty parishes, forced the peasants to move on to other places, and replaced the men with beasts of the forest so that he might hunt to his heart's content'.[18] This story, so often repeated by the chroniclers, was almost certainly exaggerated.[19] It may occasionally have happened that villagers were forced to quit their homesteads but it should be emphasised that the expulsion of the original inhabitants was in no way integral to the creation of forests. Afforestation involved not wholesale eviction of the local inhabitants but the imposition of a new code of law upon them. And so long as they agreed to abide by the new laws, those who had traditionally lived and farmed the wooded areas were generally permitted to stay. As the landscape historian Oliver Rackham has helpfully clarified: 'all land, even roughland, in eleventh-century England belonged to someone and was used. The king's deer added to, and did not replace, whatever was already going on.'[20] Undoubtedly though, local inhabitants found their lives much harder than they had previously been. The new forest laws may have allowed the woodland dwellers to stay put, but they ensured that the animals and timber they had once exploited were now effectively placed beyond their reach.

In order to protect the king's deer, the forest law prohibited the hunting, not simply of deer, but of all animals in the royal forests, save by special licence. Likewise the setting of primitive traps and snares was forbidden. Unrestricted hunting, it was reasoned, would disturb the king's game, as well as prove an impossible temptation to poaching for many. Thus William prohibited bows and arrows within the royal forests and insisted on the mutilation of dogs in and around his forests, in order to prevent them running after his deer. He ordered that all large dogs have their toes removed – a procedure known as 'lawing', and described by one later authority as follows: 'the mastive being brought to set one of his forefeet upon a piece of wood eight inches thick and a foot square, then one with a mallet, setting a chissell two inches broad upon the three claws of his forefoot, at one blow doth smite them cleane off'.[21] The king's deer were to remain untouched under all circumstances: even should they enter fields and damage crops, landowners had no choice but to stand by and let the animals be. For any inhabitant brave or foolhardy enough to kill deer in the face of these harsh laws, severe penalties were imposed.[22]

Unsurprisingly, these policies left many of William's new subjects feeling deeply dissatisfied. The lords that held manors in newly afforested areas admittedly kept hold of their lands, but lost their right to exploit the most valuable resources contained within them. Their plight is illustrated by an account of the afforestation of three settlements in Hampshire: Nether Wallop, Over Wallop and Broughton. Prior to afforestation, the lord of the manor had enjoyed 'honey and pasture to make up his farm, and wood for building houses'. By the time of the Domesday Book (produced in 1086), all three settlements were in the royal forest of Buckholt; the king's men, it was lamented, now had these things, and the reeve was left with nothing.[23] A few favoured subjects managed to retain some rights in their afforested woods. The Bishop of Worcester, for example, though he lost 'the honey and the hunting and all profits' from his wood at Ripple in Worcestershire, nonetheless retained the right to pasture his pigs in the forest and to cut wood for his own use.[24] But these were small pickings from the table of riches they had once enjoyed, and the grounds for the chroniclers' displeasure were real indeed.

Within a few decades of the Conquest, the world of hunting had changed markedly. William had introduced a programme of land management to ensure the preservation of woodland and deer. It is not known exactly when William embarked upon the construction of royal forests, but Domesday shows that several royal forests (*foresta regis*) were in place by that date.[25] By the end of his rule, he had established twenty-one royal forests, encompassing many fine reserves of uncultivated woodland protected from logging and exploitation. Perhaps his greatest legacy was the creation of his Nova Foresta (the New Forest) – a forest of ancient woodlands and wilderness heaths that remains largely intact today, earning the area national and international status.

But most of his subjects saw the matter very differently. A right once universally held and widely exploited had been lost by the unfortunate few living within the king's forest, and although outside the forests these rights remained intact, since nothing but the king's whim determined what land was taken into the forest, all had reason to fear this development. For them, the forest law did not look like a responsible programme of forest management but an oppressive and unwelcome act of royal power. The policies William promulgated to protect his noble quarry left his barons and bishops with little but second-rate hunting land, and transformed hunting into a contentious and politicised issue.

Matters were not improved by the succession of his son. At his death in 1087, the Conqueror bequeathed his English kingdom to William, his second, and favourite, son. William II was a quarrelsome and irreligious man. Short and stout, blond-haired and ruddy-skinned, he enjoyed the pleasures of the chase as much as his father, and was determined to protect the forests he had created.[26] He did, however, extend the benefits of his royal hunting prerogative to favoured subjects – a cheap way of rewarding royal service. He did so by granting landowners rights of 'chase' and of 'warren'. Rights of chase varied widely, but they usually gave the landowner the exclusive right to hunt deer, and sometimes entitled him to imprison poachers as well. By vesting all rights in the landowner, these grants of chase effectively removed the ancient hunting rights previously held by the landowner's tenants. A right of warren gave its holder exclusive hunting rights over small animals, such as hares, rabbits, foxes, wildcats and pheasants, on his land; the charter named exactly which animals it covered. Though such animals were considerably less valuable than deer, they were not entirely without worth, and their meat and pelts could bring a useful profit to the hunter. And just like the rights of chase, warrens extinguished the hunting rights of tenants and occupiers in favour of those of the landowner.[27]

Grants of chase and warren were not numerous in the eleventh century. They were made so infrequently that they had little impact on most people's lives. Yet, just like the forests, they hint at a significant shift in assumptions respecting ownership of the country's wild animals. In Anglo-Saxon England, the right to kill wild animals had rested with the occupier of the land on which they were found: tenants, no matter how humble, had been permitted to trap and snare any wild animals on their land, and neither king nor landowner had the authority to interfere with this. In granting rights of chase and warren, the king claimed the power to remove these rights from tenants and bestow them upon the landowner. In effect, these concessions made it clear that the right to protect hunting in a given area was vested in the king alone.

In reality, however, William's subjects either did not grasp or did not care about the shift in policy that charters of this nature implied. Those with any voice objected only to the Crown's failure to grant more hunting charters, not to the principles that informed them. It was the royal forests, not the chases or warrens, which formed the focus of their complaints. Though few were affected by grants of chase and warren, many were directly affected by the policy of afforestation, and they deeply resented these encroachments on the best hunting land. William's chroniclers rarely failed to voice their dissatisfaction with the royal forests, alleging that the king had increased the penalties for interfering with them, ordering that those who shot at his deer would henceforth have their hands cut off, and those who disturbed them would be blinded. The monk and scholar William of Malmesbury even claimed that William put to death those who took his deer in his forests, though as no records from the forest courts have survived, there is no way of establishing whether this penalty was ever actually imposed.[28]

In a fitting end, William II was himself killed – 'struck by an arrow aimed carelessly' – while hunting in the New Forest in 1100.[29] Whether this arrow was shot by accident or design is unknown, but his chroniclers never failed to read into the event divine retribution for the barbaric rule of his father and for his own countless sins. As John of Worcester concluded, 'This showed without doubt a miraculous vengeance of God'.[30]

Three days after William's fatal hunting accident, his younger brother, Henry I, was crowned at Westminster. Henry not only held on to William II's additions, but proceeded to add considerably to the royal forests. A new royal forest on the eastern edge of Leicestershire was amongst the earliest of his creations.[31] He then made afforestations in Bedfordshire and Yorkshire, and by the end of his rule most of the county of Essex appears to have lain within the bounds of the forest.[32] His chroniclers took a dim view of these policies. William of Newburgh claimed that 'from his ardent love of hunting, [he] used little discrimination in his public punishments between deer killers and murderers'.[33] Harsh forest laws may have protected royal hunting, but were bought at the price of universal, biting dislike.

Henry was an obsessive hunter. He was present in the New Forest at the time of his brother's death, 'immoderately attached' to the sport in the opinion of one of his chroniclers, and known to absent himself from the woes of government and disappear hunting in his forests for days.[34] Boar-hunting was one of his favourite sports, and it may have been Henry who added the boar to the list of animals protected by the forest laws.[35] He built himself a house at Beaumont on the north side of Oxford and a hunting lodge at Woodstock, and there enclosed a park within a stone wall seven miles long. William of Malmesbury wrote that 'He took a passionate delight in the marvels of other countries, asking foreign kings to send him animals not found in England – lions, leopards, lynxes, or camels – and he had a park called Woodstock in which he kept his pets of this description.'[36]

The evidence for the importance of hunting to the Norman kings is overwhelming. A central plank of policy for William the Conqueror and his two sons was the creation, maintenance and protection of the royal forests and it can fairly be assumed that hunting ranked high on their list of priorities. But documenting the existence of the forests is far easier than answering the simplest of questions concerning their use. Did the kings hunt personally in their forests, or was the hunting performed by their servants? And if the kings did themselves hunt, how exactly did they hunt, and did their hunting differ from that of the English overlords who had hunted there before them?

An account book – the 'Establishment of the King's Household' – that survives from the reign of Henry I helps us to answer some of these questions. The 'Establishment', a set of accounts for the year 1136, possibly kept by the king's treasurer, Nigel of Ely, lists in detail the payments made to over one hundred individuals working in the royal household, and enables us to provide an outline of the royal hunting staff.[37] The section on hunting lists a varied staff, including knight huntsmen, keepers of the kennels and hounds, huntsmen of the wolf hunt, horn-blowers, hunt servants, and archers (including some who 'carried the king's bow'), each earning between one and eight pence a day.[38] In addition, the king paid for the men's livery and the purchase and upkeep of numerous dogs and horses. The dogs were divided into three packs, each with specific functions: the wolf hunt, the king's pack and the main pack. The duties of the wolf hunt are self-explanatory; it contained eight greyhounds and twenty-four racing dogs; £6 a year was set aside for the purchase of horses, and twenty pence a day for the huntsmen's clothes. The remaining men and dogs were divided between the king's hunt and the main hunt. Division between these two packs was not firmly fixed, though it appears to have corresponded with the king's hunting for recreation on the one hand, and that of his servants undertaken in order to bring food to the royal table on the other. Both men and dogs shifted between the two hunts as needs changed.[39]

Just as in Anglo-Saxon England, therefore, within the royal household hunting played two distinct roles. On the one hand there was the hunting undertaken by paid servants for reasons of necessity rather than leisure: the wolf hunt, for example, whose purpose it was to keep the wolf population in check, and the main hunt, occupied with the task of procuring venison

and other foodstuffs for the king's larder. Clearly, however, for the royal
household hunting was more than a menial task to be undertaken by servants:
the king also personally hunted and employed a large and complex establishment of paid officials and specially trained hounds to assist him. The
knight's huntsmen were paid eight pence a day (the payment of a knight);
their task was presumably also to assist the king. The payments to the four
horn-blowers suggest that music was employed – in order, no doubt, to help
distinguish between the king's recreational hunting and the utilitarian hunting
of his servants. One imagines that the royal hunt was an occasion of some
importance: the king and his knights riding out in the company of numerous
dogs and servants, to the strains of hunting music, must have made a very
fine pageant.

How the king hunted is a more difficult question to answer, as there is no
information in the 'Establishment' relating directly to this problem. Given the
complexity of the hunt establishment, however, it seems likely that hunting
took many forms, according to who was hunting, and what they sought to kill.
In all, the account lists nearly a dozen types of dog: hounds, bloodhounds,
running hounds, leash hounds, big leash hounds, small hounds, big harrier
hounds, small harrier hounds, brachet hounds, racing hounds and greyhounds
are all mentioned, and this suggests that the hounds were employed in a very
wide range of roles according to the exact nature of the hunt. The breeding
and training of dogs was relatively advanced, and from this we may surmise
that hunting had indeed become an art by the early twelfth century.

A little more information about the nature of the king's personal hunting
can be gleaned from the twelfth-century chronicles, though the information
they contain is tantalisingly brief. The account of William II's death contained
in Ordericus Vitalis' *Ecclesiastical History* provides a rare descriptive account
of royal hunting in the eleventh century. It tells of William mounting his
horse, and departing at speed with a number of 'eminent men' to enjoy
a day's hunting in the New Forest. On reaching the interior of the forest,
William, Walter Tirel and a few others separated from the other hunters: 'as
they stood on the alert waiting for their prey with their weapons ready'.[40]
According to Ordericus, when Walter shot at a stag that suddenly appeared,
his arrow grazed the animal's back and sped onwards, wounding and killing
the king. Here we have a clear description of a small-scale drive hunt, with
the king and a handful of followers divided into two teams: one (the beaters)
driving the stag towards the other (the silently waiting archers). Gaimar's
account of the same incident in his *History of the English* is broadly similar.
Gaimar describes the king heading on horseback to Brokenhurst in the New
Forest, and dismounting when he saw a passing herd of deer in order 'to
shoot at a stag'.[41] Both accounts suggest that the horses are used in order to

reach quarry: the king and other statesmen enjoy the privilege of shooting at the stag, but this is done from a stationary position and not while their steeds are moving.

The few other accounts of eleventh-century hunting contained in the chronicles are couched in rather vague terms and contain little explicit detail about the nature of the hunt. They describe kings whiling away long hours hunting in the forests.[42] Furthermore, the frequency with which members of the royal household met their death suggests that hunting often involved hard riding at breakneck speed. William's elder son, Richard, for example, died before adulthood in a hunting accident. Ordericus informs us that 'whilst he was galloping in pursuit of a wild beast he had been badly crushed between a strong hazel branch and the pommel of his saddle'.[43] His grandson, another Richard, died in a similar accident in the same forest.[44] These deaths suggest that hunting in the early twelfth-century forests was a risky business, and that skilled horsemanship was an essential accomplishment for the aristocratic hunter, but exactly why there was so much fast-paced riding when it appears that the actual kill was performed from a stationary position is not entirely clear.

Descriptions emphasising the speed of the hunt indicate that something had changed since Anglo-Saxon times, as there is no evidence that the drive hunting practised before the Norman Conquest called for courageous chases through the forest. The Anglo-Saxon evidence suggests that deer were chased or driven through the woods by servants; the kill was the most revered element of the hunt, and this was performed by the lords from a hidden, stationary position. William's son – 'galloping in pursuit of a wild beast' – does not appear to be following the conventions of the Anglo-Saxon drive hunt. Had the Norman kings imported new hunting techniques, or is this simply a case of more detailed records providing new evidence for an old practice? For the present, such questions remain frustratingly impossible to answer.

By the end of Norman rule, the royal hunting privilege was firmly and unambiguously asserted. William the Conqueror had established a band of royal forests, mostly located in areas of poor soil, which were well wooded and sparsely populated, and his two sons had consolidated these holdings in considerable measure. Both had not only extended the royal forests, but, through the grants of chases and warrens, bolstered their father's claim to a unique royal hunting prerogative. Reflecting on the youngest son's rule, Ordericus concluded that Henry had 'claimed for himself the hunting of the beasts of the forest throughout all England'.[45] It was of course something of an exaggeration, but the chroniclers' frequent complaints of the Norman kings' excessive control over wooded areas were certainly born of experience.

Furthermore, there can be no question that the new monarchs viewed their forests both as valuable territorial possessions and as personal hunting grounds, to be enjoyed for recreation as well as for profit. All three kings hunted within some of the newly created forests. By the time of Henry's death, hunting was defined as a courageous and high-status activity, and it was set to dominate aristocratic life and politics for many centuries to come.

CHAPTER TWO

A Royal Affair

It is in the forests too that 'King's chambers' are, and their chief
delights. For they come there, laying aside their cares now and then, to
hunt, as a rest and recreation. It is there that they can put from them
the anxious turmoil native to a court, and take a little breath in the
free air of nature. (Richard fitz Nigel)[1]

Wild animals, which are gifts of nature, are claimed by [the kings of
England] even under the watchful eye of God ... A fact that excites
surprise is the frequent practice of declaring it a crime to lay snares for
birds ... You have heard it said that birds of the sky and fishes of the
deep are common property, but those that are hunted ... belong to the
royal treasury. (John of Salisbury)[2]

Despite the apologies of the king's treasurer – Richard fitz Nigel – for
the royal forest, the forest policies of William and his two sons provoked
a burning hatred among their subjects and John of Salisbury's searing
indictment was certainly more representative of twelfth-century opinion.
But the royal forests, the forest law, and the forest courts and officials that
the Normans had introduced, were all here to stay. Indeed, the strength
of their Angevin successors' rule in the twelfth century guaranteed their
extension for a further hundred years. It has been claimed that at their peak
in the middle of the century royal forests contained one-third of the land
in England.[3] They were highly valued both for their hunting and as a useful
economic asset, and a succession of strong kings with no need to curry favour
had no intention of relinquishing them.

The expansion of the royal forests, however, was by no means easy. Like

William II and Henry I before him, one of Stephen's first acts was to promise to relax the much reviled forest laws in a bid for support. But when civil war broke out in earnest three years later, it became clear that events in history were about to take a new turn. Despite his initial determination to hold on to his forests, Stephen soon found that not only was he making generous disafforestations in a bid to gain support for his military campaign, but that his enemies were too.

Civil war broke out in 1139 when Matilda contested Stephen's claim to the throne. War wrought havoc on the forests. Stephen and Matilda both matched their claims to the throne with claims to the forests, and set about dispensing forest favours in return for political support. Thus Matilda purchased the support of powerful nobles such as the Earl of Essex and the Earl of Oxford by granting them charters acquitting them of forest offences, enabling them to cut timber in their woods, and giving them licence to bring the land under the plough without penalty. She granted to Miles of Gloucester the Forest of Dean in return for his support – a generous gift indeed.[4] Stephen issued similar charters to loyal supporters exempting their holders from the constraints of forest law. The warring parties both used disafforestation and the sale of privileges as inducements for support, and as they did so the edifice of forests created by the Norman kings began to crumble.

Not only did the civil war cause the disafforestation of parts of the royal forests; it also severely weakened authority in those forests that remained intact. Embroiled in civil strife over his disputed throne, Stephen's attention was inevitably turned away from hunting and forests, and with royal power weakened, local magnates and humble forest dwellers united in wreaking a devastation that was as much symbolic as it was real. Stephen's chronicler considered that 'Wild animals, which before had been most scrupulously preserved in the whole kingdom ... were now molested in every quarter, scattered by the chance-comer and fearlessly struck down by all'.[5] Without trustworthy officials monitoring the forests, the forest law was effectively reduced to nothing. Stephen's chronicler noted that during the course of his rule, 'many thousands of wild animals, which formerly had overflowed the whole land in numerous herds, were so suddenly exterminated that from such a countless swarm you could soon have scarcely found two together'.[6] Undeniably, the tale is retold with a touch of artistic licence, and historians have begun to suggest that the anarchy with which Stephen's reign is usually associated has been exaggerated.[7] But the impact of the civil war upon the royal forests was certainly unmistakable. With only nominal control over parts of the kingdom, Stephen was unable to enforce petty regulations concerning the right to chop timber and hunt deer. By the end of his rule, the boundaries of the forest had retreated, and royal authority in what remained was much weakened. Events had shown that only with an iron grip on power could any monarch hold on to his hunting privileges.

The balance in favour of the nobles proved to be short lived, however, for order was restored in 1154 by Stephen's heir, Henry II, a ruthless king and a hard, hunting man – he was, according to his irreverent clerk, Walter Map, 'a great connoisseur of hounds and most greedy of that vain sport'.[8] In disapproving tones, his chroniclers recounted instances when the business of governing came second to the king's favourite pastime. In a dispute between the towns of Battle and Canterbury, for example, the Abbot of Battle travelled to the king's court at Westminster, 'but could get nothing that day since the king had gone hunting'.[9] Fully confident of his claim to the throne, and intent on regaining the royal prerogatives held by his grandfather, Henry II pushed the area of the royal forests to their greatest extent.[10]

At his coronation, Henry made good the losses incurred during Stephen's reign by restoring the forests to the extent they had been at the time of Henry I's death. The Forest of Dean was reserved to the Crown following Miles's death in 1155; and the whole county of Essex, granted away in the 1140s by a series of charters, was once more brought back into the forest.[11] In the long reign that followed, Henry steadily extended the forests yet further, adding lands in Nottinghamshire, Leicestershire, Derbyshire, Oxfordshire and Buckinghamshire, amongst others.[12]

The forests were central to royal policy throughout the twelfth century, and the reasons for this are not hard to find. They were filled with valuable natural resources; supplying food for the royal table, timber for royal building and, perhaps most significantly of all, much-needed revenue for the royal purse.[13] Many of the royal forests were farmed out; leased to men ready to cultivate the land in a way that was consistent with forest law. Walter Waleran, for example, rented land in the New Forest throughout Henry II's reign and through much of his successor's for an annual rent of £25. During Henry's rule, forest rents averaged about £125 a year – a modest, but no doubt useful, sum.[14]

Added to the money from forest rents were the larger sums that the king regularly collected in the form of forest fines. The largest fines were imposed upon those found guilty of killing the king's deer, but a host of much smaller fines were also enacted for any damage caused to the woodland they inhabited. The first of Henry's forest eyres was held in 1166. It was co-ordinated by the king's newly appointed chief forester, Alan de Neville, and raised £502 for the Crown. The contempt in which this man was held by the twelfth-century chroniclers for performing this task speaks volumes about contemporary attitudes to the forests. The chronicler of Battle Abbey, for example, recorded that 'This Alan never left off plaguing both ecclesiastics and laymen so long as he lived, in order to enrich the king. To please an earthly king, he feared not to offend the king of heaven.'[15] He was excommunicated in 1168 by Thomas Becket, Archbishop of Canterbury, for having kept his chaplain in chains.[16] Later eyres held in 1179 and 1185 raised £1,007 and £2,403 respectively.[17] When put in the context of the total royal revenue – an estimated average annual revenue of a little under £20,000 – Henry's desire to hold on to distant forests becomes readily comprehensible.

Not only were the forests a source of revenue, they were also a potent symbol of royal power. Henry's manipulation of the forest eyre of 1175, held just after he had quashed the rebellion of his sons and their supporters, indicates how shrewdly he grasped the full potential of the royal forests. Alarmed by the apparent loss of the loyalty of some of his subjects and desperate to keep what support he had, Henry II had promised the complete abolition of his royal forests during the rebellion, and issued a writ to that effect. Yet when he regained control in 1174, not only were the royal forests restored, Henry also swiftly set about punishing all those who had flouted the recently suspended laws. Earls, barons, knights and even clergy were brought to court, accused of killing deer, and heavily fined for their crimes. In Nottingham, the justiciar Richard de Lacy was moved to protest that he had not enforced the forest laws during the recent civil strife on the king's own orders and displayed the king's writ ordering the suspension of the forest laws. But his protestations were to no avail. Once fully in control, Henry refused to honour his earlier writ, and set about collecting fines for infringements with unusual vigour. He carried out his great Forest Visitation of 1175 in person, presenting to the Exchequer an exceptionally long list of fines. Over 1,100 fines were enrolled on the 1176 Pipe Roll for forest offences, ranging from sums of 5 shillings to 500 marks.[18] Many smaller amounts, accounted for in lump sums, were also recorded on the rolls.[19]

Throughout the twelfth century, the historical evidence for both the extent and the administration of the royal forests steadily improves, yet information about the actual use of the forests remains scarce, and a picture of the nature of hunting in Angevin England must be sketched from the most scanty of sources. Nonetheless, it is clear that the royal forests continued to have a value to the Crown that was not purely economic. Twelfth-century chronicles indicate that many of the Angevin kings, like their Norman predecessors, hunted personally in the royal forests, using them as recreation grounds in addition to exploiting their resources with ruthless efficiency. The twelfth-century writer Peter of Blois claimed that Henry II was 'an avid lover of the woods; when he ceased from warfare, he occupied himself with birds and dogs'.[20] The chronicler Gerald of Wales noted that even times of peace brought little rest to Henry 'for he was immoderately fond of the chase and devoted himself to it with excessive ardour', rising at the break of dawn and spending the day 'riding through the woods, penetrating the depths of the forests, and crossing the ridges of hills'.[21] Interestingly, both writers appear to relate hunting to warfare, casting the hunt as a kind of peacetime alternative to the rigours of war. Hunting was certainly esteemed as a preparation for warfare in late medieval culture, and these references suggest that it may have occupied a similar role in earlier times. Henry II spent much of his time in the hunting park that Henry I had created at Woodstock, and extended it in the later years of his reign. As he travelled ceaselessly around England on business, he stayed in the royal forests – his 'chief delights', as his courtier Richard fitz Nigel called them – where he reportedly forgot the cares of government and immersed himself in hunting.[22]

Henry's sons, Richard and John, were both capable huntsmen, and John in particular spent many hours hunting in the royal forests, taking a close personal interest in their administration and laying down minute orders on the preservation of the animals in the forests he wished to hunt. His chroniclers reported that 'he haunted woods and streams, and greatly delighted in the pleasure of them'.[23] The poet Bertran de Born even implicated his excessive hunting in his ignominious downfall:

> He loves better playing and hunting,
> Brachets, greyhounds and hawks,
> And repose, wherefore he loses his property,
> And his fief escapes out of his hand.[24]

The chronicles contain abundant evidence that hunting formed an integral element of medieval kingship, and evidence from the royal itineraries helps to shed a little more light upon the hunting that the Angevin kings clearly adored. The royal itinerary was a tour undertaken by the royal household through important administrative centres of the realm; it was a mechanism for facilitating contact between the king and those he had placed in positions of power in county communities.[25] Yet although the purpose of the itinerary was primarily political, a large and unwieldy hunting establishment, comprising dozens of men and hundreds of dogs, travelled with the king throughout the realm. In May 1212, the hunt accompanying King John included no fewer than 167 greyhounds, 38 'dogs of the pack' and 32 bercelets, all in the charge of 52 handlers. The exact composition of the pack changed from month to month, and by mid-September of the same year had grown to 300 greyhounds, 16 boarhounds, 9 bercelets and 64 handlers.[26] The accounts provide no evidence concerning exactly when or how these hounds were used, but as the pack's movements closely mirrored those of the king, it seems certain that they

2. A medieval illumination, purporting to show King John stag-hunting, but in fact produced more than a century after his death.

travelled with the king in order that he might hunt, either in the royal forests or on his subjects' lands, whenever the opportunity arose. The sheer number of dogs and men journeying with the king gives some indication of the possible scale of a royal hunting expedition in the early thirteenth century, and underscores once again that hunting was a grand and public occasion, a conspicuous display of royal might.

No doubt the king's hunting on his royal itineraries fulfilled more than a recreational role. As we have seen, an early medieval hunt could be a fast-paced and dangerous affair – hunters needed to display fine horsemanship and considerable courage to acquit themselves respectably in the course of the hunt. Hunting in company with the king was possibly a way for his favoured subjects to demonstrate their loyalty and courage, and presumably also, therefore, their fitness for war – something never far from the minds of the medieval nobility. Yet it was not only his subjects who demonstrated their strength and courage in the course of the hunt, for the king's hunt surely also served as a strong symbolic statement to his subjects. For many of his hosts, the appearance of the king's lavish hunting pack on their own lands must have been about as welcome as a visit from the tax inspectors, but they were of course impotent to raise any form of objection. The king hunted where he wished: on his own land, in his forests and, when visiting, on his subjects' land as well. The large pack of hunting dogs with which he travelled formed a potent symbol of the king's authority, and helped to remind his subjects of the true extent of his power.

Two Anglo-Norman poems from the twelfth century – *Tristan* and the 'Romance of Horn' – reinforce the evidence from the itineraries and suggest that the king's love of hunting was also shared by those of his subjects with pretensions to social status and noble birth.[27] Hunting was emphatically a kingly art and an essential accomplishment for members of the nobility. So, for example, in the 'Romance of Horn' (composed in about 1170) the noble birth of the hero cannot be concealed, despite his reduced circumstances, because of his unsurpassed skill at hunting and hawking.[28] Hunting here is not a means of obtaining food; it is an art to be studied and mastered by those with time on their hands. In the 'Romance of Horn', the king's household divert themselves with hunting in order 'to relieve boredom'; a paid huntsman was employed to undertake the more prosaic duty of provisioning the household with venison.[29] Likewise in the *Tristan* poems, the nobility turn to hunting for recreation, rather than to fill the larder. Stag hunts in the meadows are laid on for the entertainment of guests at King Mark's court at Tintagel, Cornwall. The king's huntsman, Orri, used nets and hedges to trap wild boar and deer; by such means (we are informed) he controlled an extremely well-stocked cellar.[30] In this imaginative literature, hunting is represented as part of a culture shared by royalty and nobility, and its defining feature lies in the fact that it is pursued primarily for recreation, and not out of necessity.

The aristocratic hunt was embellished in a number of ways that helped to distinguish it from the utilitarian hunting of peasants and servants. Fine clothes, ritual, music and a special language were all employed to add pageantry and status to the occasion. According to the scholar and clergyman John of Salisbury, pipes and trumpets were blown to signify a successful kill, and the animal's severed head held triumphantly before the returning hunt party.[31] The gentle hunter needed to learn a special vocabulary in order to display his knowledge of the aristocratic art of hunting: 'Be careful not to misuse any of their hunting jargon in speaking,' John warns his reader, or you will be 'branded with ignorance of all propriety.'[32] The noise of dogs, horns and hooves assailed the senses and provided a visible demonstration of the strength and power of the medieval nobility. Clothes, language, music and ritual dissections – in the medieval world such things turned the killing of wild animals into hunting, and we will hear much more about them in the pages that follow.

Though the utilitarian hunting of peasants and servants was disdained by the wealthy and powerful as a lowly activity, we should never forget that hunting was not in fact confined to the wealthy, but was an art enjoyed in some form at all levels of society. Yet what those below the level of the aristocracy hunted, or how they went about it, is difficult to establish, given the extreme paucity of evidence on this subject. All the evidence we have is contained in a few sentences written by John of Salisbury, who wrote that the poor hunted by setting snares, weaving nooses, and luring wild animals with tunes and whistles – 'trapping them in any manner whatsoever'.[33] This fits neatly with what we would expect: peasants and servants hunted for reasons of utility rather than art, and went about their business without the pomp and ritual of the aristocratic, recreational hunter. The poor hunted in the same way that they have across the globe, armed with little more than the most basic of equipment and their own knowledge of the natural world.

As a man of the Church, John of Salisbury was scornful of the time-wasting implicit in the court's love of hunting and dismissive of the rites and rituals of the aristocratic hunt – complaints that clergymen were to echo through the centuries. Undoubtedly, however, it was the iniquities of the forest laws, rather than the long hours the court devoted to the hunt, that exercised him most. He summed up the burden of Henry II's forest in the following terms: 'Farmers are kept from their fields that wild beasts may have liberty to roam over them. That feeding ground for them may be increased, farmers are deprived of their fields of grain, tenants of their allotments, the herds and flocks of their pasture, and even the bees are scarcely allowed their liberty.'[34] Such views were echoed by the scholar Ralph Niger: Henry II, he wrote, 'conferred immunity upon the birds of the air, the fish in the rivers, and the wild beasts of the earth, and made poor men's plots their feeding-grounds.'[35] These assessments reflected a widespread dissatisfaction with the royal forests in the country at large, but philosophers and churchmen complained in vain. Ruling over an empire from the Scottish borders to the Pyrenees, Henry II was an energetic and highly successful king, under no pressure to bow to the will of discontented nobles or whining philosophers. At his death, the royal forests were at their greatest extent and a complex system of forest administration was firmly in place.

Following the death of his elder son, Henry II was succeeded by his second son, Richard, though in the course of a ten-year reign, the new king was tied up with the Third Crusade, and spent no more than six months in England. Richard's constant warfare left little time for recreation, and he was not celebrated as a huntsman, though his chronicler did recount an instance of skilled swordsmanship and dashing bravery when he once chanced upon a 'very fierce wild boar'.[36] Another reference to Richard hunting appears in the chronicle of Roger of Howden, who describes him waiting to set sail at Portsmouth, and filling the unwanted delay with a little hunting.[37]

With little time to spend hunting in England and constantly pressed for cash, for Richard I the forests represented a fine opportunity to raise much-needed revenue from hunting nobles through the sale of forest privileges and exemptions from forest jurisdiction. Large disafforestation raised substantial sums; the magnates of Bedfordshire, for example, paid £200 to have the parts of their county that Henry I had afforested taken back out of the forest, and the knights of Surrey paid the same sum for the disafforestation of their county.[38] By selling off large tracts of forests and forest privileges, Richard acquired the money for his warfare, and for the first time in a century the boundaries of the royal forest began to recede.

A sole forest eyre, held in 1198, brought further revenue rattling into Richard's war chest. With his war in Normandy going badly, and the sale of forest privileges gradually drying up, Richard sought to fill his coffers by collecting in the fines due for forest offences committed in the past decade. His eyre raised £1,980 in fines.[39] According to Roger of Howden, 'by these and other vexations, whether justly or unjustly, all England has been reduced to poverty from sea to sea', and though Howden's comment was something of an exaggeration, it certainly captures the resentment that these occasional royal courts aroused.[40] Richard even ratcheted up the penalties for infringements of the forest laws. His Assize of the Forest in 1198 extended the penalty for trespass against the king's venison to mutilation by loss of the eyes and the testicles.[41] Since no records from the forest courts in Richard's reign have survived, there is no evidence that these penalties were ever used; but the threat could hardly have been better calculated to rouse the barons' ire.

King John, Richard's brother, and his successor following his death in 1199, continued the policy of reducing the area of forest, by systematically disafforesting and granting licences in return for the money he needed to pursue his ill-fated expeditions in France. He raised hundreds of pounds from disafforesting all of Cornwall and much of Devon and Essex.[42] The disafforestation of Devon was accompanied with promises that gave freedom to the inhabitants to 'impark, take all kinds of venison, have dogs, bows and arrows and all kinds of weapons'.[43] Smaller, but still considerable, sums were raised by removing parts of Staffordshire and Shropshire, Yorkshire, Sussex and Worcestershire from the forests.[44] In addition, John received money in return for charters permitting the construction of parks in the forests, and for the partial removal of the forest law. The Abbot of Dore in Hereford, for example, paid over £300 to the king in order to bring 300 acres of woodland in the royal forest under the plough and to free the land permanently from the forest fines.[45]

Notwithstanding these numerous concessions with respect to the extent of the forests, John was as assiduous as any of his predecessors when it came to enforcing the forest law. After the loss of Normandy in 1204 John resided permanently in England, and from this position he gave close attention to all his forests. By punishing petty infringements with heavy penalties, John succeeded in raising large sums from the forests, despite their diminishing size. Furthermore, his heavy-handed policy ensured that the stream of landowners seeking to get their lands disafforested and free from the law for good and all never dried up. His eyre of 1212 raised £4,486 – more than double the amount raised by Henry II's last eyre, and a considerable sum given the disafforestations that had taken place in the twenty-seven years intervening.[46] Over the course of his reign, John raised less from the forests than Henry II had, yet they remained an important means of raising revenue.

After a promising start, John's rule rapidly went downhill. His confiscation of church property, the loss of Normandy, and his heavy taxation had roused the opposition of magnates and nobles, and his aborted invasion of Poitou in 1214 provided the opening that a rebel band of discontented barons needed. On 3 May 1215, they declared against him, and following unsuccessful negotiations they drew up and sought to force him to seal Magna Carta.[47]

Consisting of a series of chapters, this historic document was designed to force the monarch to respect feudal custom regarding the raising of taxes, to provide safeguards against the king's arbitrary behaviour, and to confirm the people's rights under common law. It is commonly and rightly heralded as a legal landmark, for it subjected the king to the law of the land for the first time in history. Yet it is surely significant that, along with such weighty matters, the barons did not forget their grievances over the royal forests. Here was an opportunity to restore hunting land and rights to themselves, and a clause in the forty-seventh chapter of Magna Carta duly ordered a reduction in the number and extent of the royal forests, decreeing that 'all forests that have been made such in our time shall forthwith be disafforested'.[48] The following chapter ordered an immediate inspection of 'all evil customs connected with forests and warrens'.[49]

In such unsettled times, however, the document was doomed to failure. John had agreed to the terms of Magna Carta merely to gain time, and he immediately attempted to have it annulled by the Pope, who issued a papal bull saying that it was 'not only shameful and base, but also illegal and unjust'.[50] By the time civil war broke out in earnest, just three months later, it was a dead letter. On the brink of defeat by Prince Louis of France, John's timely death from dysentery in October 1216 spared the nation a second humiliation at French hands. When the regency council, led by William Marshal, proclaimed his son King Henry III, the English barons flocked to his standard. Louis was forced to retreat.

Yet though the Angevins managed to cling to the throne, the discontent that had been sparked almost a hundred and fifty years earlier by William's first forest laws continued to fester. With the failure of Magna Carta, the barons' many grievances — including their demand for reform of the forest laws — remained unaddressed. Legal wrangling over hunting rights in the forests continued between the barons and the new king's regents. Their hand strengthened by the fact that Henry was still a child, the barons and bishops ultimately prevailed, and within a couple of years they had successfully wrested a far more comprehensive document from the Crown.

CHAPTER THREE

The Forest Charter

No one, at his peril, shall hunt in the king's forests, parks, or chaces or take ... any beasts without the king's special licence ...[1]

Although John had managed to evade the terms of Magna Carta through consummate politicking and outright deception, Henry III, his son and heir, could not escape its provisions so easily. Following John's death, the barons issued amended versions of Magna Carta in 1216 and again in 1217, and the new king was bound by this final document. Even the Pope could not save him now. In the course of these revisions, however, the barons had removed the clauses regarding the royal forests. It is testimony to the seriousness with which they viewed the issue that the failure of Magna Carta was swiftly turned into an opportunity for a more comprehensive reform of the forests. In 1217, after a year of hard bargaining between Henry III's regents and the bishops, barons, earls and nobles, a fresh document, addressing the multiple grievances that had divided successive monarchs and their barons for the previous century and a half, was presented to the king, and duly granted.[2]

This, the Charta de Foresta, promised two major concessions. Firstly, it codified the forest laws and mitigated their harshness. The penalties for unlawful hunting were relaxed. The 1198 penalty – loss of eyes and testicles – was substituted in 1217 with imprisonment for up to a year and a day, with release at any time if bail could be found. No longer would poachers be punished by death or mutilation; fines, imprisonment or exile were henceforth the maximum penalties that could be imposed. The Charter also limited the 'lawing' of dogs (the removal of their toes) in land close to the royal forest. From 1217, dogs would only be lawed in places where the practice had existed at the time of the coronation of Henry II. Hunting and travelling though the forests with hunting dogs remained strictly prohibited, but the punishment for poaching was brought more in line with the expectations of common law.[3]

Secondly, and more significantly, the Charter disafforested all lands annexed by Henry II and his sons. In other words, by a stroke of the pen, the boundaries of the royal forest were redrawn once more, so that the land these three monarchs had placed within its borders was now freed from the forest laws. But whilst simple in principle, the implementation of this element of the Charter proved far from simple in practice, and took almost a century to accomplish, owing to endless confusion over the precise changes that each of the three monarchs had made.

In 1218, the regency council determined to resolve the matter and ordered twelve knights in each county to undertake a survey of their county, in order to establish where the new boundaries of the forest should lie. The knights willingly seized this opportunity to redraw the forest boundaries, busying themselves perambulating their counties, and invariably constructing new forest boundaries that were very much more in their interests than in those of the king. The knights of Huntingdonshire, for example, who had undertaken their survey before even receiving orders from the king to do so, announced that the whole county, which had previously lain within royal forest, had been afforested by Henry II. They concluded that all, save a few of the king's own private woods, should therefore be taken out of the forest. Subsequent surveys in other parts of England produced verdicts that were just as little to the regents' liking by claiming similarly extensive disafforestations.[4] Though the regents were unwilling to accept these surveys, they were desperate for money to finance their war in France, and consequently granted a number of concessions in Surrey, Sussex and Rutland.[5] In their aftermath, the chronicler Roger of Wendover recalled that 'not only men, but dogs also, who used formerly to [have their toes cut], enjoyed these liberties'.[6]

But the barons' victory was not long lived. On 9 January 1227, when Henry III declared himself to be of age, many of the concessions forced from his regents were swiftly overturned as the new king attempted to claw back the forests lost in the previous decade. The very day following his assumption of power, Henry summoned the knights responsible for the surveys in Shropshire, Leicestershire and Nottinghamshire, and asked them to explain why their forest boundaries excluded land that he believed should lie within; similar hearings were later arranged for other counties.[7] In front of the king's person, most were quick to admit that their earlier surveys had been made in error, and in return for amending their surveys as the king saw fit they received his royal pardon. In this way, Henry established a new set of forest boundaries by the end of 1228.[8] But even with these disafforestations, the hated system essentially remained in place. In 1232, the Waverley annalist noted that eight years had passed since the Forest Charter; 'But alas!' he continued, 'the yoke of slavery is now become more burdensome, and conditions worse than before, especially with regard to the forests.'[9] And although the issue of the forests was raised again during his reign a number of times, the barons got no closer to seeing the central tenets of the Charter fulfilled, as time after time, Henry placated his irate council with royal promises that were simply never carried out.

Not only did Henry successfully evade honouring the central demands of the Forest Charter, he also upheld the forest laws in a fashion that many of his subjects perceived to be unduly oppressive. Although the physical penalties of old had been cast off, this still left ample scope for fining and imprisoning those caught engaging in wrongdoing in the forest and, just as his predecessors had found, fines from illegal hunting, tree-felling and farming could form a valuable source of revenue. Henry's constant money worries inclined him to exploit this stream of income as hard as any. Two chief justices, Robert Passlow and Geoffrey of Langley, both of whom displayed unusual zeal in the role, brought considerable wealth to the royal war chest by these means, though their royal favour was bought at the price of universal dislike. The St Albans chronicler Matthew Paris declared that Passlow had convicted clerics and laymen, nobles and commoners for manifold breaches of the forest laws simply in order to enrich the king. His courts, Paris continued, had imposed such heavy penalties that many were flung into prison, others were stripped of their goods and forced to eke out a bare existence in want and misery, and yet others became homeless beggars.[10] Paris's verdict on his successor, Geoffrey of Langley, was no less harsh. Langley, he wrote, had performed his duties cunningly and wantonly, impoverishing men of noble birth for taking 'a single small beast, a fawn or a hare' found wandering in the fields.[11]

Perhaps the most eloquent testimony to the contempt with which the forest laws were held, however, comes not from the written word, but from the actions of those whom the forest law penalised. The full force of the barons' disgust is apparent in a series of depredations in the Derbyshire forests throughout the course of Henry's rule. A forest court held at mid-century revealed that William Ferrers, Earl of Derby, had helped himself to no fewer than 2,000 of the king's deer between 1216 and 1222. Like any great aristocratic householder, the earl needed large quantities of venison for his family and servants; nonetheless, this number greatly exceeded his personal needs, and was surely designed to show contempt for the king's prerogative, rather than to provide food for his table.[12] The poaching raids in this instance were fuelled by an ongoing conflict between the Ferrers family and the Crown over land that had been seized by the king from Ferrers following the

Battle of Evesham in 1265 and given by Henry III to his son Edmund, Earl of Lancaster. By the time the forest court eventually assembled to address the matter, Ferrers had long since died and the king was forced to display his displeasure by imposing cripplingly heavy fines on the earl's surviving huntsmen instead.[13]

But the king's firm action only added to local tension surrounding the royal forests, and the conflict continued to simmer in the following years. The ongoing disgust of the great Derbyshire family at their exclusion from the county's finest hunting land was made apparent in their campaign of civil disobedience organised in the 1260s. A forest court, held nearly twenty years later in 1285, assembled to consider this grave matter. Of over 500 charges laid before this court, the Earl of Derby (now Robert, Earl Ferrers) once again figured as the most serious offender. He was presented for having hunted on three separate occasions in the Campana Forest with a 'greate compeny of knights', each time taking some forty head of deer and driving a similar number out of the forest. This was a large-scale invasion of a royal forest; thirty-eight offenders were named, though the numbers involved were undoubtedly higher since death had carried many (including the earl) to their graves in the intervening years. Most were men of position and many came from places far from the Campana Forest.[14] Once more, it is clear that this posse of well-born gentlemen was not in the forest in search of a free haunch of venison. These incursions were undertaken by Ferrers and his supporters to show contempt for the king's forests and preserves and to challenge the foundations of his rule.

On Edward's accession, the barons still hoped to see the promises contained within the Forest Charter fulfilled. The Charter had promised to set the boundaries of the forest back as they had been before the reign of Henry II, but progress had stalled in the half-century since then because no one could agree where these boundaries had lain. Edward I's rule was punctuated by fresh, though ultimately vain, attempts to resolve this issue, and at the end of his reign the problem of the forests remained essentially unresolved. In response to pressure from the barons, Edward had made a number of minor concessions, but had failed to carry out the root and branch reform promised in the 1220s. At the time of his death, few of his subjects were satisfied that the promises of the Forest Charter had been met.[15]

In the event, the substantial disafforestations demanded by the barons were delayed until the reign of his son, Edward II, crowned in 1307. An unpopular king from the outset, Edward, despite a shaky grasp on power, managed to avoid addressing forest grievances for the best part of a decade. In 1316, however, on the back of humiliating defeats in Scotland, he was finally forced to bow to his baronial opposition and agreed to recognise the perambulations that his father had ordered in 1300. He subsequently clawed back some of these concessions, but these minor gains failed to survive the breakdown of social order that occurred following his imprisonment, and subsequent murder, in 1327. His queen, Isabella, and her favourite, Roger Mortimer, struggled to maintain control of the kingdom during the regency of his son, and with only a frail hold on power they judiciously conceded baronial claims and ordered earlier perambulations to be observed. The boundaries of the royal forests, so long and so jealously guarded by a series of monarchs, began to recede for good. One century late, the substantial disafforestations promised in the Forest Charter finally took place.[16]

It is unlikely, however, that the disafforestations which occurred materially affected the lot of the commonality in the way that might be expected. In theory, where forest status was removed, that land and the wild animals within could be freely hunted by all; the animals and birds belonged to those who found them, though no one was allowed to trespass on their neighbour's land in their search. But although disafforestation undeniably opened up hunting in large tracts of woodland to the commonality, it was the barons who had fought to secure this change, and it was ultimately they who benefited from it.

In the event, thirteenth-century disafforestation did little more than orchestrate an exchange of hunting rights between the Crown and magnates – bishops, earls, nobles. Whenever the king and barons reached agreement on reductions in the extent of the royal forest, expensive royal charters had to be obtained to confirm the changed status of the land. These sometimes explicitly transferred the rights to venison that the king had formerly enjoyed to the holder of the Charter. A charter granted to Geoffrey fitz Peter, Earl of Hereford and Essex, gave him parts of the Forest of Huntingdon 'as fully as the king had it'.[17] The earl lost no time in constructing a network of foresters and personal courts, to protect his deer from illegal hunting, that closely modelled those found in royal forests. Private foresters and keepers, once largely employed only by the king, now became part of many large noblemen's ordinary retinue. And the lives of the small farmers and peasants who lived in or near the forests continued to be subject to their tyrannical rule.

Where the new charters did not grant their owners exclusive hunting rights, powerful landowners simply employed illegal ruses to ensure that the best hunting land was enjoyed by them alone. In the scramble for the newly opened areas of forest during the thirteenth century, local magnates were frequently drawn into unseemly and often illegal afforestations of their own. The Abbot of Newminster, in 1280, 'put in defence' part of the recently disafforested Northumberland, effectively turning it into his own private game reserve, and using force to ensure that it remained as such.[18] Similarly, Earl Reginald illegally afforested most of the Blackmore Vale in Dorset – locally known as the White Hart Forest, after Henry III had found there a white hart so beautiful he ordered it be spared.[19] The Bishop of Ely appropriated part of the royal Forest of Huntingdon. When the king's foresters went to enquire into the grounds upon which he had done so, they were met by the bishop's bailiff and three priests, armed with book, cross and candle, who sent them away with threats of excommunication.[20] Illegal though such actions might have been, wealthy magnates frequently had sufficient power to bully their neighbours into silence. In no time, the best disafforested hunting land had fallen into the hands of the rich and powerful. Wherever good woodland was removed from the royal forests, its occupiers set about creating the same kinds of structure as those used by royalty to protect their hunting from interlopers: it thus remained 'forest' in all but name. For the small hunter, depressingly little changed. Thousands of acres were removed from the royal forests and returned to the commonalty in the thirteenth century, yet it hardly heralded the dawn of a new era of hunting for all.

Whilst disafforestation greatly increased the number of hunters, not a single acre of new hunting land was added thereby. And with more people chasing after the same number of wild deer, the stage was set for an unending conflict over who might hunt what deer, and where. Conflicts between king and nobles were as old as William the Conqueror's first forest laws, but during the thirteenth century, new battle lines, lines which failed to position royalty against nobility so neatly, began to be drawn. Wealthy neighbours, who had long conspired together against the king, were now frequently found in conflict with each other. A long-running squabble between the Abbot of Whitby and the Earl of Lancaster was typical of many. The earl's forests contained numerous fine deer, but as there were no fences they periodically wandered on to his neighbour's (the abbot's) land. As soon as they did so, the abbot (according to the earl), directed his scouts to set nets and snares at the boundary. He then ordered his servants to terrify the deer with dogs and shouts so that they turned and headed back to the boundary. Of course in their flight they were caught in his nets. 'This he does every year, to the destruction of the deer and the damage of the Earl, by what right the jury know not.'[21] Throughout the thirteenth century, much woodland remained unfenced, and the potential for petty squabbling between neighbours over the deer that roamed it was seemingly infinite.

The truth is that successful hunting practice rests upon a delicate and contrived balance: hunters may kill, but while doing so they must also ensure that enough grazing deer survive to enter next year's field. Though successful in providing this protection, the Norman forest laws had forced the nobles to pay the price, and as their power increased in the twelfth century they simply refused to continue to pay. The Forest Charter was the barons' victory. No longer would they be excluded from the elevated sport of kings; no longer would they endure the inconvenience of the king's marauding deer on their own land. But as the victorious barons surged on to the hunting scene in large number, they were soon forced to confront the unpalatable fact that there was no corresponding leap in the number of deer for them to hunt. Ultimately, then, the Charter displaced the conflict over hunting rather than resolved it. In pursuit of good hunting, barons and magnates, once united against the king, were now divided amongst themselves. With a growing number of hunters, preserving and hunting deer required greater subterfuge, cunning and force than ever before.

Following the implementation of the Forest Charter in the thirteenth century, a clearer picture of the methods of hunting starts to emerge. There are no descriptive or literary accounts for a further one hundred years, but one of the Angevin kings' legacies was an increasingly efficient system of forest administration. In an attempt to preserve the king's deer, royal officials closely monitored all activities in the forests, and kept careful records noting any wrongdoing they encountered. Though the forest records were assembled for a very different purpose, they offer a unique insight into the medieval world of hunting.[22] Together with a handful of household accounts that have survived from the thirteenth century, it is possible to piece together the place of hunting in medieval society.

For the wealthy, those who hunted for pleasure rather than profit, hunting was an intensely social activity. A nobleman rarely hunted alone; a deer hunt was an expedition to be undertaken by a party of half a dozen men or more. Fathers, sons, brothers, friends, landowners, tenants, clergy and laity came together to while away the hours in pursuit of wild animals. And although hunting was primarily a male activity, women did sometimes go hunting with their households as well. For example, in 1280 Matilda de Mortimer was caught poaching in Whittlewood Forest with members of her household, and in 1334 Lady Blanche de Wake was presented for having taken one stag and two hinds from the Forest of Pickering.[23] Frequently landowners are found entertaining their visitors by taking them to their woodlands in pursuit of game. The Earl of Gloucester, for example, one night 'after dinner ... went to his wood of Micklewood' with a number of his dinner guests and their dogs.[24] When Joan of Acre came to visit Joan de Valence at Goodrich Castle in Herefordshire in April 1297, she brought her pack of dogs so that her party might hunt in the Valences' woods.[25] In 1265, Eleanor de Montfort's household lodged both her own dogs and her visitors' packs – fifty-two dogs in all, more than half of which did not belong to her.[26] Good hospitality demanded that guests be entertained not only with food and drink, but also with dogs and hunting, and hosting a hunting expedition was a valuable means for landowners to demonstrate their wealth and largesse.

The possession of woodlands in which to go hunting was of course the privilege of the wealthy, and this helped to mark deer-hunting as a high-status activity. The hunt provided a unique opportunity for each individual to display his strength, courage and skills; and for the same reason, hunting occupied a unique place in cementing relationships between neighbours and allies. Thus Philip Marmion, Lord of Tamworth, hunted in Cannock Forest with a large number of minor local lords and neighbouring knights; the hunts usually ended with the freshly slaughtered deer being hauled back to one of the households for convivial feasting and drinking.[27] The expeditions were social occasions, but also a way for Marmion and his neighbours to display their hunting prowess and, in some measure, their worth.

However, although the authority for these expeditions lay with the landed elites, the hunting parties were often in reality much more inclusive affairs, composed of those of gentry status and of lesser rank, including servants. The evidence from the hunting career of John Giffard, a thirteenth-century baron possessing the manor of Brimpsfield, Gloucestershire, indicates the socially mixed nature of many a medieval hunting party. Giffard regularly hunted, both in his own woods and illegally in those of his neighbours, often with much the same party of hunting friends. His regular hunting companions included Thomas de Morton, Anselm Basset and Geoffrey Arblaster, all of a similar status to his own, but they also included two of his servants, Ralph Daubeny and Walter Ball.[28] Likewise Marmion, Lord of Tamworth, hunted with men of considerably lower social status than himself: his hunting companions in Cannock included not only his huntsman, but also his cook.[29] Elsewhere, poaching records reveal local lords hunting in the company of huntsmen, chaplains, haywards, woodwards, parkers, other household servants, and local villagers.[30] The boundaries dividing medieval society were rather less clear-cut than we sometimes imagine. Trusted servants and villagers skilled in handling dogs or with an intimate knowledge of local woodlands, though they did not personally own hunting land, were not necessarily excluded from the sport they offered.

For hunting magnates such as Giffard, much of the importance of the hunt was symbolic and recreational, yet even here a number of more prosaic considerations underpinned their interest in hunting. The extensive woodland owned by wealthy landowners might contain a thousand deer or more along with countless smaller wild animals, providing a valuable source of food for the household. But the appetite of a large household placed heavy demands on the estate's produce, and could easily outstrip the venison a landowner was able to provide through his personal hunting. Alongside the recreational

hunting of the landowner, therefore, was a separate hunting staff, charged
with the task of bringing deer and other wild animals from the forest to the
table.

Nowhere were the demands for venison and the operations of a professional hunting staff greater than in the royal household. As feasts and banquets
approached, the king's foresters received detailed instructions to deliver
so many head of deer to the palace. The scale of royal feasting during the
thirteenth century is simply staggering. Consider Henry III's Christmas dinner
in 1251: his forests yielded an astonishing 430 red deer, 200 fallow deer, 200
roe deer, 200 wild swine, 1,300 hares, 450 rabbits, 2,100 partridges, 290
pheasants, 395 swans, as well as crane, pigs, hens, peafowl and salmon for
this occasion.[31] This was feasting on an exceptional scale, even for the royal
household, and rarely were the forests plundered to such an extent. In an
average year, Henry III took around 800 deer, mostly fallow deer, from his
forests, as well as over 80 wild boars.[32] In the light of such figures, Henry's
reluctance to cede the demands of the Forest Charter even in woods that he
never visited is readily intelligible.

No aristocratic household could match such feasting, but though their
banquets were smaller, the landed aristocracy exploited their woodland in an
identical way. Joan de Valence's household employed men to catch partridge
and rabbits and, following the death of her husband in 1296, a huntsman
was also employed to provide the family with venison from woods in Kent,
Herefordshire and Worcestershire. From this date, the pack spent most of
its time away from the household. Much of the meat was salted and moved
to the residence at Goodrich, where it was eaten throughout the year except
during Lent.[33] Her huntsmen almost certainly used nets, traps and snares to
kill animals in the most efficient manner possible – probably little different
from the way described in Aelfric's *Dialogues*. Though the family's woods were
used for recreation, they were also the scene of hunting of a more utilitarian
nature.[34]

With most of the finest woodland in the hands of either the king or large
landowners, the eating of venison was effectively confined to none but the
richest of families. Venison was not available on the open market: it was a
delicacy that money could not buy. For this reason, venison was integral
to feasting and hospitality; it was an edible and visible symbol of a family's
wealth and prestige. Forests and woodland, therefore, were not simply useful
for the foodstuffs they contained; they were also a unique source of social
prestige.[35]

There were significant differences in the place of deer-hunting for the
wealthy and for those lower down the social scale. For the poorest in society,
deer-hunting was not about the display of hunting prowess. Nor was it a

means to foster friendships and alliances. The chance to acquire meat and skins rather than sport was the motive for hunting. A plate of venison was a precious addition to the poor man's diet, a valuable source of protein in a society where food was too often in short supply. Alternatively, the money that could be raised by the sale of a haunch of venison provided plenty of motivation for the peasant hunter, and it was not usually difficult to find neighbours deprived by the forest laws of the right to hunt, but with the means and desire to buy venison. There was even the prospect of using the skins to turn a penny, though the risk of being caught in possession of such an obviously illegal item made holding on to deerskins a dangerous activity. A study of Feckenham Forest in the late thirteenth century reveals that about half of the men caught poaching in the forests were motivated by the need for food.[36] Although hunting was about status and display for some, we should never forget the place of subsistence hunting in medieval England.

Peasant hunting motivated by a need for food lacked the structure and camaraderie that characterised the hunting enjoyed by their social superiors. Amongst the poor, men acted singly or in pairs, their 'hunting' sometimes amounting to little more than seizing deer found dead or dying. For example, two men who found a doe 'partly eaten at the front and the back' by hounds did not scorn to feast on these paltry remains; they carried the carcass home for their own meal.[37] In similar vein, when a villager named Roger Prigge stumbled upon a dead deer in the New Forest, he 'carried it off in a sack towards Romesey'.[38] Even when the poor took a more active role in killing deer, much of their hunting was purely opportunistic. Stray wild deer wandering into gardens formed the basis of many a chance hunt by the poor. At Inglewood Forest in the 1280s, for example, William and his wife Ada enjoyed an unexpected feast after they happened upon a deer feeding in their garden.[39] Humble hunters may have enjoyed a certain thrill on locating and capturing a deer, but were no doubt primarily motivated by reluctance to see a good meal walk away. The small peasant hunter valued the product above the means of its acquisition.

Inevitably, peasant hunting was conducted without such an expensive accoutrement as a horse. At this social level, men hunted on foot, armed with simple home-made traps and snares, and usually accompanied by a solitary dog.[40] Their snares were fashioned from materials to hand – wood, horsehair, cord or rope – but though basic, they were capable of catching even the largest deer found in the forests. Some were designed to entangle the antlers and head of animals: for example, two brothers took a hind in Sherwood Forest with snares 'placed in such a way as to strangle the animal'. Others trapped the animals' feet: ropes and cords might ensnare a deer; more occasionally traps of sharpened stakes on which the deer were impaled were used.[41]

Traps and snares rarely killed the animal outright: they brought it within the poacher's reach, and other means, such as stones launched from slings, were used to finish it off.

During the thirteenth century, deer-hunting was integrated into society at all levels, but impregnated with many different meanings. For the great landowners, hunting was an outward sign of wealth and status, a form of conspicuous display, though their hunting was not entirely insulated from that of the commonalty, who might sometimes participate as servants in the aristocratic hunt. Lower down the social hierarchy, no such pretensions existed. Hunting may well have provided the poor with some measure of excitement and exhilaration, but for those on meagre diets the tangible and valuable product it promised provided incentive aplenty.

The deer was undeniably coveted as the hunting quarry *par excellence*, but the English countryside teemed with smaller animals. Wolves, foxes, wildcats, hares, conies and birds all provided exciting hunting as well as a little fur and meat to soften the harsh existence of the small farmer. Owing to the general prohibition on hunting in the king's forests, no one was permitted to hunt these small beasts there, but elsewhere the smaller wild animals could be hunted by whoever occupied the land on which they were found. The Norman kings had challenged this Anglo-Saxon principle by selling grants of warren – charters giving their holder exclusive rights to hunt the fox, hare and rabbit – but such grants had remained comparatively few, so in practice few tenants who wished to hunt the smaller animals found their right to do so restricted.

In the century following the Forest Charter, however, a dramatic increase in charters of free warren steadily encroached upon these ancient rights. Increasingly kings granted charters conferring hunting rights on particular lords for a defined area, and prohibiting all but the holder to hunt and kill there. Each charter specified the animals that it protected: hares were almost always named, but foxes, wildcats, rabbits and game birds, such as pheasants and partridges, were also often included. A charter granted to Peter des Roches, Bishop of Winchester ordered that 'no one man enter the said warren to take the fox, hare, partridge or pheasant without the bishop's licence'.[42] Another acquired by Richard de Sutton, Canon of Lincoln, permitted him to hunt hare, fox, cat, badger and squirrel.[43] For those found guilty of hunting in somebody else's warren, a fine of £10 was the usual punishment.

In the thirteenth century, and particularly from the 1250s, grants of this nature began to proliferate. Henry III granted at least sixty-nine charters for Nottinghamshire in the first thirty years of his reign, and in Derbyshire, thirty-seven lords obtained charters covering at least 121 places over the same period.[44] This pattern is mirrored in other parts of the country, and the rapid and extensive curtailment of long-established hunting rights this entailed soon began to attract the attention of the barons. Grants of warren were added to the discontented barons' long list of grievances drawn up at the Oxford Parliament of 1258 and duly presented to the king. This 'Petition of the Barons' stated that the king's Forest Charter had promised the disafforestation of royal forests 'in order that everyone might be able to hunt freely everywhere', but continued by noting that the king's grants of warrens were undermining these promised liberties.[45] But just as Henry resisted pressures to reduce the boundaries of his forests, so did he resist this call to limit his grants of warren. The aspirations of manorial lords gave rise to a steady stream of requests for grants of warren and the Crown's constant need for funds ensured that Henry rarely refused them.

Reflecting on the surge of grants of warren that occurred in the 1250s, Matthew Paris claimed that warrens were put on sale to whoever wanted them, but of course not all of the king's subjects were able to buy.[46] Grants of warren were the preserve of the rich and powerful, of large landowners with the means to purchase such expensive privileges. The barons at Oxford may have grumbled about the expense of the grants, but it was they, ultimately, who had most to gain from them. One can only guess at the silent discontent of the small hunter, deprived by such grants of the old hunting rights that the Forest Charter had promised to restore.

A glimmer of this resentment surfaced in the late fourteenth century, following the Peasants' Revolt. In 1381, Wat Tyler led several thousand peasants to London, objecting principally to the recent introduction of a new poll-tax, though also articulating a number of concerns about low and artificially suppressed wages. Interestingly, the recently created network of private hunting reserves figured on their list of complaints, and it was these, rather than the royal forests, that formed the target of Tyler's campaign. He declared 'that all warrens … parks and woods should be common to all: so that throughout the realm, in the … woods and forests, poor as well as rich might take the venison and hunt the hare in the field'.[47] The transfer of hunting rights from the king to his wealthiest subjects had not gone unnoticed, but in the event the Peasants' Revolt raised, rather than resolved, this problem.

The thirteenth century was a period of readjustment in the world of hunting, a period that saw both winners and losers. Although the Forest Charter promised, and did eventually deliver, a reduction in the Crown's hunting privileges, the benefits were not extended to all. Wherever land was disafforested, a hasty scuffle ensued to take over the hunting rights that the king had once enjoyed. Time after time the largest landowners did best, with a consequent closing down of hunting opportunities for tenants and small peasant farmers. In time, a more complex set of conflicts emerged, pitting the king against his barons, and the barons against both each other and their poorer neighbours. By the early fourteenth century, all the factors which ensured that hunting would be the source of perpetual social conflict for the following five hundred years had been put in place.

CHAPTER FOUR

Hunting Goes Tame

I will prove by sundry reasons ... that the life of no man ... be less displeasable to God than the life of a perfect and skilful hunter ... Hunters go into Paradise when they die, and live in this world more joyfully than any other men.[1]

In the wet summer of 1348, a virulent strain of plague jumped ashore at Bristol, probably carried by rats in a ship sailing from Gascony. Within weeks of midsummer, people were dying far beyond Bristol in unprecedented numbers, and rather than abating with the onset of winter, the death rate continued to soar. The deaths continued in 1349 and into the following year. The Black Death, the most devastating outbreak of plague in the country's history, had reached Albion's shores. Somewhere between a third and a half of England's population is estimated to have died.[2]

Yet those who survived discovered that population loss on this horrifying scale brought not only disruption and dislocation but also new possibilities of social advancement. Fewer people meant more resources to go round, and there were a number of winners in the newly constructed society that emerged from the devastation of the plague. Labourers found their services were now highly coveted, and were in the enviable position of being able to demand higher wages for their work. Parliament even resorted to passing Maximum Wage Acts in a vain attempt to curtail such impudence.[3] And small farmers, outstripping the number of tenant farms by a comfortable margin, were able to drive down the rents they paid.[4] Large landowners, faced with lower rents and higher wages, were amongst those who gained least, though population loss offered consolation of a very different kind even here. At a stroke, landowning families had been almost halved, and this radically changed the hunting world they inhabited. Both land and deer must have felt gloriously abundant for those who survived the Black Death, and the fifteenth century is widely regarded as the heyday of medieval hunting.[5] Large expanses of woodland with a thriving population of deer were stalked by fewer hunters than ever before. Kings and barons could hunt extensively without harming deer stocks and began to write books and poems extolling the joys of doing so.[6]

From the early fifteenth century, the growing collection of hunting manuals, poems, paintings and illuminations, along with an expanding body of court records and private papers, makes it possible to sketch the nature of the hunt in medieval England in greater detail than ever before. The earliest surviving hunting text in English was authored by William Twiti, huntsman to Edward II. His *The Art of Hunting* is a short prose treatise 'drawn up for the instruction of others', and takes the form of a dialogue between a master huntsman and his pupil.[7] Its promise of instruction, however, was only partially fulfilled. The treatise in fact offered little more than a brief description of the hare, hart, boar, roe deer and fox, along with explanations concerning the use of the horn. Much of the information it contained was rather random – how a hart's droppings might be used to establish whether the animal had been pasturing in wheat or in beans – rather than useful instruction in hunting, and its value to the historian is therefore limited.

Edward, Duke of York's *Master of Game*, written at some point between 1406 and 1413 while the duke was imprisoned for traitorous activities in Pevensey Castle, was a more substantial work. The book was largely a translation of a hunting treatise written by the Frenchman Gaston Phoebus, though the duke generally indicated where English hunting practice diverged significantly from that of his French counterparts. He opened with a lengthy prologue recommending hunting, as it 'causeth oft a man to eschew the seven deadly sins' and diverted his attention from 'imaginations of fleshly lust and pleasure'; and concluded 'that hunters go into Paradise when they die, and live in this world more joyfully than any other men'.[8] As well as praising the wholesome qualities of hunting, his handbook detailed every aspect of the medieval hunt. It went through numerous editions and provided a model for countless imitators.

The only other two Middle English hunting manuals to have survived are the *Boke of St Albans* and *Tretyse off Huntyng*, both of which contain comprehensive accounts of the quarry, the hounds and various aspects of hunting procedure. Henry V paid for no fewer than twelve hunting books in 1421, so it is likely that the medieval nobleman enjoyed the use of more than the above four manuals; nonetheless, as only these four texts survive, it is from these alone that we must reconstruct the medieval hunt.[9] Yet these manuals, along with a burgeoning imaginative literature, shed valuable light on a number of hitherto obscure aspects of medieval hunting.

It is clear, for example, that the drive hunt – sometimes called the 'king's hunt' or hunting with the 'bow and stable' – continued to occupy an important place in the world of aristocratic hunting, though fifteenth-century descriptions of the drive hunt suggest that a somewhat more sophisticated procedure had emerged. In place of the two teams that a simple drive hunt requires, the fifteenth-century bow and stable hunt called for hounds and men divided into three teams: the archers, armed with bows and arrows, lying hidden and camouflaged, ready to shoot at the moment of the deer's arrival; the beaters, sometimes mounted, whose task it was to use the dogs to flush the deer out of the woods and towards the archers; and the 'stable', unarmed foot servants positioned so as to guide the approaching deer into the silent ambush of archers. Whether the addition of the 'stable' reflects a development of practice or simply greater detail in the sources is not possible to establish; even accepting the stable to be a genuine innovation, however, the similarities between the fifteenth-century bow and stable hunt and the Anglo-Saxon drive hunt are unmistakable.[10]

Our most evocative and detailed account of bow and stable hunting is contained not in the manuals, however, but in the celebrated fourteenth-century poem *Sir Gawain and the Green Knight*. The poem recounts a series of hunting episodes spread over three days in the castle grounds of Sir Bertilak, a wealthy lord. The time of year is late December, a deer hunt has been arranged for the first morning's entertainment and, as this is the close season for hunting male deer, the hunters' attention is turned towards the female and young male deer. Rising before daybreak, the huntsmen saddle their horses, release the hounds from the kennel, and begin their morning's hunting. All the elements of the bow and stable hunt are here. Sir Bertilak and the most senior knights are in the saddle, chasing the deer through the forest with horns, hounds and cries. The stable flank the slopes, letting through the protected male deer, but holding the hinds and does within the valley. The archers are waiting in the depth of the dale, shooting the deer as they run towards them. Those that break through the ranks of bowmen are chased by the men on horseback and finished off by the dogs.[11] The poem may help to resolve the contradictory evidence for hunting in the eleventh century, which describes royal huntsmen both galloping through the forest and waiting in a silent ambush ready to shoot at the deer. These were possibly interchangeable roles for the most senior huntsmen, determined by personal taste rather than dictated by custom.

The handbooks and literary works describe the drive hunt as an endeavour conducted on a grand scale with dozens of men performing each of the different roles. So magisterial was the scale of the bow and stable hunting with which the Duke of York was familiar that he knew it as the 'King's hunt'; and Bertilak in *Sir Gawain* hunted with 'his many men', with no fewer than 'a hundred men of the boldest hunting blood'.[12] But although these events called for a large number of participants, they also promised great rewards: whole herds of deer could be driven towards the archers; dozens of beasts could be slain in a single morning. In Bertilak's woods, for example, 'By sundown, he has slain so many beasts; Does and other deer – it is a marvel to recall.'[13] The large number of hunters and servants employed was justified by the dozens of carcasses lined up at the end of the day. The drive hunt called for heavy investment in men and dogs, but it repaid this input magnificently.

But the fifteenth-century hunting literature reveals that alongside the drive hunt of old was another quite different form of hunting. The drive was a means of killing animals in herds, and in practice this meant that it was employed primarily for hunting the female and young male deer. Upon reaching maturity at around the age of five, the male deer – now named a 'stag' or 'hart' – parted from the herd and outside the mating season roamed the forest, either in a much looser herd of male deer, or alone. Though a young male deer might sometimes find itself bound up with the drive hunt, most adult males would not be captured in this way. For these, a second technique – the *par force* hunt – was employed. Hunting *par force* involved the pitting of the hunters' combined wits against the speed, cunning and strength of one mature male deer. Its rewards were both greater and less than those of the drive: in place of the dozens of slain deer that a drive might produce, the *par force* hunt promised to offer up a single animal, but this was a stag or hart – which most agreed was the greatest trophy of all.

The hunt commenced early in the morning. An inner circle of experienced hunters rose at dawn and departed for the forest in order to locate the finest hart in the woods.[14] The hart chosen, the junior hunters and their dogs split from the rest of the hunt and positioned themselves strategically throughout the forest, while senior huntsmen proceeded directly to where the hart was believed to lie. When the master huntsman sounded his horn to signal the departure of the hart from its resting place, the surrounding hunters uncoupled their hounds and followed the animal on foot and on horseback. Then followed a desperate chase of men, dogs and horses through the forest, an exhilarating mix of speed and noise with dogs barking and horns blowing. The fresh dogs earlier placed throughout the forest maintained the speed of the chase by joining the hunt as the original dogs tired. With a hart showing pluck and courage, the chase might continue for several hours, but there was no knowing when or where the hunt would end. In contrast to the drive hunt, where the animals were driven to a fixed, pre-established point, the endpoint of the *par force* hunt was unknown, and the hunters needed quick wits and an intricate knowledge of the terrain in order to pursue their quarry to the end.

The hart has magnificent qualities of speed and strength, but when eventually worn down by multiple adversaries, it abandons its flight to turn and face its opponents: it is then said to be 'at bay'. This is the moment for the kill. The master of the hunt would approach the animal and, with his sword, pierce the animal 'behind the shoulder forward to the heart'. When it lay dead, all the hunters proclaimed its death with their horns.[15] The deer was then dissected in ritual sequence, a skilled task, but one that Edward, Duke of York considered fit for woodsmen rather than hunters. The hart was turned on its back and the skin of its throat slit the length of its neck. In order to enhance their instinct for pursuit, the dogs were rewarded by being allowed briefly to tear at the exposed flesh; then joints, organs and muscles were carefully cut from the carcass in ritual order.[16]

To capture the full flavour of *par force* hunting, we can scarcely do better than turn to the foremost poet of the Middle Ages, Geoffrey Chaucer. In his words:

> And as I lay thus, very loud
> It seemed I heard a huntsman blow
> To test his horn and so to know
> Whether its call was clogged or clear.
> Comings and goings I could hear,
> Men, horse and hounds in every place,
> And all men talking of the chase:
> And how they would run the hart to death
> And how the hart, quite out of breath
> And sweating at last – I know not what!
> The moment that I heard all that,
> And knew it was a hunting day,
> My heart rejoiced and straight away
> I left my room and on my horse
> Went prancing forth without a pause
> Until I reached the hunting field,
> On which a crowd of huntsmen wheeled,
> Huntsmen and foresters renowned,
> With sets of deer- and tracker-hound.
> Fast to the forest then they ran
> And I with them. I asked a man
> Who led a pack of deer-hounds there,
> 'Whose are these fine huntsmen here?'

And civilly he answered, 'Sir,
Octavian the Emperor,
And he himself is fast nearby.'
'Well met, by God! Let's hurry,' said I.
And swiftly then did we two ride
Until we reached the forest side.
There every man was doing just
As he by laws of hunting must.
Three long notes blew the master then
Upon his great horn, telling men
To unleash and urge on every hound.
And quickly then the hart was found,
Hallooed and keenly hunted fast
Long time with shouts; until at last
The hart zigzagged and stole away
From all the hounds a secret way.
The pack entire thus overshot
And lost the scent they'd had so hot.
At once the master-huntsman knew,
And on his horn the recall blew.[17]

Chaucer captures the defining qualities of the *par force* hunt. The speed, a breathtaking dash through the woods; the noise, from horn, hounds and men; and the unpredictability, the twists and turns, the possibility of a disappointing outcome. Deer-hunting *par force* offered speed and danger, and called for skilled horsemanship and nerves of steel: as its advocates frequently emphasised, nothing but warfare made such exacting demands.

Although the fast-paced *par force* hunt only makes its appearance in the historical record in the late fourteenth century, it was undoubtedly an ancient hunting technique with a history stretching back many centuries. In essence, *par force* hunting involved little more than setting dogs on a solitary animal and we saw evidence of this in Aelfric's *Dialogues* written in the tenth century, and in the Bayeux Tapestry, produced in the eleventh. But although the *par force* hunt predated the late Middle Ages, the elaborate and complex customs and procedures that fifteenth-century writers described may have been of more recent origin. *Par force* hunting was subject to exact rules, specifying the procedure and timing of each element of the hunt; this was no informal dash through the woods after whatever the dogs put up. The selection of the hart or stag was a carefully planned event in which experienced huntsmen shared their intimate knowledge of the local terrain in order to determine where the finest quarry might lie. The chase itself called for numerous well-trained dogs: lymers – scenting hounds to track the game to its lair; harriers – faster hounds also hunting by smell, to pursue the animal in full flight; and greyhounds – hunting by sight rather than smell. Each dog possessed specific skills and was in the charge of dedicated servants (lymerers, berners and fewterers respectively) who monitored their work throughout the hunt. The horn-blowing followed complex rules, and hunters were expected to be able to understand and follow the messages that its music communicated. Even the dissection of the dead hart's body was subject to minute regulations. Chasing animals with dogs predated the Norman Conquest, but these elegant customs concerning the manner of the chase bear the stamp of the Norman aristocracy who had taken over English estates after the invasion.[18]

Perhaps no less significant than the development of *par force* hunting is the fact that it never replaced the older drive-hunting that had been practised in Anglo-Saxon England. Hunting manuals and poetry both testify to the ongoing significance of the drive hunt, and the absence of discussion about this form of hunting in French treatises confirms that it was a distinctively English form predating the Conquest. Edward, Duke of York, in his *Master of Game* based his chapter on the bow and stable hunt upon his own experience rather than the French source from which the rest of the work was derived. Indeed, the French writer upon whose work his book was based professed he could tell his readers little about 'hunting with the bow', and advised, 'if you want to know more, you had best go to England, where it is a way of life'.[19] Centuries after the introduction of *par force* hunting, the drive hunt was still current in England, and was to remain so for many years to come. The introduction of French hunting techniques did not result in the effacing of traditions dating back to Anglo-Saxon times, but in their adaptation. The Norman Invasion altered rather than destroyed older hunting patterns, leaving a wider and more extensive set of hunting practices.

So the bare outlines of the late medieval deer hunt seem clear: the drive hunt, used largely for hunting deer in herds; and the *par force* hunt, employed for hunting the solitary stag. Greater detail, however, eludes us, despite the appearance of specialist handbooks, for these leave the simplest of questions surrounding the practicalities of hunting unanswered. Small but significant details concerning the number of dogs and men needed, the type of bows to be used, or the appropriate positioning of archers, for example, are not revealed in the Middle English hunting manuals. Instead of explaining how the hunt should be conducted, they dwell extensively on the names of things and the customs and formalities that surrounded each element of the hunt. They introduce their readers to an arcane world of complex terminology, patterned horn signals and hunting cries. Each author gives the precise names for the tines on the stag's antlers (the antler, Royal, Sur-royal, and troches);

and the correct terms for the male deer at each stage of its growth: calf, bullock, broket, staggard, stag and 'hart of ten'.[20] A hart of ten, Juliana Barnes advised her readers, was to be called a 'great' hart, and on no account a 'fair' hart.[21] The manuals are a source of endless information about small social details peripheral to the main hunt, teaching their readers not to perform the hunt, but to speak about it. It is perhaps not details such as these that interest us most at the remove of several centuries, yet their inclusion is nonetheless significant. Some form of hunting, we should never forget, was enjoyed at every level of medieval society; the unrelenting emphasis on the etiquette of hunting was teaching the great and the good to hunt in a way that differentiated them from the rest of society. The manuals present a stylised form of hunting, and represent a continuing attempt to carve an exclusive aristocratic sport out of a ubiquitous activity.

Deer-hunting was undoubtedly the premier pastime of all major landowners throughout the Middle Ages, but wild deer were not the only animal they hunted. The male deer in fact was generally hunted from the Feast of St John the Baptist until Holy Rood Day (24 June–14 September), and hunting season for female deer ran from Holy Rood Day till Candlemas (2 February).[22] During these close periods, hunters by necessity looked elsewhere for their hunting, and the wild boar and the hare ranked next in importance. The wild boar had been placed under the protection of the forest laws in the eleventh century, and anything valued by the Crown was deemed worthy of the attention of the most elevated hunters. In contrast to the beauty and evasive guile of the deer, the boar was ugly and flat-footed, yet it was one of the oldest and most venerated animals of the forest and offered magnificent sport. It sought to outrun the hunter through stamina (it was capable of running from dawn to dusk) and strength (an angry boar might turn and run at its attackers, and was more than capable of killing dog, horse and man).

Once again, it is *Sir Gawain and the Green Knight* that contains the best account of this form of hunting.[23] On the second morning of Gawain's stay, Bertilak and his men once again rise early, hear mass, eat breakfast and head to the forest in their fine hunting clothes, uncertain as yet what their dogs will find. The hounds pick up the scent of a boar, and so the day is devoted to the pursuit of this solitary beast. The speed, noise and uncertain outcome that characterise the *par force* hunt are all evident:

> Soon they mount a search at the edge of a marsh,
> The huntsmen goading the hounds that had the scent,
> Rousing them fiercely, raising a frightful din.
> The hounds, hearing the shouts hurried forward
> And sprang along the trail, a throng of forty or so,

And such a riot of yelps and yaps arose
That all the rocks around rang with the sound.
The hunters, with shouts and horn-blasts, urged them on.
At that, the pack strung together and sprinted
Down a track between a pool and a beetling crag.
By the edge of a rock outcrop, near the marsh's rim,
Where rough rocks had fallen hugger-mugger,
They rushed in to flush their quarry, the hunters following.
They spread around the crag and the jagged mound
Till they were certain they'd trapped inside their circle
The beast that the bloodhounds had discovered.
Then they beat the bushes furiously, forcing him out …[24]

The wild boar was a powerful and dangerous quarry, and it was therefore fitting that only Sir Bertilak possessed the courage to kill it: when the harried boar eventually turns at bay, Bertilak dismounts and plunges his sword deep into the boar's chest, 'shattering its heart'.[25] The death was the occasion of more horn-blowing and barking, with every man shouting and hallooing, and as with all highly regarded quarry animals, its death was celebrated with a ceremonial cutting up of the body: the blood and intestines were fed to the hounds; the head cut off and the carcass carried home separately.[26]

Boar-hunting was a popular motif in fifteenth-century poems and hunting treatises, but it is notable that archival records reveal that the wild boar was virtually extinct by that date, so these courageous boar hunts were imaginative rather than contemporary descriptions.[27] This is not, however, to suggest that the *par force* boar hunt was a literary device with no counterpart in practice. The fifteenth-century poems are often the earliest surviving accounts of older tales, recording practices that had once been common but which had died out by the time the stories were printed. If these poems are indeed based upon the memory of earlier traditions, it enables us to push the date that *par force* hunting became established in England back before the first written accounts. The native population of wild boar became extinct at some point in the thirteenth and early fourteenth centuries, indicating that *par force* hunting had become established in England by that date at least.

The only other animal that merited the attention of the aristocratic hunter was the hare, which Twiti had considered 'the most marvellous beast that is in this land' – a judgement with which many other writers agreed.[28] Unlike the boar, it was common and widely hunted throughout the Middle Ages. Medieval authors recommended hunting it *par force* with scenting-hounds – though, inevitably, a much reduced number. The Duke of York considered that 'any poor gentlemen with a couple of greyhounds … could have a good run with the hare, even though he might not possess a horse'.[29] Its status amongst aristocratic hunters is indicated by the brief ritual that accompanied the hare's capture: the death was marked with horn-blowing and a ritual distribution of the animal's head and intestines to the dogs.[30]

Although the literature of the fifteenth century provides a level of detail concerning hunting procedures that surpasses anything that survives for earlier centuries, there is inevitably much that it does not reveal. All our fifteenth-century sources have a definite and unashamed focus on the grandest and most magnificent elements of the hunt. The less extravagant (and no doubt far more common) forms of hunting are obscured. The bow and stable hunt, for example, was represented as grand spectacle, a conspicuous display of wealth and power. But although none chose to write about it, the outline of a humbler form of hunting is discernible beneath the grand aristocratic deer drives. It is not hard to envisage the key elements: a handful of skilled beaters with a single dog guiding deer to one or two archers. Writers were not concerned with such inconsequential affairs, yet there is no reason to doubt that they were practised in England throughout the Middle Ages. The drive was the stuff of courtly extravagance, but the same techniques were also practised on a smaller scale by hunters of more simple means, or – more likely – by those with no right to be in the forest at all. We are reminded once again of the complexity of English society; although late medieval literature describes a world of courtly hunting confined to the elite, the reality is that hunting was never sharply confined to one section of society.

Hunting literature generally has little to say about the illegal hunter, but the medieval poem 'The Parlement of the Thre Ages', in which the narrator figures as a poacher, forms a notable exception. In contrast to the tapestry of noise and movement described elsewhere, silence and stillness are the hallmarks of the lone poacher; and fine clothes are replaced with camouflage – 'Both my bow and my body I leaved like a bush'.[31] Poaching was a common activity, and this poem provides a useful insight into the way in which the illegal poacher might proceed.

> Lightly I dropped my leash and let it fall
> And bid my dog lie down by the bole of a birch;
> I checked the wind by the way it stirred the leaves
> And stalked him stealthily, not snapping a stick,
> And crept to a crabapple tree and took its cover.
> At last I bent my crossbow, bound to take him,
> Drew to the handle, the arrow trained on his heart.
> The buck beside him brought up his nose
> And stood there sniffing, straining after a scent.

I could only stay where I was, not stir a foot,
For if I twitched or moved or made any sigh,
All my wait and my sport were lost.[32]

Much of the hunting practised in the Middle Ages did not fit neatly into the categories provided by the hunting manuals. A hunt might be a planned, formal affair, or an impromptu event triggered by the chance spying of a deer. Men hunted singly and in large groups; for recreation, or because they needed the food; legally and illegally – at all times drawing upon a shared repertoire, endlessly reinvented in countless different contexts. Our medieval sources, rooted as they are in the aristocratic hunt, fail to capture this diversity, but any historical account of English hunting needs to make an effort to do so.

Inevitably, there is much less evidence concerning the ways in which the small farmer and peasantry hunted. The hunting manuals of the fourteenth and fifteenth centuries paid only the most cursory attention to the traditional trapping and snaring techniques of the poor, and imaginative literature had nothing to say at all. Of rabbits, for example, the Duke of York did 'not speak, for no man hunteth them but the bish-hunters' – by which he meant low-bred fur hunters.[33] Yet these animals were important to the poor, who were much more likely to hunt pheasants, partridges, wildcats or rabbits than the larger animals favoured by the social elite.[34] Most stock was slaughtered and salted down in the autumn owing to the lack of fodder to feed them through the winter, so small wild animals and birds provided a welcome addition to the meagre winter diet of the poor. Not only small mammals, but even badgers and squirrels, could be eaten, and the furs, hides, skins, horns and bones could all be put to some use – the hide of badgers, for example, could be usefully sewn into shoes for poor men.[35]

A handful of illustrations of peasant hunting are contained in two medieval prayer books: *The Luttrell Psalter* and *Queen Mary's Psalter*. The *Luttrell Psalter*, completed in the early fourteenth century for Sir Geoffrey Luttrell of Irnham, Lincolnshire, is unique amongst medieval manuscripts in the numerous scenes of everyday life it contains; and *Queen Mary's Psalter*, produced at roughly the same time, though less concerned with depicting daily life, does contain an extensive collection of images of animals. Both include some images of the techniques of the peasant hunter. In *Queen Mary's Psalter*, for example, we find an illustration of a peasant hunting with traps: a man, his humble status betrayed by his simple tunic, is illustrated trapping a partridge in a net several feet long stretched over a wooden frame.[36] Another illustration shows two women hunting for rabbits – one placing a ferret in the rabbits' burrow, and the other prepared with a net to catch the fleeing animal.[37] The *Luttrell Psalter* depicts the use of ferrets in the same way.[38] Hunting on foot with

batons, as illustrated in the Bayeux Tapestry, is also depicted in both psalters.[39] The illustrations are in line with other forms of evidence which suggest that the poor hunted for small birds and animals with the assistance of traps and nets. Beyond this, however, greater detail concerning how the poor hunted in medieval England is sorely lacking.

3. A peasant netting a small bird using a net on a pole.

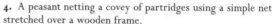

4. A peasant netting a covey of partridges using a simple net stretched over a wooden frame.

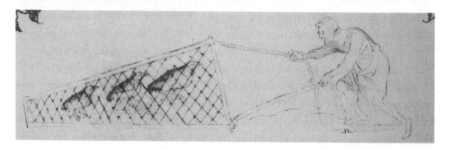

5. Women using nets and ferrets to catch rabbits.

The century following the Black Death is widely regarded as something of a golden age in the history of hunting, the reduction in population creating a straightforward increase in hunting opportunities. By the late fifteenth century, however, the population was gradually beginning its inexorable rise once again. England's population perhaps doubled during the next two centuries, and this growth placed new strains on the medieval network of forests and woodland, ultimately forcing the wild deer hunting enjoyed since the Norman Invasion to give way to a new form better fitted to the changing world.[40]

The impulse for change was the loss of trees. The growing population all needed to be fed and housed, and this in turn placed pressure on the deer's protected woodland. Fifteenth-century church-building required wood in large quantities, and families needed wood for house-building as well as for fuel for heating and cooking. The nascent lead-, iron- and copper-smelting industries, cornerstones of the late medieval economy, all needed wood for furnaces. As the trees fell, so agriculture quickly put the cleared land to new uses. Sheep-farming had become established following the Black Death when land was plentiful and hands were scarce, and it continued to expand into the cleared woodlands. The pressures on the deer's habitat were relentless, and the extent of land covered by wooded forest progressively reduced.[41] With the woods went the wild deer, and the hunting elite was forced to find new ways of preserving its ancient sport in this harsh new world.

One response was to limit the number of hunters, as the Norman kings had effectively done with their forest laws. The Norman kings had appropriated much of the best hunting land for themselves, stripping large numbers of forest dwellers of the right to hunt. The Forest Charter of 1217, though slow to be implemented, eventually restored their rights, causing a rapid increase in the number of subjects who could hunt and a corresponding and entirely predictable decline in the number of deer. By its provisions, all, from the grandest magnate to the smallest cottager, were entitled to kill not only deer, but any wild animals they found on their land. But surely, the hunting elite was now asking, the line had to be drawn somewhere? Should the humble really be permitted to partake in the sport of kings and nobles? Following the Charter, the number of subjects who could hunt had rapidly increased; unfortunately the numbers of huntable wild animals had not kept up. Hunting magnates who had so strongly opposed restrictions on their own hunting in no time found that wild animals were too precious and too few to be freely hunted by all, and introduced a new form of limitation – the game laws – to ensure that the finest hunting would be for them alone.

The first Game Law was enacted in 1389 by Richard II, prompted (it was claimed) by the observation that 'butchers, shoemakers, tailors, and other low persons, keep greyhounds and other dogs, and at times when good Christians on holy days are at church, hearing divine services, go hunting in parks, rabbit-runs, and warrens of lords and others'.[42] To prevent such outrages, it restricted the right to own hunting dogs to those who possessed land worth 40 shillings or more a year in rent, and ordered that any man in possession of less must keep his dogs fastened up or have their 'claws cut'.[43] The king gave the bill his consent, adding that the accoutrements of the peasant hunter – 'ferrets, hays, hair-pipes, cords' and other devices used to follow the 'sport of gentlefolk' – should also be prohibited. It was warmly welcomed by the hunting elites, and many further additions, governing the ownership and use of hunting dogs, traps and nets, were made throughout the fifteenth century. The game laws grew into a sprawling and unwieldy body of legislation, proving in time to be more durable, and possibly even more hated, than the much-reviled forest laws.

The game laws eroded the principles of the Forest Charter. Where the Charter had proudly restated the right of all to hunt wild animals on their own land, the game laws now removed that right. A form of means testing was introduced, with only the wealthy landowners allowed to hunt on their properties. When deer destroyed his woodland, or when hares or rabbits nibbled his crops, the smaller farmer could do nothing but stand by and watch the destruction. This was a clear attempt to limit hunting to a certain class. In place of the royal prerogative, the expanding gentry introduced new restrictions for hunting based upon wealth rather than divine royal right.

The game laws protected deer from the threat posed by the peasantry, but as much hunting land was still unfenced in the fourteenth century, the threat posed to the hunting gentleman by his wealthy neighbours was no less great. Wild deer wandered freely from one family's estate to another's, and one had to hope that the neighbours were not hunting too vigorously or the deer's visits to one's own land were sure to become more infrequent. In fact any hunting in a given area would deplete the local deer stocks, so a large landowner needed to find ways to limit his neighbours' hunting if he wanted to be sure that enough remained for his own entertainment. The solution was the construction of deer parks. Imparking involved no more than placing fences around one's land so that the deer could not escape. Inside the newly created park, a breeding programme provided a healthy supply of captive deer for its owner. Stock could be added by constructing deer leaps within the park walls – openings which allowed neighbouring wild deer to jump into the park, but from which they were unable to exit. The park provided its owner with a ready supply of deer: its walls ensured that the pleasure of hunting them was reserved for none but himself.

The park was not an invention of the late Middle Ages. There is evidence of parks in pre-Conquest England, and the Domesday Book reveals the existence of about thirty-five parks, hunting areas securely enclosed by timber paling and sometimes reinforced by a ditch.[44] The century following the Conquest saw a fresh wave of park construction.[45] Imparking was an expensive business. Clipstone Park in Sherwood Forest, for example, had been enclosed in the 1170s for the considerable sum of nearly £90, but within a decade yet more money was needed for repair of the paling.[46] Nonetheless, a growing economy in the thirteenth century provided the means for many more noble and knightly families to construct their own private parks and, in the century following the Charter, the number of parks increased rapidly, only slowing down in the early fourteenth century, a consequence both of the end of disafforestation and of the Black Death.[47] After the ravages of the 1350s, the labour required to build park walls was more expensive than ever before and with the drop in population the demand for protected hunting reserves was attenuated, but as population crept ever upwards from the late fifteenth century the attractions of a private park became more apparent. It has been estimated that nearly 2,000 parks existed at various times in the Middle Ages.[48] They were an enduring feature of the world of medieval hunting.

Late medieval estate records illustrate the careful efforts with which park owners attended to their deer.[49] There were two moments during the year when the deer's need for protection was greatest: the mating and fawning seasons, and the coldest winter months. During fawning and the rut, deer need to be left undisturbed, so park owners routinely employed extra men to oversee their parks at these crucial times. On the estates of the Bishop of Durham, for example, special 'watchers' were brought in during the month in which female deer fawned (the fence month) to ensure that the deer were left undisturbed.[50] The other perennial difficulty for park managers was the winter, typically a period of high mortality, particularly in areas where the deer were many and the resources few. Park owners' responses to this problem included the building of shelters and the provision of food. If cover was inadequate for the number of deer, sheds were built to protect the animals from the harsh winter. In order to ensure sufficient food for the deer, other stock was removed from parkland, and if this still left the deer malnourished, more positive action was taken, such as the putting out of hay, oats or browsewood for the animals' grazing. In Needwood Chase, Staffordshire, nearly 400 cartloads of browse were cut for the deer in the winter of 1417–18.[51] Besides providing winter feed, landowners used breeding programmes and regular head counts to control and monitor the deer populations in their parks. A carefully managed park required constant human intervention; and it takes some artistic licence to describe the deer contained within it as 'wild' animals.

So the creation of these parks changed the nature of hunting in subtle yet important ways. In open woodland, a deer was a wild animal – yours to take whilst on your land, but out of your reach as soon as it sauntered on to land where you had no right to be. When a deer jumped through a deer leap into a park, it was transformed from wild animal into private property. And how different was hunting a wild animal in an open forest from hunting a deer enclosed in a park with no hope of escape. The beast was always destined to encounter its owner's own park gates; no matter what its strength, speed or guile, its fate was sealed, if not that day, then surely on another. The deer parks successfully ensured a healthy population of fine deer, but they also introduced an artificial form of hunting with captive, and sometimes semi-tame, deer.

The modern innovation of parks was a source of pride to many Englishmen. One officer to the army proudly stated that 'The kingdom of England is adorned with fine hunting, for there is such abundance of parks, full of venison: fine red, roe and fallow deer, and when the ladies resort there for entertainment they take singular joy in shooting with the bow and killing these beasts.' But an observer from across the Channel saw the matter quite differently: 'Killing a beast in a park is not hunting,' he censured, for 'if it is in a park it is caught already. It is not to be wondered at that the English ladies kill them with a bow, for the poor beasts go where they want them to go, of necessity.'[52] Whatever their merits, deer parks continued to expand in the late Middle Ages and, as more land was brought into private parks, the number of truly wild deer necessarily went into decline.

We should of course take care not to exaggerate the speed at which open forests were replaced by enclosed parks. Parks had existed prior to the Norman Conquest, and they developed continuously from that date, more quickly when the economic and political conditions were ripe, and more slowly when they were not. The two systems, therefore, existed in tandem throughout the medieval period. Further, parks could be of considerable extent, and if they were large enough they sheltered animals that were wild rather than tame. The largest medieval deer park, Clarendon Park, measured 4,500 acres; hunting in such a space bore strong similarities to hunting in open woodland.[53] And, of course, considerable expanses of forests and unfenced woodland, controlled both by the Crown and by the landed elites, continued to form the location of much recreational hunting. Nonetheless, the trend towards hunting animals in enclosed spaces is unmistakable, and any romantic notions of medieval hunting we may have are sorely challenged by the reality of a growing network of protected reserves, harbouring semi-tame deer.

Yet artificial as parks may have been, they reflect a sensitive awareness on the part of the hunters of the need to balance their hunting with available resources. Hunting and preservation are always two sides of the same coin, and the fate of the wolf, which had always been free of all hunting restrictions, illustrates why. The wolf, along with the fox, was considered a 'noxious' animal; a danger while alive, and of little value dead beyond the pelt that could be used for mittens and cloaks if its foul smell could be removed. Wolves not only threatened livestock, they were also a threat to human life, and tales of country children being taken by old wolves losing their teeth and speed abounded in medieval folklore. They were to be hunted and killed, and there was no penalty for their destruction. The only restriction was that they might not be hunted in the royal forests – since (the Norman kings reasoned) the temptation for a suitably armed hunter to take a shot at a deer would surely be impossible to resist.[54]

The abundance of wolves throughout England in pre-Norman times is attested to by the Saxon name for January: 'wolf-month'; and they were still sufficiently numerous in the early twelfth century for Henry I to maintain a considerable wolf-hunting staff.[55] Place and field names in north Derbyshire suggest they were particularly numerous here, though they were found in most parts of the land, and made fine hunting during the close season of other animals in the depths of winter. A thirteenth-century French writer confidently described the wolf as a beast 'which most people have seen', but his fifteenth-century English translator was at pains to stress this was only the case 'beyond the sea'. By this date, unrestricted wolf-hunting had reached its logical conclusion: the eventual extinction of the wolf.[56] By the late fourteenth century the wolf population in Britain had dwindled considerably, and they are thought to have died out at some point in the following century. In the late sixteenth century, one writer considered, the wolf 'be not found in any place'.[57] Efforts to maintain a population of deer were certainly contrived, but without artificial methods of deer preservation this most noble and beloved of the native animals would certainly have shared the wolf's fate.

Hunting's very nature was always destined to change. The wild-deer hunting introduced by the Norman kings had rested upon large expanses of uncultivated yet protected woodland, but the pressure on this land down the years was unremitting. First the nobles demanded a share of the hunting woods, then population growth encouraged landowners to put their woodland to other uses. With more hunters fighting over ever less land, the wild-deer hunting of the Middle Ages was gradually forced to give way. In its place emerged a related but different sport. Hunting magnates carved out their own private parks, and invested large sums in modern fencing designed to keep the deer in and the poachers out. A new form of tame hunting had emerged which, though it initially coexisted with the wild deer hunting of an earlier age, was destined to replace it.

CHAPTER FIVE

The Tudors

[Robin Hood and the Knight] washed and dried their hands together,
And sat down to their dinner;
Bread and wine they had in plenty,
And sweetmeats from the deer.[1]

Even the most committed hunters were distracted from the thrill of the chase for much of the second half of the fifteenth century. Between 1455 and 1485, England was torn apart by a series of bloody civil wars as the two branches of the ruling Plantagenet family fought over the right to the Crown. Temporarily, the smaller civil skirmishes between hunting magnates were put to one side, as country gentlemen found themselves involved in an unwanted war with far higher stakes. The eventual outcome was one that few had envisaged. In the summer of 1485, as Henry Tudor gathered his forces in France, Richard III's frail grip on power began to loosen. Meeting with his rival on 22 August in battle at Bosworth Field, two of Richard's leading commanders abandoned his cause, and the king himself was killed as he led a last desperate charge at the heart of his enemy's army. The throne passed to Henry Tudor – the last remaining representative of the Lancastrian line, and one whose claim to the throne would in normal times have been far-fetched at best.[2]

His claim to the throne might have been tenuous, but Henry VII proved himself a strong and able leader. From the outset of his reign, he was determined to bring order to England after thirty years of civil war and social unrest. He faced two insurrections during his reign, as pretenders claiming a closer dynastic link to the Plantagenets challenged his rule. Both were swiftly and brutally repressed. Henry ruthlessly enforced royal fiscal rights, building up reserves sufficient to free him from the constraint of frequently requesting money from Parliament. He died in 1509 after a twenty-four-year reign, little loved, yet bequeathing the inestimable benefits of a safe throne and solvent government to his second son, Henry VIII.[3]

Besides tightening up the civil administration, Henry had also attempted to ensure the better management of England's woodland during his reign. Like so many monarchs before him, Henry VII was a keen huntsman. Throughout his reign, he took a personal interest in his hunting establishment, and in 1507, just two years before his death, he still went out hunting and hawking every day, apparently unhindered by his failing eyesight.[4] He was also an ardent defender of the royal hunting prerogative. Weak government and civil commotion had always resulted in looting and despolation in the forests, and the Wars of the Roses had opened new opportunities for unscrupulous hunting magnates and gangs of poachers, just as in earlier years. For a generation, local gentry and others had become accustomed to taking deer in the forests with little interference from the royal foresters, and one of Henry's first acts as king was to appoint new foresters in an attempt to set his forests back in order. The long lists of wrongdoers prepared for his first forest eyre, held in 1488, show how widely the forest laws had been disregarded in recent years, with the forest officers often more deeply implicated in the plunder than the neighbours they were supposed to police.[5] Corrupt officials were removed and replaced by men who had been loyal during the recent war with Richard III − Sir John Savage and his sons, for example, were rewarded with valuable offices in Feckenham Forest, Malvern Chase and numerous other royal parks.[6] With the new foresters in charge, Henry had taken important steps towards restoring the medieval network of royal forests.

His son and successor, Henry VIII, was introduced to stag-hunting in childhood and developed a passion for the sport which never left him. As a young man he declared that hunting was a means to avoid 'Idlenes the ground of all vyce and to exercise that thing that shall be honorable and to the bodye healthfull and profitable'.[7] As an adult, he was considered a skilled hunter, frequently rising early and spending as many as eight hours a day in the saddle out hunting for deer, not uncommonly wearing out several horses in the process. Following stags and boars for up to thirty miles, he never seemed to get tired and only heavy rain kept him indoors.[8] In the 1520s, Richard Pace, his secretary, wearily informed Cardinal Wolsey of His Highness's devotion: 'the king rises daily, except on holy days, at 4 or 5 o'clock and hunts 'til 9 or 10 at night. He spares no pain to convert the sport of hunting into martyrdom.'[9]

The hunt infused every aspect of the new king's life. His love letters to Anne Boleyn were embellished with tales of his day's hunting exploits, and sometimes accompanied by the buck or hart he had killed; a dead hart, for example, was sent with a missive describing it as 'hart's flesh for Henry'.[10] Foreign ambassadors as well as his officials murmured frequent complaints about the king's hunting delaying or disrupting business.[11] In July 1526, an official approaching with letters for the king's attention was brushed aside and informed 'he was going out to have a shot at a stag'. The frustrated messenger was told to wait until evening.[12] Later in Henry's reign the French ambassador Charles de Marrillac wrote home that there 'was no news worth writing, the king being, with a small company, hunting, about 20 miles from here'.[13]

Although Henry exploited the material products of his forests as assiduously as any medieval monarch, he also used them for his own personal hunting, particularly during his regular progresses through the country.[14] Many of his efforts in the royal forests were directed at improving the hunting they afforded. In Northamptonshire, for example, he introduced a system of new and enlarged parks during the 1540s.[15] He personally viewed the ground for the new park at Hartwell while negotiations were proceeding for his divorce from Anne Boleyn, and actually extended the area of royal forest, making the first afforestations for three hundred years.[16] Using a form of persuasion that often left his subjects no choice whatever, he procured much of the country between Hampton Court and Nonsuch so that his frequent visits to his two favourite palaces might be enlivened with a little sport.[17]

The dissolution of the monasteries provided Henry with fresh opportunities to extend his hunting. He had regularly used these as hunting stops on his progresses earlier in his reign; now they were used to extend his own private network of hunting preserves.[18] In all, thirty new palaces and hunting lodges were built after 1535 and, by the time of his death twelve years later, he owned a total of fifty residences, containing some 200 parks. Over half a million pounds had been spent on their construction.[19]

Henry VIII bequeathed more than hunting palaces. He even turned his pen to writing poems extolling his favourite pastime:

> Pastime with good company
> I love and shall until I die
> Grudge to lust, but none deny
> So God be pleased, thus live will I
> For my pastance,
> Hunt, sing and dance,
> My heart is set,
> All goodly sport
> For my comfort:
> Who shall me let?[20]

His hunting, however, was brought to a swift end at the age of forty-four, when he fell from his horse in a jousting tournament.[21] The accident crippled one leg and left him a chronic invalid. His only consolation now lay in food and drink, which he continued to consume in immoderate quantities to the inevitable detriment of his waistline: in his last few years he measured an unfortunate four and half feet round the waist. Yet this large and uncomely figure notwithstanding, Henry VIII continued to hunt into older age. He turned to hawking, a sport for which he had 'shown no affection' in younger years, and his hunting became a little gentler. The long progress was abandoned in the 1540s, and his hunting confined to the royal palaces in which he resided. Mounting blocks were built in favourite hunting parks so that 'the King's grace may not only get upon his horse easily but light down upon the same'; and bridges were built in Woolwich marshes for Henry 'to ride over the ditches a-hawking and a-hunting safely'.[22] Towards the end of his life, though needing the assistance of several servants to clamber up to the stand, his enthusiasm remained undimmed.

In addition to slowing the pace of his hunting, Henry became more interested in the drive hunt. At Hatfield in 1541, he presided over a drive hunt in which over 200 animals were killed in one day.[23] This was a magnificent display, intended, in no small part, to impress his French counterpart – the French ambassador was invited to proceedings and urged not to forget to tell his king what he had seen.[24] His palace at Hampton Court was fitted with a specially constructed enclosed paddock for drive-hunting.[25] The drive hunt, though taxing the king's skill at shooting, was a poor relation of the athletic, horseback hunting he had once enjoyed, but Henry continued to guard his hunting privileges no less jealously than before.

Throughout his life, and regardless of his state of health, Henry VIII devoted his considerable skills and energy to maintaining the royal forests, though the external pressures on these protected reserves were becoming ever more acute with the passage of time. The decline of the High Peak Forest in north-west Derbyshire illustrates the Crown's losing battle. The High Peak was a remote and wild expanse of woodland, but its isolated situation did not protect it from the local inhabitants' encroachments in their search for a living. On a hunting expedition to the forest in 1526, Henry became alarmed that there appeared to be so little grass left for the deer, and appointed commissioners to inquire into illegal grazing by horses, cattle and sheep. Reporting two years later, they found no fewer than five herds of cattle (amounting to 903 animals) in the place of the two that the forest regulations allowed, as well as over 4,000 sheep and 320 horses. It was little wonder that the deer stocks had gone into serious decline.[26]

By the time the Earl of Shrewsbury was appointed Chief Forester of High Peak Forest two decades later, the situation had deteriorated yet further.

Shrewsbury found a great number of sheep in the forests, 'whereby the feeding for the deer is utterly consumed, and thereby also the said deer are forced to flee out of the said forest for their relief whereas they be killed and destroyed'.[27] He ordered the impounding of several hundred sheep (most met their death in the process), and set up an inquiry into the condition of browse and pasturage. But his actions were too little, too late. By the 1550s, following a succession of severe winters, his foresters were forced to report that the famous old forest was 'a champion and plane place wherein no wood groweth'.[28] So many deer had died or strayed out of the forest that only a single herd of thirty was left. The foresters issued a statement requesting a stay on all hunting for six years, optimistic that this might encourage the breeding of this small herd – a vain hope that was soon to be disappointed. The human and economic pressures on the royal forests were remorseless, and this time they prevailed.

Although Henry and his courtiers continued to enjoy the hunting of wild deer through the first half of the sixteenth century, wild deer-hunting was becoming a pastime that increasingly few of his subjects were able to experience. Outside the royal forests, deer hunting in open woodland had been almost entirely replaced by the hunting of semi-tame deer in private parks. A few red deer could be found in the wild in some of the more remote woodlands – Dartmoor, High Peak Forest and Sherwood, for example – but most were bred and reared in enclosed parks, and the smaller, and more common, fallow deer were almost always found in parks.[29] Hundreds of parks existed by this date, and the claim made by Tudor writers that deer-hunting in 'spacious forests' was superior to all other forms of hunting was in reality little more than a lament for times past.[30] A private park protected by an expanding set of game laws and numerous gamekeepers was an obligatory component of any country estate, highly valued both for the hunting and for the venison that it produced, but the park provided an artificial form of hunting, a sport that was tamed and domesticated when contrasted with the medieval hunting of old.

The form of hunting may have changed, but the sport retained its pivotal place in upper-class life. Training in the art began in childhood and was an integral part of any young gentleman's education.[31] One mother was reassured that her son's summer had been 'virtuously spent in hawking and hunting, with such other pastimes as beseemeth such a one to use'.[32] It was the form and process of hunting rather than the end product that marked hunting out as a gentle pastime. As the writer and physician Andrew Boorde noted in his handbook on health, hunting was for 'great men', who 'do not set so much by the meate, as they do by the pastyme of kyllying it'.[33]

No celebration or special occasion was complete without a little hunting, and providing sport was an integral part of Tudor hospitality. For example, when the gentleman John Quennell of Chiddingfold, Surrey, stayed at the house of his friend Thomas South to celebrate a baptism, the party was enlivened with a little illicit hunting in the neighbours' grounds. Several members of the party broke into Odiham Park after the christening supper was finished, killing five deer and getting lost in the process: Quennell himself did not emerge until the following morning, when he had to ask for directions. In Lancashire, a bridegroom's companions lured him into unlawful hunting the night before his wedding: all had the misfortune to be caught by the keepers before any real damage was done. Whether the young groom made it to the altar the next day is unfortunately not recorded.[34]

No less important than the social role played by hunting was the large and valuable quantity of meat it produced. The value of venison can hardly be exaggerated: it was, literally, beyond price, integral to feasting, a symbol of honour to guests, and unavailable on the open market. Large landowners needed venison both for their own table and (no less importantly) to distribute as largesse to friends, family and neighbours. The produce of parks was thus variously consumed fresh by the household, salted for the winter, or given away. This range of uses is demonstrated by the Howard family in Suffolk. Their deer park at Framlingham contained several thousand head of deer and in most years something between one and two hundred deer were given away to local gentry, churchmen, friends and family.[35] Likewise the Lisle family gave away much of their venison to friends and relations, as well as sending many gifts of small game and hunting dogs.[36] The custom of giving was an important symbol of a great house's power, consolidating social networks and relationships; and the exclusion of rivals from this cycle of gift-giving and the refusal of gifts were both every bit as significant as the exchanges that did occur.[37]

The wise park owner took especial care to ensure that his gifts were appreciated by his richer and more powerful acquaintances. For example, in Gloucestershire, Henry, eleventh Lord Berkeley, shrewdly sent yearly gifts of venison, salmon and pies to the queen, 'to judges, great officers of state, privy councillors and lawyers, whereof he reaped honour and profit a hundred times more than the charge'.[38] But the exchange of game was by no means confined to large landowners, royalty and courtiers. The custom extended right down the social hierarchy, with smaller householders giving gifts of hares, rabbits, partridges and pheasants – gifts that befitted their humbler means.

Parks were a precious possession, valued both for their hunting and their venison, and their owners invested large sums in gamekeepers and in constructing and maintaining wooden fencing in an attempt to protect them. But protecting a huntable population of deer was an uphill battle, one that required much more than the provision of wooden pales and gamekeepers.

Park owners needed the assistance of a national system of protection and regulation, and Parliament readily obliged with the appropriate laws.[39] Throughout the Tudors' reigns, new game laws were steadily unfurled, providing ever greater protection for the park owners' deer. A law prohibiting hunting at night or in disguise was introduced; another making it an offence to keep nets without a licence soon followed; these and similar acts were frequently passed through Henry VIII's reign. But though the game laws may have protected deer, they further underscored the disappearance of older medieval hunting practices. Wild deer had once roamed free over wide tracts of woodland, the hunter's capacities, rather than his park walls, constraining his ability to capture them. By the sixteenth century, deer were private property, enclosed in parks and rigorously protected by the long reach of the law.

Though parks were highly esteemed, their existence was under increasing pressure throughout the century. Early in the Tudor period, the creation of parks slowed dramatically as landowners tried to exploit their land in other ways. Stagnant land values and low rents throughout the fifteenth century encouraged them to reconsider how they managed their estates, and the appeal of selling off woodland for other uses could be hard for a cash-strapped landowner to resist.[40] Once estates had become fragmented, old hunting grounds were invariably put under the plough, and there was little prospect of the land being restored to hunting once this had happened. Following Henry VIII's dissolution of the monasteries, many of the forests carefully stewarded by the clergy down the centuries were sold off and cleared by new owners keen to get their hands on the money the timber could raise.[41] Hunting remained the pre-eminent pastime of gentlefolk, but everywhere the trees were going down, and with them the deer's habitat was irrevocably lost. With this steady reduction in the amount of woodland cover, deer-hunting was forced to carve out a niche in an increasingly hostile environment.

Thus the sixteenth century witnessed a heightening of the conflict that hunting had always provoked. As land to hunt over became more scarce, the temptations for all ranks of society to turn to trapping and snaring deer whenever the opportunity presented, and regardless of whether they owned them or not, inevitably increased. Hunting was capable of pitting one family against another in the most acrimonious way, and conflicts between neighbouring landowners remained an indelible part of the hunting world. In Yorkshire in 1544, for example, the Star Chamber was presented with a typical such squabble between two magnates in Richmondshire. Shortly before his death in the 1540s, Sir James Metcalfe had apparently 'nourished up 11 tame red deer about [his] house in Redale', and suspicion fell upon his neighbour, Lord Scrope, when it became apparent that all eleven had strangely disappeared. Admitting that 'he knows not who has killed them', Sir James's heir, Christopher, nonetheless called on an elderly uncle who claimed to have 'known and seen Lord Scrope hunt in the forests on many other occasions' and added that 'the voice of the country' shared his belief that a servant of Lord Scrope was responsible for the death of the missing deer.[42] Perhaps the illegality of the hunting had served to heighten the thrill of the chase through these Yorkshire forests; it certainly continued to fuel the feud between these neighbouring magnates. And there was nothing unusual about these events in Yorkshire; Star Chamber records for several counties are filled with similar cases. The only winners were the lawyers, who grew fat on the charges that such trials incurred.[43]

With the decline in deer, hunters began to take more interest in small game – the pheasants, partridges and hares. But, of course, as more hunters went after them, the numbers of small game risked going into decline. Although the game laws already offered some protection, more laws were soon considered necessary to shield these too from the traps and snares of the masses. Henry VII extended the game laws to pheasants and partridges, and Henry VIII forbade the hunting of hares in the snow.[44] Wherever the hunting elites found pleasure in hunting, there they extended their game laws in order to protect it. Game laws were proving a flexible and useful tool, endlessly adaptable to changing hunting tastes.

The game laws may have successfully protected the gentry's hunting, but this protection could only be bought at a price. Laws which took away the right to trap and snare wild animals in the common fields, and which forbade the poor to hunt even on their own land, were obviously socially divisive, and a less desirable outcome of the game laws was the social tensions they created. Cases of poaching which reached the courts allow us to glimpse the hatred that seethed in rural communities amongst those excluded by the game laws from the hunting fraternity. In 1524, for example, a spate of poaching in his North Mimms estate provoked Sir John More to take his grievances to Star Chamber. In a lengthy deposition, he told of the night when three yeomen, a parish priest and ten others, 'with force and arms riotously, with bows, arrows, coats of defence and other weapons defensible', assembled at midnight, broke down the poles of his close and took six of his deer. They ripped two fawns out of the bellies of two does, and 'in despite set the said buck's head with a stick in his mouth' towards his mansion house. Before leaving they killed a further two young deer, hacking them to pieces and leaving them on the ground where they lay.[45] This was an emphatic and symbolic rejection of the manor's authority and of all that it stood for; such incidents were frequent in the troubled century that followed.

Poaching trials contain recurrent evidence of defiant and rebellious behaviour. In Lancashire, poachers flung stag heads at the door of the keeper's lodge.[46] Elsewhere bands of poachers dined riotously and publicly on their ill-gotten gains in local inns. In Wiltshire, William, Earl of Pembroke and keeper of Clarendon Park complained to Star Chamber of deer-stealers who had feasted on a poached buck in 'vaunting manner', rejoicing 'that they had ... killed and taken the said buck to the great dishonour of your subject'.[47] The game laws may have offered legal redress to the park owners who suffered such losses, but the trials they produced illustrate the hatred that simmered in rural communities.

In 1548 a spate of rioting broke out across the country.[48] The main centres of revolt were Norfolk, Devon and Cornwall, but fully half of all English counties witnessed insurrection to some degree, triggered by deeply rooted rural discontent centred upon high prices and enclosures, and frequently fuelled by religious controversies as well. Though ostensibly unconnected with deer and the game laws, it is nonetheless significant that parks and deer were a common target of the rioters' fury. Beginning in Norfolk, rebels visited the estates of the gentry, cast down hedges and began slaughtering and eating the deer.[49] The pattern was then repeated in one place after another. During the Suffolk Rising, agricultural labourers and cloth-workers attacked deer parks and their keepers, killed deer and ate the meat.[50] In Oxfordshire, rebels attacked Sir John William's parks at Thame and Rycote and 'killed all the deer'.[51] The government's response was to introduce yet more game laws: Edward VI's law of 1549 made it a felony to enter forest or park at night or in disguise with the intent to hunt.[52] But such repressive legislation, though it might offer greater protection to these precious animals, further stoked the embers of discontent. The riots were suppressed, but the resentment that parks and game laws provoked was not so easily put away.

The killing and eating of deer which accompanied the riots in the late 1540s was filled with symbolism. The country's parks and game laws ensured that venison was a foodstuff consumed by none but the great landowners, their families and friends. It was food that could not be purchased, the nation's most potent marker of wealth and privilege. The eating of deer, therefore, was not simply a mindless act of vandalism by a hungry peasantry; it was also a political action laden with significance – a symbolic overturning of the established order. Initially royal forests, and then the game laws, had endeavoured to establish ownership of these beautiful wild animals. Both were resented equally by those who were excluded, and this bitterness had long found expression in social action as well as in lore and legend.

Nowhere is this illustrated more clearly than in the tales of Robin Hood. These tales were a diverse body of stories recounting different incidents but each featuring much the same well-known cast of characters, and they circulated widely among all ranks of society in late medieval England.[53] Just as the characters were largely unchanging, so was the location: the king's northern forests. And although these ballads and stories ranged over a diverse set of topics dear to the Tudor mindset, the hunting and eating of the king's deer was a frequently recurring motif.[54] Robin and his men dine off such dainties as venison pasties and the 'noumbles of the deer' – the sweetbreads, widely considered to be a delicacy.[55] In one of the best known tales, 'The Gest of Robyn Hode', the king is served up his own deer – illegally poached by Robin and his men.[56] In other tales, men were outlawed for crimes against the king's venison: they took refuge in the forests, where of course they continued to poach and plunder the king's finest deer.[57] The taking and eating of deer was a staple of medieval legend, but it was usually a story, a humorous depiction of the way one might wish the world to be rather than a statement of the way things actually were. In the mid-Tudor rebellions, however, the wholesale and audacious plunder of the royal forests was occasionally translated from legend into reality. Whether in story-telling or real life, the privileged status of venison imbued the eating of deer by ordinary people with a symbolic importance that never failed to amuse and entertain.

Just as the king's forest laws had once caused resentment among the nobility, so the nobles' own game laws were now resented in turn. A growing population, ever hungry for the woods and forests, was in constant competition with the gentry's deer, and this competition sharpened the edge of social conflict. In the Tudor period, hunting was justly revered as an ancient tradition of the royalty and nobility, but its practitioners proved no more successful at removing the discord and strife surrounding hunting than their forefathers had been. It was a conflict set to continue for many years to come.

CHAPTER SIX

Elizabeth and the Puritans

Of all the pleasures in country and court
Hunting with hounds is the pleasantest sport.
Though painful it may seemeth, yet health it doth bring:
It is a pastime for a duke or a king
    Merrily chants the hounds in the wood:
    Most men it delights, the noise is so good.[1]

What Christian heart can take pleasure to see one poor beast to rent, tear and kill another? (Philip Stubbes)[2]

Henry VIII's numerous wives had borne him eleven children and, on his death in 1547, the throne passed to his only living son, Edward VI, then a mere nine years old. However, Henry's failure to provide clear instructions regarding his rule set in motion a chaotic and relentless religious upheaval, with the Crown passing next to his great-niece, Lady Jane Grey, for a fleeting nine days, then to his first daughter Mary, who died five years later. In 1558, the throne passed finally to his second daughter, Elizabeth, whose mother Anne Boleyn he had had executed in 1536 when Elizabeth was a mere two years old. Little of the relationship between king and daughter is known, yet Elizabeth inherited at least one thing from her wayward father: a passion for sport in general, and for hunting in particular.

Elizabeth's childhood had been spent in the care of governesses and tutors at Hatfield House, on the estate confiscated from the Duke of Buckingham following his fall from favour and beheading in 1521, and much of her time there had been devoted to learning the arts of hunting. As a girl of just fifteen she had cut the throat of a fallen stag with her own hand.[3] By the

6. As the most senior person present at the hunt, Queen Elizabeth is invited to take the first cut of a newly slaughtered stag.

time she succeeded to the throne at the age of twenty-five, the young queen was an enthusiastic and accomplished horsewoman and hunter, who regularly followed the hunt on horseback. Since aristocratic hunting custom dictated that the most important personage present should be invited to slit the captured stag's throat with a knife, Elizabeth was frequently dignified with the honour of dispatching the stag – a role that she admitted much 'gratified' her.[4] One of the sixteenth century's most popular hunting books, *The Noble Arte of Venerie*, included a woodcut illustrating the royal huntsman passing Elizabeth a knife to open the belly of a stag.[5] On one occasion she demonstrated her mercy by sparing a hart which had taken to water, and 'ransomed' its ears instead.[6] Though her successor, James I, dismissed her legacy – 'being a lady whose sex and years were not so apt to that kind of recreation' – her ability as a hunter should not be underestimated.[7]

Elizabeth used her extensive hunting estates to entertain foreign dignitaries, and was in turn provided with hunting by her subjects on her progresses or tours around the country. On her stay at the Earl of Leicester's Kenilworth estate in July 1575 she was fêted with particularly extravagant festivities lasting nineteen days and with no expense spared.[8] Hunting in the Kenilworth deer park was the centrepiece of the revelries. Robert Laneham, one of the earl's employees, declared that the sport had been a 'pastime delectable in so high a degree ... there can be none any way comparable to this'.[9] A visit to her own park at Clarendon in 1574 was enlivened with a magnificent drive hunt, during which, according to one eyewitness, no fewer than 340 bucks were killed.[10]

The drive hunt had always been central to Elizabeth's hunting, and as she neared old age she evinced a marked preference for it. With the queen in her late fifties, Lord Montague provided entertainment of a suitably sedate nature during Her Highness's sojourn on his estate at Cowdray. He had a special bower constructed in his deer park from which Elizabeth and her ladies-in-waiting shot at deer rounded up and driven towards them; the queen apparently killed 'three or four' on this occasion.[11] She also continued to hunt on horseback well into old age. At the age of seventy-seven she was said to be well and 'exceedingly disposed to hunting, for every second or third day she is on horseback and continues the sport long'.[12]

As a keen hunter, Queen Elizabeth was inevitably interested in the protection of her forests and, with a growing population, the need for vigilance was as great as ever. In mid-century it was discovered that in a single year the keepers of Needwood Forest in Staffordshire had cut and sold 841 wagon-loads of timber.[13] Other northern forests fared little better, and in 1564 she reached the pessimistic conclusion that 'The woods and deer of all our forests and chases and also of all our parks by the north Trent be much spoilt, wasted and destroyed both by the inordinate taking, felling and browsing of the woods and also by the killing of the game and deer.'[14] Her chief forester was charged with tightening up all the forest laws and courts in the northern forests, though his efforts with the recalcitrant locals (like those of many chief foresters before him), were only partially successful.

Hunting was of course not simply the preserve of the monarch. It remained the pre-eminent pastime of the nobility and gentry, and proverbs affirming the close connection between hunting and gentility abounded. 'He cannot be a gentleman which loveth not hunting and hawking,' announced one authority; and 'he cannot be a gentleman which loveth not a dog'.[15] A steady stream of treatises and handbooks for gentlemen hunters (and for those aspiring to join their ranks) was published through the sixteenth century. Even the nobleman's servants were provided with books instructing them in the art of accompanying their master hunting – reminding us once again that the pastime was in reality less exclusive than the hunting literature of the time proclaimed.[16] The *Boke of St Albans*, the late fifteenth-century hunting treatise, was reprinted some twenty times between 1486 and 1615.[17] Other fifteenth-century books went through numerous imprints, and new works on hunting, horsemanship and dogs added to this growing body of literature. The appetite for reading about hunting was seemingly insatiable.

For gentlemen hunters, the hart of course remained the quarry *par excellence*, hart-hunting being described variously as 'honourable and delightful' and the 'noble arte'.[18] Sixteenth-century hunting manuals presented the chase as training for war, a stimulant to health, an antidote to idleness and a distraction from baser forms of entertainments; and provided the interested reader with ever more detail about every aspect of the hunt.[19] Furthermore, they show that the hart hunt had changed little since the early fourteenth century, when Edward II's huntsman William Twiti had produced the earliest hunting manual. Many customs dated back several centuries: the analysis of footprints, droppings and the height of branches and boughs broken by the deer's head to select an animal to hunt; the use of bloodhounds to flush the deer out and running hounds to pursue it; the setting of relays to take over the hunt as the original dogs tired; the use of bows and arrows to maim a fleeing deer and mounted swordsmen to cast the fatal blow; the ritual dissection of the slain deer's carcass, and the reward thrown to the dogs. How far such customs were really being practised in the enclosed parks in which deer were now invariably hunted is open to question, but the ideal of the medieval deer hunt was certainly still being peddled by sixteenth-century writers.

Just as in earlier hunting treatises, there was a strong emphasis in much of this literature upon the correct forms of speech and address. Page after page was filled with the correct terms for the parts of the animals, for their ages, footprints, excrement, mating, 'noises and voices', young, tails and fat, as well as with detailed information about the proper terms for the dogs and correct use of the horn. As the most highly rated animal, the most extensive vocabulary was inevitably reserved for the hart, in particular its 'head' or antlers, as this determined the age of the animal and thereby its suitability for hunting. In wholly typical form, Gascoigne advised his readers: 'The thing that beareth the Antliers, Royals, and toppes, ought to be called the beame, and the little clyffes or streakes therein are called gutters.'[20] After endless information about the correct name for each head at every cycle of its growth, there followed six illustrations describing the correct vocabulary for the heads depicted: 'This is called the Burre'; 'This heade should be called a Crowned toppe'; 'This heade should be called a palmed toppe', and so forth.[21] But although no animals were accorded such complex and extensive language as the deer, no aspect of the gentleman's hunt was too lowly to escape a special vocabulary of its own. A gentleman seemed to be expected to know even the correct terms for the noises that each animal made: 'An Harte belloweth: a Bucke groyneth: a Rowe belleth: a Bore freameth: a Hare & a conie beateth or tappeth: a Fox barketh: a Badgerd shriketh: an Otter whineth: & a Wolfe howleth.'[22] With a vocabulary of such complexity, it is little wonder that sixteenth-century gentlemen continued to claim that hunting was for kings, not peasants.[23]

Interestingly, however, the drive hunt, which had figured so heavily in medieval hunting literature, had largely disappeared by the sixteenth century. Elizabeth, as we have seen, was routinely entertained with elaborate drive hunts, but the pretence that many of her subjects regularly participated in drive-hunting had by now been dropped. Of course, it is far from certain that drive-hunting had ever been widely practised outside the royal court, our earlier evidence deriving largely from literary, rather than archival, sources; nonetheless the drive had occupied an important symbolic place within the medieval hunter's horizons. By the sixteenth century, the deer drive had lost its powerful conceptual hold, and the reasons for this are not hard to fathom. Keen hunters faced an unrelenting and expensive struggle to maintain a huntable population of deer, and so the indiscriminate and large-scale slaughter of the deer drive was a luxury that failed to convince, even if only as an idea rather than a reality.

In place of such profligate waste a more conservationist alternative – the deer course – had emerged. Deer coursing involves setting two dogs upon one deer in an enclosed space; it is a form of competition between hounds, the purpose being to see which will chase the deer the more successfully. A few large estates had a permanent structure specially designed for the coursing of deer. At Ravensdale in Derbyshire, for example, there was a course stretching one mile in length and about eighty yards wide enclosed by two parallel hedges.[24] The course at Clarendon Park was slightly longer, and enclosed by fencing rather than hedges.[25] The most elaborate deer courses would also have had pens at their start to contain the deer, and a standing or lodge along the course, from where spectators could view the event. At Lodge Park in Gloucestershire, for example, the course was described as having 'hansome contriv'd Pens and Places, where the Deere are kept, and turn'd out for the Course'.[26] The sport could equally be enjoyed without the luxury and expense of a dedicated deer course and standing. Posts and rope could be used to construct a satisfactory temporary enclosure, as was doubtless done in many smaller English deer parks.

The practice of deer-coursing predates the sixteenth century. The deer course at Windsor Little Park, for example, was probably constructed in the middle of the fifteenth century; and that at Ravensdale has been dated as far back as the fourteenth.[27] Despite these antecedents, however, deer-coursing reached the peak of its popularity during the early modern period, a development which must be related to the increasing pressures on deer-hunting at this time. Coursing guaranteed entertainment for both today and tomorrow, and offered an intelligent use of scarce resources.

The hunting handbooks, however, devoted little attention to the sport of deer-coursing – perhaps they considered that chasing deer in enclosed pens lacked the dignity this noble beast deserved. They focused proudly on hunting, and the space that might have been filled with instructions for deer-coursing was filled instead with detail about the hunting of smaller animals, including even the hunting of vermin – an activity that had traditionally been held in very low esteem. The sixteenth-century hunting manuals display an undying commitment to the sporting values of an earlier age and an attempt to preserve them in an ever changing world.

The hare hunt, for example, was always signalled by sixteenth-century writers as worthy of the attention of the gentleman hunter; Sir Thomas Cockaine even reversed the usual order of things by describing the hare hunt ahead of that of the deer in his hunting treatise.[28] The challenges posed by the hare were unique and intricate. This small, furry mammal of course posed no threat to the lives of either hunters or their dogs, yet sixteenth-century huntsmen were full of praise for the hare, its virtues and qualities considered by one writer to be 'verie great & many'.[29] The attraction lay in the subtlety and challenge of the hunt. Running in zigzag lines, doubling back and forth, crossing, turning and winding, before breaking into a straight run at speed that might continue for several miles, the hare taxed both the speed and the tracking ability of the hounds, and provided exercise and spectacle for the hunter. Hare-hunting called for great skill, and this elevated the sport into a noble pastime fit for kings.

The scale of the hunt was small. Handbooks recommended just two huntsmen, possibly a third; it mattered little whether they were on foot or on horseback. One of the hunters led the hounds as the hare darted one way and then the next. His task was to encourage the dogs with horn and cries to seek out and chase the hare, to track it in its dancing path, to follow it as it doubled and turned. The other hunter hung at the back of the hunt and encouraged any dogs that fell behind. The handbooks were full of stories of crafty hares that had taken to water, tucked themselves in the gaps in stone walls, or hidden amongst sheep after running for two or three hours to escape the hounds. As befitted an animal hunted by the gentry, the hare's death was marked by the blowing of the horn, and by ritual dissection of its body. First it was skinned and the gall removed. The dogs were then rewarded with bread and other morsels dipped in the hare's blood, before the animal's head was cut off and its remains thrown to the dogs. Though its flesh was not highly rated, many hunters no doubt preferred to take their quarry home to put in the pot, but the hunting handbooks tended to play down utilitarian hunting of this nature. They described the hare hunt as a form of entertainment for men of leisure, concluding that 'the Hare maketh greatest pastime and pleasure'.[30]

The rabbit or coney, although its flesh made finer eating than the hare's and its skin had a number of practical uses, was much less highly rated by the huntsman. Where the hunted hare sped away above ground, the rabbit darted below and the hunting consisted in fetching it from its burrows for the dogs to kill. Writers recommended two or three spaniels or curs to drive the animals into their burrows, and ferrets to send in after them. Sixteenth-century writers considered it a low sort of hunting, useful for the table but peripheral to the main business of the hunt. In Cockaine's short treatise, it did not even merit a mention.

The hunting of vermin, by contrast, was attracting a greater degree of interest by the sixteenth century. Hunting manuals devoted increasing space to vermin and predators – foxes, badgers, wildcats, polecats and otters – low-status quarry that medieval writers had frequently neglected to consider. Each presented its own challenges to the hunter and demanded a degree of skill and, in a world of declining deer stocks, any animal that taxed the hunter's talents was worthy of consideration.

The common fox was slowly starting to emerge from its long-held position of obscurity. The animal was considered false and crafty: preying on country farms, it was a pest, fair game for all. Late medieval writers had declared that the season for foxhunting lay between the Nativity and the Feast of the Annunciation (25 March), though as foxes were unwanted vermin these dates were probably routinely neglected.[31] It was most commonly hunted with traps and snares by farmers who wanted to rid their land of pests, but members of the gentry also hunted the fox with hounds in the name of sport. An animal with a strong scent that could be successfully pursued by dogs, it had always had its place in hunting – The Master of Game, for example, had thought 'the hunting for the fox is fair, for the good cry of the hounds that follow him so nigh and with so good a will'.[32] Sixteenth-century hunters evinced a clear preference for hunting the fox with hounds above ground, and in order to be sure of a good chase in the open, the hunters needed to stop the foxes' burrows. Thus the well-organised huntsman began his preparations well in advance, establishing the location of the foxes' earth, and stopping it up at night with twigs and earth while the fox was abroad searching for food. The attraction lay in watching the hounds at work, and as dog breeding and training improved in the early modern period, the artistry involved in pursuing the fox became more pronounced.[33]

Yet more lowly than the fox was the badger. A slow, nocturnal animal, much given to sleeping, the badger was hardly the quarry of serious hunters. Feeding off carrion, poultry and rabbits, fruit and nuts, never straying far from its set, and unable to run from the hounds at speed, it was dismissed by The Master of Game as a beast the hunting of which hardly 'needed any great mastery'.[34] Yet the badger was also a large and strong animal, capable of ferociously attacking the hounds, and most writers devoted a few pages to the hunting of the badger. They recommended setting dogs close to the badger's set. If the dogs could take it before it entered, a powerful fight between badger and dogs ensued; the badger was prepared to fight to the bitter end, and was hard to kill. If the badger went underground, it was hunted with hounds specially trained to hunt below ground. There was no season for badger-hunting and no ritual cutting up of the body – it was, after all, mere vermin.[35]

Through these hunting handbooks, with their detailed instructions for each element of the hunt, shines an intimate knowledge of nature. In the words of one writer:

> The things that you are to observe in this exercise (to my skill) are, that you know the nature of beasts which you hunt, their wiles, the time and season when they should be hunted, the places where they remain in winter, and where in summer, the winds which they fear and flee from, to find them out, to know their courses, and whether they be for land or water …[36]

The huntsman needed a well-trained and sensitive eye to read the signs on the landscape that enabled him to locate animals to hunt: the size and colour of droppings to judge the sex and age of a hart; the scratchings on the bark of a tree to tell the size of a boar; the depth of a footprint to determine the direction in which a hare was headed. Broken ground, fresh soil, disturbed dew, a freshly formed cobweb and other such tokens told the initiated hunter the way and time an animal had passed. The hunters read minute details to establish not simply what animals had recently visited, but also their age and sex.

But the pastoral idyll that sixteenth-century writers presented was only partially accurate. Although hunters certainly did possess an extensive knowledge of nature, their hunting was embedded in a more prosaic world of competing claims to own the land's natural resources. Sixteenth-century hunters faced a constant struggle to maintain a population of animals to hunt. The greatest conflict centred upon the deer, which had always been the source of petty squabbles between hunting magnates, who in turn had long united to battle against the encroachments and depredations of their poorer neighbours. But as hunters turned their attention to vermin and smaller game, these too became a more precious and coveted commodity. The steady expansion of population that occurred in the sixteenth century only intensified the centuries-old struggle to preserve woodland and wild animals.[37] In essence, an ever more populous country was holding to older hunting traditions in increasingly unfavourable circumstances.

Alongside these age-old pressures of population, however, emerged a new form of pressure, with a radically different origin. The conflicts caused by competing claims to own the wild animals were as old as the centuries, but the dissenting voices that emerged in the middle of the sixteenth century were of more recent vintage. For the first time, a coherent intellectual and religious opposition to hunting was articulated. It came from the Puritans and their views on hunting were without precedent. They objected to their neighbours' hunting not from the narrow concern that it encroached upon their own, but simply because they thought it was wrong. An intellectual, rather than economic, force was starting to emerge.[38]

The Puritans were haunted by numerous concerns about every aspect of human morality and behaviour, including both the wasting of time in recreation and the misuse of the lesser beasts. Hunting and blood sports were therefore obvious targets. In their view, the animals were God's creation: they had been given to man – for his use, but not for his abuse. Killing animals for food was part of God's plan, but to make sport out of the process was frankly contemptuous of his creation. Undoubtedly, these religious reformers also disliked hunting for the time-wasting, profanity, hard drinking and excess with which it was often associated, but it is important to recognise that their complaints went far beyond these moralistic concerns. The Puritans were the first to articulate a consistent and coherent attack on cruelty to animals, a distinction that has rarely been acknowledged by subsequent generations of hostile critics.[39]

Yet despite their genuine concern about the misuse of animals, the Puritans tended to be somewhat selective in the sports they condemned. In effect, it was sports such as cockfighting and bear-baiting – overwhelmingly, though not exclusively, patronised by the lower orders – that attracted their strongest criticism, whilst the more aristocratic pastime of hunting largely escaped condemnation. Let us consider, for example, their response to the ancient sport of bear-baiting.

Bear-baiting had held an important place in English society for several centuries; it was a sport beloved of kings, nobles, civic elites and the populace alike. It consisted in a contest between one bear and several dogs. The bear was tethered to the ground, and dogs were set loose to attack it either singly, or (if the bear was particularly powerful) two, three or even four at a time. The spectators watched and marvelled at the strength of the bear, and at the courage and ingenuity with which the dogs attacked this terrifying opponent. Spectators usually paid nothing or a few pence in order to watch, and a bear-bait could usually be guaranteed to draw a large crowd.

It sounds somewhat brutal, but bear-baiting was not an amusement confined to the roughest and lowest. In fact bear-baiting, like so many blood sports, had followers in the highest social circles. Richard III found the sport so entertaining that he established the post of Royal Bearward, which ensured that a royal servant was on hand to entertain the court with bear-baiting at all times.[40] In the following hundred and fifty years the sport continued in royal favour, being a particular favourite of Elizabeth, who regularly summoned the bearward to the royal palaces to amuse herself and her foreign dignitaries. It made, in the opinion of one courtier, 'very pleasant sport', and Elizabeth frequently entertained illustrious guests by calling upon the bearward to perform his duties.[41] And what was good for royalty was also good for others in the nation's ruling circle. Many great households and civic corporations maintained their own bear and bearward, both to entertain visitors and to demonstrate their wealth and sophistication.[42] In sixteenth-century Nottingham, for example, the borough court had ordered the mayor to announce all forthcoming bull- or bear-baitings, so that all 'his bredren' might 'see the sport of the game after the old custom and usage'.[43]

But although bear-baiting was patronised occasionally by the wealthy, the crowds that gathered around the bearpit were overwhelmingly composed of men of more humble means. When not required to stage stately bear-baitings for royalty, the royal bearward was free to make a profit by entertaining the public in a more homely fashion. These baitings took place at a bearpit at Southwark known as the Bear Garden, usually on Thursdays and Sundays. Entrance cost somewhere between one and three pence (the price varied according to the quality of the seat). This garden (according to one visitor) was 'a round building, three stories high, in which are kept about a hundred large English dogs, with separate wooden kennels for each of them'.[44] Alongside these dogs, the Bear Garden held around twenty bears, as well as numerous bulls, horses and monkeys – anything in fact that might be expected to put up a good fight against a dog. A show at the Bear Garden consisted of regular bear-baitings and some rather more curious combats staged between dogs and other animals. One visitor described seeing 'a pony with an ape fastened on its back' set loose amongst dogs. He concluded that the spectacle of the pony kicking amongst the dogs, with some hanging from its ears and neck and all accompanied by the screams of the ape, was 'very laughable'.[45] Aristocrats and ambassadors certainly visited the Bear Garden; nonetheless, the labouring poor were the mainstay of the crowds that filled the arena.

There could be no claiming that bear-baiting served some useful purpose. In the eyes of the Puritans, it simply gathered unruly crowds delighting in the suffering of animals. When the scaffolding at the Bear Garden in London fell down during a bear-baiting on a Sunday in 1583, it seemed obvious to religious reformers that God was punishing sinners and they used the incident to protest loudly against the sport.[46] The uproar was quieted when Elizabeth decreed the closure of the bearpit on Sundays and moved the bear-baitings to Thursdays, but the affair made plain the hostility the ancient game now aroused.

The Puritans' response to hunting proper was more complex and less uniform. Implied in their pleas for the better treatment of animals was a clear criticism of hunting, and a few brave souls did go so far as to articulate a case against the ancient sport of kings and nobles. Philip Stubbes, for example, in 1584 declared that hunting for sport alone was wholly unlawful: 'I never read of any in the volume of the sacred Scripture that was a good man, and a Hunter ... for our pastimes, and vain pleasures sake, we are not in any wise to spoil or hurt them [beasts]'.[47] But few were willing to express their position in such forthright terms. Most adopted a somewhat vague language, such as the clergyman George Walker, who wrote that to kill animals 'with cruelty and with pleasure, delighting and rejoicing in their destruction ... is a kind of scorn and contempt for the workmanship of God'.[48] Some Puritan gentlemen even continued to hunt. Nicholas Assheton's religious leanings, for example, did not prevent him from spending much of his time hunting deer and coursing hare, and nor did they prevent him celebrating a good day's hunting by drinking until he was as 'merry as Robin Hood'.[49] Likewise, Sir Edward Lewkenor, a model of godly Puritanism, had no qualms about keeping his hawks and hounds; this was fitting (in the opinion of one commentator) 'not only in regard of the abilities of his estate, but ableness of mind ... [Lewkenor] knew right well to put a difference between the use and the abuse'.[50] Hunting still garnered support in the most powerful quarters, and many beleaguered Puritans no doubt reasoned there was little point inviting unnecessary opposition here. In sixteenth-century England, it took a bold spirit indeed to challenge the chief recreation of royalty and nobility, and though many clergymen urged the need to treat God's creatures with respect, most diplomatically left their listeners and readers to work out for themselves quite where this left hunting.

For the present, therefore, the hunters had little to fear. Elizabeth was a keen sportswoman, diligently maintaining her own forests and encouraging the deer parks without permitting unduly harsh penalties for the common poacher. She delicately trod a careful line between all those with an interest in the wild animals of the countryside. Yet these were troubled times, and the menacing signs of future conflict were everywhere apparent. Landowning magnates continued to hunt, to tend their parks and to defend their privileges, but as one preacher ominously warned his congregation in the year of Elizabeth's death, 'there would be no hawking or hunting in heaven'.[51] Hunting's enemies refused to be silenced.

CHAPTER SEVEN

Two Sporting Monarchs

If they came to watch him [while out hunting] he would passionately swear and ask the English nobles what they would have. They would answer, they came out of love to see him. Then he would cry out in Scottish, 'God's wounds! I will pull down my breeches and they shall also see my arse.' (Of James I, 1610)[1]

By the start of the seventeenth century, complaints about blood sports had been rumbling for several decades, but the change of succession in 1603 brought no support for the critics. The new monarch, James I, had a love of hunting that was perhaps as obsessive as that of the Norman monarchs five hundred years before. His triumphal progress from Scotland to England following his accession to the throne was punctuated by a number of impromptu hunting expeditions. At Widdrington Castle in Northumberland, for example, the king 'suddenly beheld a number of deer ... [and] according to his wonted manner forth he went and slew two of them'; while at Worksop he 'hunted a very good space, very much delighted'.[2] It soon became clear that James's enthusiasm for the hunt was not to be buried under the responsibilities of government and, together with his son, he was to frustrate the ambitions of the Protestant reformers for a further half-century.

James maintained that he needed to hunt frequently to protect his health from the toils of kingship, proclaiming at the outset of his reign, 'how greatly we delight in the exercise of hunting, as well for our recreation as for the necessary preservation of our health'.[3] In an attempt to justify his prolonged absence from government, he informed his Privy Council that open air and exercise were necessary 'even in the strongest bodies'.[4] It was a form of self-medication that he took extremely seriously.[5] His progresses around

7. The foreground of Richard Blome's illustration of 'unharbouring ye stagg' captures the moment at which the stag has just started from its resting place and the ready positioned hounds and riders begin their chase in earnest. In the background a stag hunt in full flight is depicted.

the country regularly took him through hunting ground and, just like his original progress into England, were invariably enlivened by days of long hard hunting.[6] His secretaries often complained of delays in getting his signature, with incidents such as the following – the king 'kept long his bed, having hunted hard yesterday and the day before' – being all too frequent.[7]

Foreign ambassadors were no less inconvenienced by the king's predilection for hunting. Only months into his reign, the Venetian envoy reported that 'for the next twenty days [the king] will be without his council, away upon a hunting party, and everything is at a standstill', and subsequent envoys frequently made similar complaints.[8] In 1624, he upset the French ambassador by failing to give him his undivided attention during the negotiations for marriage between his son and Henrietta Maria (he was much preoccupied at that time by the recent capture and killing of 'Cropear'– a stag that had long outwitted the hunters).[9] Like many, he gave up hunting with dogs in his later years, but even when too old to ride with the hunt, he loved to 'come at the death of the deer and to hear the commendations of the hounds'.[10]

James's love of the sport was so great that it led him, averred his critics, to neglect his duties. In 1604 Archbishop Hutton told Robert Cecil that he would like to see 'less wasting of the treasure of the realm and more moderation in the lawful exercise of hunting, both that poor men's corn may be less spoiled and other of his majesty's subjects more spared', and Lord Harington, Queen Elizabeth's godchild, was similarly troubled by the new king's excessive appetite for hunting.[11] Following several days given over to hunting and drinking during the King of Denmark's visit in 1606, he concluded that the hunting world had been turned upside down, with 'the beasts pursuing the sober creation'.[12] But Hutton, Harington and others of a Puritan bent complained in vain. However much strict Protestants at court abhorred the king's conduct, they were impotent to influence the king's degenerate ways.

Besides spending huge sums on his hunting (one estimate for a six-month period in 1613 put the bill at nearly £60,000), James devoted considerable attention to the royal forests.[13] Within months of ascending the throne, James issued a proclamation that he intended to put into execution all laws against killing game which had recently fallen into abeyance and further proclamations were issued throughout his reign.[14] At the time of his accession, the amount of land covered by forest law was still considerable (despite the tendency of both Henry VIII and Elizabeth to sell Crown rights in the forests in return for ready money), but much of the land was now enclosed and farmed for timber. James was determined to set the clock back, to exploit his royal forests fully as a source both of revenue and of recreation. Of these twin aims, the protection of recreation often came first. James generally opposed his courtiers' plans to lease or sell parts of the royal forests in return for revenue. The Earl of Southampton, for example, needed to exercise the most delicate diplomacy in getting the king to agree to the leasing of woods in his Northamptonshire forests.[15]

James also asserted his royal hunting prerogative. He claimed a right to hunt all the game in England, and if he announced his attention to hunt in a particular part of the country, the landowner was required to stop hunting in that area until he arrived. A letter written to Robert Cecil, later Earl of Salisbury, in July 1604 indicates James's attitude to his subjects' estates:

> It is now time that ye prepare the woods and park of Theobalds for me. Your part thereof will only be to harbour me good stags, for I know ye mind to provide for no other entertainment for me there than as many stags as I shall kill with my own hunting ... it will be easy for you to

harbour a great stag amongst the sweet groves about your house … But in earnest, I lose all this year's progress if I begin not to hunt there upon Monday come eight days, for the season of the year will no more stay upon a king than a poor man.[16]

Providing good hunting was a valuable way for his subjects to curry favour, and one aristocrat was moved to complain vociferously when a neighbour killed 'a fair, large, bold and crop-eared buck of especial note' that he had expressly reserved for His Majesty's imminent visit.[17] It should be stressed, however, that providing good hunting for the king was not a matter that landowners could choose to refuse. Gentlemen in Bedfordshire and Hertfordshire were instructed to reform their farming practices in order to remedy the scarcity of game in both counties, and the king left them in no doubt as to the consequences of their not obliging.[18]

When confined to London, James enjoyed the more limited pleasures that the city could offer. He rarely failed to visit the cockpit at St James's Park (it was once noted that the sport there had made him 'very merrie') and he regularly enjoyed the spectacles at the bearpit.[19] Early in his reign he took his family to watch a lion pitted against a bear, and it was perhaps because he enjoyed it so much that he later ordered the construction of 'an especial place' to bait the lions kept in the Tower with 'dogges, beares, bulles, bores, &c'.[20]

Even James could not ignore the groundswell against sports and pastimes emanating from his godly subjects, however, and his response was characteristically diplomatic. In 1617, following disputes about Sunday recreation between Puritans and Catholic gentry in Lancashire, he issued his Book of Sports, rebuking Puritans and other 'precise persons', and explicitly authorising and promoting the Sunday sports and rural festivals they denounced as profanations of the Sabbath, pagan in origin, and occasions of sin.[21] In a gesture of conciliation, he conceded that bull- and bear-baiting, plays, bowling and other such 'unlawful' pastimes should not be permitted on the Sabbath day, but this concession was insufficient to appease his Puritan critics. In 1618 James transmitted orders to the clergy throughout England to read the declaration from the pulpit; but so strong was the opposition that he prudently withdrew his command. As ever, he behaved so as to create the minimum number of enemies. His limited attack on sports and pastimes was not enough to keep the Puritans happy, but his generally successful rule forestalled the issue.

For those of his subjects not inclined towards strict Protestant beliefs, it was very much business as usual in the world of hunting. Few landowners aspiring to gentry status could afford to live without a private deer park of their own. One estimate suggests that the gentry owned some 850 parks in the early seventeenth century, ranging in size from 20 acres to 1,000 acres.[22] The diarist and traveller Fynes Moryson thought that 'Parkes are now growne infinite in number, and are thought to containe more fallow Deer, than all the Christian World besides'; and estimated that any family with an annual income above £500 had a park.[23] Large landowners of course owned several. The Percy family, the great magnates of the north, owned twenty-one parks in Northumberland, Cumberland and Yorkshire, containing over 5,000 head of deer, as well as several others in their southern estates.[24] Just as in earlier times these private parks, whether large or small, served the dual purpose of providing their owners with recreation and food. Thus, for example, a Leicestershire squire, Sir Philip Sherard, reported that he kept a small herd of thirty deer both 'for his pleasure and the service of his house' in his 20-acre park at Stapleford.[25]

Despite the effort and expense that park owners invested in paling for their parks, the gentry poached each other's and the king's deer indefatigably and the Star Chamber and forest courts were kept busy trying to adjudicate between all sides. John Welcome, for example, a person of 'very quarrelsome and contentious disposition' had the impudence to hunt in Sherwood Forest when James himself was hunting there – the last of a series of illegal hunting expeditions in the forest, and the final straw so far as Gervase Lee, the local Justice of the Peace, was concerned. He alleged that Welcome had frequently taken deer, pheasants and hares and carried them to alehouses where he had them prepared and made 'great jollity and sport' whilst feasting upon them. Welcome was heavily fined, and their quarrel thereby dismissed from court.[26] Countless attorneys in all parts of the country made a good living from feuding neighbours such as these.

But the parks, though ubiquitous and highly coveted, were a poor relation of the medieval forests that had once formed the location of most men's deer-hunting. Park walls, breeding programmes and winter feeding all helped produce a growing population of deer, but these deer were semi-tame and this changed the nature of hunting in a fundamental way. One contemporary critic of parks, William Harrison, questioned 'whether our buck or doe are to be reckoned in wild or tame beasts or not' and concluded that hunting in parks was 'more meet for ladies and gentlewomen to exercise … than for men of courage'.[27] The accuracy of his comment is suggested by Lawrence Wright of Snelston in Derbyshire: some of his deer, he admitted, 'were reduced to that state of tameness that they would take bread at the hand'.[28] Hunting, by definition, is the pitting of human skill against the forces of nature; the chasing of tame animals in an enclosed space is a degraded form of that contest. The park may have preserved deer, but it did not preserve the deer-hunting that earlier generations had enjoyed.

Deer enclosures were just one response to the changing nature of the English countryside. Another solution was to hunt other animals that existed in greater abundance, and as an expanding population placed ever greater pressures on the deer, large landowners turned their attention to small game. They resorted to Parliament, which obligingly produced a stream of fresh game laws intended to provide greater protection of small wild animals. Parliament tightened up the game laws in 1603, and again in 1606, by imposing stiff fines on the sale or purchase of animals killed contrary to law, and raising the qualification for owning guns, bows, crossbows, nets, ferrets and dogs.[29] But these new laws placed great pressure on the poorest hunters, who had traditionally hunted for small animals rather than deer. A gamekeeper's warrant issued in 1620 justified the appointment in the following terms:

> Persons of meane qualitie in our counties of Northampton, Huntingdon, and Rutland do usually commit many disorders in hunting, tracing and poaching with beagles, hounds or mongrills, coursing with greyhounds, using setting-doggs, engines or netts, shooting with crossbows or gunnes ... to the great decay and spoil of the several games of hares, pheasants, partridges, ducks and other fowls.[30]

As ever, the desire to hunt and consume the country's wild animals outstripped the provisions of nature, and for those in power the most obvious solution was to restrict the hunting of the common man. As a result, by the seventeenth century, persons of 'meane qualitie' were more rigorously excluded from ancient traditions of trapping and snaring small wild animals than ever before in history.

James's second son, Charles I, a sickly child with a speech impediment, seemed unlikely to follow in the footsteps of his sporting father, yet when thrust into the limelight on the death of his elder brother Henry in 1612, Charles undertook a remarkable programme of self-improvement, and did indeed become a huntsman to rival his father. Within a few years of his accession to the throne in 1625, Charles had transformed himself into a dignified, kingly figure every bit as impressive as his counterparts on the continent. In an effort to adopt a fitting regal comportment, his dress, speech and deportment were overhauled. Improving his hunting skills was inevitably an important component of the monarch's refashioning.[31] Sir Simonds D'Ewes remembered some dashing feats of heroism from the young prince whilst hunting one summer at Bushbridge in Surrey, but also worried that there was something unhealthy about Charles's close examination of every part of the carcass of a dead stag.[32] By the time he had become king, his hunting frequently caused him to be absent from business – a fact regularly commented upon by foreign ambassadors, sometimes in none too flattering tones.[33]

But though he adopted the demeanour of a king, Charles's refined tastes and new-found love for hunting and the arts put pressure on the royal budget, rapidly increasing the Crown's debts and exacerbating his problems with Parliament. His closeness to the deeply hated Duke of Buckingham caused displeasure at court and his high Anglicanism, bordering (claimed his critics) on Catholicism, made him unpopular in the country at large. In 1629, troubled by an increasingly uncooperative Parliament, Charles reached the foolish conclusion that he could dispense with Parliament and manage the kingdom's affairs on his own. Thus began the king's ill-fated eleven-year 'Personal Rule'.[34]

As if this was not enough to alienate his subjects, Charles next pursued forest policies that outraged the many inhabitants, both high and low, who resided within the boundaries of the royal forests. The royal forests had formed a significant source of revenue for the most determined medieval monarchs, but by the time that Charles inherited the throne, they had long ceased to make a sizeable economic contribution to royal coffers. The Tudor monarchs and James I had sought to raise revenue from the forests through the old policy of disafforestation and a more recent policy of timber-felling. James, for example, had disafforested woods of little use for hunting, such as Melchet Forest in Wiltshire, Pamber Forest in Hampshire and Galtres Forest in Yorkshire; and felled nearly 2,000 oaks in the New Forest and elsewhere for the use of the Royal Navy.[35] Charles continued to pursue both of these policies, but he also investigated the possibility of reviving some of the most hated forest policy of the Norman and Angevin kings.

The many laws concerning the cutting of trees, planting of crops, grazing of sheep and lawing of dogs that had so infuriated the residents of the medieval forests had long ago fallen into disuse. Successive kings had found it prudent to modify the operation of the forest laws in order to keep the inhabitants happy. In place of the endless fines for farming in the forests, tenants usually paid small rents and enjoyed a number of perquisites, such as extensive common grazing and the right to collect a limited amount of timber for fuel, as a form of compensation for the inconvenience of the king's marauding deer. The forest courts no longer enforced hefty fines for minor crimes against the vert and venison. Unsurprisingly, therefore, the combined income that the Crown pocketed from rents and fines from the royal forests was dismally low. It was a problem the cash-strapped king was eager to address. Desperate for sources of revenue following his rejection of parliaments and the onset of his Personal Rule, Charles saw the royal forests, still considerable in extent, as a possible purse, and ordered his courtiers to re-examine the disafforestations of earlier monarchs and the disused forest laws.

Following these investigations, Charles came to believe that a revival of medieval forest boundaries would not only reverse the forests' declining fortunes, but was also within his royal rights.[36] In 1632, he instructed his attorney-general, Sir William Noy, to initiate a new forest policy. In an act of breathtaking bravado, Charles attempted to turn back the clock by hundreds of years: Noy claimed on behalf of the Crown areas that had been disafforested in the reign of Edward I, over three hundred years earlier. Charles and his advisers dug out from the royal chests surveys of the forest boundaries undertaken in the thirteenth century, and denied the legitimacy of the disafforestations that had taken place in subsequent years. Next he revived the forest eyres, or courts, in order to try the forest dwellers for the countless infringements of the old laws they had committed in the past three centuries.

The policy was introduced first in the Forest of Windsor, then in the Forest of Dean and, following limited successes in these two forests, Noy's successor, Sir John Finch, extended the policy to the Essex forests in 1634. In each county the pattern was the same: large areas were brought back into the royal forest and the system of forest courts was revived. The Earl of Warwick was moved to protest that his land in Essex had lain outside royal forest for more than three centuries, and asked for time to produce the charters so that 'we might still enjoy with quietness the possessions of our ancestors which had bin oute of the Forest for three hundred and thirty yeares'.[37] Finch refused the request and Charles's self-appointed forest court returned the whole county of Essex as being within the royal Forest of Haining.[38] In Northamptonshire, where the forest boundaries were re-examined in 1637, similar enlargements took place. All three of the Northamptonshire forests were considerably extended: in one of the most extreme cases of enlargement, the number of villages in the Forest of Salcey swelled from six under the old boundaries to forty-two under the new.[39]

In consequence of these actions, men and women, both rich and poor, in the newly afforested areas became subject to laws that had not been in force for several generations. In the Forest of Dean, royal officials gathered evidence of over 800 forest crimes, some dating back forty years. Besides a few found guilty of stealing deer, the court records included people accused of taking a few branches, building cottages, enclosing land, and chopping timber.[40] Inhabitants of Chigwell were found guilty of forest offences ranging from the killing of a fawn to the keeping of an unlawed dog.[41]

The motivation for the whole exercise was of course pecuniary, and those found guilty were fined large sums for their crimes. In Northamptonshire, over £80,000 in fines was demanded by the Crown; and in Gloucestershire, fines from the Forest of Dean court totalled some £130,000.[42] Inevitably the king was unable to collect such sums, and the totals raised were significantly lower than the fines the courts imposed. Indeed, the king had arguably never expected to collect fines of this magnitude. The fines were sufficiently high to convince most large landowners of the necessity of exempting their estates from the forest laws, and in place of paying the forest fines, most entered into an agreement with the king to disafforest their land instead. Charles was employing an old trick that King John had exploited so successfully four hundred years earlier. Once again, a severe forest eyre had the king's subjects queuing up to offer sums of several thousand pounds to be quit of the forest for ever.

Much of the land in the royal forests had been leased or granted at well below the market rents, and Charles's policy may to some extent be justified as a attempt to raise the forest revenues to a more acceptable level. For contemporaries, however, the reversion to medieval forest boundaries seemed arbitrary and unjustifiable. Reflecting upon Charles's actions a decade later, the commentator Anzolo Correr considered that 'The question of the forests is more difficult and more odious [than ship money]. It seems to be a question of depriving men of their property which they have held for many centuries without the Crown raising any claim.'[43] It was this arbitrariness that rankled; for, as his critics pointed out, if the king could claim large expanses of his subjects' land as his own royal forest, what outrage might he commit next?

As a fiscal expedient, Charles's restoration of forest law attained a measure of success; politically, though, it was a disaster, adding to the catalogue of complaints and grievances some of his most powerful subjects already held against him. Following the failure of his religious policy in Scotland, Charles was forced to call Parliament in 1640, and the newly assembled House of Commons did not hesitate to address Charles's forest eyres and the decisions they had made. In August 1641, in a humbling moment, Charles was forced to give his royal assent to Parliament's statute for the 'Certainty of Forests', repudiating the forest eyres and setting the boundaries of the royal forest back to their positions at the start of James I's reign.[44] But neither this nor any of his many other concessions was sufficient to dispel the discord that now existed between Crown and Parliament. The tensions continued to increase, first with Parliament's execution of the Earl of Strafford and then with the king's attempt to arrest members of Parliament in early January 1642.

Days later, as Charles finally realised how weak his grip on power had become, he fled the capital and the country slipped into the first Civil War.

CHAPTER EIGHT

Civil Wars and the Decline of the Deer

Divers lewd and disordered persons ... have in great assemblies, and in riotous manner, unlawfully chased, killed and destroyed many of his majesty's deer. (1642)[1]

The said Parke was in the time of his late Majesties [Charles I] Raigne replenished with Wood and Deer, which have been shamefully destroyed by the late Usurped Authority, and much of the land plowed and sowen. (1660)[2]

Charles's flight from London, on 10 January 1642, precipitated a civil war that lasted for four bloody years. The last Royalist army was not defeated until 21 March 1646, and the war wound down to a decisive close on 5 May when Charles surrendered. But the peace proved transient and by 1648, following Royalist uprisings in Wales, Kent and Essex, the nation was at war once again. This time, Parliament's New Model Army made short work of the king's rebellion. Now that he was tarnished as an ungodly king who had wantonly reopened the civil war and who could never be trusted to make a settled peace, Charles's fate was effectively sealed. In the following December, the House of Commons, purged by the army of its moderates, set up a court to try Charles for treason. What followed was effectively a show trial. After three days' deliberations the court declared their guilty verdict. On 30 January 1649 the king was beheaded in front of a huge crowd at Whitehall. By Act of Parliament, the monarchy and House of Lords were abolished and the government of the country transferred to Parliament's hands.[3]

Given the complex and unprecedented turmoil of the 1640s, it is quite surprising to find that Parliamentarians nevertheless had the time and energy to outlaw some of the sports that had so troubled them during the first half of the seventeenth century. In 1642, in the midst of political chaos and on the brink of the outbreak of war, Parliament serenely turned its attention to the Paris Bear Garden, situated just a few miles east of Westminster at Bankside, and the site of bear-baitings and bull-baitings every Thursday. No doubt objecting to the riotous behaviour of the crowds as much as to the actual baitings, the House of Commons ordered the garden's owners to forbid 'the Game of Bear-baiting in these Times of Great Distractions'.[4] In the same year, legislation prohibiting any 'Game, Sport, or Pastime whatsoever' on the Sabbath was also introduced.[5]

This order, however, did not quite have the desired result, for although the bear garden obediently shut its doors when ordered to do so, it promptly reopened them as soon as the government's attention was turned elsewhere. By the following year, the actors who were accustomed to using the garden to perform plays on other days of the week were complaining that the bear-baiters were preventing them from using the stage. Parliament responded by repeating its prohibition of bear-baiting at the Paris Garden, but reports of bear-baitings in the newspapers in 1645 indicate that this order was also flouted.[6] This game of cat-and-mouse continued for over a decade. Every year or so the House of Commons repeated its general prohibition of bear-baiting, but the London newspapers indicate that the sport continued largely uninterrupted throughout the 1640s and early 1650s. Finally, in 1656, an exasperated Colonel Pride, weary of the disobedience of the bear garden, sent in the troops. On his orders, they shot all the bears to death, leaving (according to one observer) 'just one white innocent cub'. The dogs were shipped to Jamaica, and with that the doors to the bear garden were finally closed. The success of even this might however be questioned, as newspaper reports indicate that smaller private bear gardens soon cropped up elsewhere, filling the role that the Paris Garden had once played.[7]

Undeterred, Oliver Cromwell, Lord Protector of England since 1653, issued general orders against cockfighting and bear-baiting shortly after taking the reins of power. Once again, the wording of the order suggests that it was the disorder that surrounded such events, rather than the animal suffering they caused, that was paramount in the reformers' minds. By Cromwell's order, horse-races, cockfighting, bear-baiting and stage plays were prohibited, 'forasmuch as Treason and Rebellion, is usually hatched and contrived against the State upon such occasions, and much Evil and Wickedness committed'.[8] And this order, like those of Parliament, was once again widely flouted. Parliament had encountered significant difficulties in closing a bear garden close to home, and the prospect of successful reform in distant parts of the country was consequently poor.[9]

Parliament and Cromwell's protectorate lacked the resources to eliminate blood sports in the way they wished, but the policy they pursued was nevertheless remarkable. Though not the first attempt by government to interfere in sports and pastimes, this was certainly the most systematic. Since the Middle Ages, successive monarchs had periodically issued orders against sports such as football on the grounds that the game distracted young men from their archery practice, but their attempts to suppress popular pastimes had been both ad hoc and sporadic.[10] The opposition to blood sports during the Civil Wars and Interregnum was considerably more sustained. In the 1640s, Parliament assumed responsibility for deciding which recreations were fitting for the people. Of course, their various orders were born in large part of their fear of the subversive potential of any social gathering and tempered by a hefty dose of political calculation. Nonetheless, they set an important historical precedent, firmly establishing the legitimacy of political interference in sports and pastimes.

No less significant than Parliament's aggressive policies on bear-baiting and cockfighting is the fact that hunting managed to escape this clampdown on recreational sports. Puritans continued to voice their unease at the time-wasting and cruelty that in their opinion hunting involved. Thomas Burroughs, for example, a Northamptonshire minister, thundered against hunting in the following terms:

> How many Gentlemen be there, of whom when they die, all can be said is this, They were born, they did eat, and drink, and play, and hunt, and hawk, and lived like so many wild Ass-colts, never minding any thing that concern'd God's glory, or their own salvation ... and so died, and dropt into Hell?[11]

But though many of the Puritan reformers who backed Parliamentary forces during the civil wars were hostile to hunting, no clear policy against hunting was ever pursued, either during war or in victory. Of course, the case against hunting had never been so clear cut. Unlike other blood sports, hunting resulted in a useful and tangible product: food for the table. And although aristocratic hunters had for centuries downplayed the utilitarian aspects of their hunting, as criticism about the morality of hunting mounted, the sport's advocates soon realised that the useful products of hunting formed a valuable defence of their pastime.

Despite the bleak warnings of zealous preachers, some godly gentlemen had always maintained that a little hunting and hawking was part of God's scheme, and refused to give up their occasional hunting trips. Sir Bulstrode Whitelocke was an opponent of Charles I during the Civil War, yet he kept a pack of harriers at his Windsor estate, and even entertained Commonwealth grandees in the Windsor deer park; he downplayed the cruelty of hunting by stressing that the animals he hunted were 'creatures which by nature are continually in fear and dread, and that when they are not hunted, as well as when they are'.[12] Sir Edward Peyton, a Puritan squire seated at Isleham, Cambridgeshire considered hunting and hawking to be 'most commendable exercises'.[13] The lingering hold of hunting on moderate Puritan gentlemen made the obstacles to a successful attack insurmountable.

Furthermore, the hunting stakes were high: money and friends were there to be made if the right policy was pursued, and once Cromwell was in power, intellectual opposition to hunting simply melted away. Instead, the pressures on hunting during the turmoils of the 1640s and 1650s were exactly the same as they had ever been: the difficulty of maintaining a habitat suitable for deer.

Throughout the centuries, civil strife had been accompanied by the looting of the forests, and in this respect the 1640s were no different. The royal forests contained much of the country's premier hunting land, and were the source of one of the deposed king's most unpopular policies. Little wonder then that they were ransacked during the wars. In 1641, as the country slipped ever closer to civil war, riots, no doubt triggered by earlier royal policy, broke out in parts of Windsor Forest. Despite orders from the House of Commons that the deer in Windsor were to be protected, men from Egham began raiding the forest and killing the deer with impunity. In the following year, the riots spread from Surrey to the Berkshire part of the forest and the Windsor Great Park was invaded.[14] Parliament brought in the army to quell the disorder, but before stability was restored, the soldiers, growing impatient of waiting for their wages, began to join in the plunder, cutting timber and slaughtering deer. Though a handful of ringleaders was swiftly arrested and charged, it soon transpired that local residents were willing and able to continue the plunder without their leaders, and the disorder did not end until 1644. So long the mark of privilege, game became a symbolic target in these times of lawlessness and levelling uprisings, and three years of sporadic rioting inevitably resulted in extensive damage to both deer stocks and woodland.

The disorder that originated in Windsor quickly spread to other royal forests. In April 1642 a crowd armed with guns, bills, pitchforks and clubs invaded Waltham Forest in Essex, killing and wounding many of the deer.[15] Similar problems were faced by the newly appointed warden of Sherwood Forest, John Holles, second Earl of Clare. A survey produced for Clare at the end of the first Civil War, recorded 258 deer in the ancient forest; when contrasted with an earlier count of over 1,100 in the 1630s, the extent of the destruction wrought during the war years becomes apparent.[16] Soon forest officials in Northamptonshire and Essex were confronted with similar disorder.[17] In countless forests, civilians took advantage of the temporary suspension of the usual mechanisms of law and order to enter the forest and help themselves to the forbidden deer.

The royal forests fared little better in the subsequent uneasy peace. Following the abolition of the monarchy in 1649, the Long Parliament formally took possession of all the royal forests and, with a return to greater stability in the 1650s, gave the fortunes of the forests their careful consideration. But the country's finest woodland had fallen into the hands of a body of men largely clueless about their correct management, and the outcome of their deliberations was not encouraging. Like so many new owners of woodland before them, Parliament opted to sell the forests off as quickly as possible for cash, and in 1651 vested all the royal forests with trustees and charged them with the task of organising their sale. Two years later, in 1653, the trustees presented a 'Proposal to manage the forests of the late King less offensively to the people' to the Council of State. The act that followed ordered their disafforestation, sale and improvement.[18]

The proposal immediately stalled. All the royal forests were inhabited, in part at least, and those living there were far from convinced that this wholesale sell-out was in their best interest. Large landowners in the forests leased cherished hunting rights, and commoners rented land, often at favourable rents: none had a desire to see their land sold off, and petitioned the state against the proposal. To add to the difficulties, few seemed to be interested in buying the state's newly acquired forests – only four buyers appear to have come forward.[19] With Parliament preoccupied with other matters, the forest proposals were left to languish.

By 1654 it had become clear that the Act for Disafforestation was not going to yield the large sums that the government had initially hoped for, and Cromwell appointed new commissioners to make fresh surveys of the forests in order to advise how they might be used for the benefit of the Commonwealth. These commissioners admitted that the previous act 'was impossible to execute', and suggested that the government might get its hands on the money it so desperately needed by attempting to sell just four forests – Ashdown, Sherwood, Kingswood and Needwood – instead.[20] But even this radically scaled down proposal soon foundered. The Forest of Needwood, for example, was offered for sale in 1654, in order to pay the bills for the soldiers. The inhabitants of the twenty-one villages and townships affected swiftly petitioned Cromwell against the sale, arguing that the county of Stafford had already paid nearly £8,000 towards the soldiery, and adding that 'the Forest of Needwood is merely formed by nature for pleasure, no forest in England being comparable thereunto'.[21] These objections were sufficient to hold the project up and nothing was accomplished before the return of Charles II six years later. Nor indeed had any of the other three forests been sold by this time.

In place of hasty sales, the government attempted to improve the revenues from the forests by introducing better management. It resorted to such tried and tested methods as the restoration of forest courts and the reorganisation of forest administration: it was a modest return, in effect, to the ill-fated policy of Charles I. Yet despite Cromwell's best efforts, his stewardship ultimately failed. His government had no strategy to repair the devastation wreaked in the forests during the war years, and this, along with a lack of competent forest staff and effective law-keepers, fatally undermined Cromwell's laudable policy of responsible stewardship.

The problems faced in the Commonwealth's forests were mirrored in private parks across the length and breadth of the country. So long a gleaming symbol of national pride, the private deer parks everywhere were a shadow of their former glory. During the wars many landowners had been forced to stand by and witness extensive depredations in their forests by opportunist poachers and hungry neighbours. At Farnham in Surrey, for example, 'the county people ... gathered together in a great multitude, and ... killed and destroyed great store' of the Bishop of Winchester's deer in the Great Park, killing 'above twenty at a time'.[22] Nor was it simply the Royalist gentry that suffered in this way. In 1646 the Herefordshire Parliamentarian Sir Robert Harley, testified that his parks had been laid open and wholly destroyed: at least 500 deer had been killed in the process.[23] Numerous parks across the realm met a similar fate, and Parliament's attempts to prevent the slaughter of deer were singularly ineffective.

Indeed, Parliament's men were frequently involved in the plunder. The ongoing failure of Parliament to pay its soldiers' arrears created bands of angry, armed and hungry men, and the army was in fact responsible for much of the damage caused in parks and forests. Soldiers ransacked the forests either in order to fill empty bellies or in lieu of unpaid wages. In Sherwood, the soldiers justified their slaughter of deer on the grounds that 'they had fought for the deer'.[24] A Parliamentary soldier, Nehemiah Wharton, described the involvement of his regiment in the destruction of woodland in a series of letters written during the wars. At Coventry, for example, he explained:

> Several of our soldiers, both horse and foot, sallied out of the city to Lord Dunsmore's park, and brought from thence great store of venison, which is as good as ever I tasted; and ever since they make it their daily practice, so that venison is almost as common with us as beef is with you.[25]

In Northamptonshire, he wrote, 'we could not restrain our solders from entering [the Earl of Northampton's] park and killing his deer.'[26] Army officers were unwilling and often unable to prevent these depredations, and in such circumstances the preservation of deer was clearly a hopeless task. At the wars' close, forests and parks everywhere were ransacked and in a state of disarray. The Royalist gentleman John Evelyn observed 'My lord Craven's house at Causam in ruins, his goodly woods felled by the rebels'.[27] It was a pattern that was only too familiar.

The confiscation of Royalist assets and the legitimate sale of estates and deer parks tended to the same result. An act of 1649 ordered the confiscation of the estates of 'malignant' Royalists; many were leased to distant landowners who lacked the resources and inclination needed to maintain a park. Hatfield forest, for example, was leased to the Earl of Cardigan. It was said later of his stewardship that 'the Deer were killed, the ffences let down and the fforrest of Chace filled with Sheep & Hoggs'.[28] Many estates were sold during the Civil Wars and Interregnum, and their parks broken up into fields and closes for farming. The Southwell deer park, established by the Archbishops of York in the fourteenth century, was sold twice in the 1640s, and at the Restoration it was noted that the excellent park had been 'demolished in the late rebellion'.[29] Land sales were frequent in the 1650s, and the preservation of deer parks a low priority for new owners during these troubled times. Rioting, illegal plunder and land sales all tended in one direction – the destruction of deer, woodland and parks. It was just one of many problems which indicated that the government was losing its grip.

By the end of the 1650s, the future of the Commonwealth seemed uncertain. The army, in control since it had seized power in 1649, was growing increasingly dissatisfied with the way events were unfolding. Months before his death in September 1658, Cromwell had named his eldest surviving son, Richard, his successor, but whereas Cromwell was a fine soldier and accomplished statesmen, his son was little more than a country farmer, and the army was no doubt correct to fear for the future of the Commonwealth under his control. It recalled the Rump Parliament dissolved by Cromwell in 1653, which immediately and unceremoniously dismissed Richard as Lord Protector, but which, it soon emerged, had no strategy for the power vacuum that this act created. With no signs of imminent progress, George Monck, one of the army's most capable officers, began to explore the possibility of restoring the monarchy. Early in 1660, he recommended that Parliament should invite Charles II to return, and his suggestion was warmly welcomed by a war-weary Parliament. In April 1660, a treaty restoring the monarchy ended the disintegrating Protectorate, and on 25 May Charles landed at Dover to take up the reins of government. He reached London on the 29th. King

Charles II took power under the terms his father had conceded in 1641. For most, it was the long overdue putting back of the world to rights.[30]

The legacy of two decades of turmoil was decidedly mixed for the devotees of the hunt. In one key respect hunting emerged as strong as ever, for the intellectual attack that its opponents had formulated through the sixteenth and early seventeenth centuries had been shaken off. Puritans had long expressed disquiet about the morality of hunting, yet once in power they had shown no enthusiasm for attacking the pastime of the rich and powerful. With the Restoration, they were decisively cast out of the political realm, and all prospect of a serious attack on hunting was lost. With their demise, hunting was to thrive, safe from any significant intellectual or moral attack, for well over two hundred years.

But although the moral drive against hunting had failed, the world of hunting never fully recovered from the events of the 1640s and 1650s. In the event, it was not intellectual change but the age-old force of a hungry populace that proved decisive in consigning deer-hunting to history. After two decades of conflict, wood, pales and deer had all been plundered, and the fine deer-hunting enjoyed earlier in the century was no more than a distant memory. Although the Restoration marked a return to the old order in many senses, with respect to hunting it proved impossible to turn the clock back.

As so often in the history of hunting, a decisive lead was given by the royal household. The restored monarch was handsome, popular, frivolous and spendthrift. Like his father and grandfather before him, he had been introduced to hunting as a child and developed an interest that continued throughout his life.[31] The diarist Samuel Pepys noted 'a great match of hunting of a Stagg the king had' in August 1666, in which 'the king tired all their horses and came home with not above two or three able to keep pace with him'.[32] Once settled on the throne he immediately turned his attention to restoring the royal forests. In an effort to rebuild the ruined woodlands, he accepted various presents of deer from both abroad and home and imposed a three-year stay on hunting in the newly stocked forests. The carriage for a parcel of deer sent from the Duke of Brandenburgh in 1661 came to nearly £200, and a further £50 was spent the same year on the transport of stags from the Duke of Oldenburgh.[33] The bill for transporting thirty-three 'Jermayne Deer' for Waltham Forest came to nearly £150.[34] Some of his own subjects offered deer from their own meagre stocks. The gift of 300 deer from English noblemen for Charles's forests at Windsor, Waltham and Enfield early in his reign was no doubt gratefully received.[35] In return, Charles annulled Commonwealth sales of forest territory, and handed out baronetcies to gentlemen who helped him to restock the royal parks. He began to reassert the royal hunting privileges of old, and in 1688 even set about creating a hunting park close to Buckingham Palace – enclosing the Green Park and stocking it with imported deer.[36] Yet these efforts made a small dent on the damage caused by two decades of war and neglect. Despite committed efforts to restock the Forest of Windsor at the Restoration, the deer declined from 3,066 in 1607 to a meagre 461 in 1697.[37] In other royal forests the deer had long since vanished; in Yorkshire and Lancashire, so great were some of the losses that the king was left with no option but to remove forest status altogether.[38]

His brother and successor, James II, was every bit as keen on hunting. While king he hunted regularly and in addition to the Royal Buckhounds, maintained a pack of foxhounds and a pack of harriers. He hunted while in exile, but had been rather too occupied with other matters to devote much time to the royal parks during his short reign in England.[39] His usurper, William III, however, had both the time and inclination to attend to the royal forests. After assuming power in 1688, William, a fine and athletic huntsman, built up the deer park at Hampton Court, and made a committed effort to preserve deer in the royal forests: he was the last monarch to do so. In a cruel twist of fate, he died after a bad fall from his horse in the park he had earlier created at Richmond Park.[40] William's sister-in-law and successor, Queen Anne, continued the tradition of royal hunting. Her favourite hunting seat was Windsor Forest where she kennelled the Royal Buckhounds. When she became too old to ride, she ordered the creation of 'rides' throughout the forest, wide pathways that enabled her to follow the hunt in her carriage.[41] All of these monarchs helped to raise the fortunes of the royal forests in the years following the Restoration, though none was able to reverse the damage caused by the civil disruption of the 1640s and 1650s.

The Hanoverian kings were less interested in the chase than any of their predecessors, and under their rule the modest advances in the fortunes of the royal forests stalled. When George I was taken deer-hunting in the Windsor Great Park, he apparently soon grew bored with the activity and finished the day with some shooting of ducks.[42] His son, George II, took a little more interest, and announced that Wednesdays and Saturdays were his 'hunting days', but as a hunter he was held in rather low esteem – it was claimed that he had the dogs' paws chopped so as to limit the chase to a pace he could manage.[43] His successor, George III, a lover of hard exercise, took a discernibly greater interest in the hunt, and throughout the later years of his reign his exploits with the Royal Buckhounds were regularly reported in the pages of the sporting press.[44] Although remnants of the royal forests still survived at Dean, Epping and Windsor, the king and his buckhounds spent most of their time chasing tame animals brought to the hunt in a cart and set loose, rather than wild deer. Following the decline of his health in 1811, his

son the Prince of Wales was appointed regent until crowned George IV in
1820: at this point the future of royal hunting looked uncertain. With a new
king more interested in gambling, womanising and drinking than in hunting,
the position of deer-hunting in the royal forests had never been lower.

Meanwhile, the country deer parks that had been so carefully created
and jealously guarded by generations of gentlemen had fallen into a hopeless
state of disrepair. Though many large landowners set about replenishing their
parks, they were no more successful in restoring their former glory than
their royal peers. The fortunes of Sheffield Park may stand as an example of
many. The park had been in existence since at least the thirteenth century,
but on the death of the seventh Earl of Sheffield, Gilbert Talbot, in the early
seventeenth century, the estate passed to absentee lords and the park entered
a period of prolonged neglect. By 1637, much of the park was rented to tenant
farmers, though in a survey of that date, the earl's steward, John Harrison,
nonetheless noted that 'this Parke is very well adorn'd with great store of
very Stately Timber and not meanly furnished with fallow Deare, the number
of them at this present is one Thousand, whereof Deare of Auntler is two
hundred'. During the Civil Wars and Interregnum, however, much of this
wood was felled. In 1651 George Sitwell, a Renishaw ironmaster, bought 200
oak trees to convert into charcoal for his furnaces, and on his frequent returns
to the lords for more wood, he unfailingly found a willing seller.[45]

Despite the loss of Sheffield Park's woodland, there was apparently still
some hunting at the Restoration, since the estate's records indicate that in
1664 they were sending venison to London, but the lords' continued absences
eventually undermined the viability of the park. In the 1670s, the deer were
removed and the land converted piecemeal to agricultural and industrial
pursuits. By 1693 the park wall, measuring eight miles in circumference in
1637, was reduced to three; the deer and timber had gone and the lodge was
in ruins.[46] Yet the rents from this remodelled estate were no less profitable
to its absentee lords. The growing population and changing economy had
fundamentally altered the ways in which profits might be made, and deer
parks were a luxury that increasingly few felt able to afford. With a growing,
land-hungry population, many large landowners were forced to conclude that
there were more economic uses for their assets, and one by one, the great
landowners abandoned their attempts to rear and protect deer.

The deer parks had gone into decline, and of the native red and fallow deer
virtually none remained. Wild deer were now largely confined to the remote
plains of Exmoor and Dartmoor.[47] For most sportsmen, the only chance of
enjoying a taste of the ancient noble pastime was to join a pack in pursuit of
a 'carted' deer – a semi-tame animal brought to the place of meeting in a
cart. The hunting involved turning it loose and setting the dogs to follow it,

while the hunters followed the chase on horseback. Too precious to be killed, the dogs were prevented from harming the deer, and the deer was returned to the cart so it might be taken home and set loose for hunting another day.[48] Carted-deer hunting had been introduced to the Royal Buckhounds in the 1780s and by the following decade it appears that most deer hunts, both royal and otherwise, were in fact chases after carted deer.[49] Deer that could be guaranteed to provide a particularly lively chase were even named, and their exploits reported in the sporting presses. In the 1790s, a deer called Compton was fêted for his 'most determined courage and inexpressible speed'.[50] Two beasts named Moonshine and Nightflyer were almost as highly revered.[51] From this point, however, accounts of deer-hunting tended to emphasise the absurd rather than the aristocratic. The popular sporting journalist Robert Surtees scoffed at the hunting of carted deer and a writer in the *Sporting Magazine* considered it 'the lowest of all possible sports', with neither 'stimulus nor science'.[52] But despite the low esteem in which those who considered themselves to be true sportsmen held carted-deer hunting, by the early nineteenth century most deer-hunting took this neutered form.

Although stretches of royal forests and private woodland survived throughout the eighteenth century and beyond, they no longer offered the kind of sport that earlier generations had enjoyed. Deer remained a high-status possession, valuable both as a symbol of gentle status and for their

8. This picture illustrates the reality of deer-hunting by the end of the eighteenth century: a tame deer, taken to the hunt in a cart, released and recaptured when the 'hunting' was done. This photograph appeared in *Country Life* in the late nineteenth century, but the practice had become established over a century earlier.

9. Burley House in Rutlandshire (built by Daniel Finch, second Earl of Nottingham, between 1694 and 1705) replete with its deer park. In contrast with the dangerous wild deer that earlier generations had hunted, the animals here appear tame and unlikely to pose any threat to potential hunters.

venison. They graced the country's diminishing forests and private parks in a largely ornamental capacity, and with the virtual disappearance of wild populations of deer, the fiction that park owners 'hunted' was finally laid to rest. In the game acts passed after the Restoration, deer were removed from the list of 'game' animals: they were no longer considered wild, but were classed as 'property', so attacks on them were not poaching, but theft. Not that this change in definition in any way softened the social conflict that these beautiful creatures continued to provoke. Deer remained every bit as potent a source of discord as they had ever been – the target of opportunistic poachers, of large, armed gangs of organised deer-stealers, and even of the occasional prank carried out by high-spirited sons of the gentry.[53]

Nor did redefining deer as property rather than game diminish the seriousness with which the nation's lawmakers viewed deer-stealing. Most notoriously the Black Act of 1723 restored the death penalty for the stealing of deer – though intended as a temporary measure it sat on the statute-book for over a century. A host of other activities connected with deer stealing – the possession of traps, trespassing at night, or trespassing in the company of a lurcher – were made capital offences by the same act, though in common with most of the capital statutes passed during the eighteenth century the full rigours of the new laws were rarely applied.[54] Deer-stealing and the Black Acts gave rise to some of the most violent instances of social conflict in eighteenth-century England, and at first sight it appears as if little had changed in the position of deer-keeping. The appearance of continuity, however, is deceptive. In contrast to the centuries-old conflicts over forests, hunting and deer, eighteenth-century deer-stealing crises were not primarily an assertion of ancient hunting rights. Deer-hunting disappeared along with the populations of wild deer: though no less acrimonious, these were modern disputes about private property rather than about ownership of the gifts of the natural world.

For centuries, people and deer had competed for access to finite natural resources, and as the balance between the two forces changed, so the wild-deer hunting introduced by William the Conqueror had adapted and evolved. By the eighteenth century, the pressures of population decisively gained the upper hand. From an all-time low of about two million following the Black Death, population had slowly risen to something in the region of six million by 1650. The majority of the people were endeavouring to scrape a living from the land, and the steady rise in population placed pressure on wealthy landowners' old custom of reserving large tracts of the best land exclusively for the hunting of deer. The Civil Wars of the 1640s shattered the uneasy equilibrium that had existed throughout the Tudors' and Stuarts' rule, and at the Restoration no one proved able to repair the damage.

But none of these developments heralded an end to the place of hunting in elite society. Exclusive hunting rights had been the privilege of royalty and nobility for hundreds of years, and were to remain safely intact in the new social world created following the Restoration. Hunting would once again adapt to a changing society, though new and radical measures would be called for to preserve the ancient pastime in an increasingly modernising world.

CHAPTER NINE

A New Era Dawns

And God said, Let us make man in our image, after our likeness: and let them have dominion over the fish of the sea, and over the fowl of the air, and over the cattle, and over all the earth ... (Genesis, 1: 26)

Game Laws are contrary to the liberties of mankind. God himself, the Creator of all things, gave man a right to kill and eat the birds of the air, the beasts of the field etc. (*Gentleman's Magazine*, 1753)

With the deer population reduced to a fraction of its pre-Civil War size, England's hunters were forced elsewhere, and the small mammals were as attractive as any other. Hare, pheasants and partridges had long been on the margins of the hunting world, but hunting small game had slowly become more fashionable with the hunting fraternity during the Tudor period as the pressures upon deer-hunting had become ever more acute. Of course, small game, like all forms of wildlife, had been poached and plundered on a large scale during the Civil Wars and Interregnum, but the return to order in 1660 was accompanied with optimism that stocks could be rebuilt if appropriate measures were taken. The Cavalier Parliament duly set about constructing new laws to protect small game from the unlimited hunting of the masses. The result was the Game Act of 1671, and though Parliament had been passing game acts for several centuries, this one marked a decisive break with its antecedents.[1]

Like the many game acts before it, the 1671 act prohibited the killing of game (now defined as partridges, pheasants, hares and moorfowl), by all except 'qualified persons', but it radically raised the bar for qualification. Henceforth, only owners of land worth £100 a year or the eldest sons of esquires, knights and nobles (and their gamekeepers) were eligible to kill game.[2] Even allowing for the effects of inflation, this was a significant increase from the earlier qualification of 40 shillings and sharply reduced the number of qualified persons.[3] The act authorised qualified landowners to appoint their own gamekeepers to police the illegal hunting of any unqualified persons on their estates; a later act of 1691 gave them almost unlimited power to resist poachers.[4] Like many later additions to the 1671 act, this set high penalties for any infringement of the law – a £20 fine, or a year's imprisonment and an hour at the pillory. The new legislation was a punitive response to the audacious and illegal hunting that landowners had had to endure during the recent troubled times, and displayed an unshakeable commitment to preserving hunting as the unique privilege of the landed elite. Parliament was serious in its intent to preserve hunting for none but the wealthiest few.

Yet despite these draconian laws, so far as the mass of the population was concerned, the continuities after 1671 were probably as striking as any changes. Certainly that tranche of society possessing land valued somewhere between £10 and £100, which had previously enjoyed the privilege of being qualified hunters, was now technically removed from the protected class. But the older £10 qualification had already been high and farmers, tenants and labourers of humble means had long ago been excluded from the legal hunting fraternity. Although the 1671 qualification was ferocious, a steady stream of game laws since 1389 had effectively extinguished the right of the poor to hunt hare, pheasant or partridge centuries earlier. These new qualifications were arguably a squabble amongst their social superiors that had little relevance to them.

Between the king and his wealthiest subjects, however, a novel and very real shift in power occurred with the passage of this act.[5] Since the Norman Invasion, a long succession of kings had claimed the royal prerogative to hunt wherever they pleased – a right that James I had actively exercised as late as the 1620s. The 1671 act did not remove this royal right, but it did extend it to qualified landowners. Earlier game laws had confined the gentry's hunting rights to their own estates. The law of 1671 allowed a qualified person to kill game on *anyone's* land unless specifically warned off, thereby making their right to hunt universal. At a stroke, all the nation's small wild animals, not only those hopping over private estates, but also those found in the country's woods and commons, became the exclusive property of one social class: the landed gentry. Just like the king, the qualified landowner enjoyed an unlimited right to hunt wheresoever he pleased. It created a breed of 'petty princes', grumbled one critic, '[who] claim the privilege of prowling for prey, without control, on their neighbour's land'.[6]

Moreover, the 1671 act not only vested exclusive game rights in the hands of a tiny minority, it also established the supremacy of their game rights over all ordinary property rights. Anyone living in the country admittedly possessed the right to warn a neighbouring hunter off his land, but if the neighbouring hunter was his own landlord, that right might prove difficult to exercise. Furthermore, even when warned away from private land, the unwanted hunter could only be pursued in the courts for trespass, not for any damage to crops that his hunting may have caused. These game laws, therefore, bore more than a passing resemblance to the forest laws introduced by the Norman kings so many centuries before. Justly might the great legal theorist William Blackstone despair that where 'the forest laws established only one mighty hunter throughout the land, the game laws have raised a little Nimrod in every manor'.[7] It was a principle that many of those excluded found hard to accept.

Yet although the act has widely been regarded as unjust, repressive and socially divisive, it was intended in some measure to restore an older and purer form of hunting. Much of the attraction of hunting has always lain in the excitement of pursuing an unfettered animal across open land, the pitting of human wits against the speed, strength and cunning of an untamed animal with the risk that the animal might outwit the hunter. Of course, throughout the Middle Ages the hunting of truly wild animals had steadily declined, and with respect to the deer – the most highly coveted animal of all – this concept had become something of a fiction long before the Civil Wars. But the legislation of 1671 helped to recreate something of the wild hunting of old. Valuable game animals did not confine themselves to the estates of qualified men – they wandered across commons, farms and gardens owned or occupied by the unqualified majority. However, rather than fence the animals in, the Game Act extended the huntsman's horizons by enabling him to enter his neighbours' land with impunity. The hunter's abilities, rather than the extent of his estate, now formed the only boundaries that circumscribed his hunting.

And just as strong kings in the Middle Ages had added to their forest laws when they had had the power to do so, so did Parliament six hundred years later. Another twenty-four principal statutes were added in the next hundred and fifty years, increasing penalties, clarifying terms, filling in loopholes, and ultimately leaving no aspect of the unqualified hunter's activities untouched.[8] Where the 1671 act had laid down new qualifications for hunting, subsequent acts attempted to regulate a wide range of the illegal hunter's activities. An amendment to the 1671 act, for example, prohibited the possession of snares, 'hare-pipes', nets, and other 'engines' that might be used to hunt game, as well as the keeping of 'greyhounds, setting-dogs, ferrets, coney-dogs, and

lurchers' by unqualified persons.[9] The possession and sale of game, prohibited
early in James I's reign, was the subject of a series of further laws passed
between 1693 and 1707. Initially the law penalised the possession of game
without good explanation, but in 1707 all buying, selling and possession
of hares, partridges and pheasants by unqualified persons was outlawed,
thereby ruling that game was the exclusive property of the qualified elite
– untouchable by lesser mortals.[10] In its endeavour to close down the illegal
market in game, later in the century Parliament even imposed a ban on
the sale of animals lawfully killed by a qualified person.[11] Hunting at night,
qualification or no, was strictly forbidden, and in 1711 new penalties for this
transgression were introduced. The 1671 act, therefore, was simply the first
of a series of ever more aggressive measures to protect the small game of the
qualified gentleman. It was the bedrock of a solid body of laws constructed
over the eighteenth century that was to remain unreformed until 1831.

The 1671 act and its many later additions were clearly in the sole interest of
those who passed them. The 1 per cent of the population qualified according
to the game laws' provisions made up a tiny fraction of the whole population,
but all the Lords and nearly all the Commons who passed the laws were
qualified persons. Each modification and amendment was solidly backed
by Parliament: even the introduction of a new tax on game was positively
welcomed, in the hope that this would help to deter unlawful hunting and
the illegal sale of game. As qualified nobleman, Lord Suffield observed,
the system was 'one of exclusion [whose] chief enjoyment consists in the
possession of that which your neighbour has *not*, and perhaps *can not* have'.[12]
It was a privilege for which the qualified were more than happy to pay.

Yet the game laws equally stand out as a singularly ill-fashioned and
incoherent body of legislation. The original game law was muddled in
language and intent. Opponents delighted in repeating Blackstone's observation that the 1671 act contained six grammatical errors and gleefully
noted that it could only have been the work of 'boorish country esquires and
stupid fox-hunters'.[13] This shaky foundation was then extended in a piecemeal
fashion, responding to crises as they happened. New laws overlaid the old;
none of the old laws were repealed and they frequently contradicted the latter
additions. The resulting game code was filled with anomalies. In the words
of one critic, the whole body of the game laws was 'arbitrary, unjust, absurd,
and contemptible'.[14]

Many of these absurdities centred upon the use of the word 'esquire' – a
'very loose and vague description' in the opinion of the legal writer.[15] The
1671 Game Law stipulated that 'The sonne or heir apparent of an Esquire, or
other person of higher degree' was qualified to hunt, but said nothing of the
rights of the said esquires. According to the letter of the law then, though

an esquire owning land worth £99 a year was unable to kill the game on his lands, his eldest son could. If his land was worth £100, he and his eldest son could both kill game; but his younger sons could not. Furthermore there was a host of problems surrounding the definition of an 'esquire', which, though central to the 1671 act, Parliament had failed to clarify. It was a problem that one 'Country Gentleman' and critic of the game laws eloquently exposed:

> I would gladly know what the true and determinate Meaning the word Esquire is; I do not believe the Law has determined its true Sense, and for my Part, I have no clear Idea of what it is, though I give that Title (if it is one) to many of my Acquaintance; but do not know by what Right they claim it.[16]

The 'Country Gentleman' was quite correct: Parliament had failed to determine the 'true sense' of the word 'esquire', and as there was no legal definition of an esquire it was left to the courts to decide. In practice, however, they proved far better at deciding who was not an esquire than in establishing with any certitude who actually was – much to the humiliation of those who brought their cases to court.[17]

It was no doubt for this reason that the law was interpreted with a wide degree of latitude. As the musings of our self-styled 'Country Gentleman' indicate, rural dwellers knew instinctively who amongst their neighbours was an 'esquire' and who was not, though they were often unable to explain the foundations of their judgement. Eighteenth-century letters and diaries reveal that the tranche of small landowners and large farmers that had technically lost their qualification to hunt in 1671, in fact continued to enjoy the pleasures of the chase – with the approval, and sometimes even in the company, of their social betters. Joseph Page, for example, an Essex yeoman worth something under £100 a year, often shot with the local gentry, and even aped the medieval custom of sending gifts of game to his friends and neighbours.[18] Other diarists recorded hunting with their servants, an activity which though illegal posed little threat to the maintenance of law and order, and was unlikely to be pursued in the courts. Eighteenth-century rural society was for the most part consensual, and most JPs prized cordial relations with the substantial families in their district above strict adherence to the game qualifications.

Yet even granting that many middle-ranking farmers and landowners were suffered to hunt, there can be no escaping the conclusion that the game laws made their authors many enemies. Despite centuries of game laws restricting and removing the once universal right to hunt wild animals, most rural inhabitants still held to the common law principle of *ferae naturae* – that wild animals were without owner. They simply disagreed that small birds and mammals living in the wild could be owned by any but he with the wit or skill to catch them. As Smallman Gardiner, one critic of the game laws, stated: '[not] shall all the world alter my Opinion, that we are as much entitled to the Gifts of Nature, as the most powerful Men the Kingdom produces'.[19] It was a view endlessly repeated throughout the eighteenth century by a wide range of commentators, and the game laws, no matter how sensitively enforced, were fundamentally at odds with this belief. Those making a living off the land held a world view that could not easily be reconciled with that of their rulers, and despite numerous and passionate defences of the game regime by those who were qualified, the hostility and opposition of those who were not refused to go away.

Besides this objection to the principles underpinning the game laws, there was also widespread criticism born of more material considerations. The gentry's predilection for hunting placed a heavy burden on their tenants and neighbours. Peasants and farmers had traditionally hunted small wild animals not simply for sport and for food, but also because, left unchecked, these animals became farmyard pests. Just five hares eat nearly as much as a small sheep. They destroy young corn, bark fruit trees, and nibble turnips, causing considerable damage to the farmer's crops. Speaking of hares, one agricultural writer informed his readers that 'the quantity they *eat* is considerable, but small in comparison to the *waste* they create. Before a hare will make a meal of turnips, she will taste, perhaps, ten, without meeting one to her tooth … the turnip thus partially bitten, is, as a food, thus entirely lost to the farmer, and to the community'.[20] Large populations of hares, therefore, were disastrous to the farmer.

Pheasants and partridges, though less voracious than hares, nevertheless feed at the farmer's expense. Pheasants feed on the wheat crop and, to a lesser extent, upon barley and clover, whilst partridges live mainly on clover, cereal and grain.[21] Both birds might cause great damage to a farmer's crops. The agricultural writer William Marshall considered that the destruction caused by 'an inordinate quantity of game … is in a manner inconceivable' and argued fervently, though ultimately in vain, for a more equitable and productive use of the land in areas practising game preservation on a large scale.[22] A poor run of harvests at the end of the eighteenth century left many rural communities short of grain and the sight of these hungry animals foraging upon the land can only have added to their worries.

As has often been the case, laws hated by a wide cross-section of society were held in universal contempt and widely flouted. Inevitably, the farmers, in whose gift the preservation of game ultimately lay, were ill disposed to play their part so long as they had so much to lose and so little to gain. As

one critic pointed out, if the farmers are 'not allowed to sport themselves ...
they will either destroy the Game out of resentment, or let the poacher do
it for him'.[23] Even the most ardent defenders of the game laws were forced
to admit that the current regime made it difficult to gain the co-operation of
tenant farmers in preserving wild mammals.

At the bottom of the social scale gangs of armed poachers resorted to
bloodshed and violence to restore rights they felt Parliament had unjustly
taken away. Landowners responded by petitioning an obliging Parliament
for ever more severe game laws, and by introducing increasingly barbaric
forms of protection to their land. Weapons such as spring guns and mantraps
became an indispensable component of any hunting landowner's estate.
Spring guns were concealed guns that shot indiscriminately when unwittingly
triggered by a hidden tripwire. Mantraps were designed to ensnare offenders
in their metal jaws: names such as 'the Body-squeezer', the 'Thigh-cracker'
or 'the Crusher' give an idea of the effect desired.[24] Both contraptions were
intended as deterrents, and their use was accompanied by prominent notices
in the local papers warning would-be trespassers of their existence. But
their intended victims, the poachers, usually became adept at detecting and
disarming them, sometimes even resetting them against the keepers. Instead,
these weapons were too often the cause of injury to innocent bystanders,
not least children. The three sons of a Suffolk admiral, for example, were
all seriously injured by a single shot from a spring gun, and at one Suffolk
estate, Moseley's at Rushbrooke, no fewer than five innocent victims were
injured by spring guns in the 1820s.[25] It was certainly not unknown for their
use to have fatal results.[26] Well might Henry Zouch, a prominent Justice of
the Peace, lament that there were 'persons assembling themselves together
in the night in companies, armed with firearms, clubs and other offensive
weapons ... impatient of rule and contemptuous of authority'.[27] Villagers
were indeed utterly contemptuous both of the exclusive game laws and of
the methods used to uphold them.

So in the century following the Restoration, the world of hunting was
changed immeasurably. The noble and beloved deer had been entirely eclipsed
by the small animals that had long been peripheral to the real business of
hunting, and in the process a clear realignment in the social context of the
sport took place. Hunting had always been divisive, but deer-hunting had
traditionally pitted large landowners against each other, rather than against
their poorer neighbours. The old squabbles between neighbouring landed
magnates receded under the new regime, and a clear and stark class divide
now took its place.

As the status of different animals changed, the very nature of hunting began
to undergo subtle changes as well. The small animals now classified as 'game'

had been hunted for centuries, but as large numbers of hunters turned their attention towards them, hunting techniques inevitably evolved. It is not that older hunting techniques were effaced, for some facets of hunting were the same as they had been in the Middle Ages. But alongside old traditions, the eighteenth century witnessed many innovations, and changes were multiplying at an unprecedented rate.

Consider, for example, the hare. Hunting the hare had always been revered. The animal's ability to run for miles at high speed, all the time twisting, turning and doubling back upon itself, made it difficult to capture, and raised the esteem with which hare-hunting was held. Short of larger mammals to hunt, sportsmen inevitably became ever more enthusiastic about their old friend the hare during this period. One writer, Nicholas Cox, considered that 'of all Chaces the Hare makes the greatest pastime and pleasure'.[28] Another, Gardiner, described hare-hunting as 'delightful, but not dangerous ... moderate, but not so laborious'.[29] Many writers turned their pen to extolling the virtues of the hare hunt, and the sport continued to flourish throughout the eighteenth century.[30] Indeed, there were more packs hunting hares than there were foxes as late as the 1830s.[31] Furthermore, they hunted in a fashion little different to the way practised in the Middle Ages. The eighteenth-century hare hunt was a genuine descendant of the hunting enjoyed in earlier times.

Alongside this ancient form of hare-hunting across open land, the related sport of hare coursing was also rapidly gaining in popularity. Coursing is a test between two greyhounds: its requirements are simple – just two greyhounds and a live hare are needed. The two dogs are released at the same time; the one that kills the hare is declared the winner and, as with horse-racing, bets are usually placed upon the outcome. Though medieval writers had rarely thought to describe coursing in detail, it had no doubt been popular for centuries. Certainly, by the sixteenth century an elaborate set of rules governing the procedures was in circulation, so it seems reasonable to assume that the sport was quite widespread by that date.

Throughout the early modern period coursing resembled traditional forms of hunting more closely than the modern sport of coursing that was soon to emerge. It was usually conducted on unenclosed land, and finding the hare was an integral element of the sport. The coursers traversed the land, either on foot or on horseback, casting their eyes up and down the fields in search of a hare or beating bushes to stir them from their forms.[32] The coursing took place on whatever patch of unenclosed land the hare was found. The informal and unstructured nature of traditional hare coursing is illustrated in James Seymour's painting *A Coursing Party*, completed in 1738, which shows three riders, two greyhounds and one dead hare, all situated in an unenclosed rural setting. The animal was found and coursed in its natural habitat, and the lack of enclosure made the escape of the hare one possible outcome of the event.

In the eighteenth century, as coursing became more popular, so did the nature of the sport begin to change, and as the occasional and informal meets between greyhound owners were gradually transformed into an organised pastime, the sport became increasingly artificial. In 1776, Lord Orford and twenty-five other gentlemen established a coursing club which sponsored annual meets in Swaffham in Norfolk. Other counties soon followed suit, and in time-honoured fashion the regional clubs were soon competing against one another. The result was large matches that gathered crowds of several hundred people, often with large sums staked upon the outcome.[33] With large crowds and stakes, the finding of the hare could not be left to chance: to be certain of a good day's sport, live hares needed to be captured beforehand and set free at the appropriate moment. And in order to be certain that one dog would defeat the other, an enclosed arena was desirable. The sportsmen no longer began their day's sport casting about in search of a live hare, nor did the hare have any real chance of escaping its pursuers – and two key similarities between hare hunting and hare coursing were thereby eroded.

This was as nothing, however, to the changes that occurred in the hunting of pheasants and partridges, which was slowly being transformed beyond recognition during this period. For centuries, pheasants and partridges had been snared at ground level, using a combination of nets and traps. Dogs pointed at the birds and keepers spread the nets, whilst the sportsman, perhaps mounted, perhaps on foot, controlled and observed the proceedings. The hunter might have an enjoyable day's sport with little more than a few handfuls of grain and a well-trained dog.[34] It was a gentle pastime. Guns, though most huntsmen had one by this point, were considerably less popular than nets and snares; a knowledge of the birds' habitat, however, was fundamental. The sporting writer Nicholas Cox considered that understanding the haunts of fowl – whether the edge of rivers or brooks, the dry part of overgrown fens or half-drowned moors or the hollow vales of heaths and plains – was the 'thing of greatest moment for the fowler'.[35] The hunting was slow, and though the rewards might be significant, it had not seriously undermined the population of small game.

In 1735 the *Sportsman's Dictionary* informed its readers about the art of 'shooting flying', describing it as the 'best and most diverting way of shooting'.[36] Shooting birds 'on the wing' – or 'shooting flying' – involved no more than shooting the bird while it was in the air. Owing to the limitations of the gun – a muzzle-loading piece fired by flint and steel – it remained a difficult feat for most of the eighteenth century, but a stream of small improvements to the gun in the second half of the century removed some of the technical impediments to shooting flying. In the 1780s, Henry Nock's patent breech enabled guns to shoot harder and quicker, and this in turn enabled the gunmakers to cut the barrel to 30 inches, making it far easier to wield and use.[37] Double barrels began to appear in the late eighteenth century.[38] This series of minor modifications to the gun increased the ease with which birds might be shot in flight, and helped to transform shooting flying into a skilled and fashionable pastime.

Its appeal lay in its unique combination of simplicity and skill. One advocate considered that the sport's rules were of 'no signification; a good gun, a cool and steady aim, and practice; [also] the nice difference in aiming at or before the mark' were all that were needed to make a good flying marksman.[39] A proliferation of publications educating sportsmen in the purchase, use and care of a fowling piece were soon on the market, and in a matter of generations the use of nets and lime, so long the mainstay of hunting small game, had been relegated to the margins.[40] At the end of the century, one writer could justly claim that 'the rage for shooting was never at a higher pitch than at present' and 'that the art of shooting flying is arrived at tolerable perfection'.[41] And by the early nineteenth century, all other means had 'long since been superseded'.[42]

Initially the culture and style of shooting flying resembled that of earlier trapping methods. The individual sportsman walked the land with his dog in search of small flocks of birds; a setter or pointer helped him to locate the birds, and he shot at the birds wherever he found them.[43] The knowledge of the birds' habitat and nature that was so important to the early modern fowler was no less important to the hunter who shot flying. It was soon realised, however, that the full capacities of the new flintlock gun were not exploited by this method. The loading process of the flintlock enabled the hunter to shoot about four or five times a minute, but he was unlikely to shoot so often if he and his companion adhered to the old method of shooting at small flocks of birds wherever they found them. There was scope to test one's marksmanship more rigorously if a means of bringing more birds before the shooter could be designed.

In order to use new technologies more efficiently, the 'battue' hunt was born — a continental import, introduced to England around the turn of the century. In the French battue hunt, shooters and beaters walked a line through a covert sheltering plentiful game. The birds were flushed from their covert, and the shooters, supported by gun loaders and spotters, took aim. As the birds emerged, the still of the countryside was broken by a frenzy of shooting and clouds of gun smoke. Hunting in this way, the skilled shooter can bring down dozens of birds in a matter of minutes. The skills required by

10. Samuel Howitt's beautiful engraving of two gentlemen out with their dogs, 'shooting flying', published in 1807. The engraving depicts a blend of modern technologies combined with the older practice of walking the fields in search of wild game birds and shooting them in their natural habitat.

the battue are greater than those called for by the old method, now known quaintly as 'walking up', but by the same token, the rewards far outweigh those of traditional methods. Far more birds could be killed by this means than with a day's solitary shooting.

The spread of battue hunting was limited before the 1840s, and most sporting handbooks continued to instruct their readers in the arts of walking up rather than battue hunting.[44] Even practitioners of the new mode of shooting appear to have rationed the amount of the time spent battue shooting and continued with the walking-up method of old through much of the season. Colonel Peter Hawker, for example, author of a popular shooting handbook and one of the early nineteenth century's finest shots, spent most of the shooting season on solitary hunting expeditions with his dogs: his battue hunts were occasional affairs punctuating a shooting season conducted upon more traditional lines.[45] Yet the gradual spread of the battue was unmistakable, much to the consternation of more traditionally minded sportsmen. Traditionalists took exception to the extensive slaughter that the grand battue hunt might involve and railed against the introduction of this 'abominable Gallic System'.[46] During the 1820s, numerous correspondents to the *Sporting Magazine* voiced complaints about the new system, dismissed by one correspondent as being 'unworthy of any gentleman aspiring to the title of an English sportsman', and by another as 'cruel, selfish, and unmanly'.[47] The sportsman and writer William Daniel, ordinarily a staunch defender of country sports, thought that the lists of game killed in certain areas revealed 'such wanton registry of Slaughter, as no Sportsman can read without Regret'. He wished that some of the country's most celebrated marksmen would 'in Mercy forbear such terrible Examples of Skill'.[48] But the outrage expressed at the modern French system is testimony to the growing importance of the battue, and hints at the changing nature of small-game hunting that lay around the corner.

A successful day's hunting had always been measured to some degree by the number of beasts killed, but the capture of a particularly old or elusive stag was rated far above the killing of several smaller, younger deer – those classified simply as 'rascal' or 'folly'. Hence medieval handbooks that devoted page after page to explaining how a deer's age could be ascertained from its antlers. Hence also James I's distraction and delight at the capture of old Cropear in 1624. As battue hunting gradually became established in the nineteenth century, however, there was a decisive shift of emphasis. With the introduction of modern technology, hunters were able to kill larger numbers of wild animals than ever before. On the manors of Sir Richard Colt Hoare in the 1790s, the average head of game shot was 760, but in just three decades this almost doubled, rising to 1,270.[49] At the great shooting estates in north Norfolk, a successful day's hunting might occasionally result in as many as fifty head of game being killed by each shooter;[50] and in 1824, a shooting party on Lord Granville's Wherstead Estate in Suffolk killed upwards of 1,000 head of game in just two days.[51] For the modern shooter, it was simply the number of birds shot that mattered. In the eighteenth century there was a clear shift in emphasis, away from the thrill of the chase to the pleasure of the kill.

Change in the world of hunting was of course not new. The history of hunting had long been one of continuous adaptation to changing circumstances. Competing pressures on land and a varying ecology had decisively shaped hunting practices throughout the Middle Ages; even the oldest traditions had always had to evolve. But adjustments had been gradual, spanning the centuries rather than the decades. The invention of new technologies in the eighteenth century ruptured this established pattern of slow evolution. A quick succession of small improvements to the gun revolutionised the hunting of game, and it very rapidly upset the precarious balance that earlier generations had achieved.

In the event, however, this progress simply led the hunters back to the age-old limitations experienced by their forebears – that is, that hunting has somehow to fit with nature's provisions. Since the Norman Invasion, hunters in England had struggled to carve a niche out of their ever dwindling share of the natural resources of an increasingly populated country. Their efforts had for the most part been at least partially successful, but with the arrival of the gun and the development of the battue, the hunters' capacity to kill vastly outstripped the gifts that nature could ever supply. Draconian legislation had been drafted to ensure that game shooting was confined to a tiny elite, but no game law, no matter how exclusive or ruthlessly enforced, could preserve the game population in the face of hunting techniques such as these. The hunters had no option but to return to the tried and tested method of rearing and protecting the animals they wished to hunt.

In order to guarantee the large numbers of birds required for a successful day's shooting, keen marksmen needed to find ways to ensure a steady supply of wild birds on their land. They initially turned to simple methods to lure birds to their fields. A few strategically placed heaps of buckwheat here, an enticing pile of berries there, or some 'white pease' placed in small troughs – these and other such simple ruses were used to encourage birds to settle.[52] It soon became apparent, however, that a more thorough breeding programme was required, and landowners began to experiment with rearing large stocks of partridges and pheasants in specially constructed reserves kept free of predators.

The pheasant was scarce at the start of the eighteenth century, but the population grew steadily in the next one hundred years following the introduction of hand rearing. At first large landowners used the common barnyard hen to hatch pheasant eggs found on the estate; once able to care for themselves, the young were turned out into protected coverts, where gamekeepers fed them in times of severe weather.[53] Alternatively, landowners might send their employees into their fields in search of eggs. At Wilton, the Earl of Pembroke paid one shilling for every pheasant egg brought in from the surrounding countryside.[54] Around the middle of the century, the rearing of pheasants became more intensive with the construction of 'pheasantries' – special buildings designed to house the eggs for hatching – and committed game preservers disbursed large sums on their construction and upkeep. At Audley End, for example, almost £150 was spent each year on game preservation in the 1780s, whilst at Longleat the pheasantry cost over £200 a year to maintain.[55] The estate's servants were kept busy killing the rats, hawks, owls, crows, magpies, jays and polecats that preyed upon the game and their eggs – over 300 such predators were killed at Longleat in a single year.[56] Partridge rearing was conducted in much the same manner, though with rather less success until enterprising landowners developed a new trade in partridge eggs. In a single year, the Duke of Richmond imported more than a thousand such eggs from France.[57]

This twin strategy of importing eggs and raising them under pullets enabled game preservers to produce very large numbers of birds. It was said of the preserves of one keen hunter that 'the pheasants were as thick as sparrows on a barn-door and the hares running about like rabbits'.[58] John Byng found chicks in such number on the Duke of Marlborough's Blenheim estate 'that I almost trod on them in the grass'.[59] In Norfolk, the local newspaper reported that a severe winter in 1813–14 killed some 20,000 head of game – the figure was probably an exaggeration, though it gives some indication of the extent of game preservation being practised.[60]

By the nineteenth century, intensive preservation had become a necessity that no serious shooter could avoid, and it guaranteed the large bags that hunters desired. But it also changed the nature of the sport in significant and regrettable ways. Amongst the key attractions of hunting over the centuries had been the pitting of human skill against the speed and cunning of natural wildlife, but game that had been reared by hand and sheltered from the elements can be considered 'wild' only in the loosest sense of the term. Moreover, the intimate knowledge of the game, its habitat and its habits that had aided the hunter in earlier times had become largely unneeded with the emergence of game produced on an industrial scale by hired professionals. The hunter needed a steady aim, but did not need to read the landscape in the way that generations before him had done.

Hunting traditions necessarily adapt, but whilst change in the world of hunting was not new, the pace of change in the eighteenth century was unlike anything previously known, for the introduction of the gun altered the scale of hunting in fundamental ways. The eighteenth century marked the origin of hunting in its modern form, but it also marked the passing of many older hunting traditions. Centuries of accumulated knowledge about the habitat and customs of hares and game birds became increasingly redundant as the modern forms of hare coursing and shooting emerged; and in their place, the hunter's old friend – preservation, in the form of game laws and breeding and rearing programmes – became ever more important.

CHAPTER TEN

Hunting the Fox:
'fascinating and soul stirring sport'[1]

We give law to hares and deer, because they are beasts of chase; it was
never accounted either cruelty or foul play to knock foxes and wolves on
the head as they can be found, because they are beasts of prey. (Oliver
St John, 1641)[2]

The qualifications for hunting game had been set so high in 1671 that the
numbers involved in the eighteenth-century shooting revolution remained
small. With less than 1 per cent of England's population allowed to hunt
game, numerous unqualified farmers and smaller landowners with a taste for
country sports were forced to turn elsewhere in search of animals to hunt.
The English countryside was not lacking in unprotected wildlife – foxes,
martens, badgers, otters, squirrels and wildcats all lay outside the game laws,
and were fair game for any who set their dogs upon them. The only trouble
was that hunting them was widely regarded to be without especial interest.
In the eighteenth century, however, the fox was lifted from this category of
second-rate quarry and, in an extraordinary transition, foxhunting moved
from its marginal position to centre stage.

As we have already seen, the hunting of foxes had traditionally been held
in low esteem. Foxes were vermin and so lacked the status that had made
hunting a noble pursuit for centuries. In contrast to other coveted quarry
– deer, boar, pheasant, partridge and hare – the fox's flesh is unpalatable and
inedible; and unlike other animals of prey, the fox poses no danger to human
life. It was a simple farmyard pest of no culinary worth; hunting it was useful
rather than noble or heroic. Furthermore, the hunting of foxes had generally
been considered slow and unexciting. Foxes run fast, and in straight lines, and
the hounds traditionally reared for deer-hunting were strong, heavy animals

that ran too slowly to chase foxes effectively. For this reason, fox hunts were usually timed to take place early in the morning as the fox returned to its earth after feeding – at this hour its stomach was full and the animal was unwilling to run. The hunts were long, and the chase sufficiently slow to be satisfactorily followed on foot.[3]

In the late sixteenth century, however, foxhunting had gradually emerged from its traditional position of relative obscurity. The two foremost hunting writers of the Tudor period, George Gascoigne and Thomas Cockaine, had both devoted some attention to hunting the fox: Gascoigne, for example, considered that one could have 'good pastime at this vermin'.[4] Following the Restoration in 1660 ever more hunters began to turn their attention to the humble fox. Arthur Stringer, the author of a handbook entitled *The Experienc'd Huntsman* (published in 1714) thought he 'need not insist long upon endeavouring to recommend the Pleasure of Fox-hunting, it being much used by Kings, Princes, Noblemen, and Gentlemen; and it is certainly a brave, noble Chace for such who keep good Horses and Hounds'.[5] The growing interest in foxhunting after the Restoration, however, was more than a simple consequence of the decline of the other large mammals that hunters had traditionally pursued. The nature of foxhunting itself was changing. When huntsmen began innovating with the hounds used to hunt foxes the sport was transformed from a small-scale, slow-moving, low-status affair into one involving long and fast chases for large fields of mounted hunters. A recreation to rival the ancient sport of kings was born.

Much of the credit for these changes has been given to Hugo Meynell, a wealthy Leicestershire squire and a keen huntsman who had inherited his father's estate in the village of Quorn in the 1750s.[6] According to this account, having bought his first pack of hounds at the age of eighteen – an aristocratic pack from Wardour in Wiltshire dating back to the seventeenth century – Meynell began breeding them for stamina and speed as much as for nose. He had soon bred hounds that were fast enough to keep on terms with the fox, and so switched the hour of hunting to mid-morning, a time when the fox could be expected to run. His neighbours began to take an interest once the excitement that could be had hunting with the Quorn became clear, and skilled riders from further afield were also keen to join the hunt and demonstrate their ability to keep up with the fast-running pack. The hunt now offered a unique opportunity for the well-connected to display their riding ability to those who mattered.[7]

But although Meynell made significant improvements to the breeding of foxhounds, the foundations for the innovations with which he is credited were well under way before the 1750s. Long before Meynell began his work in hound-breeding, many foxhunters had realised that fast hounds set upon foxes at the right hour offered the promise of a hard and fast chase, and had begun their own experiments. For example, Arthur Stringer, writing in 1714, strongly urged his readers to use their fastest hounds for foxhunting: the hunting party, he advised, needed 'fleet hounds, for slow hounds signify little for that pastime'.[8] With slow hounds, a fox might run about from daybreak to just before night without successful capture – how much more preferable to have just a few fast hounds and a fast chase over ten or more miles.[9] No less importantly, the foxhunter needed a fine horse; in Stringer's opinion, if a huntsman were to chase a fox with fleet hounds with any chance of success, his horse needed to be in as good condition as a racehorse. Stringer's ingredients – fast horses and fleet hounds – form the backbone of modern foxhunting.

Though Stringer was alone in writing at length about the nature of foxhunting in the early eighteenth century, he was certainly not alone in noticing the potential for fast, exhilarating chases in pursuit of the humble fox. John Smallman Gardiner, a passionate advocate of the sport of hare-hunting, was loath to accept that the upstart sport of foxhunting had any conceivable advantages over it. Nonetheless, writing before the emergence of Meynellian science, he described a sport that already closely resembled modern foxhunting in all key respects:

> A Lover of Hunting almost every Man is, or would be thought; but twenty in the Field after a Hare, my Lord, find more delight and sincere Enjoyment, than one in twenty in a Fox Chace; the former consisting of an endless Variety of accidental Delights, the latter of little more than hard Riding, the Pleasure of clearing some dangerous Leap, the Pride of striding the best Nag, and shewing somewhat of the bold Horseman; and (equal to any thing) of being first in at the Death, after a Chace frequently from County to County ... So that, but for the Name of Foxhunting, a Man might as well mount at his Stable-Door, and determine to gallop twenty Miles an End into another County.[10]

It is clear that the origins of the fast-paced fox hunt go back further than Meynell and his work at the village of Quorn in the 1750s. The true origins must be located in the decline of deer-hunting after the Restoration. At its finest, the stag hunt had offered a relatively fast-paced horseback chase across mile upon mile of unfenced country, and the decline of the deer population deprived the hunting community of this ancient and uniquely exhilarating pastime. No native animal but the fox could come close to rivalling the deer for the quality of the chase it provided, and hunters had been quick to explore the possibility of preserving some element of the horseback chase as soon as the unstoppable demise of wild-deer hunting became apparent. Meynell was not the inventor of modern foxhunting, but he certainly did raise the previously uncoordinated efforts of hound breeders to a new level. And as more breeders began to hear about Meynell's hounds, the practice of breeding fast hounds began to spread. Ever more serious foxhunters possessed hounds capable of chasing the fox at speed over long distances. And just as with the deer and the hare and other highly rated quarry, the appeal of hunting the fox lay in the difficulty in outwitting it. As one writer commented, what makes 'foxhunting so very far superior to other sports, is *the wildness of the animal you hunt*, and *the difficulty in catching him*'.[11]

In the second half of the century, the switch to fleet hounds occurred in most parts of the country, with only a few outlying regions in Wales and northern England continuing to follow the fox on foot.[12] Speed was now everything in the fox hunt and skill at riding had become integral to the sport. Peter Beckford, a keen huntsman and the pre-eminent sporting writer of the eighteenth century, even admitted to knowing men who thought foxhunting 'is only to be followed because you can ride hard'.[13] Indeed, although most sporting writers were keen to advise their readers against hard riding, one at least had to confess that he doubted whether the 'Noble Science might not be robbed of one half of its seductions were it not so combined with the use of the horse'.[14] The speed and excitement found expression in hunting songs, as one immensely popular song by John O'Keeffe testifies:

> Thus we ride whip and spur for a two hours Chace
> Our Horses go panting and jobbing
> You Madcap and Riot begin now race
> Ride on Sir and give him some mobbing.[15]

In 1793, the Prince of Wales, never much interested in his father's deer-hunting, took to hunting foxes.[16] The sport's appeal clearly lay in the exhilaration of a fast ride: 'I hope you will get [the pack] so fast that they will run away from everybody,' he once wrote to the huntsman of the Buckhounds.[17] Within the space of about fifty years, the fox, so long disregarded as hardly worthy of a gentleman's attention, was transformed into hunting quarry *par excellence*, and the method of hunting him had reached 'a system of perfection never before known'.[18] By 1781, 'foxhunting is now become the amusement of gentlemen: nor need any gentleman be ashamed of it'.[19]

With so many riders turning their interest to the fox, every aspect of the old-fashioned fox hunt was soon transformed. The appeal of a daybreak start, for example, though it lingered amongst traditionalists throughout the eighteenth century, had by the early nineteenth century been largely eliminated. In the 1780s, Beckford thought that 'the hour most favourable to this diversion, is certainly an early one' and recommended that the hounds should be at cover at sunrise. In similar fashion, Sir Edward Littleton, owner of Pillaton Hall in Staffordshire and Master of the Cannock Chase Hunt between 1774 and 1791, left the early start unchanged throughout the years of his mastership: the hour of meeting was at 'peep of day' – generally eight o'clock, or as soon after as the light would permit.[20] During these years, chases typically lasted between one and two hours, and a descendant of Sir Edward was struck by the efficiency of the system: 'The number of foxes killed each year,' he wrote, 'shows the immense superiority of this system to the modern one.'[21] Nonetheless, the system was already on the way out, and by the early nineteenth century the early morning hunt was largely gone. 'Hunting early is *unnecessary*,' advised one writer; 'the breeds of hounds, the feeding, and the whole system is so much improved, that the majority of foxes are found and killed in the afternoon.'[22] The hunt now met at an agreeable hour in the mid-morning, and offered hours of hard riding across the English countryside. A legendary run described by the sporting journalist Charles James Apperley, under the pseudonym Nimrod, lasted for no less than two hours and fifty minutes: the fox was killed and though every hound was present at the death, only two riders had managed to stay the course.[23]

The early morning hunts of old had effectively confined the sport to the locals: a squire kept a private pack and shared his sport with his neighbours – there were no fixed times or places for meets, and only those invited joined in. But the increasing speed and excitement of foxhunting heightened the appeal for fashionable sportsmen, and the mid-morning hunt enabled keen riders from distant parts to trek several miles to join it. Inevitably, the size of the hunting field began to grow and expectations concerning the size and quality of the pack soon increased as well. Rearing a pack of hounds suitable for large, hard-riding fields was an expensive business – one contemporary estimate for the cost of maintaining a pack of foxhounds put the total at nearly £2,000 a year.[24] Traditionally, local squires of substantial means had shouldered this expense, but rising costs were making it ever more difficult for them to do so and, as a result, they turned to subscriptions – small payments to help support the hounds – in order to make ends meet. As early as the 1760s, Meynell was accepting subscriptions, though he never had more than a handful of subscribers at any one time.[25] And, as ever, where Meynell led, the rest soon followed. By the middle of the nineteenth century, only fourteen of over a hundred packs listed by the *Sporting Magazine* were supported entirely by their master; all the rest were funded, in part at least, by the subscriptions of paying members.[26] As one keen foxhunter observed: 'a committee is the order of the day; the new mode of doing things by subscription is introduced'.[27] As they began to disappear, the private packs were held up as a token of hospitality and generosity and there was no shortage of conservative commentators ready to lament the passing of the good old days, but the trend towards professionalisation was unstoppable.[28] By the early nineteenth century, a pack of foxhounds was increasingly likely to be a professional outfit, with hounds and a master maintained, in part at least, by subscription.

The growing size of the field did not simply necessitate changes in the organisation of foxhunting, it also led to changes in the very nature of the sport. Since the sixteenth century, much of the appeal of hunting had lain in watching hounds work upon the fox's trail. The fox has a strong scent, but one that fades quickly, and the huntsmen need well-trained hounds if they are to keep on terms with the fox. Indeed, early modern writers had usually devoted considerably more attention to the rearing and training of the hounds than to the actual hunting of the fox. The great hound breeders of the eighteenth century were similarly inspired by a delight in watching their trained hounds at work. It is unlikely, however, that many in the large fields of riders that hunted with them shared this interest. For most foxhunters, the sheer challenge of remaining mounted provided all the excitement they needed. One sports writer confessed that 'many people go out for the sake of the riding part only; the hunting is a minor consideration'.[29] For the average rider in the field, the sport offered hard, exciting riding with a strong competitive element, and conversation at the evening's hunt dinner turned upon the performance of one's fellow riders and not upon the work of the foxhounds. As one gentlemen observed, foxhunting had become 'a thing to brag about'.[30]

The problems posed by a large field of hard riders, or 'thrusters', were noted in the early 1780s by Beckford: 'if you can keep your brother sportsmen in order, and put any discretion into them,' he wrote, 'you are in luck; they frequently do more harm than good.'[31] And writing a few decades later, Sir Charles Knightley, Master of the Pytchley Hunt between 1809 and 1817, opined that the problem had worsened in the intervening years, with the quality of runs declining, despite the fact that the 'hounds never were better managed than now'. Much of the problem was simply that fields were becoming larger: 'where in former days there were fifty men out there are now three hundred'. For the competitive rider, a large field added considerably to the excitement, but for this Master of Foxhounds, it simply increased the number of hard riders and thrusters insensitive to the work of the hounds.

Formerly five or six men used to ride hard, and if they knew but little of hunting, they generally knew when the hounds were on scent and when

not. At present everybody rides hard, and out of three hundred, not
three have the slightest notion whether they are on or off scent ...[32]

Committed hound breeders continued to rail against the 'immense
ungovernable fields' with which they had to hunt, but much of their work
was dependent upon the subscriptions paid by these large fields, and each
party had little choice but to seek an accommodation with the other.

   Towards the close of the eighteenth century, the long fast runs that had
put the sport on the map were enlivened yet further with the introduction
of jumping – or, in contemporary parlance, 'leaping'. There had always
been some element of jumping, but the enclosure of the three midland
counties that formed the cradle of the sport – Leicestershire, Rutland and
Northamptonshire – introduced jumping on a scale never previously known.[33]
As each county was extensively enclosed after 1760, the expansive open fields
over which the hunters had once ridden were transformed. The old open
common fields were divided up, and each new landowner erected fences and
hedges around his plot. Though initially just thorn seedlings protected by
a rail, these fences nevertheless needed to be jumped and, as the seedlings
grew, large hedges had to be negotiated. It all added a new dimension of
excitement. Foxhunting now promised breakneck jumping as well as fast
runs, and its popularity continued its steady rise.[34]

   The sport's growth was encouraged yet further in the middle of the
nineteenth century when the new railways made it possible for hunters to
widen the field of their hunting. Though initially feared by the hunting
fraternity – 'a trebly accursed revolution' – in the opinion of one writer,
the railways ushered in a new phase of the sport's growth, rather than its
demise.[35] From the 1840s, Victorian trains were equipped with horseboxes,
and this enabled keen huntsmen to hunt over a far wider territory than before.
An early-morning train from London would take hunter and horse to a mid-
morning hunt in the Shires for a little over £3, a trifling sum for a wealthy
Londoner, and season tickets were available for the truly committed.[36] The
sporting Londoner, travelling by train to distant meets, even figured in some
of the sporting literature of the time. Robert Surtees's John Jorrocks, for
example, took advantage of the opening of each new train line to visit new
hunting country, each time combining hunting with business – 'hunting one
day and selling teas another'.[37] The railways inevitably increased the size of
the field yet further, particularly those of the fashionable midland packs, and
helped to consolidate the position of foxhunting in rural life.[38]

   As foxhunting rose in status, it took over some of the rituals associated
with deer-hunting in earlier times. The killing of the deer, for example, had
been dignified with a degree of formality; it was an honour accorded to the

most senior person present, and the carcass of the slayed deer was dissected and carted away following strict conventions. For the low-status fox, hunted on foot and with traps and snares, such flattery was unknown, but as wealthy gentlemen turned their attention towards foxhunting the dispatch of the fox rose in importance. Being present at the kill was all-important, as was the offering of the fox to the hounds: 'When he is caught,' wrote Beckford of the fox, 'I like to see the hounds eat him eagerly.'[39] Writing in the middle of the nineteenth century, Delabere Blaine described the 'funereal honours bestowed upon' the dead fox: his brush, pads and head or snout were cut off, and the carcass held up to the pack and then thrown at it.[40] The particulars, Blaine added, differed from one pack to the next, each practising its own variant of this basic script. The huntsman's 'whoo-whoop' at the death of the fox was borrowed from stag-hunting. The custom of giving the brush to the first rider at the kill was invented, and the practice of 'blooding' – daubing the faces of children or new hunt members with the fox's blood – was also developed.[41] So too was a complex vocabulary of hunting terms, and the sporting handbooks provided their readers with long lists of the correct technical terms for each aspect of the hunt, just as the earliest hunting treatises published centuries before had done.[42]

As with all high-status hunting, fine clothes were an essential part of the experience, with the fashionable Leicestershire hunts leading the way in this respect, as in so many others. A travel writer commenting on the hunt at Meynell's Quorndon Hall observed that the company on a field day 'go out with as much ceremony as to court, their hair always being dressed'.[43] According to Nimrod, in the early nineteenth century the Meltonian was known by 'the exact stulze-like fit of his coat, his superlatively well cleaned leather breeches and boots, and the generally apparent high breeding of the man'.[44] And the post-hunt socialising was no less glamorous: the start of the Quorn's hunting season, for example, was celebrated with 'splendid entertainments' given by Mr Meynell to his friends.[45]

For most of the eighteenth century there was no formal dress code, beyond the need to be seen in fine attire, but in the final decades of the century, foxhunters switched to the red coats that are now their hallmark. For example, the fashionable Taporley Club in Cheshire, founded in 1762, switched from blue to red coats in 1769, at the same time as they switched from hunting the hare to the fox.[46] In the 1770s, the subjects of George Stubbs's paintings were frequently painted in red frock coats, and by the following century the tight-fitting red scarlet coat, adorned with five brass buttons, had become de rigueur.[47] By the nineteenth century, one writer considered the issue of clothing 'a matter of too much importance to admit of my neglecting'.[48] Gradually the sport was invested with the smartness and

11. Henry Alken, the leading British sporting artist of the early nineteenth century, captures all the key elements of the modernised fox hunt in this illustration for Nimrod's *Life of John Mytton*: the large field, the red hunting coats, and the riders' speed, 'leaping' and mishaps.

pageantry that befitted a gentleman's status. Hunting the fox had become a fashionable pursuit.

The property qualifications required to shoot game effectively shut all but the most privileged 1 per cent of society out. But with no qualification needed to hunt foxes, the sport's defenders could legitimately claim that anyone could participate, that skilled horsemanship, not wealth or status, was the only qualification. The Prince Regent even claimed to have raced a Brighton butcher at a Sussex hunt for over an hour, a story which though untrue was at least plausible.[49] Advocates of the sport frequently made bold claims about the ways in which it fostered class ties. For example, John Conyers argued that 'the humblest man in the population, provided only he be decent and well-behaved, may ride by the side of a duke when both are in pursuit of a fox, but in what other country but dear old England could such a sight be seen?'[50]

Of course, although foxhunting was technically open to all, these proud claims of social equality need to be approached with some degree of scepticism. This is not to deny the existence of modest packs formed by small farmers and tradesmen, with low subscriptions and a relatively modest social base of support. Such packs certainly did exist, and no doubt they offered much entertainment to those who hunted with them, but a fashionable sporting gentleman would scarcely be found in their midst. Packs were not socially integrative affairs – subscriptions, dress codes and the custom of accepting new members only by invitation all helped to ensure that every foxhunting man found his place in a pack fitting his social status.

The fashionable packs springing up in the midlands were technically open to any who could pay the annual subscription, but the social obligation to turn up with fine horses and in expensive clothing considerably raised the cost of joining the hunting fraternity.[51] The combined costs of subscription to a smart pack, appropriate attire and the maintenance of a horse ranged somewhere around £100 a year, and sharply limited any downward drift of the sport.[52] Indeed these requirements were considered so weighty by one commentator that he considered foxhunting scarcely more open than hare-hunting, despite the high property qualification needed for hunting the hare. The fox-chase, he opined, no doubt had its delight, 'but of such sort as cannot be heartily enjoyed except by persons of ample fortune and circumstance'.[53] In the opinion of another writer foxhunting was a pastime 'exclusively appertaining to gentlemen'.[54] From humble origins, foxhunting was rapidly becoming a high-status pursuit, attracting fashionable, moneyed sportsmen. Foxhunting may have been open to farmers and landowners disqualified from shooting game, but it was, as one commentator observed, 'too costly for the poor'.[55]

One final development in the world of eighteenth-century hunting worth noting is the gradual exclusion of women, for the development of new forms of foxhunting not only made an old pastime more elitist, it also appears to have decisively pushed female hunters outside the hunting fraternity. A scarcity of sources prior to the eighteenth century precludes detailed discussion of female hunting in the medieval and early modern periods, though it is well known that women did ride to hounds throughout this time. Records of poaching in the royal forests indicate that women were involved in hunting as far back as the thirteenth century, and estate papers from the sixteenth and seventeenth centuries reveal that female household members sometimes accompanied their male relatives at the hunt.[56] The female monarchs – Elizabeth and Anne – certainly rode to hounds, and as so often in the world of hunting, the lead provided by royalty was followed in aristocratic families throughout the land. At the same time, however, it is clear that no matter to which period we turn, women occupied a marginal position on the hunting field and we should be wise to forget any romantic notions of sexual equality on the hunting field before the eighteenth century.[57]

Despite this, it does appear that the emergence of modern foxhunting was accompanied by a discernible contraction of women's opportunities for hunting. In the eighteenth century, commentators began to declare that there was something unnatural about the sight of a woman hunting alongside men. The Scottish poet James Thomson captured this unease in his most celebrated poem, *The Seasons*:

> But if the rougher sex by this fierce sport
> Is hurried wild, let not such horrid joy
> E'er stain the bosom of the British fair.
> Far be the spirit of the chase from them!
> Uncomely courage, unbeseeming skill,
> To spring the fence, to rein the prancing steed,
> The cap, the whip, the masculine attire.
> In which they roughen to the sense and all
> The winning softness of their sex is lost.[58]

A combination of harder and faster chases and changing notions of femininity caused ever more commentators to declare that female participation was inappropriate. John Cook, in his treatise on hunting, wrote that women were 'more in their element in the drawing-room or in Kensington Gardens, than in the kennel or the field'.[59] And to the celebrated Robert Surtees there was 'a wide difference between ladies hunting and ladies coming to see the hounds off. They are as much in their place at their meet as they are out of it tearing across country.'[60] He cited reasons such as their tendency to keep 'the whole field in alarm lest an accident happen', and the fact that their presence deprived gentlemen riders 'of the agreeable change and variety which their society makes in the evening' in support of his argument that the ladies should keep clear of the hunting field.[61]

But at the same time as declaring that foxhunting was not a fit sport for women these writers make it clear that women still 'occasionally [graced] the field with their presence', despite social disapproval and the inconveniences posed by their clothing and the necessity of hunting side-saddle.[62] Lady Elizabeth Belgrave, for example, hunted with the Belvoir during the 1820s: Captain Russell noted she was 'out galloping about' one fine morning.[63] The *Sporting Magazine* contained occasional reports of women on the hunting field. In the 1830s, one correspondent lamented the fact that only Lady Kaye was out hunting – her companions Lady Suffield and Mrs Villiers being kept indoors by ill health and other commitments.[64] Perhaps most celebrated of all was the Marchioness of Salisbury, who acted as Master of the Hatfield Hunt after her husband's death in 1793.[65] The *Sporting Magazine* enjoyed providing its readers with colourful accounts of her exploits in the saddle: 'Out of a field of fourscore her ladyship soon gave honest Daniel the go-by; pressed Mr Hale neck and neck, soon passed the whippers-in, and continued indeed throughout the whole of the chase to be nearest the brush.'[66] The Marchioness of Salisbury continued hunting until her seventieth year, and her death in 1836 was much lamented in hunting circles.[67] Doubtless, such women were very much the exception to the rule. Melton Mowbray, the heartland of fashionable hunting, was an avowedly masculine world until women and families began accompanying their husbands during the hunting season in the 1850s, and it was not until the second half of the nineteenth century that women joined fathers, brothers and husbands on the hunting field to any significant degree.

This temporary disappearance of women was more than compensated for, statistically at least, by the growth in male followers and did nothing to slow the rise in popularity of foxhunting in the century following 1750. As hunting fields grew, however, the problem that has always plagued hunters raised its head once more: the increase in foxhunters soon led to a predictable decline in the number of foxes. From time immemorial, the fox had been free game for all, but hunting literature from the sixteenth century suggests that even by this date a little surreptitious preservation was being practised. William Harrison, for example, writing in 1577 believed that foxes would have been 'utterly destroyed' many years earlier had they not enjoyed the protection of hunters, preserving them in order to 'have pastime withal'.[68] Though Harrison, along with many other commentators, took a dim view of the practice, it is no doubt owing to this that the fox had not followed the boar and the wolf to extinction in the late Middle Ages. Nonetheless, stocks were low at the time that Leicestershire squires began experimenting with new sport with them, and as foxhunting surged in popularity, their numbers went into freefall. More radical forms of protection were clearly needed.

By the end of the eighteenth century the problem was only too apparent to the founder of modern foxhunting: in 1793 Meynell took his hounds out of Leicestershire in order to 'enable a stock of old foxes to get up again'.[69] But by this time the sport had many zealous converts, and few shared the old master's foresight or taste for self-denial. Remarkably, the so-called vermin had become a valuable and highly coveted commodity.

Initially masters of hounds experimented with such old tricks as hand-rearing cubs and preventing their hounds from killing caught foxes. In order to encourage the growth of a new population of foxes, landowners either planted artificial coverts of gorse or blackthorn in which the newly introduced foxes could lie, or rented appropriate land from their neighbours.[70] A few of the sporting handbooks contained hints on the hand-rearing of fox cubs, and one enterprising huntsman even visited France in search of huntable foxes to bring back to England.[71] Colonel Joliffe, who had the Merstham Hounds, sent a man across the Channel in search of foxes, though since he returned with no more than six brace, the effort was presumably discontinued.[72] By the early nineteenth century, no pack regularly hunting foxes could continue without devoting considerable attention to the task of rearing a huntable population of foxes: 'fox-hunters and their friends use all possible exertions to protect the breed, and increase the numbers,' observed one commentator.[73] As foxhunting continued to increase in popularity, however, it rapidly became apparent that these local efforts to hand-rear small populations of foxes were inadequate to the task: there were simply too few foxes left to allow the newly fashioned sport of foxhunting to thrive.

Much of the foxhunters' difficulty lay in the fact that foxes were notorious for killing farm animals and, perhaps most seriously of all, for disturbing the game birds so carefully preserved by the shooting fraternity. Their wishes were in stark conflict to those of many of their neighbours, and readers of the *Sporting Magazine* were full of helpful suggestions as to how this uneasy relationship might be managed. One correspondent, writing under the name of 'Brush', pleaded with keen game preservers to catch foxes on their estates with muffled traps and send them to the nearest kennel if it agreed to unbag them far from the preserves.[74] Hunt your country regularly, exhorted another keen foxhunting man, or you will never succeed in encouraging the owners of your coverts to preserve.[75] One correspondent advised foxhunters to remunerate the keepers of coverts more generously, and suggested that if foxhunters were to pay them for each fox found by the pack, rather than for each cub they reared, the keepers of coverts might fulfil their duties more assiduously.[76] Lord Fitzwilliam, for example, paid the owners of coverts in his country between three and five guineas for breeding up foxes, but he also employed his own set of keepers and paid them half a guinea for every fox that was actually found – a system that was effective, but beyond the purse of most hunts.[77] One reader described the case of a large landowner who had instructed his agent to inform those of his tenants who had 'shown a contrary Disposition, by destroying Foxes ... or otherwise interrupting Gentlemen's diversion' that the need to preserve was a pre-condition of the renewal of leases.[78] The problem with this suggestion, however, was that many large landowners were also game preservers, and not even the most optimistic of foxhunters could expect shooting landlords to bully their tenants into preserving foxes. Despite the hopes of some foxhunters that the countryside might be managed in such a way as to increase the number of foxes, there was an unavoidable tension between the foxhunters on the one hand, and farmers and game preservers on the other, and this augured ill for the maintenance of a healthy fox population.

It seemed that the only solution to the curse of blank days was to keep a ready supply of foxes at hand and turn them down in a place where they could be hunted. These captive foxes released in the wild were known as 'bagmen' and their use had become sufficiently established by the 1780s for Beckford to devote a few pages to describing the best way of making sport out of them. Like most huntsmen, Beckford objected to the practice. In his opinion a fox confined in a small place and transported many miles 'must needs stink extravagantly': with a powerful scent, weakened for want of food, and with limbs stiff from confinement, the bag-fox was too easy a prey for the hounds, and most writers shared Beckford's view that hunting a bag-fox was a very second-rate form of sport.[79] As a hunter in Surtees's *Mr Sponge's Sporting Tour* so astutely noted, 'the mere retaking of an animal that one has had in hand before is not calculated to arouse any very pleasurable emotions'.[80] Nonetheless, the practice was widespread in the first half of the nineteenth century and was fundamental in enabling the sport to develop.

The question for most packs, therefore, was where to procure these bagmen. The market took care of this problem. In the early nineteenth century, a commercial trade in continental foxes based at Leadenhall Market emerged and, by mid-century, about a thousand foxes a year were being imported from Holland, Germany, France and Scotland.[81] From the outset, however, foxhunters evinced a clear prejudice against the continental foxes, which they judged inferior to the native English breed, and the market quickly geared up to providing these highly sought after English foxes. It was supplied by gangs of fox-stealers operating in parts of England where foxes were preserved. Early in 1828, the *Sporting Magazine* reported that sixty brace of foxes had been taken from the Quorn and forty brace from the Pytchley by a well-organised gang crossing Leicestershire and Northamptonshire with their traps, nets and wires.[82] A member of the Taporley Hunt claimed that a certain Mr Fletcher of Liverpool had regularly employed men to hunt foxes in the Cheshire countryside paying them at the rate of £2 a fox.[83] But these thefts served only to exacerbate the problem that had given rise to the trade in the first place. In 1826, one foxhunter claimed he could 'never recollect so great a scarcity of foxes [in Oxfordshire] as during the present season ... attributed principally to the enormous extent to which the traffic in foxes is carried on in Oxford'.[84] Essex and Norfolk were also reported to be 'fearfully stripped'.[85] In the 1830s, Surtees expressed his surprise that any foxes remained to be hunted in the countries surrounding London, 'finding, as they do, a ready and safe market'.[86] Trading in indigenous foxes was no more than a short-term solution, doing nothing to increase the number of native foxes and threatening to 'destroy the sport of others and ... shortly put an end to their own'.[87]

With so much effort going into importing foxes and planting coverts, it was not uncommon to prevent the hounds from killing, so that the hunters might return to hunt another day – a feat that was not always so easy to accomplish in practice.[88] At mid-century, Delabere Blaine had stern words for foxhunters who actually killed the foxes they hunted. There were enough fox-killers around, he warned, 'without the aid of hounds', who should be prevented from killing their quarry at all costs: 'murdering foxes is a wanton and useless prodigality', he added.[89] George Templer, hunting in south Devon, kept about twenty bagmen on hand to insure against blank days, and trained his hounds to catch, but not kill, foxes. He claimed that one of his foxes, nicknamed the Bold Dragoon, had been turned down and recovered no fewer than thirty-six times. Reverend John Russell, who regularly hunted with the Templer pack, provided the following account: 'whether he were a wild fox or a bagman, such was the hard riding and such the obedience of the hounds to a rate, that, nine times out of ten, the animal was picked up before them, without a hair of his skin being broken'.[90] England was by now a populous and industrialising country and hunting could only thrive in conditions that were wholly artificial.

As foxhunters took to breeding foxes, a clear contradiction in the rationale of the sport emerged. The hunt was ostensibly there to serve the needs of the farmers: it existed to kill the vermin that plagued their farms. But the foxhunters also insisted that they alone were entitled to kill foxes and woe betide any farmer who dared to take the destruction of foxes into his own hands. In the 1820s, a new word entered the English language. In that decade, the *Sporting Magazine* began referring to 'vulpicides' – by which it meant people who killed foxes with utilitarian, rather than sporting, intentions.[91] In the absence of any legal sanction prohibiting the killing of foxes, a social convention emerged, and as the foxhunters assiduously imported, bred and reared a new population of foxes, so did they successfully implant the notion that vulpicide was a despicable act. The American novelist Harriet Beecher Stowe, visiting England in the 1850s, observed, 'It seems that killing a fox except in the way of hunting is deemed among hunters an unpardonable offence.'[92] Her observation was entirely correct.

Francis Grose, the English antiquary and humorist, provided a typically light-hearted account of the social pressures that the foxhunting fraternity placed on would-be vulpicides:

In a visit to a friend, at a great town in the North, I accompanied him to the public bowling-green, where I saw a very genteel looking man, who seemed to be shunned by every body. By accident, entering into conversation with him, I found him a very well-informed, polite, and agreeable gentleman. On my way home, I could not help taking notice of what I had observed; and enquired of my friend the cause of this

gentleman being thus evidently disregarded. 'Cause enough,' answered
he; 'that fellow is the greatest scoundrel upon earth.' – 'What has he
done?' said I – 'Has he any unnatural vices? Has he debauched the wife
or daughter of his friend? Or is he a bad husband or father?' – 'We don't
trouble ourselves about his amours or connections,' peevishly answered
my friend; 'but to do the fellow justice there is nothing of that – he is
besides both a good husband and father.' 'What then, has he committed
a murder, or been guilty of treason?' 'No,' added my friend – 'besides,
we have nothing to do with his quarrels, and don't trouble our heads
with his party; we have nothing to say against him on those subjects.'
'What then, in the name of Fortune, can it be! Is he a cheat, a black-
legs, or an usurer?' 'No, no!' replied my friend, 'no such thing; but if
you will have it, know then, that good-looking plausible villain, in his
own farm-yard, shot a bitch-fox, big with young.' – Recollecting that
my friend, and most of the gentlemen on the green, were staunch foxhunters, my wonder ceased.[93]

With so much effort going into the creation of a huntable population of foxes,
the 'subtle, pilf'ring foe' had been transformed into a precious commodity.[94]
And as with all the animals that men have particularly liked to hunt, the
humble fox had been transformed into a source of bitter conflict.

Through the trade in fox cubs, a steady breeding programme and hunting
practices that did not involve killing, the foxhunters managed to maintain a
huntable population of foxes, but the question of land was a different matter.
As well as a reliable flow of foxes, foxhunters needed access to large expanses
of land on which to hunt them, and with the British population more than
doubling in the first half of the nineteenth century, the pressure on land
was increasing as never before. Fields of several hundred horseback riders
were capable of inflicting serious damage to fields, fences and crops, and the
attitude of many foxhunters did little to alleviate the tension.

As foxes were vermin, foxhunters had always believed they had a right to
enter anyone's land in pursuit of their quarry and, in a ruling of 1788, that
right had been confirmed. Mr Justice Buller declared that a hunter might
pursue a fox across another man's land, though added he must not cause
damage to fences or fields 'more than is absolutely necessary'.[95] The ruling
was used by the foxhunters to enter other people's land as they pleased, and
frequently with too little regard for the destruction they caused. Depressed
agricultural prices in the early nineteenth century, along with the bad
behaviour of many hard-riding foxhunters, shook the tolerance of the rural
community, whilst the importation of foxes undermined the principle upon
which the sport was based.

The simmering tensions that the modern form of foxhunting caused were brought to a head in the case of Essex and Capel. The Hon. and Revd William Capel was Master of the Old Berkeley, a pack hunting in Buckinghamshire and Hertfordshire; and the Earl of Essex, a large landowner in the Berkeley's territory, was the Hon. Capel's half-brother. The two men hated each other with the kind of visceral loathing of which siblings are truly capable. In 1808, as the half-brothers' personal feuding escalated, the Earl of Essex made a formal complaint about the damage done by the Old Berkeley Hunt on his land, but his warning shots went unheeded. A few months later, when a gate had been closed to the hunt by Lord Essex's keepers, dozens of riders deliberately broke through fences and entered the earl's land in pursuit. Lord Essex brought an action for trespass and won his case. He was awarded a mere shilling for damages, but was nonetheless highly satisfied with the outcome. The Buller ruling of 1788 was overturned. The Chief Justice had dismissed the defendant's plea that the Old Berkeley hunted in order to kill vermin, and established the principle that foxhunters could be sued for trespass by any farmer who objected to their activities.[96]

But this ruling did nothing to hinder the growth of the sport. Unable to shelter behind the law, the foxhunters realised they needed the goodwill of the farmers over whose land they wanted to ride. The arrogance of many of the early hard riders gave way to a more conciliatory approach; masters of the hunt began seeking prior permission to hunt over land, and compensating farmers for any damage caused. Farmers were in any case usually well disposed to foxhunting in principle. Whilst many remained unqualified to shoot pheasants and partridges, most could nevertheless hunt, and their generally conservative leanings predisposed them towards the local hunt and all it stood for.

In the century following 1750, the obstacles to the enjoyment of hunting were arguably greater than at any earlier time. Population doubled between 1800 and 1850, and industrial cities experienced mushroom growth, along with all the social problems attendant upon this. It was the period of the industrial revolution and not a time favourable to the emergence of a new form of hunting. Yet by the middle of the nineteenth century, the ancient tradition of hunting with hounds had found a new place in this modernising world. By importing and breeding foxes and through negotiation with landowners, foxhunting had successfully adapted to the demands of nineteenth-century society. From informal, local beginnings, an organised and sustainable field sport with national appeal had been created, and foxhunting's position as 'the only chace in England worthy of the taste or attention of a high bred sportsman' was undeniable.[97]

CHAPTER ELEVEN

'A busy and anxious
disposition to legislate'

Sir Matthew White Ridley considered ... that the Bill, while it left coursing, shooting, fishing &c., the amusements of the higher classes, untouched, infringed too much upon those of the humbler classes ...

Mr Brotherton hailed the measure as a further step in civilisation ...[1]

The decline of the native deer population had a number of consequences, but the demise of hunting was not one of them. In place of the deer hunt that had fascinated huntsmen down the centuries, new activities better fitted to the changing environment had emerged. But as shooters carefully reared their quarry and foxhunters devoted their energies to breeding new packs of foxhounds, novel pressures were starting to gather around hunting. The moral objections that had been quieted with the demise of the Puritans in the middle of the seventeenth century were resurfacing once again. Throughout the eighteenth century, and particularly after 1750, an increasing number of writers and thinkers turned their attention towards humanity's proper relation with the animal world. In philosophy, in poetry and the arts, and in religious thought, writers began to express concern about cruelty to animals. And although the hunting community initially escaped any criticism for their activities, it was simply a question of time before such thinking was turned against this ancient pastime as well.

In some respects, eighteenth-century concern about cruelty to animals was a descendant of the opposition to animal sports that the Puritans had mounted. As the eighteenth century drew to a close, a growing number of clergymen reiterated the Puritans' claim that God's will was the comfort and happiness of *all* his creatures. Like their forebears, they maintained that though this did not deprive man of the right to kill animals for sustenance, it did mean he had no right to torment or harm any beast. They urged that animals had been 'sent for our use, but not for our abuse'.[2] Any mistreatment of animals was a 'betrayal of the confidence that God had reposed in man';[3] it was 'sinful and adverse to the divine law';[4] 'an act of impiety, or a trans- gression against the plainest principle of religion'.[5] And simple though this injunction to avoid mistreating God's creation might be, it had a very wide sphere of influence, for the range of activities that these clergymen regarded as abusive was large indeed.

In contrast to previous centuries, however, when the only significant objec- tions to animal cruelty had hailed from religious belief, the eighteenth century also witnessed the emergence of secular arguments in favour of compassion for animals. One early and significant proponent of this view was the political philosopher Jeremy Bentham, who not only argued for the greatest happiness of the greatest number, but also maintained that that number included the animal creation. 'The question is not,' he famously wrote, 'Can they reason? nor, Can they talk? but, Can they Suffer? Why should the law refuse its protection to any sensitive being?'[6] Others appealed to the secular argument of Michel de Montaigne, originally advanced to rather little effect in sixteenth-century France, that animals had a certain claim not to be tormented by humans.[7] As one writer put it: 'we ought, therefore, upon principles not only of speculative philosophy, but of common humanity, to avoid the infliction of every unnecessary disaster [upon animals]'.[8]

These arguments, both religious and secular, had significant ramifications for every aspect of man's treatment of animals. Every sport involving animals – racing, hunting, coursing, cockfighting – was denounced; the overwork of horses was censured; and the cruel rearing and slaughter of animals destined for the table, combining cruelty with greed and vanity, were also uniformly condemned. These writers picked over such varied problems as riding post-chaise, the docking of dogs' and horses' tails, swallow-shooting, and the dissection of live animals in universities. No aspect of man's treatment of animals was beyond analysis and criticism in this burgeoning literature advocating the more humane treatment of animals.

But although a new generation of reformers and humanitarians was starting to ask weighty questions about humanity's proper relation with the animal world, there is scant evidence that their philosophical and theological reflections penetrated deep into English society. Interest in animal cruelty was certainly increasing, but no more than one or two books were printed each decade, which suggests that animal cruelty cannot be ranked amongst the burning concerns of the day.[9] Furthermore, although ever more books and tracts were being printed, this does not in itself prove that the material was widely read and digested. Sermons and tracts did not circulate in large numbers, and their popularity (or lack of it) with the reading public is surely indicated by the fact that few were ever reprinted. What the reading public made of these earnest arguments is difficult to say, though it is not impossible that they fell upon deaf ears. I found some evidence of this when I started researching this topic a decade ago, and discovered that a book published mid-century, James Macauley's *Essay on Cruelty to Animals*, was held at the Cambridge University Library. To my surprise, the pages had not even been cut – the book had survived a hundred and fifty years, but had never been read. There certainly was a committed minority of poets, writers, philosophers and humanitarian reformers opposed to mistreating animals in any form, but how well do poets and philosophers ever reflect the views of most of us? The printing and sale of a book is no indication that its content was even read, still less that it reflects the beliefs of the society that produced it.

It is arguably the newspapers, both national and local, that provide a more accurate barometer of public opinion, and there is little in these publications to suggest that the public was interested in the animal protectionists' message. Animals were frequently discussed in the columns of the newspapers, but they were not romanticised as suffering creatures to be pitied and protected, and one is left questioning how deeply the animal protection message penetrated provincial England before the nineteenth century.[10]

But the public's indifference to animal protection, though great, was not quite total, for there was one strand of the protectionists' case that fell upon more receptive ground. Most of the philosophers' and clerics' pontificating was routinely ignored, but their criticism of popular blood sports such as cockfighting and bull-baiting was much more warmly received. The newspapers paid far greater attention to a small number of popular blood sports than to any of the other issues associated with the animal protection debate. Within a matter of decades, sports which had been enjoyed in some form since the Middle Ages were being roundly condemned as barbarous, uncivilised, unenlightened and cruel. Newspapers printed sensationalist stories of instances of working-class bloodlust and cruelty at such events, and unanimously declared bull-baiting an 'inhuman and barbarous practice', a 'scandal to humanity'.[11] Those who took part were 'Christian Savages, who delight in inflicting torture';[12] the ancient pastime was now considered 'Unchristian and barbarous'.[13]

It is not, therefore, that the press entirely ignored the animal protection debate. Rather, it simplified it, reducing the complex web of complaints and concerns expressed by philosophers and clerics to just one simple point. In the process, criticisms of hunting were entirely filtered out, and working-class blood sports such as cockfighting and bull-baiting stood alone as the only form of cruelty about which the respectable citizen needed to be concerned. But though this distinction held fast in the early nineteenth century, events were to prove that the reformers had unwittingly unleashed a powerful set of arguments about the use of animals for recreation that later generations would effortlessly extend to hunting.

Much of the horrified outrage that poured from the newspapers was grounded in the claim that the contest between the bull and its attackers was hopelessly uneven, that there was something intrinsically unfair and unsporting about the whole affair. In Lincoln, for example, the animal baited was just 'a small bull about two years old';[14] and in Bury St Edmunds, a 'persecuted creature' and 'poor beast' were baited.[15] Capel Lofft, a barrister, writer and ardent opponent of bull-baiting, wrote: 'I hear that this noble but wretched animal was perfectly gentle and inoffensive when turned out.'[16] Another journalist complained that 'so broken was [the bull's] spirit, or so inoffensive was it in its nature ... that it was led along without any resistance, like a lamb'.[17] But a bull is a large and powerful animal, and if it is a question of the relative size of dogs and victim that constitutes cruelty, it might reasonably be expected that the concerned animal lover should be far more worried about foxes than bulls. Yet one searches the newspapers for concerns about cruelty to foxes in vain. All that is to be found is a grim procession of normally sweet-tempered bulls, mangled, bloody, and torn beyond recognition.

Perhaps the most puzzling aspect of this account of bull-baiting, however, is that it flatly contradicts earlier descriptions of the ancient custom. Eyewitness accounts of bull-baiting throughout the centuries provide scant evidence for the gentle and harmless bulls of the Victorian imagination. In the sixteenth and seventeenth centuries, foreign visitors and English diarists had occasionally recorded their own experiences of bull- and bear-baiting, but they never encountered passive and docile bulls. Instead, they watched powerful bulls which, though tethered, usually made a very good show of attacking their assailants.

Over and over again, these sources describe a sport in which the bull (or occasionally the bear) made short work of his canine assailants. This, for instance, is what Thomas Platter saw in 1599:

> a large white powerful bull was brought in, and likewise bound in the centre of the theatre, and one dog only was set on him at a time, which he speared in such a masterly fashion, that they could not get the better of him, and as the dogs fell to the floor again, several men held the sticks under them to break their fall, so that they would not be killed. Afterwards more dogs were set on him, but they could not down him.[18]

Many other witnesses provided similar accounts. In 1710, according to Von Uffenbach: 'about thirty dogs, two or three at a time, were let loose on [the bull], but he made short work of them, goring them and tossing them high in the air above the height of the first storey'.[19] The Duke of Wisterberg noted that 'four dogs at once were set on the bull; they, however, could not gain any advantage over him, for he so artfully contrived to ward off their attacks that they could not well get at him; on the contrary, the bull served them very scurvily by striking and butting at them'.[20] Finally the agriculturalist John Houghton wrote: 'I believe I have seen a dog tossed by a bull thirty, if not forty foot high; and when they are tossed either higher or lower, the men about strive to catch them ... Notwithstanding this care, a great many dogs are killed, more have their limbs broke ...'[21]

The eyewitness accounts of bull-baiting found in travel journals and diaries form a sharp contrast to the endless stream of poor, innocent, inoffensive bulls that offended Victorian opponents to the sport. This observation is not intended to vindicate bull-baiting from the charge of cruelty; well-trained dogs could seriously injure the bull, and sensational reports about cruel acts committed by the human spectators probably had some basis in fact.[22] Furthermore, a case could certainly be made for cruelty to dogs. Given that a dog would attack whatever its owner told it to, setting it on an animal twenty times its size might well be construed as cruel. But if bull-baiting was cruel, it was not cruel in quite the way that the sport's opponents claimed. A bull-bait was a fair contest between reasonably matched animals, and in this it differed remarkably little from the wholly uncontroversial pastime of hunting. Needless to say, however, most critics of blood sports went to very great pains to reassure their readers that no hostility to hunting should be detected in their criticisms of bull-baiting.

Consider, for example, the work of John Lawrence. Lawrence was a vet who wrote extensively about sports; he reviled bull-baiting, which involved finding pleasure in 'witnessing the lingering tortures and excruciated sensibility' of an animal.[23] Foxhunting was quite different: 'no true and lawful, that is to say, rational, useful, and delightful sports, would be interrupted by this regulation ... I shall be found ... a willing, although perhaps a weak advocate, for all those sports, which inspire mirth and hilarity, and promote health.'[24] So baiting an animal involves 'lingering torture', whilst hunting it is 'rational, useful, and delightful'. Yet one is still left wondering, what exactly are the grounds for distinguishing between the two ancient pastimes in this way?

There are in fact three different types of blood sports with which we are dealing. In animal fights, two animals of equal strength and size are put into the ring and left to fight, usually to the death. Animal-baiting consists in tethering one large or particularly ferocious animal, such as a bear or bull, to the ground, and setting dogs loose, usually one at a time, in order to attack it. The baited animal has no chance of escape, in fact it does not generally seek to escape; the baited animal is powerful and uses its strength in its defence. *Par force* hunting also involves using dogs to attack another animal; this time, several dogs are set loose to attack and kill a solitary animal. This animal is not tethered but not necessarily wild; it uses its speed, or 'cunning', rather than strength to elude capture and thereby defend itself. All three sports have many differences, but the similarities are no less striking. In their essence, they are contests, between animals, but orchestrated by men. The strongest grounds for distinguishing between hunting animals on the one hand, and fighting and baiting them on the other, is to suggest that the former is conducted through need, whilst the latter are pursued purely for entertainment. Yet, as we have seen, the large-scale importation of foxes and use of bagmen in the nineteenth century give the lie to the argument that foxhunters were motivated by anything other than the pure thrill of the chase. One is forced to contemplate the possibility that the differences between hunting and baiting were very much less clear cut than the simple arguments of the humanitarian reformers implied.

Despite the questionable foundations of the reformers' case against bull-baiting, public outrage over the persistence of the sport continued to mount, and as it did so, politicians soon turned their attention to bull-baiting and cockfighting as well. Criticism that had originated in newspapers and drawing rooms rapidly transmuted into a divisive political and class wrangle that was to last nearly forty years.

The first bill to attack blood sports was Sir William Pulteney's Bill for Preventing the Practice of Bull-baiting, introduced in 1800.[25] It had the narrow goal of outlawing (in Pulteney's words) 'the savage custom of bull-baiting', but despite gathering considerable support in the House, it faced eloquent and lengthy opposition from Sir William Windham, the Tory MP for Norwich.[26] Windham derided the bill as evidence of 'a busy and anxious disposition to legislate on matters in which the laws are already sufficient', and owing in no small part to his impassioned defence, the bill was lost by just two votes.[27] Windham had successfully tapped into a widely held concern that by interfering in men's private pleasures, Parliament was stepping into new and dangerous waters. 'It should be written in letters of gold,' declared *The Times*, 'that a Government cannot interfere too little with the people; ... whatever meddles with the private personal disposition of a man's time or property is tyranny direct.'[28] It was a powerful critique, and one that protected working-class blood sports for a number of years.

Two years later, undeterred by Pulteney's defeat, John Dent introduced a similar measure to Parliament. His bill gained strong support in the Lower

House, and two pamphlets in its favour were promptly published.[29] Once again, however, Windham spoke at length against the bill; and once more the bill went down to defeat.[30] In 1809, Lord Erskine, an eccentric animal lover and the former Lord Chancellor, introduced a third bill, this time a broader measure to protect domestic animals.[31] Despite Lord Erskine's efforts to distance himself from the earlier, narrow attempts to prohibit bull-baiting, the measure was ridiculed by Windham as 'A Bill for harassing and oppressing certain classes amongst the lower orders of the people'.[32] Though the bill was initially sent to committee by forty votes to twenty-seven, a few days later the House reversed its decision, and the bill was withdrawn. Erskine made a second attempt to introduce animal protection legislation in the following year, but once again his bill was lost. With that, the matter languished in Parliament for a number of years.[33]

Finally, a new champion of animal rights emerged in the person of Richard Martin – dubbed by his friends 'Humanity Dick' – the owner of very large Irish estates and keen practitioner of all field sports.[34] In 1822, Martin introduced a bill to prevent cruelty to cattle and horses, which later that year received royal assent.[35] This 1822 act outlawed acts of cruelty to farm and draft animals, but did not in fact outlaw bull-baiting in the way Martin and his supporters had hoped: bulls had been expressly omitted from the final act by a government sensitive to the criticism that it was meddling in spheres it had no right to touch.[36]

This omission kept the reformers busy for the next decade, but the precedent set by the landmark 1822 act made their task rather easier. In 1835 they secured the passage of the Protection of Animals Act, which extended protection from livestock to domestic animals and made it illegal to keep any place for the fighting or baiting of any animal, wild or domestic.[37] Overnight, enjoying a bull-bait, bear-bait or dogfight became a criminal offence, and fines and prison sentences served to convince anyone who might think otherwise. This act, consolidated and extended to include cockfighting in 1849, was the first major piece of legislation passed to prohibit blood sports; and (to the chagrin of nineteenth-century reformers), it also proved to be the last.[38]

The outcome of these new laws was initially mixed. Bull-baiting, being near impossible to hide, was most easily suppressed and local authorities speedily and effectively used their new powers to round up those involved and consign the sport to history.[39] The latest evidence of bull-baiting in England comes from the Suffolk village of Lavenham. It had long been the custom here to celebrate Guy Fawkes Night with a bull-baiting, and Lavenham's remote location perhaps shielded it from the prying eyes of reformers and constables for a little longer than might otherwise have been the case.[40] At any rate, bull-baiting was successfully suppressed in Lavenham in 1842. Less than a decade after the Protection of Animals Act, the ancient sport had been entirely eradicated.

A cockfight or badger-bait, however, was much more easily shielded from prying eyes, and so its disappearance was far more protracted. The greatest problem the reformers faced was that the legislation provided no means of enforcement; the apprehension and prosecution of wrongdoers were haphazardly left in the hands of ordinary citizens and without proper mechanisms in place the trial and punishment of offenders were patchy. In an attempt to enforce the law more rigorously, a self-proclaimed body of 'divers benevolent persons' formed itself into the Society for the Prevention of Cruelty to Animals (SPCA) in 1824, and started collecting funds to assist individuals in prosecutions. In 1835, the society received the first of many royal patrons (the Duchess of Kent) and in 1840 Queen Victoria, a patron since 1835, granted it permission to prefix 'Royal' to its name.[41] As the new society grew in size and importance it took to hiring constables to walk the streets and apprehend offenders. Though not without danger – one of their men, a certain James Piper, died after a fracas with cockfighters at Hanworth, Middlesex in 1839 – its officer corps grew steadily, totalling 120 by the end of the century.[42]

The elimination of working-class blood sports took some time, but the general trend was clear: by the end of the nineteenth century, bull-baiting had disappeared, and cockfighting and dog-fighting had been firmly pushed underground. Sports that people of all social ranks had enjoyed for hundreds of years had been cast out of the realm owing to the changing values of a small, but powerful, minority who no longer took part. Though not the earliest attempt to outlaw popular recreations, the 1822 act was certainly the most remarkable – until, at least, the Hunting with Dogs Act of 2004. As such, it marks a turning point in the history of blood sports, and one is inevitably led to ask: why did the Victorians impose such an intrusive piece of legislation? It is a question not only of intrinsic historical interest, but also of practical moment, not least because the Victorians' campaign to suppress bull-baiting so strongly prefigures the anti-foxhunting campaign of our own times. Why do societies periodically appeal to notions of humanity in order to stamp out the recreations that other people enjoy?

One argument that we have to reject is that this was the spontaneous flowering of a new compassion for animals. As we have seen, such sensitivity can certainly be found in poetry, literature and art, but it is much less evident among the rest of society. Throughout this period, cruelty to animals was ubiquitous. Animals were used in every aspect of life, and were inevitably much abused in the process. For most people, animals were there to fill stomachs, work machinery and move things about: the concept of the pet, an animal simply to be loved and enjoyed, was a luxury that the majority could not afford. Animals could be seen everywhere: horses, donkeys, dogs, cats, cattle, sheep and poultry filled streets, markets, gardens and fields. The sight, sound and smell of animals were an inescapable part of everyday life. People's lives and homes were shared with animals, and there was little room for sensitivity and compassion in this world, and ample scope for cruelty and ill use.

Even if we were to grant that the reformers were genuinely concerned about animal cruelty, there is something suspicious in the targeting of blood sports. Of all the forms of cruelty that animals might face, cockfighting and bull-baiting were surely the least of their worries. A cockfight was a combat between two evenly matched animals fighting freely. The concept of a fair fight was also intrinsic to the sport of bull-baiting, and by the late eighteenth century, the sport was in any case already very much on the decline. Cockfighting and bull-baiting both bore more than a passing resemblance to all forms of hunting and coursing, but neither of these sports attracted criticism of any real note. Furthermore, the systematic abuse and overwork of the millions of horses that powered the English economy was surely a greater evil than any of the uses to which animals were put in the name of sport. Blood sports were marginal forms of cruelty in a society in which the use and abuse of animals were extremely widespread. If the Victorians *really* cared so much about animals, why did they not focus on more pressing cases of cruelty?

The answer may be found by switching our gaze away from the animals and back to ourselves. All this fuss was not really about the animals, but about us. The newspapers cared not about the piteous cock or poor mangled bull, but about the human spectators who watched their struggles and laughed. Animals naturally fight, but these are fights orchestrated by humans for their own pleasure, excitement and financial gain. In arguing that bull-baiting and cockfighting should no longer be tolerated, the literate classes were promoting their own vision of a progressive and compassionate society.

Inevitably, it was the poor that needed to be saved, and the oft-used accusation of class bias is not too far from the mark. With the exception of a small but dedicated core of wealthy gentlemen who continued to support cockfighting, the poor were the primary supporters of most forms of animal fighting and baiting by the early nineteenth century. According to one writer, bull-baiting was popular with 'the most unfeeling, and least humane, part of the very lowest, and most abandoned orders of the people ... *brutes*; the very scum and refuse of society'.[43] It was hardly an accurate description of working-class bull-baiters, but it was certainly what many of the educated classes liked to hear. Animal cruelty, it made plain, was something perpetrated by other people.[44]

By casting the perpetrators of cruelty as ignorant and unenlightened, Victorian reformers inevitably defined themselves as in the vanguard of progress and civilisation; this was a way for the middle classes to reaffirm their status as humane and enlightened individuals. The ignorant masses needed to be saved from their wickedness, but fortunately there was a well-meaning middle class, willing and able to do the saving. One politician declared his support for John Dent's 1802 bill by arguing that 'he who had a just notion of [the people's] dignity, and wished to raise them in the scale of being, would try to cultivate their minds, to polish their manners, and to instruct them in the principles of morality and religion'.[45] Preventing 'the people' from participating in bull-baiting was of course an integral part of this process of raising the poor from their degradation. And it is surely no accident that the campaign addressed a very marginal form of cruelty. In contrast to legislation governing the use of dogs and horses, which would have been certain to have significant economic ramifications for the large number of individuals who exploited animals in order to earn a living, the suppression of bull-baiting concerned very few people, and it was easy to support the cause at no personal cost. It all served to make the anti-bull-baiting message both powerful and appealing, and it is not hard to understand why the Victorian middle classes rallied to the cause so enthusiastically.

The social bias of reformers did not go entirely unnoticed, indeed such accusations have haunted the RSPCA since its inception. Though it quickly emerged as the leading body concerned with animal cruelty, busily harassing working-class coach drivers and taking petty cockfighters to court, the charity was supported by funds generously donated by many a sporting gent. Some of the society's most distinguished members were foxhunters and shooters; none saw a conflict in their allegiance to the two causes. Richard Martin, a keen hunter and sponsor of the 1822 act, dismissed charges of hypocrisy by arguing that hunting and shooting were 'amusements of a totally different character', and the society's inaugural meeting was chaired by Fowell Buxton, a keen shooter who once killed 500 birds in a week as a bet.[46] The chair of the society's 1839 general meeting, Viscount Mahon, sought to reassure his listeners that he did not think that 'innocent amusements, such as fishing and shooting, come within the objects of the Society', but supporters of the RSPCA continued to challenge their leaders' allegiance to field hunting and shooting. At the next year's general meeting, a hostile question from the floor about the cruelty of hunting elicited the following response from Lord Dudley Stuart:

No doubt the stern advocate for humanity may object both to hunting and steeple-chasing as unnecessary, and shooting and fishing would of course come within the same rule; but I think these objections to our national sports may be carried too far, and, so long as unnecessary cruelty is avoided, I see no reason to cry them down on the score of inhumanity; and I believe it is generally admitted, that the sports of the field, if unavoidably attended with a certain degree of suffering on the one hand, produce, on the other hand, many advantages which might fairly be brought forward as a set-off against the alleged cruelty of such practices. (Hear, hear.)[47]

No wonder that the RSPCA was periodically castigated as a tool of class oppression.[48]

Occasionally the press spoke in defence of working people's traditional recreations. Sydney Smith, writing in the *Edinburgh Review*, for example, objected that 'A man of ten thousand a year may worry a fox as much as he pleases ... ; and a poor labourer is carried to a magistrate for paying sixpence to see an exhibition of courage between a dog and a bear!'[49] But it was the men of ten thousand a year, not the poor labourers, who wrote the laws, and very few public commentators were troubled by this inequality.

Yet although the great and the good of Victorian society were almost universally supportive of their new laws to protect animals from cruelty, they had unwittingly set in train a reform movement that in time would prove to have a momentum of its own. As *The Times* had warned when Parliament made its first attempts to suppress bull-baiting: 'whatever meddles with the private personal disposition of a man's time or property is tyranny direct'. Like so many, it had soon come round to the idea that this small intervention might not be such a bad thing – it concerned only the 'dispositions' of the poor, after all. The problem was that each incursion into working-class blood sports helped to establish a little more firmly the principle that Parliament might indeed, quite legitimately, meddle with 'the private, personal disposition of a man's time'.

It was simply a question of time until such rhetoric would be used against its creators.

CHAPTER TWELVE

Game Laws in the Nineteenth Century

Oh! if only pheasants had but understanding, how they would split their sides with chuckling and crowing at the follies which civilised Christian men perpetrate for their precious sake. (Charles Kingsley)[1]

A pheasant is more of a pampered creature than a peasant ... Game, game! We have heard too much about it, and had too little of it. (Joseph Arch)[2]

The abolition of bull-baiting and cockfighting had no immediate consequences for the hunting and shooting enjoyed by the social elite. The occasional opponent of the new legislation warned darkly that meddling in the pastimes of the poor set a dangerous precedent, but their mutterings fell upon deaf ears, and the next few decades failed to see their dire warnings fulfilled. It looked as though the practitioners of field sports had nothing to fear from the moralising of humanitarian reformers. Instead, their concerns were of a much more familiar nature: the perennial struggle to preserve a huntable population of game in the face of unrelenting pressure on natural resources.

Nowhere were these struggles more acute than in the rapidly changing sport of shooting. With no legal market for game but a consistently high level of demand from the urban middle classes, a black market inevitably emerged, and professional poachers quickly appeared to supply the demand. Many were small-time operators working individually and opportunistically, but many worked together in professional and highly organised gangs of a dozen or more armed men. Deadly night-time conflicts between armed poachers and the large estates' gamekeepers were only too common.[3] With the looming presence of armed gangs of poachers, landowners and preservers employed large numbers of gamekeepers to watch over their precious game. Keen preservers might employ over a dozen men in this capacity, and in heavily preserved counties, the number of private gamekeepers easily outstripped the police.[4] The switch to small game after the Civil Wars seemed to have created a cycle of violence and repression that could not be broken, and these conflicts over the rightful possession of small game posed a problem far greater than humanitarian reformers.

As successive parliaments added to the principal Game Act passed in 1671, the discord surrounding the hunting of small game only increased, and in the following century the game laws' opponents became both more discontented and more resourceful. Farmers destroyed the eggs of pheasants and partridges, poached discreetly, and turned a blind eye to suspicious figures prowling at night; villagers used force, cunning and deception to trap and snare the small animals they had enjoyed of old. Nor could these be called trivial matters. Joseph Arch, an agricultural labourer and the first president of the Farm Workers' Union, looking back to his childhood in the 1820s and 1830s recalled, 'it was hardly an exaggeration to say that every other man you met was a poacher'.[5] Small game had taken the place that deer had once occupied: a precious, protected species that none but the privileged few could legally hunt, and the source of an unending social conflict.

By the early nineteenth century, few could deny that repressive legislation provided a poor defence for game while providing a prime target for popular discontent, and the pressure for reform was mounting. In 1827, some of the gentry's more aggressive forms of game protection, such as mantraps and spring guns, were made illegal, and in 1831 a new Game Act was passed.[6] The 1831 act removed the archaic property qualification and replaced it with a system of certification – anyone with the means, regardless of rank, could now purchase a certificate which permitted them to kill game. In effect, it restored the common law principle that the right to kill game rested with the occupier of the land on which it was found. The harsher punishments were abolished, and the market in game was legalised: all those with a game certificate were henceforth entitled to sell game. It was long overdue: the new law made a clean sweep of most of the old game laws, introducing the reforms which critics had been calling for for nearly half a century. The ancient hunting privilege, it appeared, had been abolished.

The appearance of reform, however, was more than a little deceptive. The 1831 act removed social privilege from the letter of the game system, but a Parliament overwhelmingly packed with qualified gentlemen had no intention of relinquishing its precious hunting rights so easily. Inserted in the act was a small protective clause authorising any landowner to keep game rights in any of the land he possessed, regardless of how it was currently used. In other words, the landowner was entitled to retain exclusive game rights on the land that he leased to tenants, as well as to enter that land in pursuit of game at will. It was a clause that many a landowner had every intention of exploiting.

For many tenant farmers, very little changed after the 1831 act. Just as before, they found themselves excluded from the sport, but not protected from the damage done by the shooters and by the game itself. The real beneficiaries of the Game Act were the urban middle classes, and the dealers who supplied them with the game they so coveted. By satisfying this powerful and vocal group, the 1831 act helped to mute the discontent that had made the game laws so controversial and socially divisive in the eighteenth century, but it did little to relieve the grievances of many a tenant farmer.

For the rural poor, from whose ranks the majority of the country's poachers was drawn, it did nothing at all. Their ideas about ownership of wild animals remained fundamentally at odds with those embodied in the game laws. Consider, for example, William Garman, a Norfolk labourer who found himself in court for snaring a hare: 'he saw it as he passed,' he told his accusers, 'he thought he might as well have it as anyone else.'[7] The rural poor persisted in their belief that wild animals were the property of whoever had the wit and skill to catch them. Later in the century, Joseph Arch repeated the centuries-old justification that the poor had given for the poaching: 'The plain truth is, we labourers do not believe hares and rabbits belong to any individual, not any more than thrushes and blackbirds do.' A labourer with a family to feed, he continued, did not believe that hares 'have been created exclusively for one class of the community'.[8] The new system of certification, priced far beyond the means of even the most affluent labourer, was wholly removed from their belief that game was the rightful prey of whoever found it, and it was not by such means that the village poacher would be lured away from his illicit activities.

The failure of effective reform in 1831 can be attributed in part to internal developments in the sport of shooting in the first half of the nineteenth century. Guns were continuing to evolve and, as they did so, the shooter's capacity to kill increased exponentially. In 1807 the detonating lock was patented, and in the following decade it was sufficiently improved to start replacing the flintlock.[9] The detonator sharply increased the speed of loading, cutting it in some estimates to a quarter, and inevitably also increasing the rate at which birds could be killed. In the 1850s, the breech-loading shotgun was becoming popular, which enabled the shooter to change charge and shot quickly and easily for different animals, and this too increased the rate at which the marksman could fire.[10]

As the shooter's capacity to kill increased, it once again became necessary to devise new ways of structuring the shoot so that this capacity was exploited

A GOOD DAY'S WORK IN THE COVERS—COUNTING THE BAG

12. This engraving – 'A good day's work in the covers' – by an unnamed author appeared in the *Graphic* in 1882. Slaughter on this scale vastly outstripped what nature could supply and could only be sustained by the extensive rearing of game birds.

to the full. The outcome was the 'drive' – a close relation to the battue, imported from the Continent some fifty years earlier. In early forms of battue hunting, the shooters moved forward in a line through the covert. The birds were shot low and flying away – both factors making the shooting relatively easy. In the drive, the shooters remain stationary and the birds are driven out of their coverts towards them by beaters. The goal is to get the birds flying forwards high and fast, increasing the difficulty of bringing them down considerably. Although most modern writers prefer to distinguish between these two forms of hunting, nineteenth-century writers, somewhat confusingly, tended to refer to both as the 'battue'.[11] A contemporary description of the drive hunt is contained in Louise Cresswell's *Eighteen Years on Sandringham Estate*, published in 1887. Cresswell was a tenant farmer at Sandringham, embroiled for the best part of two decades in an acrimonious conflict with her royal landlord over the damage his preservation did to her crops. Nonetheless, her account of the royal hunting party contains more than a little touch of admiration:

> The boys and beaters are stationed in a semi-circle some distance off, and it is their place to beat up the birds and drive them to the fences,

the waving flags frightening them from flying back. On they come in ever increasing numbers, until they burst in a cloud over the fence where the guns are concealed. This is the exciting moment, a terrific fusillade ensues, birds dropping down in all directions, wheeling about in confusion between the flags and the guns, the survivors gathering themselves together and escaping into the fields beyond. The shooters then retire to another line of fencing, making themselves comfortable with campstools and cigars until the birds are driven up as before, and so on through the day ...[12]

With better guns and a well-organised drive hunt, game bags inevitably continued to increase in size. This can be illustrated by comparing the average head of game shot by Lord Malmesbury at Heron Court in Hampshire in the period up to 1840 with averages recorded elsewhere after this date. On laying down his gun in 1840, Lord Malmesbury carefully counted up the shots recorded in his game books during the previous thirty-nine years, noting that he had killed 54,802 head. This averaged almost 1,500 head of game each year.[13] In subsequent decades, the annual heads of game on similar-sized estates rose ever upwards. In 1836, The Times reported a grand battue on the preserves of Lord Mostyn, at Pengwern, Flintshire, during which nearly 500 head of game were killed.[14] Three battues in the neighbourhood of Salisbury in 1845 had killed over 1,100 head of game.[15] By the late 1850s, the great shooting estate of Elveden in Norfolk was recording seasons in which totals of 5,000 head a year were not unusual.[16] Reflecting upon this change, The Times opined that

> Formerly gentlemen considered shooting a pursuit which united exercise and sport; they would go out with their dogs, and if they killed two or three head of game, they were satisfied. Latterly noblemen and lords of manors had got into the practice of preserving game to the amount of thousands upon thousands, and recently they had adopted a foreign custom, to which they durst not give an English name – the battue.[17]

There was admittedly something more than a little nostalgic about this assessment: the battue had been established for a good half-century by this point, as had its concomitants – preservation and large bags. Nonetheless, the more modest shoots that The Times described had certainly existed in the none too distant past. Lord Albemarle, looking back in old age at the battues he had enjoyed at Holkham in Norfolk in the 1820s, considered that 'the quantity of game killed in three months was probably not much more than it is now the fashion to slaughter in as many days'.[18] Although mid-nineteenth-century commentators had a tendency to romanticise the simple shoots of their younger years and their less sophisticated ancestors, there can be no denying the very real increase in the size of game bags that occurred throughout the century.

As so often in the history of hunting, the royal household was leading by example, its superior wealth enabling it to create a hunting establishment of the kind about which small landowners could only dream. Prince Albert, the young Queen Victoria's husband, was a keen hunter, and shortly after the marriage, game preservation at Windsor Great Park was noticeably stepped up: under his guidance, its game stock increased fivefold. Albert also extended the range of his preserves over the neighbouring Bagshot Park in order to ensure that as much of his carefully reared game was shot by him and his friends as possible.[19] His devotion to the sport was the envy of some, but the ridicule of others, as an account of a day's shooting organised by the Duke of Buckingham at his seat at Stowe for the king and five other noblemen makes clear. About fifty beaters drove the game from the covert in the direction of the stationed shooters. According to *The Times*: 'The ground immediately in front of the shooters became strewn with dead and dying; within a semi-circle of about 60 yards from His Royal Highness, the havock was evidently greatest.' The total head of game shot by the party was reported to be 200 hares, 100 pheasants and one snipe. Prince Albert shot 114 hares, 29 pheasants and the only snipe killed.[20] More than 300 animals were killed in a single morning's sport. The unease with which some nineteenth-century commentators viewed shooting parties on this scale is not difficult to comprehend.

In this context, it is little surprise to find that shooters were unwilling to loosen their grip on the nation's small game. Instead, preservation was the order of the day. The shooters pursued a three-armed strategy based upon extensive rearing programmes, large armies of professional gamekeepers, and the rigorous enforcement of the game laws. But whilst these measures helped to preserve the shooters' game, they did nothing to extinguish the conflict that hunting provoked. Between 1833 and 1843 no fewer than forty-one gamekeepers were killed by armed poachers, and many more had been seriously wounded.[21] In the same period, around a third of all prosecutions in some counties were for game offences.[22] By 1844 committals under the game laws had reached 4,500 a year, double the figure before the game law reform of 1831.[23] The preservers had yet to devise a system that preserved game and social harmony in equal measure.

Opposition to the game laws was taken up in Parliament in the 1840s by John Bright and the Anti-Corn Law League. Following decades of public opposition and parliamentary intransigence, a realistic prospect of reform was for the first time possible. In 1845, following mounting agitation, Robert Peel's Conservative government appointed a select committee to investigate the operation of the 1831 Game Act. Fifteen government-selected members were appointed and J. H. T. Manners Sutton was appointed chairman.

In the next three months, thirty-nine witnesses, most of them farmers, were called to the committee and examined. Several testified to the damage that game, particularly rabbits and hares, caused to crops, and complained bitterly of their shooting landlords' refusal to compensate for this damage when sudden increases in the game population made the losses unusually high. Farmers routinely complained of damage done to the tune of £100 or more, and one Norfolk farmer, occupying about 6,000 acres, even claimed to have suffered several thousand pounds' worth of damage to his crops.[24] Though most rented their farms on low rents on the understanding that they were situated in the midst of hunting preserves, their grievances centred on the fact that the quantity of game could increase from one year to the next, particularly if the landlord stepped up his preserving activities, causing rising costs to the farmer with no recompense.

Outside Parliament, the general public, overwhelmingly hostile to the game laws, looked on with interest and excitement. In Aylesbury, for example, a public meeting of 'gentlemen, farmers and other interested parties' was held at the County Hall in February 1845 to discuss the repeal of the game laws. Declaring that 'while they [the game laws] afforded amusement and luxury to a few privileged individuals, they were ruinous to the well-being of the nation at large', the meeting threw its weight behind Bright's reforming endeavour.[25] Like many, the gentlemen and farmers of Aylesbury were hoping that the time for far-reaching reform had at last come.

In June 1846, the game committee met to agree its final report.[26] But the government, which was hostile to game law reform, had a majority on the committee, and the outcome consequently fell far short of the hopes of many. Needless to say, Bright's draft report recommending the complete abolition of the game laws was not accepted. Instead, the committee adopted a series of resolutions proposed by the chairman, Manners Sutton, concluding that game was a form of property like any other, and calling for such continued protection for game as was consistent with other forms of property. There was some modification of the severity of the poaching laws, but the principle of the laws remained intact. As so often in matters of game legislation, Parliament showed itself to be little more than the organ of the wealthy, hunting gentleman.

So for the next few decades, it was very much business as usual for all the players in this ongoing drama. From the farmers' perspective, nothing significant came of Parliament's attention to the game laws in the 1840s, and their discontent continued to fester. The preservation of game injured the farmer's crops but brought him no tangible benefit. Their position was captured by the rural commentator Richard Jefferies in a series of essays entitled the *Amateur Poacher*. His fictional poacher, 'Old Oby' declared that 'if I was to walk through their [the farmers'] court yards at night with a sack over my shoulders full of you-knows-what, and met one of 'em, he'd tell his dog to stop that yowling, and go indoors rather than see me'.[27] The preservation activities of a farmer's landlord were considerably more costly than the occasional law-breaking of the poachers.

Lower down the social scale, a potent cocktail of primitive weapons and a sense of bitter injustice helped to stoke the conflicts caused by the game laws. Many at this social level felt cheated of the gifts of nature that their ancestors had rightfully enjoyed, and articulated their discontent in stark class terms. James Hawker, a lifelong and unrepentant poacher, recalled the time in his youth when he had been unfairly locked up for seven days for getting an old widow without coal a bundle of sticks. 'Ever since then,' he declared, 'I have Poached with more Bitterness against the Class. If I am able, I Will Poach Till I Die.'[28] Joseph Arch spoke of the 'smothered anger' occasioned by the game laws in rural communities.[29] Nightly pitched battles, murdered gamekeepers, and villagers who had seen nothing: these were the tactics of the powerless when Parliament refused to address their legitimate request to share in the hunting of the countryside's wild animals.

And, of course, the game bags just continued to grow. In 1861, the Prince Consort bought the Sandringham estate for his eldest son, Albert Edward, the Prince of Wales, another keen royal shooter. Ten thousand pheasants were raised from eggs each year and vast sums were spent on planting woods and coverts designed to encourage the largest possible concentrations of birds.[30] Preservation on this scale was of course exceptional, but the competition for game bags was felt at every level. Critics complained about 'the ridiculous spirit of emulation, which tempts men to vie with each other in the matter of bags'.[31] Shooting prowess was always measured in the number of birds killed.

Reform was delayed until 1880, when Gladstone's government passed the Ground Game Act.[32] This act gave all tenants the right concurrent with that of landowners to kill hares and rabbits, though not winged game. The rights conferred by this act were inalienable, and could not be withheld by any lease or contract. The act therefore put farmers in control of the vermin on their farms, and gave them the right to protect their crops from hares and rabbits. Though winged game was not included, the act was sufficient to cause the farmers' hostility to the game laws to melt away. Indeed, the farmers were so pleased with this compromise that this division of the rights to kill winged and ground game between owners and occupiers remains to this day.[33]

Yet, although farmers were now granted the right to carry and use their own guns to shoot rabbits and hares, they, along with the wider rural community, were strictly forbidden from using them to participate in the sport of their social betters. Shooting pheasants and partridges remained the exclusive pastime of the social elite. It is testimony to the strength of rural conservatism that so many remained strangely acquiescent in their ongoing exclusion from the ancient sport of kings.

With conflict between farmers and shooters dissipated, the future of shooting was assured. The drive grew in popularity, guns became more efficient, and the size of bags increased inexorably. In 1896, a record 3,113 pheasants were killed in one day's shooting at Sandringham, and fifteen years later that record was surpassed when in the course of a day's hunting in an estate in Buckinghamshire 3,937 birds were brought down.[34] The Elveden estate in Norfolk consolidated its place as one of the best-known sporting estates in England, regularly entertaining royal visitors such as Edward VII and the Duke of York (later George V). Under the stewardship of Lord Iveagh, shooting at Elveden was conducted on a grand scale with the most elaborate attention to detail. No fewer than seventy men were employed in the game department, twenty-four of them kitted out in fine livery. Shooting parties usually consisted of eight or nine guns: for this number, more than 100 beaters were hired, each dressed in a white smock with red collar and a hat with a red band. It was considered a poor day's sport if fewer than 1,000 head of game were killed, and the whole operation was sustained only by rearing 20,000 pheasants each season.[35] It was, of course, an uneconomic use of the land, a form of conspicuous consumption for the leisured elite. The great shooting estates of the late nineteenth century had become wholly artificial hunting reserves, a desperate attempt to carve out a protected wildlife sanctuary in an ever more populous country.

Despite this, changes in the world of agriculture at the end of the nineteenth century, in particular a downturn in prices, helped to consolidate the position of game shooting in the English countryside yet further. As prices fell, so did profits and rents, and all those earning a living from the land were encouraged to look elsewhere for income. The continuing popularity of shooting made game preservation a profitable area in which to expand. Although preserving game had historically hindered more efficient agricultural exploitation of land, low agricultural prices turned this around. In the late nineteenth century, a fine shooting estate was better business than agricultural improvements, and many commercially minded landowners began to expand in this area. The result was commercial preservation on an industrial scale.

Game preservation guaranteed both income and birds for those involved, but it is doubtful whether the sport it created can fairly be considered hunting

as we know it. At the heart of the hunter's craft down the centuries had been
the acquisition of an intimate knowledge of the animals' habits and habitat,
an ability to read the natural environment for clues about the comings and
goings of the animals within it. At its finest, the actual hunt involved the
pitting of wits of the hunter against a wild animal unconstrained by man-made
boundaries. On the great shooting estates of the late nineteenth century,
these qualities no longer held. Such estates were not simply preserving birds,
they were actually producing them, and their quarry was not wild at all. Nor
did the hunter locate and kill his prey in its natural environment. Professional
gamekeepers reared the game, and hired beaters brought it within the reach
of the shooter. The successful shooter was a skilled marksman, not an experienced observer of the countryside. Just as earlier generations had discovered,
extensive preservation was bought at the price of ultimately degrading the
nature of the sport they sought to protect.

The old skills of tracking prey that had traditionally formed part of the
hunter's art now rested in the hands of the poacher. Jefferies's fictional 'Old
Oby' explained his success in the following terms:

> The reason I gets on so well poaching is because I'm always at work out
> in the fields ... I watches everything as goes on and marks the hares'
> tracks and the rabbit buries, and the double mounds and little copses as
> the pheasants wanders off to in the autumn ... So I knows every hare
> in the parish, and all his runs and all the double mounds and copses,
> and the little covers in the corners of fields.[36]

Oby's close relationship with the countryside taught him where the animals
lay and, like generations of hunters before him, he used this knowledge to go
about trapping and snaring his prey. James Hawker, operating in the midland
counties, expanded on the same theme in his autobiography written at the
end of the century. In tones reminiscent of an earlier time, he described how
one could track a hare as it 'creeps in to a Resting Place for the Day' after a
long night in search of food.[37] Listen out for the Lark's song, he advised, the
first sound before daybreak, for as soon as the hares hear it, they return to
their forms and 'a Hare will be on you almost Before you can se it'.[38] Hawker
spoke of his delight in 'tracing the Little Footprints in the Snow', concluding
that it was 'Grand to Learn the Habbitts of Game'.[39] And Frederick Rolfe,
the king of the Norfolk poachers, reflecting on a career encompassing both
poaching and gamekeeping, concluded that it was 'a verry interesting life for
the man that will study nature ... he must study wether, and all the signs of
wood craft, the call of birds, and the flight of Wood Pigons in the wood at
night, and distinguish the different sounds, and there are a lot of different

sounds in the woods at night ... The wind and the stars are his guide.'[40] All of
these poachers spoke the same language as the writers of hunting handbooks
in the sixteenth and seventeenth centuries. They describe the woodcraft
that had long assisted the successful hunter, and their evocative descriptions
of their relationship with the natural world are a far cry from the shooters'
carefully kept game books and neatly written tables listing personal totals of
game killed.

Things rarely stand still for long in the world of hunting, yet the pace of
change in the hunting of small game in the century and a half after 1750
stands out as truly remarkable. The adoption of the gun to 'shoot flying',
and a series of steady improvements to the gun, remarkably expanded the
hunter's capacity to kill. The annual slaughter rapidly spiralled upwards,
and the shooters inevitably turned to punitive game laws and preservation
on an industrial scale in order to produce a large population of huntable
game. This was not the first time that the hunters' enthusiasm for their
pastime had degraded the nature of their sport: one is reminded of medieval
deer-coursing, or of the huge slaughters of deer so beloved by the Tudor
monarchs. Preserving the essence of hunting in the context of a changing
society has posed problems for generations of hunters and was not a novelty
of the eighteenth century. Nonetheless, the scale, pace and extent of change
after 1750 were all without precedent. In the process of game protection the
shooters severed their relationship with the natural world and refashioned
wild animals into a form of private property. Their sport could no longer be
considered 'hunting' in any traditional sense of the word, and it consequently
no longer merits a place in a book about the history of hunting.

CHAPTER THIRTEEN

Hunting Attacked

With the very best motives, the legislature had, for many years past, been putting down one after another the sports of the poor man – while they had never touched the sports of the rich. (*Hansard's Parliamentary Debates*, 3rd series, cclxxvi (19883), vols 2 and 6, col. 1665)

Neither pain nor death should be turned into matter of amusement. (Freeman, 1869)[1]

For a minimum of suffering [foxhunting] provides a maximum of recreation. (Trollope, 1869)[2]

When early Victorian society proudly passed its ground-breaking animal cruelty legislation, few had thought for a moment that the principles underpinning it could be turned against its creators' own recreations. By confining its attention to captive animals, the 1835 Protection of Animals Act had posed no threat to the outdoor pursuits of hunting and shooting: only the actions and sports of the poor lay within its scope. But within decades, reformers were arguing that the distinction between captive and wild animals was spurious, and that wild animals should be offered the same protection as their domestic cousins. Victorian reformers, it turned out, had unleashed an unwelcome force, more durable and more powerful than they had ever intended.

From the outset, the anti-hunting movement was rooted in the left-leaning, urban intelligentsia, a spiritual home that it has arguably never entirely left. Their case was stated with unexpected bluntness in 1869 by the liberal historian E. A. Freeman (later appointed Regius Professor in History at Oxford). His withering attack on foxhunting published in the liberal *Fortnightly Review* summarised the arguments that have formed the mainstay of the anti-hunting movement ever since. At the heart of his polemic was an accusation of hypocrisy against foxhunters for condemning the horrors of the bullring, but refusing to admit the 'deliberate and wanton' cruelty of their own pastime. 'Is there any difference in principle,' he asked, 'between foxhunting and bull-baiting, so that foxhunting can be right and bull-baiting is wrong?' His answer was an unambiguous no: 'Strip foxhunting of its disguises, and its principle, is, as Windham allowed, exactly the same as the principle of bull-baiting.'[3]

In suggesting a likeness between baiting and hunting Freeman had touched upon a problem that one earlier writer had called a 'dangerous string' – though it was something that those intent on suppressing bull-baiting had always been loath to address.[4] For hunting's supporters, it had long been an unshakeable article of faith that their sport was 'essentially different' from baiting, and through most of the nineteenth century few were interested in challenging the grounds of this distinction.[5] It was precisely this task that Freeman undertook six decades later with such relish.

For Freeman, the similarity between the two sports lay in the role of the human participants – those spectators, whether on foot or mounted, watching dogs attack other animals for no greater cause than their own entertainment. In baiting, the dogs attacked a large, tethered animal: the bull or bear used its strength to parry the dogs' attacks, rather than seeking to escape. In hunting, by contrast, the dogs were set upon a freely roaming animal, which used its speed rather than strength to elude the dogs. But whatever the procedural differences between baiting and hunting, Freeman believed that the sports shared one crucial characteristic: both were practised for pleasure rather than need: 'Can any modern foxhunter honestly say that his hunting is done with the legitimate object of getting rid of a noxious animal in the quickest way?' At the time that Freeman posed the question, not even the most ardent of foxhunters could claim that it was. With the preservation of foxes being practised on an extensive scale, there could be no disputing Freeman's assertion that foxhunters were motivated by something other than the useful task of eliminating a farmyard pest.

Inevitably, Freeman's piece brought a number of keen hunters to the defence of their sport, and within a couple of months the *Fortnightly Review* had published a response by the novelist (and keen foxhunter) Anthony Trollope.[6] Trollope flatly denied that the huntsman either sought, or gained, pleasure from the fox's pain, arguing that 'no man goes out foxhunting in order that he may receive pleasure from pain inflicted'.[7] As for the charge of unintended cruelty, rather than deny it, Trollope simply countered, not unreasonably, that far greater cruelty was daily endured by the cab-horse, the half-starved dog and the caged bird, and suggested that the animal protection movement might achieve more by directing its efforts elsewhere. Sketching an argument that later defenders of hunting would develop in greater detail, Trollope even suggested that the system of modern foxhunting brought positive benefits to the fox, transforming it from unwanted vermin into an animal so precious that it enjoyed unparalleled protection during its lifetime: 'Until it comes upon him that *ineluctabile tempus*, he has a good time of it among animals'.[8] For Trollope, the fuss about an animal so inconsequential as the fox was broadly incomprehensible.[9]

The exchange between Freeman and Trollope made a minor splash amongst the chattering classes, but the controversy it elicited soon died down, and life continued much as usual amongst the hunting fraternity.[10] By the 1860s, the old local packs had largely been replaced by subscription packs with a professional huntsman, and in the 1880s there were some 150 packs of foxhounds scattered throughout England: most had somewhere between twenty and fifty couple of hounds, but some of the smaller private packs remaining had no more than a dozen couple.[11] The sport was put on a more organised footing with the creation in 1856 of an informal committee of masters who met at a London club, Boodles. The committee's primary role was to arbitrate in quarrels between neighbouring packs over the ownership of coverts or the extent of their country. In the 1880s, this was replaced by a more formal body – the Association of the Masters of Foxhounds.[12] By such means foxhunting was being organised on a more professional basis.

Leicestershire and parts of Northamptonshire and Nottinghamshire remained at the forefront of the fashionable, moneyed hunting world. The cost of following the hunt here was high and the sport was socially exclusive. A subscription to the Fernie Hunt in Leicestershire, for example, cost £25 a year in the 1890s, and the necessary clothes and horses raised the overall outlay considerably.[13] Yet despite the undisputed expense of hunting in the shires, foxhunters remained wedded to the belief that foxhunting in the provinces was a democratic affair, open to all comers regardless of means. The late nineteenth-century sporting writer Major Whyte-Melville, for example, described a provincial field 'consisting of the Squire, three or four strapping yeomen, a parson, and a boy on a pony', but there was a certain degree of idealisation in this depiction of a simple, rustic foxhunt.[14] Even in the provinces, the expenses of subscriptions, clothes, horses and leisure time during the working week combined to make foxhunting an expensive pastime, and helped to reserve the sport for families of independent means and the occasional successful farmer. George Race, Master of the Cambridgeshire Hunt from 1840 to 1910, advised the would-be foxhunter as follows: 'Let him first place himself beyond poverty, and provide against a rainy day, and then enjoy himself as much as he pleases in the health-giving joys of our English field sports.' Hunting, he made clear, was not for a 'man who has a family to support by his daily labour'.[15]

Perhaps more significant than any widening of the social constituency of foxhunting at this time was the increasing participation of women. The redevelopment of foxhunting in the eighteenth century had been accompanied by a marked contraction of female opportunities on the hunting field, but by the close of the following century, Trollope could convincingly preface the chapter of his *Hunting Sketches* about 'The Lady who Rides to Hounds' with the assertion 'that the number of such ladies is very much on the increase'.[16] Whereas earlier writers had complained of the inconvenience of attending to the needs of female horse-riders, Trollope confessed that he '[liked] to see three or four ladies out in a field'. In his opinion, with a few women out, 'improved feelings prevail as to hunting, and the pleasanter will be the field'.[17] His novels of the 1870s depicted women on the hunting field as a normal part of country-house life. Mrs Spooner, in *The Duke's Children*, for example, was a woman who 'does nothing but hunt';[18] and in *The Eustace Diamonds*, when Lady Eustace was introduced to the field, she found it enjoyable if not a little expensive.[19] And though Trollope may have been unusually enthusiastic about the increasing presence of women on the hunting field, he was certainly not alone in noticing this change.[20]

A relaxing of the standards of acceptable female dress may have been partly responsible for the influx of women from the 1870s, since it had been above all the constraints of female attire that had hampered women's ability to ride to hounds earlier in the century. For women in the nineteenth century, the side-saddle was obligatory, but it was not only more difficult to ride across country when seated side-saddle, it was also more dangerous, owing to the difficulty of extricating oneself from the saddle in the event of a fall. Furthermore, the customary long habit – a woman's dress had to be long enough to cover both ankles amply in order to be respectable – was at risk of catching on obstacles and added considerably to the perils. A handful of women had always braved the risk, but the high number of accidents and their severity was a serious impediment to female foxhunting and helped to restrict the number of women on the field. It was not until the second half of the century, when female riders began to adopt new riding outfits that protected them from this 'needless and peculiar risk', that women returned to the hunting field in any numbers.[21]

First ladies' riding skirts became shorter, and then, although the conventions of Victorian society decreed that women remained seated side-saddle, the creation of the ingenious 'safety skirt' helped to lessen the dangers. The safety skirt was loosely fixed to a woman's waist, so that in the event of a fall it came off at the waist and remained attached to the saddle, leaving the dismounted female rider in breeches.[22] The safety skirt was initially viewed with some distaste: one female hunter who had adopted it in the 1870s reported that 'a great many of the ladies in the neighbourhood "cut her" because they declared she rode in such indecent clothes'.[23] Yet by the 1880s, shorter safety skirts were becoming widespread, and in 1884 the Quorn Hunt even made their use compulsory, reasoning, 'better a live lady in breeches than a dead one in a habit'.[24] It all helped to extend the appeal of hunting to women yet further. In the year that the Quorn made safety skirts compulsory, one writer declared that 'the number of women who hunt now is at least tenfold as compared with a dozen years ago', and added that now about thirty of every three hundred hunters with the Quorn were women.[25]

Yet despite the increasing number of female riders, women remained largely outside the formal hunting organisations. The fashionable Fernie Hunt, for example, had just four female members in over two hundred in 1872 – most hunted unofficially rather than as members in their own right.[26] Many hunts continued to refuse admittance to lady members; some only opened their doors to women after the Second World War.[27] It was even more unusual for women to take on any form of official responsibility. Apart

13. Despite innovations in ladies' hunting attire, foxhunting for women was no easy matter: a finely dressed Edwardian huntswoman tackling a ditch while mounted side saddle.

from the occasional season during which a woman held the reins following her husband's death, there were no female masters of foxhounds in the nineteenth century, and only six before the outbreak of war in 1914.[28] Prior to the Great War, the institutional structures of foxhunting were overwhelmingly masculine, and women's presence on the hunting field, though steadily increasing, was largely decorative rather than managerial.

The incursion of women into the hunting field was the most visible change in the world of nineteenth-century foxhunting, but it was by no means the only one. Along with a growing number of female converts in the second half of the nineteenth century, an increasing number of men were participating in hunting, contributing to a further expansion in the size of fields. The development of the railways helped to fuel this growth by making it easier and cheaper to travel to distant meets. By the end of the century, most of the railway companies offered competitive deals to travelling hunters in the form of season tickets lasting for between three and six months and with return day tickets priced at just one and a half times the single fare.[29] Larger fields, however, put greater strain on the fox population, and the hunting community continued to grapple with the problems posed by a shortage of foxes.[30] Most hunts were necessarily involved in the business of preserving foxes and managing coverts in order to keep their operations afloat. This required masters to make contact with those who farmed or owned the land where foxes were most likely to breed (the coverts) and encourage them to ensure that the young fox litter survived through the spring and summer months. Some hunts were spending up to £300 a year in payments to keepers and farmers for each litter of foxes they provided on their lands.[31] By contrast, that other feature of early nineteenth-century foxhunting – the trafficking of foxes – had fallen into complete disrepute, as the response of the hunting community to a case of fox-buying at the turn of the century amply demonstrates.

In 1900, the following advertisement in the *Gloucester Citizen* reached the attention of the Duke of Beaufort, Master of the Beaufort Hunt: 'Fox cubs wanted, to turn down, any number.'[32] The purchaser of these fox cubs was a man named Ellison, a horse and carriage salesman of Clifton, Bristol, and in an attempt to get to the root of the matter, a gentleman wrote to Ellison in his keeper's name expressing an interest in supplying some fox cubs. Ellison's reply was as follows:

We can take all you can get, if strong, healthy and fit to turn down in a strange country 150 miles off, and are giving 5s. to 7s. 6d. each packed on rail carriage forward; you can get some sugar-boxes in Thornbury at 3d. each, will hold two or three each; put in some hay or straw, and nail on the top again, giving them plenty of air-holes, and will send you cash when put on rail, and labels where to send them to. Let us know by return how many you can get during the next few weeks. Will keep strictly private nobody else will know – same as with others in Gloucestershire we are getting from.

By publicising the incident in *Baily's Hunting Directory* and chastising the wrongdoers, the Masters of Foxhounds' Association clearly hoped to shame those involved and put an end to the invidious practice of buying and selling foxes. It is more likely, however, that it simply helped to push the trafficking of foxes underground rather than eradicating it. Throughout the Edwardian era, *Baily's Hunting Directory* continued to report shortages in some areas. In the 1904–5 foxhunting season, *Baily's* reported on the availability of foxes in around half of the hunts in England and Wales. Of these, the majority reported that foxes were plentiful, but between a quarter and a third of packs reported a shortage of foxes in at least one part of their country, and between 10 and 15 per cent returned gloomy reports such as the following: 'foxes are very scarce'; 'the supply of foxes is rather short'; and 'not enough foxes'.[33] With subscribers paying handsomely for the privilege of foxhunting, the incentive for masters of foxhounds to ensure against too many blank days was clear, and one imagines that the custom of buying foxes must have continued surreptitiously in some areas.

Owing to the care and expense that were lavished on the rearing and protection of fox litters, ownership of the foxes had the potential to provoke bitter disputes between neighbouring hunting packs, and quarrels were by no means unusual. The columns of the hunting fraternity's foremost publication, the *Field*, were filled with regular reports of foxhunting disputes – usually between foxhunters and farmers, but sometimes between neighbouring packs as well. One such incident concerning Charles Manners, sixth Duke of Rutland and Master of the Belvoir Hounds, must stand as an example of many. Manners had assumed the mastership of the Belvoir territory following the death of his father in 1857, but from the outset his mastership was punctuated by struggles over vulpicide. His difficulties began in 1863, with the descent of a foxhunt one January morning into farce. The hunt had started well, with both fox and hounds heading at speed across two fields, but as the riders followed in pursuit, the duke was informed that a man had shot the fox and hidden the carcass. In order to reward the hounds, the duke asked for the carcass, and was no doubt stunned when the farmer refused to deliver it: 'a short struggle took place between the two, which ended in both rolling over, with the Duke on top'.[34] The duke then retrieved the fox, and gave it to the hounds.

Though the duke's conduct is more than undignified, a surprisingly large number of contemporaries were sympathetic, both to his plight and to his response. According to the *Field*, he was shortly presented with an address 'signed by nearly every farmer in the Belvoir Hunt, expressing their regret and indignation at such unsportsmanlike conduct in shooting a fox'.[35] Even the magazine *Punch*, usually so quick to ridicule upper-class pretensions, lent its sympathy to the duke on this occasion.[36] Yet notwithstanding this outpouring of sympathy from all quarters, the duke had no legal recourse in order to punish the farmer, who, like any other person, was perfectly entitled to kill foxes by whatever means he chose. Even such an elegant and well-placed huntsman as the Duke of Rutland could do no more than appeal to his neighbours' morality and sportsmanship in his endeavours to preserve the fox.

As if the difficulty of maintaining a huntable population of foxes was not enough, Edwardian foxhunters had to contend with the burgeoning humanitarian movement as well. In the 1890s, the opponents of hunting coalesced around a most unlikely reformer – a hitherto obscure intellectual and one-time member of the RSPCA, Henry Stephens Salt – and criticisms of hunting began to be expressed more forcefully than ever before. There was little in Salt's background to hint at the progressive social thinker that he was to become: he had enjoyed a privileged childhood and the advantages of an education at Eton. After four years studying Classics at Cambridge, he returned to Eton to marry the daughter of his tutor and take up a position as master at his old school: it seemed as though his graduation as a member of the establishment was complete. But Salt's impeccable credentials were tarnished by his habit of fraternising with socialists, and following the departure from Eton of his close friend and brother-in-law Jim Joynes because of his public contact with the American radical Henry George, Salt's position at this bastion of tradition became increasingly untenable. Having managed to save a modest pension of £160 a year, he retired to Tilbury in Kent to pursue a simple life in harmony with nature, sacrificing material wealth for intellectual riches. There he wrote essays and books and entertained his many friends, amongst them such illustrious figures as George Bernard Shaw, George Meredith, John Galsworthy, Ramsay MacDonald, Havelock Ellis and William Morris.[37]

In 1891, disillusioned with the RSPCA's conservatism on the question of blood sports, Salt founded his own rival organisation: the Humanitarian League. The League was an association of left-leaning individuals, an intellectual home for freethinkers, vegetarians, feminists, Fabians, rationalists and other thinkers, and it actively campaigned for the more humane treatment of both animals and criminals. Amongst those involved in the Animals' Defence wing of the League were the Liberal MP George Greenwood, the vegetarian Howard Williams, the socialist and pacifist Edward Carpenter and the mystic Edward Maitland: this gives a fair indication of the political and ideological leanings of those whom the League attracted.[38] The Animals' Defence campaigned in a wide sphere of animal cruelty, ranging from zoos, circuses and performing animals, to the use of animals in the development of vaccinations and in scientific experiments; and it was inevitably concerned about the use of animals in sport as well. The League quickly emerged as the nation's foremost critic of 'blood sports' – the expression was one that Salt himself coined – initially targeting coursing and carted-deer hunting, or, as they had taken to calling them, the 'spurious sports'.[39] Hares, they argued, were not coursed in the wild, but in an enclosed space; and carted deer were raised and kept in captivity. As they were not strictly wild animals, it seemed easiest to extend the principles of earlier reforms here, and the League hoped that a combination of persuasion and new legislation would soon consign both sports to history.

With Salt's encouragement, a Berkshire chaplain and former foxhunter the Reverend J. Stratton spearheaded the campaign. Stratton lost no time in busying himself with organising petitions and deputations, and overseeing the writing of countless letters and pamphlets. He chose as his target the queen's Royal Buckhounds, considering it 'a very useful peg ... on which to hang an exposure of the cruelty of stag-hunting'.[40] The idea behind this was to encourage the Palace to provide a moral lead to the nation's stag-hunters. Stratton hoped that the abolition of the Buckhounds would set a fine example that others involved in the hunting of carted deer would be proud to follow. And he seemed initially to have a promising chance of success, as the queen not only did not hunt herself with the Buckhounds, but her household even sent a reply to his enquiries stating that 'the Queen has been strongly opposed to stag-hunting for many years past'.[41] To Stratton's despair, however, this stated opposition failed to translate into the positive action the reformers desired, as neither queen nor Parliament wished to take the matter any further. When asked in Parliament whether it would abolish the Buckhounds, the government responded that the matter would require 'mature deliberation', though it took no steps to begin that process.[42] The upshot was that Victoria continued to maintain a well-equipped Royal Buckhounds, and the government continued to foot the bill.

Though later heralded as an early success in the League's campaign against blood sports, the eventual demise of the Royal Buckhounds in reality had little to do with the League's reforming efforts. Parliament and the Palace resisted all calls to disband the Buckhounds and it was eventually not humanitarian concerns, but the less edifying force of economics that brought an end to the 600-year-old institution. In 1901, when Edward VII acceded to the throne, a parliamentary select committee was appointed to make economies in the royal household, and as the new king had no interest in deer-hunting, it was decided to save £6,000 by axing the Royal Buckhounds. The select committee considered the possibility of replacing them with a pack of royal foxhounds, though eventually shied away from this option on the grounds that it would be wrong to use public money to subsidise a specific sport.[43] But in spite of the League's optimistic hopes, none of the dozen or so other deer-hunting packs in existence followed this lead. It was the upheaval of war that finally accomplished this. By 1919, no more than four packs survived.[44]

Nor should the disbanding of the Royal Buckhounds be thought to represent any shift in the royal household's long-standing allegiance to the traditional aristocratic pastimes of hunting and shooting. Though Victoria did not hunt, her husband and other close members of her family did, and she remained fully immersed in the hunting world. When she visited Sandringham in 1889, for example, she was formally greeted by thirty-six members of the West Norfolk Hunt. Her descendants were all keen hunters and shooters: George IV, Edward VII and George V all hunted foxes, and in 1921 the Prince of Wales was painted in full hunting pink by the fashionable sporting artist Alfred Munnings.[45] Indeed, Queen Victoria might be regarded as very much the exception to the rule.

The League spearheaded the campaign against coursing and deer-hunting, but it was not entirely alone in its opposition to blood sports, and it success- fully harnessed the anti-hunting sentiment of a wide circle of intellectuals of a similar frame of mind. Radicals and socialists were attracted to its mission to expose cruelty in high places, and had a natural sympathy for the League's objectives. The League was joined in its opposition to carted- deer hunting, for example, by the socialist newspaper, the *Clarion*, which campaigned against royal patronage of the sport at Hurlingham. The whole lot were dismissed by one hunter as 'malcontents who in the guise of humani- tarians, bolshevists or what not crop up in all times and in all the hunting counties'.[46] It was an unflattering but not entirely misleading description of the anti-hunting movement. The great and the good of Edwardian society were overwhelmingly opposed to the meddling cant of the Humanitarian League, but there was nonetheless a handful of like-minded individuals on the intellectual fringes willing to join them in their crusade against cruelty perpetrated by the social elite.

But whilst the League managed to harness the anti-hunting sentiment of a number of allied political organisations, it was frustrated throughout its existence by its failure to gain the support of the nation's foremost animal protection society: the RSPCA. During its campaign against carted deer-hunting, for example, it rapidly became apparent that support from the society would not be forthcoming – hardly surprising given that the society's president, the Duke of York, was himself partial to stag-hunting. The League was prompted to ask, 'what has become of the Society for the Prevention of Cruelty to Animals that it never seems to have made a persistent stand against this barbarity in high places?'[47] It was a question that the RSPCA preferred not to answer.

The RSPCA equally failed to support Salt's campaign against beagling (hunting hare on foot with a pack of hounds) at his old school, Eton. The situation here was complicated by the fact that both the headmaster and the provost of the school were members of the local committee of the RSPCA in the Windsor and Eton district. In 1902, Ernest Bell of the Humanitarian League wrote an open letter to the school's headmaster, Dr Edmund Warre, requesting that the hare-hunting that the boys currently enjoyed might be substituted with a drag hunt, a move which he thought would be 'no physical loss but much to the moral gain of the boys'.[48] Dr Warre declined to follow this suggestion, and added, 'I have never been given to understand that the society has condemned the hunting of wild animals. If it does, ought it not at once to enlighten its subscribers upon this point, so that they may not be contributing to its funds under a false impression?'[49] As for the RSPCA, one may judge from the decision of the local Windsor and Eton branch to re-elect Warre as a member that their sympathies lay with the beaglers rather than the League.[50] Like an earlier generation of hunting supporters of the RSPCA, Warre simply could not understand how the charge of cruelty could apply to him.

On the legislative front, the League was no more successful. Despite the emergence of increasingly vocal criticism of carted-deer hunting and coursing by liberals and intellectuals, Parliament remained staunchly opposed to change of any kind. Anti-hunting and coursing bills were introduced nearly every year between 1893 and 1912, but only two received a second reading and both of these failed.[51] General animal protection bills were minutely scrutinised by sporting MPs to make sure that no attack on hunting was surreptitiously slipping through. For example, Lord James of Hereford's Cruelty to Wild Animals in Captivity Bill, introduced in 1900 in the midst of Stratton's campaign against the Royal Buckhounds, was intended to protect animals in menageries. The Peers, however, thought they detected a concealed attack on rabbit-coursing and carted-deer hunting, and would not pass the bill until a clause protecting these two sports had been inserted.[52]

For the most part, foxhunters had very little to worry about. The League was a fringe organisation and Parliament was implacably opposed to its anti-hunting message. In 1884 a number of sportsmen responded to the emergence of the League by founding the National Sports Protection and Defence Association, but its transient existence points to the confidence of the foxhunters in the security of their sport. The following year it changed its name to the Field Sports Protection and Encouragement Association, and declared that its interest was the preservation of hunting, shooting, horse-racing, fishing and coursing.[53] Its stated purpose was to 'link together sporting interests', so that should any one field sport be attacked, a stronger defence could be constructed.[54] But the society appears to have been largely inactive. In the 1880s, the traditional country pursuits of hunting and shooting looked so secure that few of their practitioners were convinced of the need to establish defensive organisations.

The reformers' only real success before 1914 was the Protection of Animals Act (1911) – the work of George Greenwood, the Liberal MP for Peterborough and long-time member of the Humanitarian League.[55] Greenwood succeeded where others had failed, not because times had changed, but owing to his shrewd decision to exempt blood sports from his bill's remit. The 1911 act consolidated the existing legislation, raised the maximum fines for cruelty, and added to the list of offences 'the commission or omission' of any act likely to cause unnecessary suffering and cruelty. The act also made it an offence to inflict mental as well as physical suffering. Nonetheless, powerful hunting interests dictated the final shape of the act. All wild animals were of course excluded – this law was to protect only 'captive and domestic animals'. And even with this proviso, its passage through Parliament could be secured only by attaching clauses which underscored the legality of hunting. 'Carted' deer and 'bagged' foxes were explicitly excluded (this rested on the argument that they became 'wild' again once they were released); and (should any doubt remain), the bill expressly permitted the 'coursing or hunting of any captive animal'.[56]

By the late Edwardian period, the League had accomplished no measurable success, but was gaining considerably in self-confidence. Having at first confined its campaigns to forms of hunting which made use of tame or captured animals, namely coursing and carted-stag hunting, it was soon daring to declare publicly against the hunting of wild animals as well. Indeed, Salt had had hunting – 'this amateur butchery' – in his sights since the outset, declaring it to be 'the most wanton and indefensible of all possible violations of the principle of animals' rights. If animals – or men, for that matter – have of necessity to be killed, let them be killed accordingly; but to seek one's own amusement out of the death-pangs of other beings, this is saddening stupidity indeed!'[57] But though many of his friends in the League doubtless shared Salt's views, the organisation hesitated to express its opposition publicly, wary of attacking an ancient custom, the premier pastime of the country's leaders. In the years before the outbreak of the First World War, however, their resolve strengthened and crystallised in 1915 in the publication of an edited collection of essays, ominously titled *Killing for Sport*.

Salt's introductory note to the volume attributed the abolition of the Royal Buckhounds to pressure successfully applied by the League, and indicated its willingness to take new steps against the 'anachronistic' sport of hunting.[58] Eleven essays by different writers followed; most were concerned with various aspects of hunting and shooting in England, though one considered the big game hunting practised in distant parts of the Empire. The essays expanded upon the criticisms of Freeman, now nearly half a century old, and responded to some of the arguments that hunting's advocates had developed in the intervening years. An unmistakable and recurring theme amongst the contributors was that of class. Could it be any accident that the plebeian sports of cockfighting and bull-baiting had long ago been suppressed, but that the hunting, shooting and fishing of their social superiors continued unmolested? they asked. Greenwood, sponsor of the 1911 act, touched upon the obstacles posed by a legislature overwhelmingly packed with hunting gentlemen. No doubt embittered by the compromises he had been forced to make, he commented sarcastically upon a hereditary chamber which throws 'the aegis of its protection over the pleasures of rich and poor alike, and where the high-souled, high-bred scions of a time-honoured aristocracy magnanimously defend the cherished institutions of our forefathers against the attacks both of blatant democrats and sickly sentimentalists!' The accusation of class bias was to form the backbone of the abolitionists' case against hunting for several decades to come.

Running throughout the collection, however, was an older and more general complaint about hunting, similar in tone to that which the opponents of bull-baiting had once articulated: blood sports, they argued, were, in all their forms, 'a relic of savagery' – they simply did not belong in the modern world.[59] Though not unconcerned about animal suffering, these writers were haunted by the spectre of supposedly civilised men deriving pleasure from animal suffering far more than they were by the actual suffering. For not only was hunting cruel, it also injured the person who took part. As G. B. Shaw wrote: 'the man who enjoys [sport of this character] is degraded by it'.[60] And this, of course, was already a very well-established argument. The Puritans had worried about how God would judge men for mistreating animals and eighteenth-century critics of bull-baiting had been concerned about its tendency to degrade those who took part. The same argument would be reformulated several times in the twentieth century as well. Indeed, it has formed the most durable critique of a wide range of recreations involving animals that their opponents have ever articulated.

The League was no more effective in its attack on the hunting of wild animals than in its earlier campaign against the 'spurious sports' and the movement was formally disbanded in 1919, soon to be replaced by new organisations with fresh enthusiasm for the fight.[61] For all its efforts, it had never been more than a fringe organisation: surviving for just under thirty years it was a short-lived and wholly unsuccessful first attempt at extending the legislation of the early nineteenth century to the sports of the upper classes.

A far greater upheaval in the world of hunting was occasioned by the Great War of 1914–18. With the outbreak of war, both hunting and the bills to prevent it abated, and the hunting world was rapidly transformed. For many of the nation's hunting packs, the obstacles to maintaining the sport during the war proved insurmountable. A hundred and seventy thousand horses were mobilised in the fortnight after war was declared, and a scarcity of food for hounds made it difficult for some hunts to continue.[62] With the nation's fittest men away fighting, much of the natural constituency of hunting was removed at a stroke; and with only women and older men remaining at home to hunt, the sizes of fields contracted sharply. Subscriptions fell rapidly, and as there was something a little unseemly about those fortunate enough not to be on the battlefield enjoying themselves on the hunting field, the operations of most hunts were scaled down. A few hunts closed and many others reduced the size of their packs and the number of days they hunted. The New Forest Hunt Club, for example, reduced its hunting from four days a week at the outbreak of war to half that by the end.[63] Not that this in any sense diminished enthusiasm for foxhunting, for as many of those who continued to hunt discovered, smaller fields could still offer good sport. As one master observed: 'There was no one out to head foxes, no indiscriminate halloaing, and hounds, not being over-ridden, did most of the work themselves.'[64]

Furthermore, the contraction of hunting during the war years proved to be no more than a temporary phenomenon, and with the return of peace in 1918 the sport revived with remarkable buoyancy. In 1920, Baron Richard Greville Verney, a keen foxhunting man and the nineteenth Baron Willoughby de Broke of Compton Verney in Warwickshire recalled:

> Many people thought, some perhaps hoped, that foxhunting in the British Isles was doomed. It appears that the former are likely to experience a pleasant shock of surprise, while the latter – if there be any – may be disappointed ... Foxhunting will surely survive from its own innate qualities.[65]

The war, he continued, had simply increased the number and ardour of foxhunting's supporters.[66] The sport received further encouragement in 1919 when Edward, Prince of Wales began to hunt in Leicestershire. Between 1923 and 1928, Prince Edward and his brothers, the Dukes of Gloucester and Kent, took rooms at Melton Mowbray for the season and patronised fashionable hunts such as the Beaufort and the Quorn.[67] And it was not simply royalty that returned to the hunting field after 1818. In most parts of the country, the number of people riding to hounds continued to rise: by the middle of the 1920s many hunts were restored to their former glory and others entered a new period of expansion.[68] The growth of foxhunting appeared to be unstoppable.

The rising popularity of foxhunting should not be confused, however, with a broadening of its social base of support, for hunting in inter-war England overwhelmingly remained the pastime of a moneyed and leisured elite. Admittedly, most packs welcomed the participation of local farmers, but the significance of this custom was perhaps less than many of hunting's supporters proclaimed. After all, the kind of farmers that rode to hounds enjoyed large incomes and high social status compared with much of rural society, and the hunting dress code in any case ensured that they were not mistaken for full subscribers. The followers of most hunts were divided into three groups: members, dressed in scarlet coats and top hats; subscribers, donning black coats and top hats; and farmers or covert owners in check coats and bowler hats.[69] Despite occasional cries to the contrary, the observation of social status was important in inter-war society, and the dress code was used to maintain social distinctions on the hunting field.

If farmers were welcomed to the hunt in their workaday tweeds, members, subscribers and visitors were all expected to don clothing of the finest quality when hunting. The reason always given for this was that smart clothes served as a compliment to the Master and the hunt, but in reality this close attention to dress was more complex. Clothes were thought by one writer to be 'the only really important part of hunting'; and the hunting correspondent of *The Times* thought his hunting 'would lose much of its attractions' if stripped of the fine clothes.[70] Another even suggested there might be a psychological reason for foxhunters' care with their clothes: 'imagine the psychological effect of feeling decently fitted out with an extra bit of polish on the boots and the hunting whip ... even down to the little silver band. You'll feel just like the cat's whiskers and probably his cuffs too, ready to go out with the best.'[71] No matter what the reason, however, the need for fine clothes raised the cost of participation, and was one more way of helping to keep foxhunting an exclusive pastime. Foxhunting, reflected one former master of hounds, was taken for granted in certain circles: 'it was the inevitable hall-mark of social status' and 'not a sport for poor people'.[72]

If the social composition of the field changed little after the war, however, the gender composition did change, and quite dramatically. During the war, the number of female masters of foxhounds had doubled from six to twelve, and many others took over the reins in an unofficial capacity.[73] With so many men away at war, the proportion of the field comprised of women inevitably increased as well: for example, 70 per cent of the riders with the New Forest Hunt Club during the war were women.[74] Both of these developments survived the social readjustments occasioned by the return to peace. The number of female masters continued to rise steadily in the inter-war years, and although the gender balance of fields inevitably changed with the return of the troops in 1918, women continued to make up a larger proportion of the field than at any time prior to the war.[75]

Once again, the increasing participation of women was associated with changes in female hunting dress. During the 1920s riding astride, so long frowned upon as unbecoming for a lady, at last became socially acceptable. Indeed, just a few decades earlier, one writer had believed that 'the matter of seat and saddle would seem to be so absolutely fixed by ancient custom ... that it is hopeless to expect a revolution in this respect'.[76] Yet by the end of the war this revolution had begun to take place, and through the 1920s and 1930s an increasing number of younger women opted for the cross-saddle.

Not that riding astride was entirely without precedent. The feminist reformer Lady Florence Caroline Dixie had caused something of a scandal in the 1880s when she had taken to wearing breeches and riding astride – though her advocacy came to an abrupt end a few years later when she turned against hunting on ethical grounds, declaring she had 'come to regard with absolute loathing and detestation, any sort or kind or form of sport which is produced by the suffering of animals'.[77] But Lady Dixie was hardly representative of her sex: she was considered by *The Times* to go 'much further' than most women's rights advocates, and hunting and feminism generally had very little in common.[78] Three decades later, a supporter of riding astride had to admit that 'people turn up their eyes and cluck on seeing women and girls riding astride', and added that hunting astride was not taken seriously in the Shires.[79] Indeed, Lord Annaly, Master of the Pytchley from 1902 to 1914, refused to give the white collar to any woman who rode astride.[80] So whilst women in breeches were not entirely unheard of in the Edwardian years, it certainly took a brave soul to ditch her side-saddle prior to the outbreak of war.

The cross-saddle had a number of advantages over the side-saddle. It was less expensive, as were the clothes worn with it, and, being much lighter, it also enabled a woman to ride a smaller and cheaper horse. Mounting and dismounting were easier and it gave the rider better control over the horse. Most importantly, perhaps, the cross-saddle offered greater safety in the event of a fall, as the rider was more likely to be thrown clear.[81] Nonetheless, the conversion to the cross-saddle was by no means total in the inter-war years, as many of the older generation accustomed to riding side-saddle preferred to remain with what they knew. Many found the side-saddle more comfortable and more secure and preferred riding the larger, faster horses that the side-saddle necessitated. The widely held belief that a woman looked more elegant seated side-saddle no doubt inclined many others to eschew the modern trend for the cross-saddle.[82]

Just as with earlier generations of foxhunters, many packs continued to be troubled by periodic shortages of foxes, but by the inter-war years the commercial trade had been entirely suppressed. With the emergence of a significant anti-hunting movement, hunters could no longer afford to discuss matters such as bag foxes and hand-rearing in public, except of course to emphasise their own revulsion at these tactics. In the opinion of the hunting correspondent of *The Times*, 'handling foxes except for the purpose of destroying them is a most distasteful idea'; he also dismissed hand-feeding fox cubs as 'a ghastly travesty of natural foxhunting'.[83] Discussion of these techniques had filled the pages of the *Sporting Magazine* a century earlier; now they were considered beyond the pale for a hunter with any self-respect. Yet despite this, the pressures on masters of foxhounds to provide good sport were as great as ever before, and an extraordinary pamphlet written by Robert Churchward, joint Master of Foxhounds of the South Shropshire Hunt before resigning for reasons of conscience, suggests that finding truly wild foxes to hunt remained a constant problem for hunts in many parts of the country.

By the 1930s, it was unthinkable to advertise publicly for cubs, but Churchward indicated that local hunts could offer assistance of a more gentlemanly nature. He recalled giving this kind of help during his tenure as joint Master to a neighbouring hunt where the supply of foxes had run dry. He ordered his keepers to keep a lookout for a litter of cubs that could be suitably transported across country, and when the selected cubs had reached an age to fend for themselves, he ordered his staff to block up the holes to stop them getting out. The next day he arranged for someone from the neighbouring hunt to come down one Sunday and get the cubs. It was all done very secretly, he recalled, and in conversation the cubs were referred to as 'roses'.[84] The secrecy with which local fox populations were maintained makes it very difficult to gauge the extent of such practices in the 1920s and 1930s, but hunting, as we have seen, necessarily depends on a carefully managed environment and controlled population of huntable animals. Responsible hunting is invariably artificial to some degree, and there was nothing unusual about the measures taken to preserve foxes in the inter-war years. Clearly, however, with the emergence of a noisy opposition to hunting, it became expedient to claim that foxes were naturally occurring in the wild, and that hunters preformed a useful service by limiting their numbers. By the 1930s, the behind-the-scenes work necessary to maintain a huntable population of foxes had become extremely difficult for the hunting community to acknowledge.

As a master of foxhounds that had resigned for reasons of conscience, Churchward was a highly unusual opponent of hunting, yet he was by no means alone in his opposition. Indeed, the anti-hunting movement proved just as resilient to the dislocation of war as hunting itself had been: bills to prohibit hunting and coursing started again as soon as peace returned, though the powerful hunting lobby in Parliament continued to block all change. Beyond the Amendment Act of 1921 which stipulated that coursed animals should have 'a reasonable chance of escape', coursing and hunting in all forms were left unchanged.[85] But whilst the intransigence of Parliament helped to protect field sports, it also served to harden the resolve of anti-hunting reformers, and the anti-hunting movement refused to disappear.

In the inter-war years, the movement coalesced around the newly created League Against Cruel Sports (LACS). The society was founded in 1924 by two members of the RSPCA, Henry Amos and Ernest Bell, both frustrated by the RSPCA's refusal to challenge the hunting and shooting so beloved by the nation's elites. The LACS became the public face of the anti-hunting movement and like its predecessor was avowedly anti-establishment, deriving much of its support from urban intellectuals. It enjoyed the support of a number of Labour MPs in the 1930s, yet proved to be no more successful in securing significant legislative change than its predecessor had been.[86]

Like Henry Salt's League, the LACS focused heavily on coursing and carted-stag hunting, though it broadened its attack to include foxhunting and the hunting of wild deer.[87] It attempted to attract the attention of members of the public by using the personal columns of The Times to advertise its existence, and by organising public meetings wherever public interest existed. In Taunton, for example, meetings to coincide with the starting of the stag-hunting season on Exmoor were regularly held throughout the late 1920s. In familiar language, the League condemned the stag hunt as 'cruel and degrading'. One opponent of the hunt, a Mr Walker King who had started life as a follower of the pack but abandoned the sport for reasons of conscience, dismissed the blooding of children as 'a relic of barbarism unworthy of a civilised people'.[88] What the people of Taunton made either of the hunt, or of LACS's opposition to it, is difficult to say. According to The Times, one such meeting was noisily attended by the hunt's supporters and the League's speakers were greeted with hunting cries and the blowing of horns – but then The Times was hardly an impartial observer of the conflict between sportsmen and abolitionists.[89]

As for the RSPCA, this august institution continued to derive much-needed support from members of the hunting fraternity, and maintained its steadfast opposition to any attempts to meddle with their favoured pastime. After the First World War, the RSPCA elected the Prince of Wales at first as their patron and later as their president – his attachment to shooting and foxhunting notwithstanding.[90] Though the society periodically prosecuted sportsmen for occasional acts of cruelty, it was reluctant to become embroiled in the hunting debate, despite evidence from its own polls that a majority of its membership was opposed to some forms of hunting. The unanimous decision of the Manchester branch to take steps to abolish blood sports was swiftly followed up by a letter from the General Secretary of the RSPCA declaring that the society had no intention of working for the abolition of hunting in any of its forms.[91] Over 70 per cent of RSPCA members polled in 1929 supported a ban on hunting carted deer, yet just two years later an anti-hunting member of a local committee was asked to resign because her attitude annoyed hunting members.[92] In 1938, the Harrogate branch welcomed the patronage of Lord Bingley – joint Master of the Bramham Moor Hunt.[93] As late as 1926, the society refused a bequest of £10,000 which had been made conditional on its opposition to vivisection and blood sports.[94] The RSPCA was unshakeable in its resolve to leave the nation's hunters to pursue their pastime in peace.

It is a measure of the abolitionists' success in politicising the hunting issue, however, that the complacency the hunting community had previously shown towards the anti-hunting campaign dissipated in the inter-war years. Prior to the First World War, the future of hunting had looked so secure that the hunting defence organisations had struggled to mobilise the support of their followers. The emergence of more vocal anti-hunting organisations during the inter-war years persuaded many that their old confidence in the establishment was no longer appropriate, and in December 1930 the inaugural meeting of the British Field Sports Society was held.[95] Near the end of the decade *Baily's Hunting Directory* reported that 'the Society's task of protecting sport against the ignorant but violent attack of anti-sport societies had not grown less'.[96] The society became a highly effective spokesman for the hunting view in Parliament, Whitehall and the press, and flourished with the Duke of Beaufort as chairman and with the active support of the foxhunting and stag-hunting fraternity.

What wider society made of the hunting issue is much less clear. The newspapers split along predictable lines: left-wing papers were unlikely to be sympathetic to hunting, whilst those right of centre had little time for the reformers. In the pages of that bastion of the establishment, *The Times*, for example, hunting was a recognised and fully reported sport. Until the

Royal Buckhounds were disbanded, reports of their activities were regularly published, and the decision to disband was also reported in full.[97] Elsewhere, fixtures were listed, personalities interviewed and good hunts and kills well documented, and though its coverage of hunting declined during the inter-war years, it nevertheless continued to employ its own hunting correspondent. As polling did not develop until the 1950s, what readers made of the issue is unknown. All sides could confidently claim that their view represented the voice of the majority, though it is doubtful how much it mattered to any outside the small wealthy minority that enjoyed hunting, and the urban intellectuals that actively disapproved.

In the century prior to the outbreak of the Second World War, foxhunting continued to increase in popularity, rising numbers of women joined the field, and the sport's place in upper-class society became ever more secure. The disruptions of the First World War, though considerable, proved to be no more than a temporary setback in foxhunting's inexorable rise. At the same time, a noisy opposition to hunting was starting to emerge, yet Parliament remained remarkably unmoved by this vigorous protest movement. Politicians considered nearly thirty bills to prohibit these sports in this half-century: all failed. Half a century of agitation politicised the issue of hunting, but it made not one scrap of difference to the hunters themselves.

CHAPTER FOURTEEN

A New Jerusalem?

Distasteful to the British way of life. (Transport and General Workers'
Union, 1957)

War had never been kind to sportsmen, and the Second World War was no
exception: in most parts of the country hunting, coursing and shooting were
all put on hold. The War Agricultural Committee determined the rations
allocated to each kennel, and the reduced rations upon which they had to
survive inevitably forced some hunts to reduce the size of their packs – a
few even resorted to putting the whole kennel down. Many hunt members
were away fighting or otherwise involved in the war effort, so most hunts
saw a reduction in hunting days, and changes in the landscape added to
the difficulties for those who remained able to hunt: new fixtures such as
aerodromes, barbed wire and camps cut across hunting countries, making it
increasingly difficult to enjoy the old sport. With the austerity that followed
the war many hunts were slow to rebuild their fortunes. Food for kennels
remained in short supply, as did the material needed for the clothing that
hunters traditionally wore.[1] Ulrica Murray Smith, Master of the Quorn from
1959 to 1985, considered that hunting in 1945 'was rather a different picture
than before the war. No one had second horses, and the turn out had certainly
deteriorated; there were fewer people out, and of course, with no petrol,
practically no car followers.'[2] Wherever hunting continued, the fields were
small and the future of the sport generally looked uncertain.

The return to peace in 1945 reopened the divide between the hunters
and their opponents that had emerged so clearly in the inter-war years, and
initially it appeared that the balance of power was shifting. Remarkably,
Churchill's wartime heroism was not enough to spare his party a crushing

electoral defeat and with the end of war came a new government and the promise of a new society. In a landslide victory, the Labour Party was elected to government and set about building hospitals, schools, playgrounds and parks in its land 'fit for heroes'. Undaunted by half a century of failures, there was once again optimism amongst the critics of blood sports that the political tide was about to turn in their favour. The anti-hunting community was fully confident that hunting was at last on its way out.

In 1947 an assured Seymour Cocks, Labour MP for Ashfield, Derbyshire, introduced a private member's bill – A Bill to Protect British Wild Animals from Cruelty – with the intention of outlawing all forms of hunting, except foxhunting, and the coursing of rabbits and hares. The bill was of course strongly supported outside Parliament by the anti-hunting organisations, and many believed it would have government support. A modified version of the bill was debated in the 1948–9 session, but to the reformers' surprise, was strongly defeated by 214 votes to 101, with many on Labour's own front benches voting against it. As a concession to anti-hunting backbenchers, the Home Secretary, James Chuter Ede, agreed to appoint a committee of inquiry to investigate cruelties perpetrated against wild animals, provided a second bill attacking foxhunting was withdrawn. Both sides watched expectantly, waiting to see which way the tide would turn.[3]

The committee's findings, presented in the Scott Henderson report of 1951, were a unanimous victory for the hunters. The committee started from the premiss that wild animals needed to be controlled, and defined its task as establishing the relative cruelty of the different methods of control: hunting, trapping, shooting, gassing and so forth. The report's preamble ominously observed that certain animal welfare organisations urging the end of hunting had a tendency to 'concentrate on the suffering involved in [forms of hunting] and ... to overlook the suffering involved in the alternative methods of control'.[4] The committee was keen to redress this imbalance, to consider the problem in 'its complexities'.[5] Following an exhaustive analysis of each method of pest control, the committee concluded that hunting was less cruel than alternative methods, and therefore advised that it should be allowed to continue.

But the committee went considerably beyond its stated aim of evaluating the relative cruelty of different measures of pest control. Carted-deer hunting, for example, was not of course a form of control. As the committee itself admitted, 'it does not fulfil any useful function'. Nonetheless, it decided it did not involve a 'sufficient degree of cruelty to justify legislation to prohibit it'.[6] Likewise hare-coursing was considered by the committee alongside other forms of hunting, although it was clearly an entertainment, not a form of pest control. In reality, despite its intentions, the committee could not confine its discussion of hunting to the matter of pest control. Although many forms of hunting had the fortuitous benefit of controlling populations of wild animals, by the 1950s hunting was not conducted primarily as a means of control; nor was it the most efficient form of control available. The decision of the Scott Henderson committee to force hunting into the procrustean bed of pest control, whilst politically expedient, was wholly unconvincing in intellectual terms.

The report's critics were far from pleased. Deciding what is cruel and what is not is a highly subjective matter, and the committee's declaration that the hunting and coursing of both wild and tame animals were defensible against the charge of cruelty simply failed to wash. Hunters tend not to see their pastime as cruel, whilst many of those who do not hunt are convinced that it is; each group will answer the charge of cruelty in very different ways. As the founder of the British Field Sports Society, the country's foremost organisation for the preservation of hunting, had astutely commented before the committee had been assembled, 'it all depends who is put on the Committee as to what they will find out'.[7] So who was on the committee? Besides the chairman, John Scott Henderson, seven individuals with varying interests and expertise were called to deliberate the issue, but powerful hunting interests in Parliament had packed the committee with its own men: four of the seven members were either actively involved in hunting or closely connected to the sport. These were Miss Frances Pitt, Master of a Shropshire hunt; Major L. P. Pugh, vet to the West Kent Foxhounds; W. J. Brown, a regular contributor to the hunting community's foremost publication, the *Field*; and Dr Burn-Murdoch, a keen fisherman.[8] The remaining three members were a union representative, a zoologist, and the editor of the *Countryman*. No farmers and none of the anti-hunting societies were represented. Indeed, in contrast to the four representatives of the hunting community, there was only one from the animal welfare movement – the zoologist, Professor P. B. Medawar, a member of the Universities Federation for Animal Welfare, an organisation that campaigned for the better treatment of animals in zoos, farms and laboratories but which had no public position on hunting.[9] It was probably inevitable therefore that the committee reached the conclusions it did. For all the appearance of a neutral and expert investigation into the question of hunting, the report's conclusions were effectively foregone.

However flawed, the report no doubt came as a relief to the Labour government. It was by now clear that anti-hunting measures would not be quickly and quietly pushed through a docile Parliament. The government's refusal to endorse Cocks's bill stemmed from its perceived need to retain support in rural areas, and it was far from certain that it wanted to provoke conflict on the rather minor question of foxes and hares. The Scott Henderson report usefully quieted the anti-hunting lobby and enabled the government to devote full attention to its reformist legislative agenda.

Yet although the legal future of hunting looked secure in the early 1950s, the foxhunting community nonetheless faced a number of significant obstacles in the years following the peace. Through the nineteenth and first half of the twentieth centuries, the most serious problem for foxhunters had been a shortage of foxes, and though this became rather less of a problem after the war, new difficulties simply emerged instead. In the post-war period, both agriculture and the landscape were rapidly changing and the large expanses of land that had traditionally made foxhunting such fine sport were becoming difficult to find. Foxhunters have always preferred pasture to arable, but large areas of pasture had been ploughed during the war in a desperate attempt to increase the nation's output of food. With the coming of peace most of that land stayed under the plough. Changes in agriculture added to the foxhunters' difficulties. The farmers' preferences for large, open fields and their increased use of monoculture resulted in the removal of the hedgerows that had provided the mounted field with much of its interest and challenges.[10] The spread of chemical herbicides, pesticides and fertilisers interfered with foxes' scent, and some huntsmen feared for the future of the sport in the face of these modern developments. Some of the finest south midlands hunts – the Vale of White Horse, the Old Berkshire, the Vale of Aylesbury and the Heythrop – were hit hard by changes in agriculture, in particular by the switch from pasture to arable, as were many less illustrious packs in the provinces.[11] It all served to create an environment that was very much less favourable for hunting.

The problems posed by changes in agriculture, however, were as nothing compared with those posed by road-building and urbanisation. A host of building projects – new roads and motorways, airfields, factories, new towns, golf clubs, gravel pits, sewerage works – as well as creeping urbanisation carved up former hunting countries and took away tranches of land over which earlier generations had hunted. In the south midlands, for example, the building of the M4 cut through the Duke of Beaufort's once great hunting country in Gloucestershire and Wiltshire, not only dividing it in two, but also removing hundreds of acres of land.[12] The growth of Milton Keynes marked the end of the Whaddon Chase Hunt, which only remained viable by amalgamating with its neighbour, Bicester and Warden Hill country. In the west midlands, the building of the M5 and the expansion of Coventry eventually caused the North Warwickshire Hunt to disband, and the land that was left to hunt over was distributed amongst the neighbouring countries.[13] In the south of England, many of the pressures of advancing urbanisation were particularly

acute, and in some places the local hunt managed the most surprising adaptations with the urban world that was springing up around it. The Enfield
Chace Hunt, for example, hunted right on the boundary of Greater London,
and parts of the country hunted were flush with the London Underground's
Central Line.[14] Ulrica Murray Smith reflected at the end of a long hunting
career that the hounds 'certainly have more difficulties to contend with …
both huntsmen and Field Masters have a far trickier job to perform today,
and I would say that it is much more of a challenge to cross the country'.[15]
Nonetheless, despite the difficulties posed by an urbanising environment,
hunting continued to flourish, as each hunt made its own adjustments to the
changing local landscape. Modern foxhunting was by now two centuries old,
but the growth of foxhunting in post-war Britain was a triumph of adaptation
rather than tradition.

Nor did the obstacles faced by the hunting community impede the steady
expansion of the sport. At the same time as changes in the environment were
making it more difficult for hunts to continue their operations, the number of
men and women opting to ride to hounds actually increased. Fields remained
small through most of the 1940s, but by the 1950s an estimated 20,000 people
were hunting each season.[16] Rising incomes and greater social mobility both
helped to swell the ranks of hunters, and much of the growth was achieved
by a burgeoning middle class joining the hunting field for the first time. Many
of the newcomers were women and girls, who continued to join the field in
increasing numbers. After the war, the cross-saddle became almost universal
and women typically made up about 50 per cent of the field – often more
on weekdays when men were more likely to be at work.[17] In order to raise
funds, hunts needed a steady supply of subscriptions, and this encouraged
even the most conservative of institutions to look beyond their usual social
constituency for new subscribers. As one hunting stalwart put it, 'people from
outside the foxhunting classes' were starting to hunt.[18]

In the mid-1970s, there were 189 hunts in England and Wales, and the
number riding to hounds had risen to an estimated 50,000 each year.[19] There
were in addition some forty packs of harriers, hunting both hare and fox, as
well as beagles and fell packs, which were followed on foot. Hunting packs,
particularly in the perennially popular old Shires, were frequently oversub-
scribed, and long waiting lists faced those wishing to join. Even in the less
fashionable hunting counties the packs continued to thrive, and the escalating
costs of hunting in the 1970s appeared to do nothing to diminish the numbers
wishing to be involved. One estimate in 1974 was that the cost of maintaining
a horse in livery had doubled in the past decade and put the annual bill for
two days' hunting throughout the season at just over £400.[20] Of course, prices
varied widely according to what kind of country was being hunted and were

considerably lower outside the fashionable Shires. Nonetheless, the combined expenses of subscriptions and caps, horse ownership and hunting dress served to keep foxhunting a socially exclusive pastime, just as they had for earlier generations. Little surprise that one farm student in the 1970s found 'a haughty demeanour about the mounted field' which he strongly disliked.[21]

Paradoxically, however, despite these rising costs, hunting was becoming more open than at any time previously. This greater openness was achieved not primarily through an expansion of the mounted field, but through changes in the way in which hunts related to the rural communities in which they operated.

The appearance of the foxhunt had never failed to cause a commotion. The large pack of hounds, fine horses and fabulously dressed riders, all racing at speed across country formed a stirring visual display, sparking the interest of the local community. On the day of the hunt, farmhands had sometimes hung around in places where the hunt was thought likely to pass in the hope of earning a little spare cash from opening and shutting gates, or maybe even from informing the huntsman which way the fox had passed. The hunt, however, took little interest in these small services. Prior to the 1950s, the foxhunters had assiduously sought the co-operation of the farmers whose land they wanted to cross, but beyond that shown very little concern for how they were viewed by the rural community. Foxhunting was an exclusive pastime for those who rode to hounds, and the sport was not conceived as part of a common culture shared with the broader rural community.

The foxhunters' response to the appearance of car followers in the early part of the twentieth century is indicative of this attitude. When cars first appeared on British roads, masters of hounds had been concerned that the fumes masked the foxes' scent, and their prime concern was to ensure that cars did not interfere with the hunt.[22] In 1908, *Baily's Hunting Directory* reported that some hunts were refusing to allow motor cars to turn up at the meet, and asking their subscribers to park away from the meet and hack the final mile or two.[23] Inevitably, these attempts were unsuccessful, and by the late 1920s one keen hunter observed that 'if you go to the Meet you will observe a concourse of cars blocking up the highway for about half a mile'.[24] Nor were these cars simply transporting horses and riders to the meet and then returning home: many drivers were endeavouring to 'hunt from the chassis', a sport which one contemporary thought called for 'great powers of endurance, keen sight, quick decision at sharp corners, and a determination to turn the fox with precision and finesse'.[25] Few foxhunters, however, shared this writer's enthusiasm for 'hunting from the chassis'. According to *Baily's*, 'motor cars are an ever-increasing source of trouble and difficulty to Masters of Hounds' with their tendency to head foxes, get in front of the pack, and 'in these and other ways, including noise and smell, [of] spoiling sport'.[26] Others simply referred to the 'car problem'.[27] In the opinion of the foxhunting writer Reginald Summerhays, 'motor cars joining in the chase and heading foxes' was one of the less favourable sides of hunting in the 1930s.[28] By that date, it had become apparent that car followers were there to stay, and it was a development which most in the hunting community viewed in a very dim light. Lord Stalbridge, Master of the Fernie in the 1920s, could mutter ungenerously about the problems caused to the real hunters by 'the unemployed on bicycles and ladies in limousines' without worrying about whom he might alienate by such comments.[29] Foxhunting was for those who rode to hounds, and few considered it something to be shared by those without the means, interest or inclination to follow the sport from the saddle.

No doubt many of those who rode to hounds after the war felt much the same about the 'unemployed on bicycles and ladies in limousines' as those who had ridden in the inter-war years, but in post-war Britain they were very much less likely to go on the record as saying so. In the face of increasing hostility towards hunting in some parts of society, most hunts felt pressured to welcome the interest of non-riders. Those who did not ride were brought into the heart of the hunt's activities by a new institution: the hunt supporters' club. Though partly inspired by the need for fund-raising that most hunts experienced, part of the remit of hunt supporters' clubs was also to encourage the participation of those who did not ride – whether they followed on foot, by bicycle or car – and to foster stronger relations between the hunt and the broader rural community.

By the end of the 1960s, car followers were a permanent feature of every hunt and in contrast to the pre-war period most hunts claimed (publicly at least) to enjoy their support. For example, Captain David Keith, Master of the Quorn in the 1960s, told the editor of *Horse and Hounds*, 'We get a large number of cars following a hunt which is bound to increase the possibility of a fox being headed, and also causes many hold-ups to through traffic on the roads, for which the Hunt may be blamed.' He continued, however, that he 'would be the last person to discourage car-followers. Their numbers reflect the great interest in foxhunting still evident throughout Leicestershire. For example, when we met in Loughborough a crowd of about 15,000 attended the meet.'[30] Even the most exclusive hunt clubs were learning that the inconvenience of car followers was considerably outweighed by the benefits they conferred. In an era of increasing moral opposition to hunting, it was not just the farmers' support that was needed: hunting needed the broadest possible social sanction, and supporters' clubs were a valuable way of gaining such support.

And with this shift in attitude, hunting did at last become the socially inclusive sport that it had always claimed to be. In the late 1970s, the mounted

14. Foot followers of the fashionable Pytchley Hunt in Northamptonshire and Leicestershire. The appeal of spotting the fox before the mounted pack drew increasing numbers of foot followers into hunting after the war, and as foxhunting became ever more controversial, so the foxhunters' earlier criticism of foot followers became ever more muted.

field remained as exclusive as it had ever been, yet most hunts could plausibly claim that a wide cross-section of society was drawn in to the activities of the local hunt. As the editor of *Shooting Times and Country Magazine* wrote:

> Take a survey of a field, mounted, on foot, and car-borne, and you will come up with a cross-section of the population; all trades, types, so-called classes and stratas of society will be represented, each as good as the other and all bound together by a common link – a love for the best of sports.[31]

There is, of course, a certain degree of romanticisation in this account, yet it contains a fair degree of truth. In the 1970s, the different social classes did not meet at the foxhunt on terms of equality, yet meet there they certainly did.

While foxhunting was busy recasting itself as a rural sport with a broad social basis of support, its opponents were no less active. The anti-hunting lobby was put on the back foot by the setback of the Scott Henderson report, yet in no time they started up once again, just as noisy and determined as before. And with the advent of opinion polling, it was becoming more difficult for hunting's defenders to claim that they had a majority of the public on their side.

The first public opinion poll enquiring into views on hunting was conducted by Gallup for the *News Chronicle* in 1958; it showed that 65 per cent of the population approved of the abolition of stag-hunting, and 53 per cent of foxhunting.[32] Women were slightly more likely to favour abolition than men, as were those from lower income groups. Two polls of opinions on deer-hunting taken a decade later showed a slight increase in public opposition to the sport, and also revealed that hostility was greatest in urban areas.[33] The public were slower to turn against foxhunting, but the 53 per cent that had objected to it in 1958 had risen to 60 per cent by 1978, and by the early 1980s an RSPCA poll indicated that over 70 per cent of those questioned supported a ban.[34] Repeatedly, public opinion polls indicated that the strongest support for the abolition of foxhunting came from those who were female, lived in urban areas and had a low income, though it was by no means confined to this section of the population. Labour and Liberal voters were more strongly opposed to foxhunting than Conservatives, and the young more opposed to hunting than older generations. Beginning with the radical fringe, the anti-hunting and anti-coursing case was rapidly becoming a mainstream view. It was, as its critics observed, still largely based in towns, but the anti-hunting agenda could no longer be dismissed as the preserve of a handful of freethinking cranks and vegetarians.

15. Criticism of foxhunting refused to disappear after 1945 and the anti-hunting organisations became increasingly adept at expressing this criticism.

Yet despite the discernible shift away from hunting by the population at large, that bastion of the animal protection movement, the RSPCA, was as slow to change its position as ever. Indeed, when the RSPCA was called to give evidence to the Scott Henderson committee, it had spoken in favour of foxhunting, and the committee's final report had thought it 'significant that the RSPCA consider that the cruelty involved in shooting foxes is such as to make it an unsatisfactory substitute for hunting, and that they would therefore prefer hunting ... to continue'.[35] The pro-hunting conclusions of the Scott Henderson final report increased the confidence of the RSPCA in their own position, and late in the 1950s the society issued a fresh policy statement on hunting adopted at the Annual General Meeting. It opened by declaring that 'The RSPCA cannot approve of hunting for sport', but continued by specifying that the society had no objections to foxhunting, as it was the least cruel form of ensuring the necessary control of this farmyard pest. Their statement, however, though it helpfully clarified the society's position on this contentious matter, did not achieve what the society's leadership had hoped for: an end to discussion by its rank and file of the place of foxhunting in British society. Indeed, the RSPCA's new statement simply highlighted the breach between the society's leadership and its rank and file members, and left many within the movement deeply dissatisfied. Anti-hunting members questioned whether the need for control was not a little overstated: were the foxhunters after all not in the business of maintaining a stable population of foxes, rather than reducing them for good and all? As for the RSPCA's assertions about the relative cruelty of controlling foxes by hunting or by shooting, this was by now something of an old chestnut, and was a matter upon which hunters and their opponents could simply not agree.

In the 1960s, a handful of discontented members stepped up their anti-hunting campaign, but the RSPCA's ruling body – a council consisting of forty-four members – swiftly moved to close down the discussion, and expelled a number of its particularly troublesome anti-hunting members. But this attempt by the higher echelons of the RSPCA's management to prevent the reopening of debate was only partially successful, ultimately hardening their opponents' resolve and encouraging them to explore new ways of changing the RSPCA's policy on hunting. In 1970, the dissatisfied anti-hunters formed a Reform Group with just one goal: to remove those council members sympathetic to hunting and force the leadership to take their views on board.

In an attempt to bring the divisive matter to a close, the council set up an independent inquiry in 1973, under the chairmanship of Charles Sparrow, QC. His report, published the following year, proposed no more than reducing the number on the council from forty-four to twenty-two, yet this simple proposal effectively resolved the rift that had divided the RSPCA for the previous two decades. The newly elected, reduced council was a much better reflection of the society's membership: about a third of its members were directly linked to the Reform Group, and many others were sympathetic to its cause. When the policy statement on hunting came up for debate before this new council in 1976, it was passed unanimously. Their new statement read simply: 'The RSPCA is opposed to any hunting of animals with hounds.' Moreover, the old allowances for foxhunting were now abandoned: 'The RSPCA is not persuaded that foxhunting is an effective method of control in any circumstances.'[36] This was roundly dismissed by the British Field Sports Society as a 'hasty and ill-conceived statement'. In the opinion of the Hunt Saboteurs' Association, however, it was 'a major step forward' and 'a blow to the men in pink'.[37] When Richard Ryder, a long-time campaigner against blood sports, became chairman of the RSPCA in the following year, the policy shift was complete. In 1977, the RSPCA, which had long attempted to remain neutral on the issue, finally declared itself to be against all forms of hunting and polls of its membership in the 1980s charted a steadily increasing disapproval of hunting.

The loss of the RSPCA's support for hunting was a significant blow for the hunting community, though it did little to quell the popularity of the sport. Despite the increasingly acrimonious public debate that surrounded hunting, the actual sport was changing little, and the local hunt continued to enjoy the committed and firm support of a substantial minority in every rural community.

As ever, the royal household retained its close links with the hunting world. Its ancient connections with the sport were revived by Princess Anne in the early 1970s, after an unusual two decades in which the royal family had had almost no involvement in any form of hunting. But by the 1970s, foxhunting had become a contentious activity, and the princess's involvement was quickly transformed into a political matter. The League Against Cruel Sports denounced her participation, though the opinion poll they commissioned – revealing that 48 per cent of the population thought she should not hunt, whilst 37 per cent thought she should – was perhaps less condemnatory than they might have wished.[38] Meanwhile, erstwhile supporters of hunting applauded the princess's decision to hunt, and condemned the sermonising and interfering of those it did not concern. The Times, for example, declared that 'the Princess should be granted the widest freedom to follow her own bent and shape her own life'.[39] The matter was even discussed in Parliament, when the Labour MP for Rugby, William Price, asked the Home Secretary whether 'next time he goes across to Buckingham Palace he would explain to Princess Anne that the vast majority of our people are violently opposed to blood sports and are appalled at her determination to bestow royal patronage on acts of blatant cruelty' – a claim that was not quite borne out by the League's opinion poll.[40] Despite the derision of the anti-hunting lobby, she continued, with Captain Mark Phillips, to hunt throughout the 1970s.[41]

Price's interjection in Parliament also reveals the ongoing interest of a core of Labour MPs in the matter of hunting. Following the publication of the Scott Henderson report, bills to abolish hunting and coursing temporarily abated. They returned in the late 1950s, but for the next few decades Parliament remained as implacably opposed to reform as ever. A private member's bill opposed to stag-hunting was presented at three parliamentary sessions at the end of the decade, but it was offered no time by the pro-hunting Conservative government and was never debated.[42] The Conservatives remained in power throughout the 1950s and early 1960s, and held steadfastly to their long-standing hunting sympathies. The party was keen to emphasise that hunting and coursing were safe in their hands.

In such unpromising times, the anti-hunting movement abandoned its attempts to prohibit foxhunting and wisely turned its attention to hare-coursing instead, singled out in the late nineteenth century as one of the 'spurious sports'. The Humanitarian League had been confident that a plan of public education would consign hare-coursing to history, but a couple of decades' work had accomplished nothing and, nearly a century on, a new generation of opponents once again turned their attention to this, the least popular and least justifiable of the field sports. In 1964, the League Against Cruel Sports launched a fresh campaign, widely backed by public opinion and strongly supported in the House as well. In 1966, eighty-three MPs signed a motion declaring the sport 'a disgrace to civilisation', and in the same session a private member's bill to abolish hare-coursing was presented by the Labour MP for Liverpool Walton, Eric Heffer.[43] An NOP opinion poll of the following year indicated that a mere 12 per cent of the population approved of coursing, whilst 77 disapproved, and 75 per cent thought that the government should support the bill.[44] Yet despite this strong public backing for the bill, Parliament yet again showed itself to be the champion of the establishment's interests in all matters concerning field sports. Heffer's bill was debated on a second reading in 1967, but was talked out, and with that the bill was lost. Fresh bills were presented as private member's bills every year in the late 1960s and early 1970s, but all met a similar fate. Although the anti-coursing lobby could justly claim to have public support for its cause, translating public opinion into successful legislation was proving to be no easy matter.

The failure of these bills, all strongly supported by the public at large, may be put down to a number of factors. Perhaps most significant was the demographic bias inherent in Parliament itself. Opinion polls repeatedly showed that British society was not uniformly opposed to coursing and hunting. Those most likely to support the abolition of foxhunting were young, female and working class. Parliament, of course, was filled with, older, wealthy men – just the demographic that one poll after another identified as more likely to favour hunting. Hardly less important was the hunting community's increasingly vigorous and professional defence of the sport. The British Field Sports Society had long been something of a private gentleman's club for keen hunters and shooters, but as the anti-hunting clamour became more insistent, it effectively turned to the political arena to defend its interests. Unlike the numerous anti-hunting organisations, the hunting lobby was united under one banner and successfully grasped the necessity of exploiting parliamentary procedures to further its aims. For example, anti-coursing bills were generally presented on one of the twenty Friday afternoons set aside each session for private members' time. A bill's opponents needed only to talk at length, preferably on the bill preceding the anti-coursing bill, but during the coursing bill as well if necessary, to sink it at the first opportunity. To assist Conservative MPs who wished to sink anti-coursing bills, the British Field Sports Society took responsibility for preparing up to five hours' worth of information on *any* subject at short notice.[45] Such support was invaluable to Conservative MPs throughout the early 1970s and certainly helped to halt many pieces of anti-coursing legislation in their tracks.

The hunting lobby's chances of continuing to stall anti-coursing legislation looked far weaker, however, when Labour returned to government in 1975 and promoted its own anti-coursing bill.[46] As it was a government-sponsored, rather than private member's, bill, its opponents could not depend on their old strategy of talking it out, and when the bill passed its third reading with a Commons majority of 183 for and 82 against, and passed to the Lords, the prospect of reform had never looked more certain. Once again, however, the British Field Sports Society proved their sophisticated grasp of political procedures and devised a successful strategy for blocking the bill's progress.

When the bill was passed to the Lords, the British Field Sports Society swiftly called for an inquiry to investigate the issue outside the charged atmosphere of the House. Their spokesman in the Lords, Lord Denham, the Conservative Chief Whip, put the case for an inquiry in the following terms:

> This Bill seeks to remove an ancient freedom ... I do not believe that Members of any government should seek to remove such a freedom ... without letting it be seen that they have taken every step and made every inquiry reasonably necessary to assure themselves that it is right to do so. And this Her Majesty's government have not done. A Select

> Committee of your Lordships' House, with the right to hear evidence,
> would go some way to repairing this omission.[47]

The request for an inquiry was innocuous enough and duly accepted by the
government. But in a repeat of history, the select committee was constituted in such a fashion that it was unlikely to recommend the abolition of
coursing: it was composed of four Conservative peers, two Labour peers
and one bishop. After due deliberation, the four Conservatives voted that
'the Bill should not proceed', whilst the other three voted that it should.
The recommendation of the majority was of course accepted and the bill
lapsed. The British Field Sports Society was fully justified in concluding that
'the task of using parliamentary tactics to the full in an effort to frustrate
the passage of the bill ... was carried out with success'.[48] Coursing was a
sport with minority support, but the failure of the 1975 bill demonstrated
conclusively that it was Parliament, and not the wishes of the majority,
that would determine its future. When coursing was threatened, the entire
hunting community came to its defence fearful that a successful attack here
might prove to be the thin end of the wedge. However broadly constituted,
the hunting fraternity remained a statistical minority, but events proved once
more that it punched well above its weight.

The failure of the 1975 Anti-Coursing Bill largely brought an end to
private member's bills to abolish coursing. In all, thirteen were presented
before 1975, three of them government bills, and all sank as quickly as
their predecessors. No one even attempted to introduce an anti-foxhunting
measure; Parliament's response was considered too predictable. The private
member's bill had proved itself to be a strategy offering hunting's opponents
little promise of successful reform.

With Parliament so implacably opposed to any legislation, the opponents
of hunting inevitably looked beyond Parliament for ways to further their
ends. The older pressure groups, such as the League Against Cruel Sports
and the National Society for the Abolition of Cruel Sports (founded in
1932), continued to campaign for legislation in the way they knew best
– by identifying politically useful incidents and circulating details to the
press, commissioning and publicising polls, and advertising in the national
press.[49] The most striking feature of the 1960s and 1970s, however, was the
emergence of a new generation of protesters willing to get involved in direct
action: the hunt saboteurs. Within a decade, the hunt saboteurs had changed
the face not only of the anti-hunting movement, but even, in some areas, of
hunting itself.

The saboteurs had appeared in the early 1960s. The first group was formed
in Devon in 1963 with the aim of disrupting the activities of the Devon and

16. The new face of hunting opposition in the 1960s: the saboteurs – activists who took to the hunting field, rather than the streets, to proclaim their opposition to killing animals for sport.

Somerset Staghounds, and the movement expanded steadily in following years. Throughout the 1960s, numerous autonomous groups sprang up in the regions, and by the early 1970s there were seventeen active groups, southern university towns being their stronghold. The organisation was devoted primarily to sabotaging hunts by lawful means.

The saboteurs engaged mostly in low-level disruptive tactics designed to disarm the hunters and to disturb the horses and hounds. They assembled at the start of the hunt, holding placards, chanting, blowing horns and generally making their presence known. Squibs, crackers, smoke bombs and aerosols were used in an attempt to alarm horses; and anti-mate dog spray was squirted at the hounds to put them off the scent. Sometimes an advance guard of saboteurs sprayed woodlands with citronella, lemon grass and eucalyptus before the hunt began, again to put the hounds off the scent. They were memorably dismissed by Mr Justice Milmo, who rode with the Crawley and Horsham Hounds, Sussex, as a 'disorderly rabble', like 'some kinds of apes and baboons that one sees at the zoo'.[50] But the 'baboons' were nonetheless effective in their aims, and by the 1970s *The Times*' reports of the annual Boxing Day hunts contained as much detail on the antics of the hunt saboteurs as they did on the hunt.[51]

The hunt saboteurs were a minority group, yet their actions helped to change the tenor of the conflict over hunting in a discernible and long-lasting way. Hunting had always had friends in powerful places, and anti-hunting pressure groups had long been aware that this placed formidable obstacles in the way of abolition; nonetheless, for most of the twentieth century, hunting was not viewed in the British media through the prism of class. One of the most important legacies of the saboteur movement was to bring this issue to the very forefront of debate. The responsibility for this shift, however, perhaps lies less with the saboteurs than with the judiciary, and the justice they meted out when conflicts reached the courts. Though the hunt saboteurs were committed to disrupting hunts by legal means, their actions were liable to be interpreted as a breach of the peace, and they sometimes found themselves on the wrong side of the law. But in the cat-and-mouse fighting that periodically broke out between hunters and saboteurs it was not only the 'sabs' who broke the law.[52] It was not unknown for angered hunt supporters to rise to the saboteurs' provocation and take matters into their own hands, though when they did, magistrates sometimes struggled to treat the men in pink as the common criminals they had become. Throughout the 1970s, the courts displayed considerably greater leniency to hunters who had broken the law than to saboteurs committing similar crimes. Time and time again, powerful, vested interests rallied to hunting's cause when hunters found themselves in the dock, bringing the imbalance of power between the hunters and their opponents into sharp relief. It rapidly shifted the terms of the hunting debate, deflecting attention from animal cruelty and legitimate means of pest control, and focusing it on the class injustices inherent in British society.

The well-publicised case of Mrs Valerie Waters provides a vivid illustration of the prejudices that the hunt saboteurs encountered at court. Waters, a 45-year-old company director and member of the Hunt Saboteurs' Association, had attended the Atherstone Hunt with, she claimed, the sole aim of 'saving the lives of wild animals and not to cause trouble'. Yet the saboteurs' peaceful protest turned nasty when Waters was personally attacked by four members of the hunt, who poured oil over her car, sprayed paint on it, let down the tyres, and hit her in the face with a fox's brush. She not unreasonably decided to take her attackers to court, though she and her supporters were more than a little taken aback with the 'justice' she received there. Her four attackers were found guilty of breaching the peace and bound over in the sum of £50. One was also ordered to pay a further £30 in fines and compensation for damaging Waters's car. The chair of the bench, Mr Walter Chappell, however, then turned on Waters herself, declaring, 'It is not for you to take the law into your own hands. You have no right to interfere with people who enjoy foxhunting, which is quite legal.' He ordered that she too be bound over in the sum of £50, and warned she could face prison for up to six months if she refused. The case was adjourned.[53] Waters and her supporters were incensed that the victim of an assault and property crime and the main prosecution witness should be charged with a breach of the peace, and she refused to be bound over. True to their word, the magistrates sentenced her to prison for one month, and when she appealed to the Crown Court against their decision, the court dismissed her appeal.[54] The case left the saboteurs smarting, but it was not unique. Just three years later, two prosecution witnesses in a case against two men who were accused of assaulting them were meted out the same justice. Melvyn Dallas and Keith Bird, both of whom faced no charge, refused to be bound over, arguing it was 'unjust that prosecution witnesses should be penalised and subjected to the same penalty imposed on a defendant'. Mrs Whitehead, the chairman, replied, 'You will be sent to prison for six months or until such time as you have made up your minds and are prepared to be bound over.'[55] And go to jail they did. A partial judiciary spared many a short-tempered hunter from the full rigours of the law, but it is doubtful that it served the long-term interests of the hunting cause. The unequal treatment that the saboteurs and the hunters received from the courts during the 1970s made the dispute more public and more acrimonious and helped to inject a dose of class war into the hunting debate. This widened the appeal of the anti-hunting cause, and enabled it to harness the support of large numbers of men and women not interested in animal cruelty *per se*, but attracted by its call for class justice. And though it brought little comfort to the anti-hunting lobby in the 1970s, this development did in time prove to be of far greater value to the anti-hunting movement than to the hunters.

The hunt saboteurs helped to raise the profile of the anti-hunting movement, adding unexpected colour to an old conflict and ensuring that hunting rarely remained out of the news for long, but many outside the saboteur movement were doubtful that smoke bombs and aerosols would ever do much to hasten the end of hunting. The older and more established anti-hunting organisations remained convinced that nothing but effective legislation would abolish hunting, and continued to lobby the political parties for a clear commitment to a change in the law.

During the 1970s, the Labour Party emerged clearly as the most probable anti-hunting party. It had offered its support to three anti-coursing bills, but being a weak minority government, was unable to shift a Parliament that was still strongly opposed to legislation. By the end of the decade, however, anti-hunting Labour politicians had learnt important lessons from these repeated failures, and began to steer the party towards a stronger position. With so many MPs firmly opposed to any interference in blood sports, anti-hunting legislation would never succeed through private member's bills: it needed firm government backing. Through the spring and summer of 1978, the party's Home Policy Committee, with Tony Benn in the chair, debated the possibility of adopting an anti-hunting stance, and eventually passed a resolution to oppose all forms of hunting.[56] The National Executive Committee accepted the resolution, and it went into the 1979 election manifesto. The Labour Party was finally armed with the tools needed for abolition.

But 1979 was of course an election victory for Margaret Thatcher and ushered in a Conservative government. Just as the Labour Party realised what it needed to do, it was cast out into the political wilderness. In the next two decades, the occasional private member's bill was presented to Parliament, but all real hope of successful legislation had been lost. For the next two decades, the conflict over hunting, though ever increasing, was largely conducted outside the political arena.

CHAPTER FIFTEEN

A Last Reprieve

The reality is that cruelty for fun is no longer acceptable to the overwhelming majority of people in this country. (Tony Benn)

We should strongly avoid narrow-minded intolerance which could force people unnecessarily into becoming criminals and outcasts. We should resist the temptation to insist everyone must conform to what a majority opinion poll says. (Chris Patten)[1]

The Thatcher years brought everything that those with an interest in hunting had either hoped or feared. Margaret Thatcher had grown up in the small market town of Grantham, nestling in the heart of the nation's premier hunting country. Although she had never been personally involved in hunting, there could be no mistaking where her allegiances lay. The idea of using parliamentary procedures to interfere in the recreations of law-abiding citizens was anathema to her, and the hunting community was rightfully confident of the future of foxhunting after her election to office in 1979.

Even in these inauspicious circumstances, the anti-hunting lobby never entirely gave up hope of a legislative breakthrough. Early in Thatcher's first government, Lord Houghton, chairman of the League Against Cruel Sports, former Labour MP and now an active member of the Upper House, hijacked the government's Wildlife and Countryside Bill by introducing anti-hunting amendments during the committee stage in the Lords. Predictably enough, his amendments were swiftly rejected by his fellow peers. On the bill's return to the Commons, four Labour MPs proposed a further amendment to prohibit the 'use of any hound or any other dog, or dogs, for the purpose of hunting, coursing, killing or taking any such animal', though this too failed.

In a last ditch attempt to convert the bill into a measure that at least banned coursing and carted-stag hunting, foxhunting, the most strongly supported of the blood sports, was removed from the bill's remit altogether. This amendment was considerably more palatable to MPs. But even this failed yet again, though by just one vote.[2]

With the prospects of governmental reform looking so unpromising in the Thatcher years, the anti-hunting brigade directed most of its energies to attacking hunting outside the legislative arena. Their most effective strategy during the 1980s was a drive to persuade private landowners to prohibit hunting on their estates. This was already a well-established policy, begun by the League Against Cruel Sports in the early 1960s.[3] At that time, the League had begun purchasing parcels of land on Exmoor, which though small were well placed to disrupt the activities of the hunt, for each time one of the six packs that hunted there crossed League property, the League sought to prosecute for trespass. The hunters were therefore faced with the unwelcome choice of either stopping the hunt mid-chase, or continuing the hunt with the risk of a costly trespass action. For the League, the policy quickly proved its worth as both an irritant to the hunters and a useful source of good publicity, and it sought to expand the policy wherever possible: by the middle of the 1970s, the League owned twenty-four lots of land, and by the early 1980s this had increased to thirty-three.[4] In addition, the League lent its support and expertise to private landowners who wished to bring cases against hunts for trespass.

In the following decade the anti-hunting organisations began to exploit the policy far more ruthlessly, setting their sights on persuading large landowners to withhold hunting rights on their land rather than following the more expensive policy of buying plots themselves. Their greatest success came with the decision of the largest single owner of farmland in the private sector – the Co-operative Party – to ban hunting on all its estates. Anti-hunting members of the Co-op Wholesale Society had organised themselves into a group within the movement in the spring of 1981. Calling themselves the Co-operators Against Blood Sports, they drew upon the finances and expertise of the League Against Cruel Sports to mobilise a campaign against hunting on their land.[5] Less than a year's campaigning resulted in the Co-op roundly endorsing a motion to ban hunting on its land in February 1982. With the society owning some 38,000 acres of farmland, it was estimated that about 10 per cent of the country's 200-odd packs would be affected by the ban, with the impact being greatest on packs in the east midlands and south-west.[6] For the anti-hunting movement, the Co-op's decision remains one of the high points of their campaign, but the ban was viewed with predictable horror by the hunting community, and many turned out to demonstrate at the Co-operative Movement's annual parliament in May that year. A petition criticising the ban garnered 80,000 signatures and was handed to delegates, and dark threats of the death sentence that the ban passed on thousands of horses, hounds and jobs were issued.[7] The Co-op was unmoved and the ban remained in place for the next two decades.

The Co-op Society ban had been accomplished almost effortlessly, and left the anti-hunting organisations riding high on a wave of confidence. It looked, momentarily, as though those opposed to hunting might impose their beliefs on the hunters, even in the face of parliamentary intransigence. The hunt, after all, depended upon the good will of the nation's landowners. Might not more of them be persuaded to follow the Co-op's lead? County councils, often owning considerable tracts of farmland, were an obvious target, and anti-hunting organisations soon began petitioning local councils and offering advice to councillors eager to press for a ban in their area.

The policy had begun in the early 1980s, and there had even been a handful of successes before the Co-op ban. In September 1980, for example, councillors in Brighton voted overwhelmingly to ban hunting on their land.[8] The highly publicised Co-op ban of 1982 clearly added momentum to the movement, for a number of local councils instituted bans in quick succession following that landmark decision. Mid-Glamorgan, Humberside and Derbyshire passed motions to abolish hunting on council-owned land.[9] In South Glamorgan, seventy farms, covering nearly 15 per cent of the Glamorgan Hunt's country, were covered by a ban.[10] One councillor there dismissed foxhunting as a 'cruel, barbaric, and unnecessary so-called sport ... a stupid and ignorant activity'.[11] In all, fifteen councils, all of them Labour controlled, had banned hunting from their land by the end of 1982.[12] As Labour strongholds are traditionally located in urban rather than rural areas, however, the practical implications of some of these bans were extremely limited. In the London borough of Islington, for example, the council's ban on foxhunting on its land in July 1982 was undoubtedly an ideological statement rather than a practical measure. As the *Horse and Hound* drily noted, the council's ban was about 'as relevant as banning polo in Greenland'.[13]

Taken as a whole, the policy was never more than a partial success despite the occasional dazzling victory. County councils tended to reflect the proclivities of the communities they served. Thus urban, Labour-controlled councils supported bans on hunting, whilst rural councils dominated by Conservatives did not. But of course, it was precisely the latter councils that controlled much of the country's best hunting land, and their enduring support for hunting fatally undermined this attack on the sport. In Leicestershire, the heart of hunting country, a particularly hard fought battle between the hunt and its opponents was waged. As the antis had realised, a ban here would be of great symbolic importance, demonstrating the ability of hunting's opponents to interfere with the activities of hunts as illustrious and historic as the Quorn and the Pytchley.[14] Hundreds of worried huntsmen and hunt followers from nine local packs convened outside the County Hall as the council assembled to debate the issue, and were no doubt much relieved to learn the motion had been narrowly defeated by just one vote.[15] It was a bitter blow for the opponents of hunting, and the first of a number of harsh defeats.

Some in the rural community were mystified by their local councillors' attack upon long established rural traditions. Mr Stephen Hastings, the newly appointed chair of the British Field Sports Society, described hunting as part of 'our wonderful, national heritage', and discerned in these council motions 'a form of attack on the whole pattern of country life'.[16] His assessment was greeted with sympathy in many rural areas. A proposal put to Cambridgeshire County Council in May 1982 to ban hunting on its 1,150 farms failed by a considerable margin (36 to 23), and as Cambridgeshire had the largest collection of county council farms in England, this was something of a setback for the anti-hunting lobby.[17] In Somerset, a debate about the continuation of stag-hunting on the council's land brought members of the hunting community out in force, and a motion allowing it to continue was overwhelmingly supported.[18] A scattering of other rural county councils that investigated the possibility of withholding hunting rights from its leases, including Lincoln, Wiltshire, Kent, Dorset, Oxfordshire and North Yorkshire, also rejected bans.[19] Anti-hunting campaigners quickly realised that these failed motions were useful propaganda for their opponents, and began to discourage their supporters from pursuing bans in areas where success was unlikely. Since they were ultimately unable to introduce hunt bans in the areas with the finest hunting land, their policy cannot be regarded as an unmitigated success.

The general election of 1983 helped to raise the profile of the hunting issue, yet popular interest remained at a low ebb. An NOP poll of 1983 put approval of foxhunting at 11 per cent, disapproval at 65, and those wishing to see it banned at 55 per cent, though as ever, the poll revealed a significant split between parties. Amongst Labour voters, 80 per cent disapproved, and amongst Liberals 69 per cent. Disapproval amongst Conservative supporters, conversely, ran at 45 per cent.[20] The parties' election manifestos reflected their supporters' beliefs. The Labour Party repeated its 1979 manifesto pledge to end hunting. The Liberal Party meanwhile stopped shy of including any such commitment in their manifesto. Although the party's national council had voted in favour of a commitment to abolish hunting foxes, stags and hares – in addition to its existing policy against hare coursing – in May 1982 David Steel, the party leader ensured that the commitment did not reach the party manifesto.[21] The Conservatives of course held steadfast in their pledge to allow all forms of hunting and coursing to continue. Not that all their members supported this stance: one doughty Conservative supporter, John Cruddas, a small businessman from Somerset, had the idea of forming a Conservative Anti-Hunting Council, with the aim of lobbying inside the Conservative Party for a policy against hunting. 'It is going to be very tough to persuade the Conservative Party,' he admitted, 'but in time the change will come about.'[22] The time had certainly not come by the general election of June 1983, however, so another Conservative victory at the polls ensured that foxhunting remained safe for a while yet. When the government was questioned, early in the next Parliament, about its strategy with respect to foxhunting, a government spokesperson, Peggy Fenner, replied: 'The Government believes people should be allowed to decide for themselves whether or not to hunt and for this reason we have no plans for legislation to ban field sports.'[23]

The new Parliament nonetheless witnessed the by now obligatory backbench attempt to bring the matter of hunting before the House. In February 1986, under the Ten Minute Rule, Kevin McNamara, the Labour MP for Kingston upon Hull, introduced an amendment to the 1911 Protection of Animals Act extending the legal protection given to domestic and captive animals to animals in the wild.[24] The measure was intended to make foxhunting, deer-hunting and hare-coursing illegal. It had of course no chance of becoming law, though it did get the support of 133 MPs – the vast majority of them Labour – and it also succeeded in keeping the issue close to the public eye.[25] But beyond this, Thatcher's second term of government was free of political attempts to alter the legal position of hunting.

Instead, most of the political activity concerned with the future of hunting was conducted at a local rather than national level, in council chambers rather than in the Houses of Parliament. The League Against Cruel Sports continued to provide information and assistance to local councillors keen to press for a ban on hunting over council-owned land, but many of the votes in the later 1980s went against them. Between 1986 and 1987, motions to prohibit hunting on council land failed in Shropshire, Norfolk, Essex and Wiltshire.[26] In 1988, the Lake District Special Planning Board rejected moves to prevent hunting on its 20,000 acres of land. Proponents of field sports had argued that 'hunting with hounds is the most humane way to control whatever animal is being hunted', and the board had agreed by eighteen votes to eight.[27]

Throughout the Thatcher years, hunting was becoming an increasingly political issue, yet this did nothing to dent its popularity in some parts of society. Riding to hounds had traditionally been an expensive pastime enjoyed largely by the wealthy elites, and throughout the late twentieth century it

17. Hunting with the Quorn in the 1980s.

continued to attract support from the highest echelons of society. Just as ever, the royal household was deeply involved in this ancient and most aristocratic of recreations. Prince Charles took up foxhunting in 1975, at the relatively late age of twenty-six, though his fine riding skills honed on the polo field made the transition relatively straightforward. During the 1980s, Prince Charles regularly hunted twice a week, and frequented many of the most fashionable Leicestershire hunts – the Quorn, the Belvoir and the Cottesmore, for example.[28] He hunted with at least forty-six different packs, and as soon as his two sons were old enough, he took them cub-hunting – the pursuit of fox cubs – in preparation for foxhunting proper.[29] The Prince and Princess Michael of Kent also hunted regularly in Leicestershire in the 1980s, and the Queen Mother, Princess Anne and the Duke of Gloucester were all involved at the foremost annual foxhound show, the Peterborough Royal.[30]

In the Shires, foxhunting was as expensive during the 1980s as it had ever been. At the top end, an annual subscription for hunting Mondays to Fridays with a fine pack in Leicestershire cost nearly £2,000. Hunting fewer days was correspondingly cheaper – usually under £1,000 for hunting one day a week.[31] Yet this was just the start of the foxhunter's expenses. The editor of *Horse and Hound* put the price of a good hunter at somewhere between £4,500 and £6,000, and the cost of maintaining it for one year at about £3,000.[32] Furthermore, much of Leicestershire was what was described as 'two-horse a day country':

in other words, the hunting here involved such extensive galloping and jumping that the rider was advised to have a second horse to take over from the first at some point in the day; the meet cards marked a venue for second horses. Added to this was the cost of hunting dress. One authority considered that it was possible to spend £2,000, if you were 'determined to go regally bespoke', on the basic essential attire: top hat £200; coat £600; boots £700; breeches £250. Extras such as waist-coat, hunting tie, tie-pin, shirt, gloves, spurs, whip and flask all pushed the expense up further.[33] Prince Charles claimed to have 'met more farmers and more ordinary British blokes [foxhunting] than in any other exercise or sport I have ever done', but his assessment surely tells us more about the rarefied social circles in which he customarily moved than about the openness of hunting in the Shires in the 1980s.

Outside the cradle of Leicestershire where Prince Charles usually hunted, costs were somewhat lower, and it was perhaps on his occasional visits here that the Prince had met those 'ordinary British blokes'. In highly rated hunting counties in the midlands, south-west and parts of Yorkshire, full subscriptions cost between £400 and £800 a year, and in the more marginal hunting countries, a year's sport could be bought for somewhere between £100 and £300. At Badsworth in Yorkshire, for example, hunting two days a week cost £295 a year. The Banwen Miners in West Glamorgan and the Talybont in Gwent charged a mere £50 for two days a week, and the East Cornwall, £60.[34] By way of comparison, the minimum wage for agricultural labourers was £98 a week.[35] Hunting attire could be bought off the peg or second hand for a few hundred rather than a few thousand pounds – leather boots for £100, a black coat for £175, breeches for £35 and a riding cap for £25. For £300 one could look perfectly presentable and the outfit would last for many years.[36] And, of course, foxhunters here were not paying the large sums for their horses and their upkeep that the editor of *Horse and Hound* described for the Shires. Horses could be bought for a few hundred pounds, and riders helped to lower the costs of their upkeep by keeping them at home rather than in livery and doing most of the work themselves. Nonetheless, horses need exercising, grooming, mucking out, shoeing, occasional vetting, and plenty of food; as one hunter drily noted, 'however many corners are cut, keeping horses is a highly effective way of maintaining cash-flow – outwards'.[37]

When every allowance has been made, the number of people riding to hounds remained small. Although it certainly was possible to hunt with a provincial pack in Cornwall or Wales on a relatively modest income, the followers of most packs enjoyed a high standard of living and a large disposable income. A journalist working on a programme about foxhunting for the BBC World Service in the early 1990s, though no critic of hunting, nevertheless described the followers of the Portman in Dorset as follows:

The master was double-barrelled and plummy-accented and the
field comprised of a number of women with severe hair-dos and an
imperious manner, plenty of farmers, and a smattering of others whose
background and occupation were not immediately apparent from their
appearance.[38]

Terence Carroll, another journalist and a keen hunting man, described
the meet as 'an undeniably upper-crust occasion, with the "them" and "us"
clearly defined and mutually accepted'.[39] Keeping horses has always required
money. Certainly, by the 1980s incomes were higher than ever before and
this helped to bring many more into the foxhunting fold, yet the expenses
continued to prevent foxhunting from belonging to the masses.

Throughout the 1980s, most packs hunted upon traditional lines and the
sport had changed remarkably little since the nineteenth century. By now
fully half the membership of most packs was female and most hunts were
hunting over a landscape that had modernised, in parts at least, beyond
all recognition.[40] Yet the essentials of riding to hounds were the same,
and the hunting community proved resilient to change in any form. The
gradual transition from top hats and bowler hats to hard riding hats illustrates this conservative disposition. Hunting tradition was very clear about
the correct headwear to be worn by different members of the field. Hard
black riding hats were worn with red coats only by masters, field-masters
and hunt servants; others in red coats were to wear a top hat, and those
in black coats might choose either a top hat or bowler hat. Only farmers
and children enjoyed the same right as the masters and servants to wear
hard safety hats. The trouble with this arrangement, however, was that top
hats and bowler hats offered their wearer scant protection in the event of
a fall, and an increasingly safety-conscious society was becoming ever more
concerned about the number of fatal hunting accidents that occurred each
year. A few brave souls broke with convention and wore a safety hat, though
most traditionalists scorned such breaches of etiquette, and some masters
even endeavoured to forbid their use by all except farmers. Following the
highly publicised death of a prominent army officer in the 1982–3 season,
the Masters of Foxhounds Association stepped in and advised that no
member should be prevented from wearing a hard hat if they wished, but
that equally no member should be compelled to, and in the following few
years an increasing number of riders opted for the hard hat. Nonetheless,
at the end of the decade, despite the well-known safety advantages of the
hard hat, there were still plenty of top hats to be seen on any hunting field.
In a rapidly changing society, the hunting community clung to nineteenth-
century traditions with remarkable tenacity.[41]

Although the public face of hunting was very much constructed around the mounted field, the appeal of foxhunting to non-riders continued to grow throughout the 1980s, and the hunt supporters' clubs were by this point integral to the existence of most hunts. Through activities such as dances, barbecues, terrier shows, raffles, horse shows and gymkhanas, a successful supporters' club might contribute as much to the hunt's funds as the mounted field's annual subscriptions – money without which many clubs would no longer have been viable. Furthermore, the supporters' clubs brought much more than fund-raising to the hunting world: they provided a very public demonstration of support for an increasingly beleaguered sport. The cost of membership of supporters' clubs was usually kept low so as to encourage as many to get involved in the local hunt as possible, and some of the most successful clubs boasted memberships of three to four thousand. Car and foot followers formed the bedrock of most clubs, but the clubs always welcomed many others without the interest or inclination to actually follow the hunt. Some members did little more than turn up at the occasional meet. They enjoyed the link with the countryside that membership of a hunt supporters' club gave, and the hunt, in return, very much appreciated this public vote of support.

Most hunts continued to have a fairly ambivalent relationship with the more enthusiastic members of their supporters' clubs who enjoyed following the hunt in their car, though few by the 1980s could doubt that the car followers were there to stay. At a weekend meet there might be half as many followers in cars as there were on horseback, and countrywide tens of thousands probably hunted by this means. Many mounted followers struggled to see how 'unemployed youths on motor-bikes [coming] roaring up to the meet, keen to have a good day's hunting and "revving up" their engines, unconcerned about the effect the noise of their powerful machines might have on the horses' could belong to the world of foxhunting.[42] Most, however, pragmatically accepted that car followers were good for the public image of hunting. As one writer astutely observed, the car followers were 'a tangible force that has lowered some of the sport's social barriers and [formed] a formidable defence against its critics'.[43]

Following by car or on foot is necessarily a rather different enterprise to following the hounds on horseback. Cars cannot for the most part follow the hounds through fields, and herein lies the crucial difference. Whilst the mounted field attempts to keep as close to the fox and hounds as possible, car and foot followers must allow both out of their sight and use a combination of experience and guesswork to anticipate where the hounds will appear next. In place of sight, the car followers use their knowledge of the landscape and of the habits of the fox to second-guess which way the fox might run.

When the pack heads across fields, they follow the local lanes and byways to
keep close to the hounds and get out when they arrive at the place they feel
the hounds are most likely to pass. Finding a good viewing place, the foot
followers watch and wait in the hope of catching sight of the fox, possibly
even before the hounds and mounted field come into view. Like generations
of hunters before them, the foot followers read the environment for clues
to which way the fox will run: the movement of animals and birds, and of
course the noise of the hunt itself – the noises of the hounds, the huntsman's
horn, and the followers – all contain evidence as to the direction in which the
fox is moving. Following the hunt by car, therefore, involves a curious blend
of modern technologies and older hunting techniques, providing individuals
with a unique way of enjoying the countryside, watching the hounds work as
a pack, and testing their knowledge of the natural world.[44]

Though following on foot and by car was usually tangential to the main
business of foxhunting, there were a few parts of the country where following
on foot was the norm rather than the exception. In the Lake District, and
in parts of Wales and the Yorkshire Pennines, the terrain was unsuitable
for horses so packs of foxhounds were followed exclusively on foot. In the
Lakes, six recognised packs of foxhounds hunted the fells in the late twentieth
century. None was a member of the Masters of Foxhounds Association: they
had been organised in 1967 under the Central Committee of Fell Packs and
lay fully outside the governing body of the sport elsewhere in England.[45]
Until the 1980s, most of the packs hunted upon very traditional lines,
working each part of the hunt country in turn. Throughout the season, the
hunt toured the district, setting up for a week at a time at a local farm, then
moving on to the next. The farmer provided food and accommodation for
the hunt staff and kennels for the hounds in return for the hunt's services. In
addition, many of the packs offered a 'call-out' service during the lambing
period – travelling at short notice to farms troubled with lamb-killers. In the
1980s, most hunts abandoned this method of touring the country and staying
at farms, and travelled to meets on a daily basis, though the call-out service
usually remained.[46]

Hunting in the fells is very hard work. The huntsman may follow his
hounds between twenty and thirty-five miles a day over extremely hilly
terrain and few, besides a small band of very fit local hill climbers, are able
to keep close to the hounds for the whole day. Most followers aim simply
to see as much of the hunt as possible. Rather than attend the meet, they
might station themselves at vantage points where the hunt is likely to pass,
and follow the hounds as long as they are able. Others leave out much of
the walking altogether and follow by car, driving around fells, rather than
climbing them, and hoping to catch up with the action on the other side.

Few will spend much time in company with the huntsman and hounds, but many will enjoy catching a glimpse of the hounds at work and seeing some part of the day's action.[47]

Hunting with the foot packs in the fells differs in a number of key respects from foxhunting in other parts of England. Hunting here has always served a strong utilitarian purpose, with the killing of foxes coming first and the provision of sport second. Planting coverts, building earths and hand-rearing foxes were all unheard of in the fells: foxes were killed as a service to the sheep farmers, there could be no question of encouraging such a menace to the region's primary source of income. Performing an agriculturally significant function guaranteed the fell packs good relationships with the local community and few areas in England could boast such strong support for their hunts. In the late 1980s one estimate suggested that the six fell hunts had between them some 10,000 supporters, and instances of sabbing were rare.[48] Finally, hunting in the fells was socially inclusive in way that riding to hounds could never be. With no horses, the most common impediment to participation was removed at a stroke: everyone could join in. Nor did the fell packs pay any attention to dress: all that followers needed were walking boots and warm clothes. The costs of maintaining the foot packs were extremely low compared to foxhunting costs elsewhere, so membership fees were also low. In the 1990s, the average annual subscription to foot packs was between £5 and £20, a fraction of the cost of a riding membership even with the cheapest of provincial packs.[49] And the consequence of these low costs was that large numbers of people on low incomes were able to participate in the hunt. The journalist Charles Pye-Smith considered 'the majority of those who attended the Boxing Day meet [with the Pennine Foxhounds in Yorkshire] were working class. One of the joint-masters was a fitter from Wakefield; many of the followers were manual workers, shop assistants, gamekeepers and factory workers.'[50]

Yet whilst hunting continued to thrive in almost all parts of England, the ideological and political pressures working against the sport were mounting, as even some of the most conservative national landowners became embroiled in debates about allowing hunting on their land. Owning more than half a million acres and over 1,000 farms, the National Trust had within its gift a considerable coup for either the hunters or their opponents, and in the late 1980s it became the focus of a fresh anti-hunting campaign. More than once in its history the National Trust had been asked by its members to consider the morality of permitting hunting on its land. In July 1937, Commander J. L. Cather had moved a resolution at the Trust's annual meeting calling on the executive committee to prohibit hunting for sport on National Trust properties, and a member of the National Society for the Abolition of Cruel

Sports, a Mr Bertram Lloyd, had seconded his motion. It was opposed by the vice-chairman of the executive committee, and when put to the vote, was defeated by a large majority.[51] Fifty years later, however, the times had changed considerably, and a new generation of Trust members was hopeful that the organisation could be persuaded to prohibit hunting on its estates. A resolution to ban all hunting of deer, mink, hare and foxes on its land was moved at the Trust's AGM in October 1987 in the following terms: 'Hunting live animals with hounds is archaic, a remainder from a more primitive and cruel age, followed only by a very small but vociferous minority of the population. It has no place in a modern society which professes to care about its environment.'[52] In order to decide the issue, the Trust organised a ballot of its members – numbering more than one and a half million. The prospect of the vote had the unanticipated (and no doubt rather welcome) side-effect of creating a surge in applications to the Trust, caused, it was surmised, by both the pro- and anti-hunting lobbies eager to fill the Trust with their own kind. In the event, however, only 5 per cent of the members voted – just over 75,000 in all. Of these, a little under 40 per cent approved the motion – a mandate in no way sufficient to change the Trust's existing policy.[53] The conservative leanings of the organisation no doubt helped to tilt it towards maintaining the status quo.

In the face of parliamentary intransigence and the stalling of the League Against Cruel Sports's policy of land acquisition, animal welfare societies and anti-hunting organisations continued to agitate for reform in whatever way they could. The RSPCA, which had never been in the vanguard of the anti-hunting campaign, was prompted by declining membership in the early 1980s to reconsider its policy. Late in 1985, the society launched an anti-foxhunting campaign designed to appeal to grassroots members.[54] A spokeswoman declared: 'The society has been unequivocally opposed to foxhunting since 1971, but this is the first time we have expressed our views so firmly.'[55] But the society's campaigning nonetheless remained sedate. Rather than pursue the direct action or violent demonstration favoured by many within the anti-hunting community, the RSPCA stuck to its tried and tested formula of lobbying for legislative changes. In the inhospitable environment of the Thatcher years, its polite campaign for legislation inevitably got nowhere.

More forceful tactics appeared vital to many disappointed observers, and through the 1980s much anti-hunting activity was pursued by smaller, newly formed animal rights organisations involved in direct action rather than political campaigning. In 1982, the Hunt Saboteurs Association had a mere 4,000 paid-up members, yet it was extremely active at a local level, and successful in keeping the matter of hunting close to the public consciousness.[56] The annual Boxing Day hunt was by now as important an occasion in the hunt saboteurs' calendar as in the hunters', though each side tended to report the day's proceedings in markedly different ways.[57] In 1986, for example, the Masters of Foxhounds Association reported a peaceful day's hunting with about 19,000 riding to hounds and a further one million enjoying the hunts as either spectators or followers on foot or by car. The saboteurs, meanwhile, claimed that the day had seen 'more hunts sabotaged than ever before', and revelled in particular in the appearance of Mr Paul Johnson, the mayor of Grantham, greeting the hunt with a placard reading: 'Hunting is not a pretty sight'.[58] Following the Boxing Day hunts in 1987, the Hunt Saboteurs Association claimed that a hundred foxes had been saved from the 'slaughter for fun brigade'.[59] Yet the next year, 1988, marked the twenty-fifth anniversary of the Hunt Saboteurs Association. The anniversary was observed with peaceful protests, but the saboteurs can hardly have failed to notice that after a quarter-century of campaigning they still appeared a long way from achieving their aims.[60]

The hopelessness of reform through legitimate parliamentary means not only fuelled the hunt saboteurs throughout the 1980s, it also encouraged a new breed of hard-nosed activists. Members of the Hunt Saboteurs Association were sometimes involved in actions of shady legality, but publicly at least the organisation professed to promote only legal forms of opposition. A splinter organisation formed in 1984 – the ominously named Hunt Retribution Squad – had no such compunction. The squad was formed out of the ranks of the Hunt Saboteurs Association after one of its members, Eddie Caulston, was hit on the head and injured at a hare-coursing event in Liverpool in March 1984.[61] Another member explained his motivation for joining the squad to a *Guardian* journalist in the following terms: 'I have been hunt "sabbing" for the last three years. The hunts are not taking any notice of it any more. We want hunting ended. We don't believe that legislation will do it. We feel a new tactic is needed.'[62] That new tactic was violence and intimidation. Early in its history, the squad came to public attention by digging up the grave of the tenth Duke of Beaufort – Master of the Beaufort Hunt for sixty years and a lifelong champion of foxhunting. The desecration took place on Christmas night, and was clearly timed to coincide with the Boxing Day hunts and to attract maximum publicity.[63]

As an organisation committed to working within the law, the Hunt Saboteurs were keen to distance themselves from illegal activities of this kind. Nonetheless, Mr Ralph Cook, the association's research officer, could not help but comment that the Duke of Beaufort 'was a very unpleasant and egotistical fellow. He whipped a number of hunt saboteurs, including myself. He set himself up as a target.'[64] Other animal rights organisations were considerably less forgiving towards the squad. A spokesman for the moderate League

Against Cruel Sports described the squad as 'simply a bunch of terrorists [that] should be exposed and stopped', adding 'you can't ask for a change in the law whilst breaking the law'.[65] But in the eyes of the squad, all publicity was good publicity, and following the incident it issued a statement indicating a host of other targets it had within its sights, including the royal family, the Leader of the House of Lords, Lord Whitelaw, the Defence Secretary Mr Michael Heseltine, football manager Jack Charlton, actress Jane Seymour and football presenter Jimmy Hill. It claimed it had at least one hundred members ready to use violence to stop blood sports.[66]

Strategies such as the desecration of hunters' graves and dark, unspecified threats to pro-hunting celebrities did not usher in the end of hunting, nor did it do much for the reputation of the anti-hunting movement. They did, however, serve to sharply polarise hunting's opponents. As lawful organisations sought to distance themselves from the criminal fringe, the extremists found themselves ever more isolated, and this only increased their fanaticism. The Hunt Retribution Squad was in the news once again in 1993 when army bomb disposal officers were called to defuse two firebombs near Windsor Castle at the offices of a publisher of blood sports magazines.[67] The squad claimed their action was a response to the accidental deaths of two hunt saboteurs – fifteen-year-old Tom Worby in 1993, and Mike Hill, two years earlier.

The same year marked the birth of yet another virulent anti-hunting organisation: the Justice Department, a militant group with perhaps no more than thirty members in all.[68] In July 1994, the Justice Department firebombed the house of an owner of kennels, Peter Worley. Four hoax devices at kennels in Hampshire and Sussex were discovered at the same time.[69] In late December, hoax bombs were planted at the Chiddingfold, Leconfield and Cowdray Hunt in Sussex in order to disrupt the Boxing Day hunt, and a leading member of that hunt, Nick Fawcett, also received a razor-tipped mousetrap. Fawcett called the police and the bomb disposal squad to blow up devices left at the gates of his house on a further two occasions.[70] There were at least thirty-one bomb attacks on hunts and their followers during 1994, and most were believed to have come from the Justice Department.[71] The following year, pro-hunting politicians were also targeted. Tom King, the former Defence Secretary, was sent an incendiary device after defending foxhunting in a parliamentary debate, and Michael Howard, Home Secretary and architect of the Criminal Justice Act, received an incendiary at the same time. Neither device exploded.[72] The Justice Department was a desperate fringe organisation operating wholly outside the law. It did nothing to hasten the demise of hunting, but seriously damaged the reputation of the anti-hunting movement and helped to entrench attitudes more deeply on all sides of the debate.

It was thus against a backdrop of mounting violence that parliamentary deliberations about the future of hunting took place. On 14 February 1992, the Labour MP for Hull, Kevin McNamara, once again brought an anti-hunting measure before Parliament, this time introducing a private member's bill – the Wild Mammals (Protection) Bill.[73] The measure sought to impose up to six months in prison for inflicting 'unnecessary suffering upon wild mammals' and to ban the use of dogs to 'kill, injure, pursue, or attack'. In effect, it was designed to extend the protection afforded domestic animals to wild mammals, and it was the first time the matter of hunting was to be put to a free vote in Parliament since Seymour Cocks's bill of 1947. Being brought before the House just months before a general election, the bill had no chance of becoming law, yet it had value as a potential barometer of parliamentary opinion, and of course, were the forthcoming election to be a victory for Labour, matters would look very different.

In the event, however, it shared the fate of all earlier anti-hunting and coursing measures brought before the House. After five hours of hard debate, the bill narrowly failed on a free vote to get a second reading by 175 votes to 187.[74] Most of the bill's supporters hailed from the Labour benches, though twenty-six renegade Tory MPs had voted for the measure, including two flamboyant junior ministers – Defence Minister Alan Clark and Social Security Minister Ann Widdecombe. But taken as a whole, the Conservative Party demonstrated itself to be implacably opposed to any attempt to abolish field sports. No fewer than thirteen cabinet members voted against, including most of the great and the good of the Conservative Party: Kenneth Clarke, John Gummer, Michael Heseltine, Michael Howard, Tom King, Peter Lilley, William Waldegrave, Norman Lamont, Malcolm Rifkind, John Wakeham, Peter Brooke, David Hunt and Tony Newton. The commitment of the highest ranks of the Conservative Party to defend hunting in all its forms was unshakeable. Inevitably, therefore, yet another Conservative victory at the polls a few months later stymied any further prospect of reform.

Yet McNamara's bill offered a glimmer of hope to the anti-hunting lobby. The bill had been supported by nearly 200 MPs: it had failed to reach a second reading by a mere twelve votes. There was encouragement here that the tide in favour of hunting was gradually turning, and anti-foxhunting measures continued to appear in Parliament throughout the rest of the decade. In 1993, the Labour MP for Newham North West, Tony Banks, introduced a bill to abolish foxhunting with hounds, under the Ten Minute Rule. It had absolutely no chance of becoming law, but it did provide Banks with the opportunity to speak to the House about the evils of foxhunting for a full ten minutes. He castigated the hunters as 'Disgusting, barbarous, anachronistic, hypocrites, thugs, motley villains', and questioned 'how anyone can claim to derive pleasure out of hunting down a defenceless creature'.[75] The bill got nowhere, but it had provided a very public platform for Tony Banks's bile – ten minutes that this vegetarian and inveterate champion of animal welfare undoubtedly relished.

A more credible attack on hunting came two years later, in the form of a private member's bill introduced by John McFall, Labour MP for Dumbarton. Unlike the private member's bill introduced by Kevin McNamara in 1992, McFall's was much lower in the ballot – fourteenth – which effectively ruled out any possibility of its success.[76] Nonetheless, when the Wild Mammals (Protection) Bill had its second reading in the Commons on 3 March 1995, MPs voted by a stunning 253 to nil in favour.[77] This clear-cut vote in favour of the abolition of foxhunting represented a major step forward for those who wanted to ban hunting. Never had any anti-hunting bill reached a second reading, and McFall himself called it a 'landmark and historic vote' which signalled the end of foxhunting and other 'deeply cruel activities'.[78] In fact the bill's initial success owed much to the political tactics of the pro-hunting lobby and did nothing to improve its chances of a successful outcome. Rather than risk the humiliation of defeat, pro-hunting MPs had declined to vote at all, and opted to sink the bill at a later stage. Having passed its second reading, the bill failed to reach committee stage through the filibustering tactics of pro-hunting Tory MPs, and McFall eventually dropped the clause banning hunting in order to get the rest of the bill, banning general cruelty to wild animals, into committee stage for its third reading.[79]

Though the anti-hunting aspects of McFall's bill ultimately failed, public interest in the bill ran high. Early in 1995 the House of Commons post office stated that MPs had received half a million letters and postcards to support John McFall's Wild Animals (Protection) Bill, and Downing Street was presented with a petition containing a million signatures – one of the largest ever.[80] The supporters of hunting were no less active in defending their pastime. Rallies were organised up and down the country at which tens of thousands of supporters of country sports gathered to protest under the slogan, 'Country sports: the countryside united'.[81] The bill's progress was widely reported in the media and elicited endless commentary and debate. McFall's bill marked the beginning of a political and public debate about hunting that was not to be silenced for a number of years.

Hunting was under pressure from all sides. Few hunts were spared regular and noisy visits from the saboteurs and the inconvenience of their disruptive tactics. Occasionally, individual hunters even faced very serious threats to their welfare from the criminal fringe of the animal rights movement. Perhaps most worrying was the steadily increasing support that each anti-hunting measure in the House seemed to attract. Admittedly, the Conservative government continued to offer its protection to hunting, but how long would the Conservatives remain in power? Matters looked bleak at the local political level as well. A poor showing by the Conservatives in the local elections of 1993 was followed by a number of newly controlled Liberal Democrat councils voting to ban hunting on their land.[82] Even Leicestershire, the historic heart of the hunting country, adopted a ban: 'If we can win in Leicestershire, the home and heartland of foxhunting, we can win anywhere,' crowed John Bryant, of the League Against Cruel Sports.[83] In all, more than 150 local authorities had banned foxhunting from their land by the mid-1990s.[84] And finally, the National Trust's support seemed to have wavered. The future of hunting on National Trust land was looking more uncertain, after a second poll of its members reversed the pro-hunting majority of three years earlier. The Trust judiciously decided to postpone responding to this vote by setting up a scientific working party for three years but the pressure for reform was undoubtedly building.[85]

For the first time in its history, hunting was unmistakably on the back foot and the easy complacency that hunters had once shown towards anti-hunting legislation had entirely evaporated. The British Field Sports Society hired an offshoot of the advertising firm Saatchi and Saatchi to launch a much-needed pro-hunting public relations campaign, and even resorted to gimmicks such as the offer of £5-a-day hunting for children, to encourage more to get involved and dispel the public's misconceptions of the sport.[86] Few hunters could ignore the possibility that their opponents were inching their way towards success.

Threatening forces were circling above the heads of the hunters, and the leadership of the pro-hunting lobby was palpably alarmed about the future. Yet despite the public furore, at a grassroots level hunters refused to be cowed, and the sport continued quietly to prosper. Increasingly vocal public opposition to hunting did nothing to undermine the hunters' enthusiasm; it simply strengthened their identification with the sport and hardened their resolve to protect it.

Throughout the 1990s, just under 200 packs regularly hunted foxes (191 to be exact).[87] They operated over almost all of Britain, with the exception of pockets of Scotland, Lancashire and the Pennines. The sport had come a long way since its development in the eighteenth century, yet the essentials of the sport – riding to hounds in pursuit of a fox – remained unchanged. For its followers, the local hunt was an outpost of tradition in a modern, changing world. Riding to hounds remained as expensive as it had ever been. But whereas hunting had once been largely confined to those with the means to keep horses, by the late twentieth century a genuinely inclusive sport had emerged. The sport's proponents claimed that about two million took part in the sport in some way — a claim that would not only have been inconceivable a century earlier, but undesirable, given the new sport's pretensions to exclusivity.[88] This growth had been created by a sharp increase in the number of people following the hounds on foot, bicycle, or by car; and by the 1990s hunt members riding to hounds made up only a small fraction of those involved in the sport. One estimate put the number of hunt members at a mere 48,000, but suggested that a further 400,000 people regularly followed the hunt by other means. Brian Toon of the Masters of Foxhounds Association reckoned 'that over a whole season, up to a million people may be involved at one time or another if you include spectators and the thousands who turn out to watch such traditional events as the Boxing Day meet of the Quorn in Loughborough market place in Leicestershire'.[89] These were no doubt rather exaggerated claims, but Toon's assertion that many non-riders in rural communities turned out to witness, support or participate in the hunt was undoubtedly true, and in the context of the history of hunting, a surprising development. At the time of the Norman Invasion, riding to hounds had been an exclusive pastime for the rich and powerful, and it largely remained so for the next eight hundred years. During the twentieth century, however, and particularly after 1945, the social reach of hunting extended rapidly and considerably. Hunting with hounds had once again demonstrated its ability to adapt to the changing society in which it was practised. Never had hunting been more reviled; yet never had it been more inclusive too.

But how long this newly popularised form of hunting would last in the face of ever growing public hostility to hunting with hounds was open to question. When the Labour Party, the traditional representative of anti-sentiment, was elected to power in 1997, there was a widespread feeling that the anti-hunters' moment had come.

CHAPTER SIXTEEN

The End of the Road

Fox-hunting? Blimey, why do we want to talk about fox-hunting? Iraq is a very serious question, fox-hunting is not. (John Prescott)[1]

A piece of legislation which took seven years and 700 hours of parliamentary time to get on to the statute book. (John Hart, of the Countryside Alliance, on the Hunting Act of 2004)[2]

The election of May 1997 was a landmark in twentieth-century political history. A landslide victory for a Labour Party that had not held office for eighteen years changed the face of British politics and, in aspiration at least, set in train a raft of far-reaching social and economic reforms. But few special interest groups could have felt the dramatic switch in power more acutely than the hunters. The Labour Party's election manifesto had promised MPs a free vote on a hunting ban, and the House of Commons was chock full of MPs keen to see the back of the sport. The country appeared to be on the verge of green-lighting the most momentous change that had ever occurred in the history of hunting. The hunting community was teetering on the brink of disaster.

The question of hunting shot to the top of the parliamentary agenda early in Labour's first term, when the newly elected MP for Worcester, Michael Foster, a long-time anti-hunting sympathiser, drew first place in the private members' ballot.[3] His natural inclination was to use this opportunity to present a bill banning hunting, but when the whips became aware of his intentions, Foster found himself the subject of close ministerial attention, with ministers urging him to choose a less controversial issue, and warning him that hunting was a low priority for the government.[4] Foster nonetheless held true to his principles and decided to go ahead with his bill, declaring that 'the vast majority of people believe, like me, that hunting wild mammals with dogs for sport is cruel and unnecessary. I think it is a barbaric practice that should have ended centuries ago along with cock-fighting, bear-baiting and dog-fighting.'[5] At its first reading in the House of Commons, Foster's bill won the support of more than 173 MPs, and it progressed to a second reading in November 1997.

A number of onlookers viewed the ease with which the bill passed to a second reading with some alarm. For the pro-hunting community, the vote appeared to augur everything they feared, and the British Field Sports Society swung into immediate action, organising a large protest rally for the following month. On Thursday, 10 July, 100,000 hunting supporters massed in Hyde Park, to listen to rousing speeches and declare their intention to fight a ban every step of the way.[6] The rally was peaceful and orderly, but accompanied with threatening undertones. For example, Sam Butler, joint Master of the Warwickshire Hunt warned, 'This is the last peaceful march and the last peaceful rally', and the racehorse trainer and keen courser, Sir Mark Prescott, declared 'if it's a battle Parliament wants, it's a battle Parliament can have'.[7] But though the Labour back benches may have been keen for a battle, those in the front benches were most certainly not, and the new Labour government was surely no less anxious about Foster's bill than were many of those at the rally. Back in office after nearly two decades on the political sidelines, the Labour government had an ambitious programme of legislative reforms. From their perspective, hunting was a trivial issue, yet legislation would be both divisive and time-consuming. The prospect of a bill banning hunting interfering with elements of their long-delayed reform programme consumed ministers with trepidation.

The bill's progress during the next few months did nothing to ease these onlookers' concern. On 28 November, Michael Foster's bill was carried on second reading by 411 votes to 151, easily the most resounding anti-hunting vote in Parliament, and one of the largest ever votes in support of a private member's measure as well.[8] A victorious Mr Foster emerged from the Houses of Parliament following the vote, holding a cuddly fox in the air and declaring the vote a 'moral mandate' to get rid of hunting in Britain, and that 'the days of hunting are doomed'.[9] He was greeted by animal rights groups which had staged an all-night vigil outside the Commons and by crowds of supporters and well-wishers.[10] All looked good for the anti-hunting pressure groups. Opinion polls generally put the proportion of the population supporting a ban on hunting somewhere between 60 and 70 per cent, and that statistic was at last mirrored by MPs in Parliament.[11] The abolitionists were confident that the end of hunting was in sight.

Yet despite the anti-hunting campaigners' exuberance, the prospects for the bill passing at this stage were still uncertain. The Labour Party's manifesto commitment had been for a free vote, which it had duly allowed, but it had said nothing about allowing sufficient parliamentary time, something no less important for a successful outcome. In the face of the unmistakable message from the back benches that they intended to bring about the end of hunting, the government quietly held its nerve, making no promises about allowing time, but not definitively ruling it out either.

For the hunters and their supporters, meanwhile, it looked as though their worst fears were about to be realised, and the pro-hunting lobby went into overdrive. Since the late 1950s, opinion polls had revealed a slow but discernible shift in public opinion towards an abolitionist stance, but with a pro-hunting government in power before 1997, the hunting community could weather the hunt saboteurs, the doomed private member's bills and general opprobrium that their opponents heaped upon them, confident they could continue to hunt with the law on their side. After 1997, however, the House of Commons broadly reflected the position of the public, and the Commons' historic vote on 28 November 1997 swept away the hunters' confidence at a stroke. It was certainly encouraging that ministers appeared to be in no hurry to accede to the backbenchers' demands, but only the most optimistic of souls could have believed that inaction would last indefinitely. The pro-hunting lobby had a clear grasp of the challenge that lay ahead of them. They needed to convince Tony Blair and his cabinet that in the matter of hunting, the stakes were far higher than their idealistic backbenchers realised, that the backbenchers' satisfaction could only be bought at a very high political price.

As if from nowhere, a newly formed organisation, calling itself the Countryside Alliance, entered the political arena and adroitly set about occupying itself with just this task. The Countryside Alliance had in fact been formed the previous summer, and, although few in the media had picked up on it at the time, it was the Alliance that had been responsible for the successful Hyde Park rally held in July. Early in 1998, the Countryside Alliance began organising a second rally, this time publicising its involvement very clearly from the outset, and as a result the Alliance rapidly moved from the fringe of public consciousness to its very centre. The new demonstration would take the form of a meticulously planned peaceful procession from Victoria Embankment to Hyde Park. There would be no rally and no speeches. It was scheduled for Sunday, 1 March, the first day of spring, and just days before Foster's bill reached its report stage in the Commons. By late February the upcoming event was receiving extensive daily coverage in the press and over 2,000 coaches and dozens of trains had been booked.[12] The

18. The hugely successful Countryside Alliance March, 1 March 1998 – an estimated quarter of a million demonstrators participated in a peaceful rally, largely, though not exclusively, in order to defend foxhunting. The march certainly scared the new Labour government and may be credited with delaying their Hunting with Dogs Act for a number of years.

Countryside Alliance was hoping that the numbers attending this demonstration would comfortably outstrip the 100,000 that attended their earlier rally held mid-week in July.

And they did. The Countryside March was by any measure a huge success. It started at about ten-thirty in the morning, but people were still leaving the starting point at three o'clock in the afternoon: it took at least four and a half hours for the procession to pass any given point along its two and a half mile long route.[13] The police estimated that about 250,000 people attended the procession, though the Countryside Alliance claimed that something nearer to 280,000 had been present. Whatever the exact figure, it was a crowd the like of which had not been seen for many years – at least double the number that had filled the streets to protest against Margaret Thatcher's reviled poll tax. Not since the CND marches of the early 1980s had a quarter of a million people turned out to protest in public.

And if the march had been designed to scare the government away from anti-hunting legislation, it could hardly have succeeded better. The sight of so many demonstrators, even peaceful ones in wellies, put the government into a decidedly obliging frame of mind. The Environment Minister, Michael Meacher, participated in the march and told the television cameras that greeted him at Hyde Park that he 'would like to see more discussions so we can reach conciliation'.[14] Other ministerial colleagues pledged to 'listen and learn' about rural concerns.[15] Most immediately, however, the government beat a very hasty retreat from the anti-hunting legislation currently wending its way through the Commons. Foster's bill was forced to fend for itself, and collapsed in the fortnight following the Countryside March, talked out by hostile Tory MPs and finally lost through lack of time. The march must be given credit for the failure of reform in Labour's first term.

Once more, the hunting lobby had forced Parliament to back away from anti-hunting legislation. Anti-hunting campaigners had been lobbying for legislation for over a century, initially without much public support, but latterly with public backing. Throughout the twentieth century, Parliament had resisted all change, but in 1997, with a majority in Parliament opposed to hunting, the tide at last appeared about to turn. Yet the hunting minority had once again managed to thwart anti-hunting legislation. How had they done it? And who exactly was behind this new organisation, the Countryside Alliance?

Though it was not widely recognised in the media at the time, the Countryside Alliance was in fact the reincarnation of a much older organisation: the British Field Sports Society. The society needs little introduction. It had been formed in 1930 to defend hunting from its detractors, and during the second half of the twentieth century had developed considerable expertise in defending all blood sports at a parliamentary level. As the prospect of a Labour victory had become ever more real in the 1990s, the society had become conscious of its staid image, and set out to develop a more coherent and forceful campaigning voice. 'We knew that Labour would win and would probably have a big majority,' recalled Janet George, pro-hunt campaigner and leading light of the Countryside Alliance. 'It was certain that there would be yet another anti-hunting bill.'[16] It was surely no less certain that a shake-up of the British Field Sports Society, and of its tactics and strategies, was in order if the pro-hunting lobby was to continue to fight anti-hunting bills in the very much harsher political climate of a Labour government. Just before the election, the decision was taken to amalgamate the society with two other rural pressure groups: the Countryside Movement and the Countryside Business Group. Neither of these less well-known organisations had achieved much of practical note in their short lives, but both had something of inestimable value to the British Field Sports Society: powerful, moneyed backers, and plenty of them.

The Countryside Movement had been launched in 1995 by Sir David Steel, the former Liberal Democrat leader, with a grant of £400,000 from the British Field Sports Society. It proved to be both a lucrative and a controversial venture for Steel, who went on to draw a generous salary of £100,000 over the eighteen months he spent as part-time chairman of the movement.[17] The movement had the backing of the 'great, the good – and the wealthy', according to one newspaper, but despite this, was poorly managed and quickly ran into financial trouble.[18] At this point, however, it was rescued by the Duke of Westminster – one of Britain's richest men and largest landowners – with a £1 million loan that was never paid back. The founders of the Countryside Business Group, established in the same year, envisaged their organisation as a more commercial operation. It was the brainchild of a Chicago-born millionaire named Eric Bettelheim, who had settled in England after an education at Oriel College, Oxford, and was supposed to raise millions for campaigning on rural issues by encouraging rural businesses to contribute a proportion of profits to the countryside campaign.[19] Like the Countryside Movement, it never quite managed to deliver on its promises. Yet despite the difficulties that the two organisations got into, there can be no mistaking the fact that big money lay behind them both. The merger of the British Field Sports Society and these two countryside movements was a happy pooling of the older organisation's expertise and the other two organisations' influential supporters and their money.

No less significantly, both the Countryside Movement and the Countryside Business Group had their origins in the defence of field sports. The Countryside Movement had been founded with a broad remit: its goal was to spotlight a broad range of rural interests, but defending hunting in the face of a possible Labour victory had always been one of its ambitions. Its literature stressed the importance of 'protecting country life from its detractors', including a 'small but dedicated band of animal rights activists'.[20] Likewise, the Countryside Business Group was immersed in pro-hunting lobbying from the outset – as its original name, the Country Sports Business Group, might suggest.[21] Its founder, Bettelheim, was a keen shooter and the millions of pounds that he hoped to raise were earmarked for the execution of an extensive pro-hunting public relations exercise. As he remarked, 'It will take intensive effort and serious money for years to take country sports off the political agenda.'[22] All three organisations were committed to the preservation of hunting, and so of course was their offspring, the Countryside Alliance. And the hugely successful Countryside March, timed to coincide with the third reading of Michael Foster's anti-hunting bill, was essentially a mass protest, organised by the hunting lobby in defence of field sports.

Yet the newly formed Alliance judiciously chose not to brand itself as a single-issue organisation. Its march was a 'countryside' march – not a pro-hunting rally. March the 1st was widely trailed as an opportunity for anyone concerned about rural issues, be it the green belt, the state of farming, rural housing, transport or employment, to make him or herself heard. For the same reason, the Alliance avoided the overtures of leading Tory politicians eager to jump on to the populist countryside bandwagon. Their spokesperson, Janet George, stressed the Alliance's openness to politicians of all persuasions, saying, 'we hope that MPs of all parties who care about the countryside will want to take part. It's a pro-countryside march, not an anti-government march.'[23] Throughout February as the day of the momentous Countryside March drew closer, the Alliance spoke about the 'countryside' and about 'rural issues', but kept very quiet about the matter of hunting, and on the day of the march, Robin Hanbury-Tenison, chief executive of the Countryside Alliance, said simply that 'The countryside is asking to be listened to'.[24] By branding themselves as earthy representatives of rural England in all its guises, rather than as a band of self-interested, die-hard hunters desperate to halt Michael Foster's bill in its tracks, the Alliance made its message ten times more powerful. It not only guaranteed the turnout of many more marchers than would otherwise have been the case, but, and perhaps most significantly, it also changed the way that the rest of society perceived the march. It was an astute and clever manoeuvre, one of the slickest public relations exercises to be undertaken in the late twentieth century.

Not that everyone acquiesced in this appropriation of the 'countryside' by a band of societies that just months earlier had been single-issue pressure groups committed to preserving hunting. The ramblers' movement in particular had a very different perception of rural issues, and was horrified to see a small band of hunt supporters backed by wealthy landowners set themselves up as the guardians of the countryside. David Beskine of the Ramblers Association dismissed the upcoming Countryside March by arguing that 'People's emotions are being manipulated. The message is: "If you are against beautiful fields being destroyed, come to London".'[25] It was, in his opinion, a gross distortion of the facts: 'The alliance is really made up of field sports enthusiasts and a small band of rich landowners and shotgun manufacturers with vested interests.' Beskine was largely right. The Countryside Alliance's claims to be an inclusive organisation representing a wide range of rural interests, including the preservation of 'beautiful fields', were not entirely untrue. Nonetheless, at its heart, it was a pro-hunting pressure group, funded by wealthy landowners, and artfully re-branded as a grassroots rural uprising. Beskine and the ramblers, however, had no chance of making themselves heard above the professionally run and very well funded Countryside Alliance. Most of us believed that the Countryside March was a genuine expression of rural discontent, encompassing issues far beyond the narrow concerns of the pro-hunting minority.

In the event, however, the Countryside Alliance's success proved to be as short-lived as it was dramatic. Their Countryside March stopped Foster's bill in its tracks, but it did little to diminish support for the measure both within and outside the Houses of Parliament. Just after the march, the chairman of MORI, Bob Worcester said that recent polls had systematically revealed that about 63 per cent of the population supported a ban on hunting, and six months later the figures had hardly changed: a poll in December revealed that 66 per cent of the population were in favour of a ban, and only 20 per cent were opposed.[26] And those 411 MPs who had stayed at Westminster to vote in favour of Foster's bill on a Friday night rather than return home to their constituencies were far from satisfied at the turn that events had taken. Only two Labour MPs had voted against the bill – Llin Golding and Kate Hoey – and the Labour cabinet was acutely aware that their backbenchers would soon be raising the issue again. By 1998, there was an unstoppable momentum for reform of the existing hunting laws within the party, and the failure of Foster's bill had taught the reformists one vital lesson: that a private member's bill, no matter how strongly supported, would never become law unless the government gave it parliamentary time and support.

The government, however, remained unwilling to get actively involved in controversial legislation that would be certain to alienate a significant minority of the electorate. Their immediate response to backbench pressure on hunting was to stall for time. In autumn 1999, in time-honoured fashion, the Home Secretary Jack Straw agreed to set up an independent inquiry into hunting with dogs, and appointed Lord Burns, a former permanent secretary to the Treasury, as the chair. The committee's focus was not the rights or wrongs of hunting, but rather the impact of a ban on the rural economy, on agriculture and pest control, and on social and cultural life; its remit was to look into 'the practical aspects of different types of hunting with dogs ... the consequences of any ban on hunting ... and how any ban might be implemented'.[27] Ministers intended to give parliamentary time to a hunting bill once the committee had reported the following May, and their hope was that the debate would be informed by the committee's findings. But the committee had only just got under way when a new private members' ballot threw yet another anti-hunting measure before the House. Ken Livingstone, a long-standing opponent of hunting and *bête noire* of the Labour Party, came eighth in the ballot and leapt at the chance to introduce a bill on a high-profile issue traditionally dear to core Labour voters. As ministers had ruled out supporting any anti-hunting legislation before the Burns Committee had reported, Livingstone's bill had no prospect of becoming law, but it did offer the promise of embarrassing the government by highlighting its own slow progress on hunting legislation.[28] In the event, however, the embarrassment was perhaps more Livingstone's than the government's. On 7 April 2000, the bill failed to get the one hundred supporters necessary to force a vote on its second reading. The bill was lost, and anti-hunting MPs had no option but to await the report of the Burns Committee and see what action the government would take next.[29]

The report of the Burns Committee of inquiry was published in June 2000. Burns and the four other members of the committee, Dr Victoria Edwards, Professor Sir John Marsh, Lord Soulsby of Swaffham Prior, and Professor Michael Winter, had worked tirelessly in the seven months of the committee's life, travelling widely throughout England and Wales, listening to individuals representing a wide spectrum of opinion, and sifting through endless pages of written submissions. Their report provided no easy answers to the hunting debate. The introduction admitted the committee had 'not attempted to answer the question of whether or not hunting should be banned', nor 'sought to find a compromise solution'.[30] Instead it provided a considered analysis of the place of hunting in rural economy, society and culture, the problems of pest control and animal welfare, and the possible consequences of implementing a ban. The report succeeded admirably in its aim to inform debate and provide an impartial appraisal of the diverse issues involved. All sides seemed encouraged by the committee's findings, and its report provided no clear indication of which direction the government's proposed legislation would take.[31]

In the Queen's Speech the following December, the government announced its intention to introduce its hunting bill and to allow it parliamentary time.

The bill offered MPs a free vote on three alternative options: self-supervision of hunting, government regulation and an outright ban. But the eventual passage of this legislation was tortuous. The Commons voted to give the bill a second reading by a comfortable majority in December 2000, and at its second reading the following January rejected the regulation options and voted overwhelmingly for a ban.[32] Yet despite having been comprehensively backed by the Commons, the bill was equally comprehensively defeated by the Lords when it reached there in March.[33] Peers placed themselves in direct confrontation with both the government and the Commons by rejecting both the outright ban and the compromise of a statutory authority to license hunting, and instead supported the self-regulation favoured by the pro-hunting lobby.[34] Parliament had clearly reached an impasse, and when the government called an early general election, the bill failed through lack of parliamentary time.[35]

Another resounding Labour victory at the polls in June 2001, however, ensured that the issue of hunting remained high on the political agenda. The party's election manifesto promised to 'enable Parliament to reach a conclusion on this issue ... If the issue continues to be blocked,' it added, 'we will look at how the disagreement can be resolved.'[36] Yet once in office, the new Labour government showed itself no more enthusiastic about becoming embroiled in hunting legislation than its predecessor had been, and once again, all the running in Parliament was made by the backbenchers rather than the party leaders.

In October 2001, more than 200 MPs backed a Commons motion calling on the government to honour its promises and make time for a vote on banning hunting, but the government's Hunting Bill of 2002, proposing a licensing system that would permit foxhunting to continue, was not what they had in mind. The bill was amended following strong Commons support for Tony Banks's amendment proposing a complete ban, and the new bill cleared its third reading in the Commons, only to be rejected by the House of Lords and subsequently to run out of parliamentary time. Unable to continue resisting backbench pressure, the government presented a similar bill to the Commons on a free vote on 15 September 2004. Once again this was strongly endorsed in the Lower House: 66 per cent of the Commons voted in favour of a ban, a proportion which almost matched the 63 per cent of the public in favour of a ban on hunting with dogs in a 1999 MORI poll.[37] Once again, the bill was rejected by the Lords. After a period in which the bill yo-yoed between the Commons and the Lords, Commons Speaker Michael Martin finally invoked the Parliament Act on 18 November and pushed the bill into law.[38] It had been a long time coming. Seven and a half years after Labour's landslide victory, and a quarter of a century since the party had passed its first resolution opposing all forms of hunting, the Labour Party had at last achieved the unthinkable. To the delight of some and dismay of others, hunting with hounds had been outlawed in England and Wales.

Despite endless negotiations about the possibility of delaying implementation of a hunting ban just prior to the passage of the Hunting Act, it eventually came into force just three months after receiving royal assent on 18 November 2004. Having failed to protect hunting in Parliament, the Countryside Alliance pledged to fight the ban through the courts and immediately mounted a legal challenge to the government's use of the Parliament Act. None of its legal actions succeeded. The High Court ruled against the Countryside Alliance on 28 January 2005, holding that the Parliament Act was valid, and the Court of Appeal agreed a few days later.[39] An appeal to the House of Lords also failed in the autumn of 2005 when the Lords upheld the original decision.[40] A second, separate legal challenge mounted by the Countryside Alliance through the European Court of Justice, arguing that the Hunting Act contravened human rights legislation, met a similar fate: the European Court rejected the case, and a limited appeal to the Court of Appeal also failed. With all possible legal avenues explored, the hunting community was forced to accept that the Hunting Act remained in force, and were bound to abide by its provisions, if they wished to remain on the right side of the law.

The new law made it an offence to hunt wild mammals with a dog, though permitted a number of exemptions, such as authorising the use of two dogs (but no more) to flush animals out to be shot, and the use of two dogs to hunt rats or rabbits. It also shielded hunters from prosecution if their hounds picked up the scent of a fox and killed it while out of the control of the hunt. Drag-hunting – the laying of an artificial scent – remained legal, however, and most hunts, rather than disband, simply reclassified themselves as drag hunts. In this way, all the trappings of the old foxhunt were preserved: annual subscriptions continued to be paid, and regular meets were organised throughout the hunting season.

The legality of the 'accidental kill' has left open the possibility that hunters may ride out in pursuit of an artificial trail but follow a live fox in the event of their hounds accidentally chancing upon one. It is notoriously difficult to know whether a pack of dogs is chasing a line or a real fox, and this makes enforcement of the law difficult – though the hunt saboteurs have willingly embraced this new responsibility and taken to patrolling hunting country, in order to monitor the activities of the hunt. Even granting this loophole, however, it is clear that the Hunting with Dogs Act has eviscerated foxhunting and publicly stripped it of its respectability. Much of the appeal of foxhunting has always lain in its thrilling chase, and some element of this can certainly be retained in drag-hunting. But for many, the unique attraction of hunting lies in the age-old contest between human wits and the wiles of the animal world. The *par force* hunt involves selecting an animal to hunt and responding to its flight – it is the wild animal that sets the pace, not the hunters. Setting hounds on a man-made trail is a sterile activity when contrasted with the subtle challenge of the traditional hunt. Even when the hunters follow the trail of an accidentally found live fox, though it restores some part of the contest between the fox and the hunters, only a small part of the huntsman's skill is exercised. Despite the exemptions and anomalies, there can be no question that the Hunting with Dogs Act has seriously restricted hunting practice on English and Welsh soil.

Tony Blair and his cabinet had been reluctant to get involved with Foster's anti-hunting bill in 1997. In their eyes, the death of a few thousand foxes killed by the hunters each year was a trivial problem. They had their sights on far more ambitious projects: a reduction of the number of children living in poverty; a radical reform of the higher education system; an expansion of the health service. But subsequent events proved that their analysis could hardly have been more wrong. Though hunted foxes might reasonably be considered trivial in the context of human history, the government had seriously underestimated the significance – ideological, political and cultural – of those foxes. Between 1997 and the final passage of the Hunting with Dogs Act in 2004, Parliament spent an estimated 700 hours debating various abolition proposals.[41] It was a statistic that opponents of the government loved to ridicule, and there is perhaps something slightly absurd about the fact that the nation's legislators devoted so much time to the future of hunting. Nonetheless, anything that Parliament finds 700 hours to debate cannot be easily discounted as trivial.

Nor indeed was Parliament alone in devoting so much time and energy to the consideration of hunting. In the seven years that it took for anti-hunting legislation to work its way through Parliament, the public appetite for listening and talking about hunting was almost insatiable, far outstripping the enthusiasm that MPs had shown. It is sobering to realise that most of the broadsheets devoted more column inches between 1997 and 2004 to the future of hunting than to the government's child poverty agenda. The fate of British foxes was discussed endlessly, in newspapers, on political programmes, on radio call-ins and, no doubt, in pubs, bars and private homes the length and breadth of the country as well. By the time the Hunting with Dogs Act was finally passed, many commentators felt foxhunting had been analysed to death. None but the disgruntled hunters had anything left to say.

Given the extremely extensive debate about the moral rights and wrongs of hunting conducted recently it is doubtful whether any fresh insights on the morality of hunting can be offered here. The historical perspective enriches our understanding of the place of hunting in British society through the centuries, but it does not tell us whether hunting is morally acceptable in twenty-first-century Britain, nor whether the government was right to ban it. Even armed with a knowledge of hunting in history, its place in today's world will continue to divide us. Yet it is not quite time to put the history of hunting to bed. If the discussion about the morality of hunting has run its course, there are still large, and unanswered, questions about why, as a society, we cared so much. Why was hunting – either its preservation or abolition – so important in late twentieth-century Britain? We cannot accept the government's assessment that foxhunting is a trivial matter. Nor, tempting as it is, can we adopt a form of collective amnesia, usefully forgetting the time we spent reading, writing and speaking about hunting. We have to acknowledge that throughout the late 1990s, few topics attracted so much public discussion, and explore the possibility that something important to British society was at stake.

One possibility that must be quickly discounted is the suggestion that this was essentially a debate about cruelty to animals. The number of foxes killed by hunting each year was small in both absolute and relative terms, and foxhunting could not by any stretch of the imagination be regarded as a particularly pressing problem of animal cruelty in late twentieth-century Britain. The Burns Committee reported that about 25,000 foxes were killed by hunting each year, accounting for a mere 6 per cent of the fox population killed each year.[42] In effect, the number of foxes killed at the hands of hunters was a fraction of the number killed by farmers and motorists, and a drop in the ocean when contrasted with the hundreds of thousands of animals living out their miserable lives in factory farms. Just as the Victorians had selected a very marginal case of cruelty when they went out to attack bull-baiting and cockfighting, so in more recent times did the anti-foxhunters target an almost trivial animal welfare problem.[43] No doubt many were genuinely concerned about the cruelty to animals it involved, but the huge campaign mobilised against foxhunting in the 1990s was motivated by something more than these concerns.

Once again, the fuss is not about animals, so much as it is about us. If we recall the anxiety that early nineteenth-century reformers expressed about bull-baiting and cockfighting the parallels between that campaign and that of our own time emerge clearly. That a society still heavily involved in the slave trade and lacking the most rudimentary legislation governing the employment of children in factories and mines should have focused its gaze on cocks and bulls appears inexplicable if it is not fully understood that the reformers were motivated by a concern about the people taking part and not the animals themselves. Nineteenth-century reformers were striving to create a more civilised, a more humane, a more enlightened society, and abolishing blood sports was a small but integral element of this project. At the end of the twentieth century, blood sports once more became the vocabulary for a public discussion about the kind of society in which we wish to live – an opportunity to define Britishness for the new millennium.

Of course at the heart of the pro-hunting lobby were a handful of men and women who hunted regularly and wished to continue doing so. Hunting, as we have seen, is an almost timeless pleasure: the challenge of pitting human wits against those of the animal world and the sheer thrill of the chase have delighted for centuries, and keen hunters were understandably reluctant to let their pastime go. But poll after poll indicated that a sizeable minority of somewhere between a quarter and a third of the population maintained that hunting should not be banned – pro-hunting sentiment clearly extended way beyond the very small numbers of people actively involved. David Steel, in fact, was one such individual: as we have seen, Steel was a tireless spokesperson for hunting both within and beyond Parliament, yet he himself never got in the saddle and hunted; his opposition to a hunting ban stemmed from ideological and political convictions, rather than from personal interest. And in this he was certainly not alone.

The defenders of hunting listed countless reasons why hunting should be allowed to continue. As the stakes mounted in the late 1990s, everything from rural unemployment, mass slaughter of hunting dogs and the extinction of the fox to the end of the old rural way of life were used to justify the continuation of a pastime that others are out to attack. Of course, none of these dire predictions have come to pass since the Hunting Act became law, but the concerns of the pro-hunting position cannot be so easily dismissed. Underneath all the hyperbole, the defenders of hunting had a clear vision of British society, one in which the nation respectfully held on to its ancient customs despite the changing times. The supporters of foxhunting unashamedly stood for the old England of traditional values, for a society in which individuals, not government, made decisions for themselves, a place above all where tradition triumphed over progress.[44] As a letter writer to *Horse and Hound* stated simply: 'Hunting is one of the few remaining traditional pursuits that still exist in this country. We should do all we can to preserve it.'[45] The supporters of hunting wanted to hold on to what was, to conserve rural life in its integrity. And these aims were essentially the same as those that had motivated William Windham to stand in defence of bull-baiting nearly two centuries earlier. Windham had not denied that bull-baiting might be cruel, but he was a true conservative, and simply believed that the benefits of preserving traditional English pastimes outweighed the drawbacks of allowing a relatively minor form of animal suffering to continue.

Likewise, the opponents of hunting had an agenda that bore very strong parallels with the opponents of bull-baiting. They too developed numerous arguments designed to strengthen their cause, linking the abolition of hunting with class war and an end to social privilege, both of which helped to extend the appeal of the anti-hunting cause. But the most enduring argument to come from the anti-hunting lobby was their belief that it was wrong for people to take pleasure in the act of killing. It was not simply the fact of cruelty that offended them, for the opponents of hunting were sufficiently realistic to understand that cruelty to animals occurred often enough in the natural world. It was the human participation, and indeed delight, in the act of killing that consistently underpinned their opposition to hunting. As one writer in the *Guardian* summarised:

> The question before the Commons is not one of rights for animals but of morally acceptable behaviour by humans. Nor are MPs discussing whether to do nothing or something about pest control in the countryside. Foxes are a menace to farm livestock and must be controlled. That means that humans need to kill foxes. But it does not mean that humans are justified in killing foxes with the unnecessary cruelty inherent in hunting.[46]

At its heart, this was the very same argument that the opponents of bull-baiting had advanced 200 years before: acknowledging the needs of humans to kill animals, but drawing the line at making sport out of the process.

Ultimately, for all involved, both then and now, the debate about blood sports has been a debate about ourselves and our society, not about animals and cruelty, and this is why it has had such vitality. And it is for the same reason surely that the debate became so intense in the late twentieth century, at a time of great change in British politics. The New Labour grandees dismissed the importance of hunting when they at last grasped the reins of power after eighteen years in the political wilderness, but in the event proved hopelessly unable to contain the debate. Yet they failed to see that it was their own election to government that helped to fuel the foxhunting debate to which they objected so strongly. Tony Blair's election promised (or threatened) social, political and economic changes on an unprecedented scale: it was, of course, at precisely this moment that the need for a public debate on the direction of British society was at its greatest.

The passage of the 2004 Hunting Act was a historic moment, though for many it was historic for all the wrong reasons. Hunting on horseback had been the protected privilege of the wealthy few since the Middle Ages. Parliament had sometimes been impotent to protect established hunting interests in the face of royal oppression, but it had never failed to protect them from the will of the majority: popular discontent, though often present, had never posed a serious threat to hunting. Down the centuries, it had been the combined forces of population growth and social and economic change that had placed almost continuous pressure on all forms of hunting. In the end, however, the most devastating attack came from the most surprising of quarters: changes in popular taste. Through much of the twentieth century, the animal protection cause had been confined to the realms of literature, art and liberal intellectual thought; the protectionists' goal to free hares and foxes from the tyranny of hunting was no more than a dream. When Parliament became involved at the very end of the century, however, their dreams were turned into reality; their idealised vision of a humane and civilised England proved more powerful than any had expected.

CHAPTER SEVENTEEN

Conclusion

Hunting can be many things: a means of obtaining food and clothing, a display of wealth and status, an affirmation of a man's bravery and skill, a contest between human wits and the wiles of the animal world, an act of defiance against a great landowner's claims to the gifts of nature, or a remnant of tradition in a changing world. It may involve men or women, rich or poor; it may be recreational or utilitarian, legal or illegal, a timeless tradition or atavistic barbarity – the possibilities are almost endless. But in the modern world, no matter who participates in the ancient art of hunting or what form their hunting takes, their actions are never far removed from the combined considerations of land and power.

Though we should take care not to idealise the hunter-gatherer societies in which the art of hunting originated, the operation of power was certainly far less acute in non-agricultural communities. Hunter-gatherer societies have tended to be highly mobile, the inhabitants moving on from one area to another as the resources of the first become depleted, and they have not therefore usually accumulated property and possessions. The transition to an agricultural economy has invariably been associated with the private ownership of land, and this in turn prompts questions about who owns the wild animals that inhabit the countryside. Does a landowner become the owner of a wild bird when it momentarily flies over his land? Who owns the hare that hops into a tenant farmer's field – the tenant or his landlord? Does the owner of a herd of wild deer raised in his privately owned and carefully managed forest, still own the deer when they stray out of the forest into neighbouring farms? The wild birds and mammals that some wish to hunt do not fit neatly into the categories of private ownership, so advanced societies have turned to the law to confer either ownership of wild animals or the right to hunt them.

From 1066, we can trace the long history of hunters attempting to protect, preserve and possess the gifts of nature. Those best placed to acquire ownership of the natural world are those at the social and political apex, and the royal family consequently loom large throughout the millennium that we have studied here. William the Conqueror and his sons introduced their much-reviled forest laws, placing large swathes of the country under a special law decreeing that only the royal household might hunt there. But although their appropriation of the finest hunting land guaranteed them good sport and a well-stocked larder, it was bought at a high political price, and proved a source of bitter conflict with their most powerful subjects. As the English barons became more powerful in the twelfth and thirteenth centuries, the Crown was forced to compromise, and in 1217 Henry III reluctantly signed the Carta Foresta, agreeing thereby to a significant reduction in the extent of the royal forests.

Through a combination of politicking and deception, the Angevin kings successfully delayed the implementation of the Forest Charter for the best part of a century, but abiding by the terms of that document ultimately proved inescapable. In the early fourteenth century, following the death of Edward II, the Crown finally conceded baronial demands, and the boundaries of the royal forests began to recede. Yet the concessions the Crown granted did little to ease the conflicts that hunting provoked, for the Forest Charter effectively increased the number of families legally permitted to hunt, thereby increasing the pressures on the land and exacerbating the social tensions that had led to its creation. In order to protect their hunting estates, landowners turned to the construction of walls and ditches designed to keep the deer in and everybody else out, yet just like the forest laws, these enclosures were bought at a very high price. Admittedly, the park walls helped to preserve the deer contained within, but they also constrained them, and gradually transformed the deer from wild animals roaming over large expanses of unfenced woodland into privately owned and semi-tame animals restricted by the park boundaries of their owners. By the late medieval period, large mammals were usually hunted in conditions that were largely artificial.

No less significant than the physical boundaries that medieval landowners placed around their quarry, were the legal barriers in the form of the game laws they constructed. Game laws contain an implicit admission that certain wild animals, existing freely in the natural world, can no more be owned than the rain falling from the sky: they nonetheless do their best to ensure that certain sections of society may enjoy hunting and eating wild animals by restricting the hunting of others. They achieve this by defining hunting as the privilege of those in possession of a specified sum of wealth or land – the earliest game law, passed by Richard II in 1390, specified land to the value of 40 shillings a year, and this sum rose ever upwards in the centuries that followed. In acknowledgement of the fact that wild animals cannot be owned, game laws criminalise not the act of taking certain wild animals, but rather the circumstances in which they are taken. So it is owning the traps that might be used to catch a hare, and not the act of trapping it, that constitutes a crime. But the distinction does little to placate those who do not have the right to own traps, snares, greyhounds and other accoutrements of hunting. Though the game laws arguably succeeded in preserving healthy stocks of game, they achieved this only by causing widespread discontent amongst those excluded from the pleasures and rewards of the hunt. What is good for hunting has rarely also been good for social harmony.

Moreover, despite the combined forces of enclosures and game laws, the hunters struggled to protect their hunting against the pressures imposed by an ever growing population. Deer, whether wild or tame, require a large amount of land, and it is almost always possible to find a more profitable use for land than leaving it to stand as unfarmed woodland for deer.[1] Deer-hunting, therefore, implied a disregard for the true economic potential of the land: it was a form of conspicuous consumption, a very public display of a family's wealth, and an incalculable source of social prestige. But it also rested upon uneconomic use of land and entailed a deeply inequitable use of the nation's natural resources.

The Civil Wars and Restoration of the seventeenth century mark a turning point in the history of hunting. Deer-hunting had been under considerable pressure prior to the civil disorder of the 1640s, and the breakdown of social order during that decade wreaked havoc on parks and forests. During the Civil Wars, those traditionally excluded from sharing in the riches that woodland contained, entered forests and parks to chop down woodland for fuel and kill and eat the forbidden deer. A fine meal of venison on the plates of the poor signified the world turned upside down – it was a motif endlessly reworked in the tales of Robin Hood, and the symbolism of this simple act was widely understood by all. Following this desecration of woodland and deer, most parks at the Restoration were a shadow of their former glory, and despite the best efforts of many landowners to put their parks back to order, deer-hunting never again occupied the central place in elite society that it had had during the medieval period. But the history of hunting is not a story of decline. Hunting has displayed an endless capacity to adapt and evolve to changing circumstances, and the unsustainable deer hunt was swiftly replaced by new forms of hunting better fitted to the modern world.

With no more deer to hunt, hunters turned their attention to the small game – pheasants, partridges and hares – that had fared much better during the 1640s and 1650s. Yet as soon as they did so, the nature of small-game hunting inevitably began to change. As more hunters began to chase after pheasants and hares, the predictable quickly happened: their population went into rapid decline. And so the hunters returned to their well-tried expedients: draconian game laws and the arts of preservation. By such means, a reasonably stable population of small game was maintained, but this uneasy equilibrium between the hunters and their prey was shattered for once and all by the development of new technologies. A succession of small improvements to the gun and the innovation of 'shooting flying' revolutionised the face of hunting, vastly increasing the marksman's capacity to kill, and uncoupling the balance between natural resources and the size of game bags that had previously existed. The consequence was a renewed commitment to retaining the game laws and a vastly extended programme of game preservation. Once again, however, preservation proved a double-edged sword – underpinning the survival of hunting, yet at the same time also fatally undermining it. The ancient skills of reading the landscape to track wild prey were redundant for the modern shooter, and his sport could no longer be considered hunting in the traditional sense of the term.

And so, ultimately, the hunters ended up with the fox. The fox was vermin and it was necessary to keep the population in check, so hunters had been setting their dogs on the animal since time immemorial. Before the eighteenth century, foxhunting was a necessary, rather than a sporting, activity, and for this reason it was also widely disdained as an inferior, low-status form of hunting. With the decline of the deer, however, the opportunities for *par force* hunting had sharply contracted, and sportsmen began to consider the possibilities of hunting foxes *par force* in place of deer. In contrast to pheasants, partridges and hare, the fox runs fast and in straight lines and offers the prospect of breakneck chases through the English countryside. During the eighteenth century more and more deer packs abandoned the deer and began hunting the fox, and in the process foxhunting developed all the trappings of high-status hunting – fine dress, special hunting music and vocabulary, and certain arcane rituals and traditions. As foxhunting became more popular, however, just the same problems as have always plagued hunters quickly resurfaced: the population of foxes went into serious decline and, once again, the cycle of protection and preservation was set in train. Foxhunters resorted to imported foxes, hand-rearing, and preventing the kill at the final moment in order to produce a sustainable population of foxes to hunt. With these ruses the future of foxhunting was guaranteed, and it continued to thrive as a genuine, and the last remaining, descendant of the *par force* hunting introduced from France almost one millennium earlier.

Hunting is every bit as much about land and power as it is about morality. In Britain, a small country, the desire to hunt has outstripped resources since as long ago as 1066. Population growth and social and economic change have pushed relentlessly on hunting's existence, progressively taking away the large tracts of protected land that are needed for its enjoyment. Over the centuries, ancient hunting land has been put to other uses and, as a result, the area over which the hunters hunt (and even the size of the animals they pursue) has steadily got smaller. In the face of modernisation, hunters have had to fiddle and tinker so as to make their sport work in a society in which it increasingly has no place. Forest laws, game laws and the hand-rearing, protection and importation of wild animals have all been called upon to enable hunting to thrive, but the pressures on wild, huntable animals have grown inexorably. Yet in the end hunting displayed a remarkable ability to withstand the combined pressures of modernisation and population growth, adapting and re-emerging in a form better adapted to modern society. In the late twentieth century, foxhunting remained as popular as it had ever been, superbly evolved to the urbanised and industrialised society that England had become.

Instead, the greatest threat to hunting eventually came from the most surprising of quarters: an English public deeply opposed on ideological grounds. Originally the preserve of freethinking vegetarians on the radical fringe, the view that there might be something wrong in making sport out of killing animals steadily drifted from the fringes to the mainstream throughout the twentieth century. After a hard-fought battle throughout the 1990s, a Labour government eventually passed an aggressive piece of legislation, designed to outlaw all forms of hunting with hounds, and leaving the hunters nothing but the drag hunt – the pursuit of an artificial scent. And this time the future of hunting appears far less certain. The drag hunt offers fast chases, but strips hunting of many of its unique qualities. Whether a change in political winds will reverse the fortunes of this ancient sport in the new millennium remains to be seen.

Notes

1. Siegfried Sassoon, *Memoirs of a Fox-hunting Man*. London, 1928 (repr. London, 1971), pp. 196–7.

Introduction

1. *Guardian*, 6 Nov. 2004.
2. Wickham, 'European Forests', pp. 502–9, 536–45; Richardson, *Forest, Park and Palace of Clarendon*, pp. 13–14.
3. For this fascinating episode, see Isenberg, *Destruction of the Bison*.
4. See in particular, Hoffman, *Egypt before the Pharaohs*. See also Shaw, *Oxford History of Ancient Egypt*, pp. 17–43, 48–9, 56.
5. In the highly militarised Assyrian Empire hunting was the hallmark of a great warrior. The renowned Assyrian conqueror, Tiglath-Pileser I, who ruled in the twelfth and eleventh centuries BC, claimed to have slain 920 lions, as well as bulls and wild oxen, thereby forging for himself a formidable reputation as a fighter to be reckoned with. See Olmstead, *History of Assyria*, p. 64; Contenau, *Everyday Life in Babylon and Assyria*, pp. 133–5. Relief sculptures in the royal palace in Nineveh etched several centuries later further underscore the place of hunting in Assyrian culture. Palace walls illustrate King Ashurbanipal in the throes of ferocious hunting battles, victoriously slaying lions, bulls, gazelles and wild horses, a grim warning to his enemies that his skills on the hunting field would be matched on the battle-field. Barnett, *Sculptures from the North Palace of Ashurbanipal*, plates ii, v–xiii, xxxix–xliii, xlvi–liv.
6. Hull, *Hounds and Hunting in Ancient Greece*, pp. 110–12, 211–23; Anderson, *Hunting in the Ancient World*.
7. Bevan, *Representations of Animals*, i. pp. 100–30; ii. plates 1–49, esp. 15–18, 33, 41.
8. Homer, *Odyssey*, bk 17, ll. 319–360, pp. 291–2; bk 19, ll. 443–528, pp. 351–3.
9. Ruck and Staples, *World of Classical Myth*, pp. 169–70.
10. *Laws of Plato*, bk vii, pp. 215–17, 822d–824a. Contrast, however, Xenophon's *Cynegetica*, which was not opposed to the use of nets. The work is translated in Hull, *Hounds and Hunting in Ancient Greece*, pp. 110–40.
11. Strabo, *Geography*, ii. p. 255.
12. Hull, *Hounds and Hunting in Ancient Greece*, pp. 164–8. It is probable that he was referring to the Celts in Galatia rather than those in England.

13. Contrast this with the estimate of a seventeenth-century gentleman writer; he considered that the cost of keeping hawks, hounds and horses was fifty crowns whilst the value of the birds he caught with his hawks was no more than six crowns. Brathwaite, *English Gentleman*, pp. 202–3.

Chapter 1: A New Sport is Born

1. *Anglo-Saxon Chronicle*, pp. 164–5.
2. Walker, *The Normans in Britain*, pp. 31–46.
3. *Medieval Life Attributed to Asser*, pp. 13–14. See also pp. 33–4.
4. *Life of King Edward*, pp. 60–3, 78–9.
5. *Bayeux Tapestry*, plate 2 and ii (detail).
6. See also *Medieval Life Attributed to Asser*, p. 34: the royal children were instructed in 'hunting as well as other arts appropriate to nobles'. Cf. hunting in the Carolingian Empire: Nelson, *Charles the Bald*, pp. 68–9, 79–80, 93–4.
7. *Medieval ... Reader*, ed. Amt, pp. 4–5.
8. *Bayeux Tapestry*, plate 8.
9. Ibid., plate 14.
10. Oswald's letter is reproduced in Brown, *Norman Conquest*, no. 163, pp. 134–5. See also Barlow, *William Rufus*, pp. 129–30; Warren, *Governance*, p. 160.
11. Lewis, ed., *Angles and Britons*, pp. 162–4. The example dates from the twelfth century.
12. See also Sykes, 'Zooarchaeology', p. 191; Hooke, 'Pre-Conquest woodland', pp. 122–9.
13. Further detail on hunting in Saxon England is contained in Greswell, *Forests and Deer Parks*, pp. 24–41.
14. Ordericus Vitalis, *Ecclesiastical History*, ii. p. 227; *Anglo-Saxon Chronicle*, pp. 164–5.
15. Cox, *Royal Forests*, pp. 1–9; *Select Pleas*, ed. Turner, pp. ix–cix.
16. Rackham, *Ancient Woodland*, pp. 177–9; idem, *History of the Countryside*, pp. 129–30.
17. Grant, *Royal Forests*, p. 9; Sykes, 'Zooarchaeology', pp. 185–97.
18. Ordericus Vitalis, *Ecclesiastical History*, v. p. 285. Cf. William of Malmesbury, *Gesta Regum*, i. p. 505.
19. The creation of the New Forest is discussed in Mew, 'Dynamics of lordship and landscape', pp. 155–66. See also Parker, 'Forest laws', pp. 26–38; Baring, 'Making of the New Forest', pp. 513–15.
20. Rackham, *The Last Forest*, p. 40.
21. Manwood, *Treatise of the Laws*, p. 256.
22. From the *Anglo-Saxon Chronicle*: 'That who so slew hart or hind; Should be made blind', *Anglo-Saxon Chronicle*, p. 165.
23. Grant, *Royal Forests*, p. 11. In consequence of losing control over the forest produce, those holding land incorporated into the king's forest frequently saw it drop considerably in value. For example, once all the woodland of William son of Stur's manor in Sopley had been put into the king's New Forest, his holding fell in value from £10 to 50 shillings. Ibid., p. 12.
24. Ibid.
25. The Windsor Forest and Forest of Dean, for example, are both mentioned in Domesday, and the outlines of Feckenham Forest in Worcestershire are discernible. Further forests in Sussex, Lancashire and Hampshire were also mentioned in Domesday. Grant, *Royal Forests*, p. 11. See also Young, *Royal Forests*, pp. 8–10 who refers to forests in Essex, Huntingdonshire, Buckinghamshire and Oxfordshire. See also Cantor, 'Forests, chases, parks and warrens', p. 57.
26. Barlow, *William Rufus*, pp. 99–100. According to the *Anglo-Saxon Chronicle*, he 'forbade every unjust tax and granted people their woods and hunting rights – but it did not last any time', *Anglo-Saxon Chronicle*, p. 167.
27. Cantor, 'Forests, chases, parks and warrens', pp. 70–3, 82–3; Cox, *Royal Forests*, pp. 2–3; *Select Pleas*, ed. Turner, pp. cxxiii–cxxxiv; Young, *Royal Forests*, pp. 10–11.

28. William of Malmesbury, *Gesta Regum*, i. pp. 563–5.
29. The quote is taken from John of Worcester, *Chronicle*, iii. p. 93. William II's death is discussed in Parker, 'Forest laws', pp. 26–38; Hollister, 'Strange death of William Rufus', pp. 637–53.
30. John of Worcester, *Chronicle*, iii. p. 93. Cf. William of Malmesbury, *Gesta Regum*, i. pp. 503–5.
31. He established it by decree after travelling north on a royal progress and finding it teeming with game, and placed it under the stewardship of a forester named Hasculf. Grant, *Royal Forests*, p. 4.
32. Fisher, *Forest of Essex*, p. 18 and map facing p. 21. Grant, *Royal Forests*, p. 13.
33. William of Newburgh, *History of William of Newburgh*, p. 408.
34. Ibid.
35. Cox, *Royal Forests*, p. 31.
36. William of Malmesbury, *Gesta Regum*, i. p. 741.
37. For a detailed summary of the Establishment see *Dialogus de Scaccario*, introduction (forthcoming). See also the discussion in Barlow, *William Rufus*, pp. 125–6; and White, 'The Constitutio Domus Regis', pp. 52–63.
38. *Dialogus de Scaccario*, p. 000.
39. Barlow, *William Rufus*, pp. 125–6.
40. Ordericus Vitalis, *Ecclesiastical History*, v. pp. 289–91.
41. Gaimar, *Lestorie des Engles*, ii. pp. 197–200.
42. Ibid., p. 199; William of Newburgh, *History of William of Newburgh*, p. 408.
43. Ordericus Vitalis, *Ecclesiastical History*, iii. p. 115. The death of his grandson is retold at v. p. 283.
44. Barlow, *William Rufus*, p. 123.
45. Grant, *Royal Forests*, p. 13.

Chapter 2: A Royal Affair

1. Richard fitz Nigel, *Dialogus de Scaccario*, p. 60.
2. John of Salisbury, *Policraticus*, p. 22.
3. This much-quoted figure is derived from the map produced in Bazeley, 'Extent of the English forest', p. 140. See also the discussion in Rackham, *Ancient Woodland*, pp. 175–88.
4. Grant, *Royal Forests*, pp. 15–16.
5. *Gesta Stephani*, p. 2.
6. Ibid.
7. Crouch, *Reign of King Stephen*, esp. pp. 1–7. For the forests see the revisionist case put by Vincent, 'New charters', pp. 829–928, esp. 912ff.
8. Walter Map, *De Nugis Curialium*, p. 477.
9. *Chronicle of Battle Abbey*, pp. 135–7. Walter Map related how courtiers exploited the king's absence to deal with business in a way that was more in their interests than in his. See Walter Map, *De Nugis Curialium*, pp. 510–13.
10. Bazeley, 'Extent of the forest', p. 146.
11. Grant, *Royal Forests*, p. 16.
12. Young, *Royal Forests*, p. 20. Not only did Henry restore the forest boundaries at his accession, he also swiftly set about retrospectively fining inhabitants of the forests for their infractions of the forest laws during the chaos of his predecessor's rule. One of his earliest acts was to fine forest inhabitants for clearings they had made since 1135, collecting over £235 in the Forest of Essex alone. Grant, *Royal Forests*, p. 16.
13. Bazeley's in-depth study of the Forest of Dean provides the clearest evidence of this. See Bazeley, 'The Forest of Dean', pp. 153–286. See also Cantor, 'Forests, chases, parks and warrens', pp. 62–6.
14. Young, 'English royal forests', p. 10.
15. *Chronicle of Battle Abbey*, pp. 220–3.

16. Grant, *Royal Forests*, p. 16.
17. Young, *Royal Forests*, p. 39.
18. For this incident see ibid., pp. 37–8. When all the fines in the Pipe Rolls connected with this forest eyre are totalled, the amount for the year is £12,305 – an exceptionally large sum when contrasted with those of earlier eyres. Ibid., p. 39. See also Grant, *Royal Forests*, pp. 17–19.
19. Besides expanding the royal forests and rigorously enforcing the forest law, Henry also clarified the forest law in his Assize of the Forest (1184). This mostly repeated the ordinances of Henry I, though mitigated the savage punishment for which he had been reviled. It ordered fines for the first two offences, and physical punishment, probably the death penalty, only for the third: 'for the third offence ... he shall answer with his own body'. Young, *Royal Forest*, p. 29. Reprinted in full in *Documentary History*, ed. Bagley and Rowley, pp. 70–3, quote p. 72.
20. Quoted in Oggins, *Kings and their Hawks*, p. 54.
21. Gerald of Wales, *Historical Works of Giraldus Cambrensis*, p. 250.
22. Richard fitz Nigel, *Dialogus de Scaccario*, p. 60.
23. Oggins, *Kings and their Hawks*, p. 65.
24. Ibid.
25. See Church, 'Aspects of the royal itinerary'.
26. Ibid.
27. 'Beroul's *Tristran*', in *Early French Tristan Poems*, i. pp. 11–199; *Birth of Romance*, ed. Weiss, pp. 1–120; John of Salisbury, *Policraticus*, pp. 13–26.
28. 'Romance of Horn', pp. 9, 59; Hero was the orphaned son of a nobleman 'with few fiefs'. Ibid., p. 54.
29. Ibid., p. 62. The king's huntsmen are described at p. 44.
30. *Early French Tristan Poems*, i. p. 183, ll. 4083–93; p. 137, ll. 3016–23.
31. John of Salisbury, *Policraticus*, p. 15.
32. Ibid., pp. 15–16.
33. Ibid., p. 22, 15.
34. Ibid., p. 22.
35. Quoted in Grant, *Royal Forests*, p. 19.
36. *Chronicle of the Third Crusade*, bk 5, ch. 31, p. 310.
37. Roger of Howden, *Annals*, ii. p. 324.
38. Bazeley, 'Extent of the royal forests', p. 146.
39. Young, *Royal Forests*, p. 39.
40. Roger of Howden, *Annals*, ii. p. 434.
41. According to Roger of Howden, a justice of the forest from 1185, killers of the king's deer 'are to lose their eyes and their virility'. Roger of Howden, *Annals*, ii. p. 434. The Assize is given in full in ibid., pp. 434–7.
42. Bazeley, 'Extent of the forest', p. 148.
43. Grant, *Royal Forests*, p. 137.
44. Bazeley, 'Extent of the forest', p. 148.
45. Young, *Royal Forests*, p. 42. See also Grant, *Royal Forests*, pp. 136–7.
46. Young, *Royal Forests*, p. 39.
47. Warren, *King John*, pp. 226–61; Turner, *King John*. The full charter with extensive commentary may be found in *Magna Carta*, ed. Holt, pp. 316–37.
48. *Magna Carta*, p. 329.
49. Ibid.
50. Quoted in Warren, *King John*, p. 245.

Chapter 3: The Forest Charter

1. Richardson, *Forest, Park and Palace*, p. 125.
2. Young, *Royal Forests*, pp. 60–8; Carpenter, *Minority of Henry III*, pp. 60–3.

3. Carpenter, *Minority of Henry III*, pp. 68—9.
4. In 1225, the knights in Surrey, Staffordshire, Sussex, Leicestershire, Rutland, Nottingham-shire, Lancashire and Dorset all reported that substantial parts of their county should be put outside the royal forest. Ibid. For attempts to execute the Charter see also ibid., pp. 89—91, 168—9, 180—1, 384—5, 277—9, 392—3.
5. Grant, *Royal Forests*, p. 141.
6. Roger of Wendover, *Flowers of History*, ii. pp. 455—9, quote on p. 459.
7. Crook, 'Struggle over forest boundaries', p. 39.
8. These admitted major concessions in Derbyshire, Northamptonshire, Wiltshire and Sussex, but in most other English counties the boundaries remained much as they had been before the Charter. Owing to Henry's improvidence and ongoing financial problems, just a year later he was forced to make fresh disafforestations, dispensing with much of his forest in Berkshire and Gloucestershire, and with parts of Sherwood Forest. Grant, *Royal Forests*, pp. 143—4; Bazeley, 'Extent of the forest', p. 152.
9. Quoted in ibid., p. 150.
10. Matthew Paris, *Matthew Paris's English History*, ii. pp. 40, 61—2.
11. Ibid., pp. 358—9.
12. Following the Battle of Evesham in 1265, the Crown had seized all the Ferrers lands and they had been given by Henry III to his son Edmund, Earl of Lancaster.
13. Cox, *Royal Forests*, pp. 155—6.
14. Ibid., pp. 161—2.
15. Grant, *Royal Forests*, pp. 154—9. Edward I is also known to have hunted personally in his royal forests. See, for example, Parker, 'Forest of Cumberland', p. 16.
16. Parker, 'Forest of Cumberland', pp. 159—65.
17. Bazeley, 'Extent of the forest', p. 141. See also *Select Pleas*, ed. Turner, pp. cxi—cxii.
18. Bazeley, 'Extent of the forest', p. 142.
19. Ibid.
20. Trench, *Poacher and Squire*, p. 37.
21. Ibid., pp. 56—7.
22. Forest records have been reprinted in several places. See, for example, 'Pleas of the Forest', ed. Wrottesley, pp. 123—80; *Calendar of New Forest Documents*, pp. 44—300, *passim*; *Select Pleas*, ed. Turner; Parker, 'Stories of deer-stealers', pp. 1—30.
23. Coss, *Lady in Medieval England*, p. 67.
24. *Select Pleas*, ed. Turner, pp. 34, 98—9.
25. Woolgar, *Great Household*, p. 53.
26. Ibid., p. 193.
27. Birrell, 'Who poached the king's deer?', p. 12.
28. Idem, 'Great thirteenth-century hunter', pp. 55—7.
29. Ibid., p. 65.
30. See, for example, *Calendar of New Forest Documents*, nos 205, 206, 208, 209, 214, 216, pp. 98—104.
31. Rackham, *History of the Countryside*, pp. 119, 134—5.
32. Ibid., p. 136.
33. Woolgar, *Great Household*, p. 115.
34. On this point see also, Birrell, 'Deer and deer farming', pp. 112—26, esp. pp. 122—3. See also, Austin, 'Castle and the landscape', pp. 73—5. Austin argues that some of the venison hunted at Barnard Castle in County Durham was traded rather than used for domestic consumption. He concludes that hunting there was 'much more than a sport; it was a business'.
35. Rackham, *Ancient Woodland*, p. 185.
36. Quoted in Young, *Royal Forests*, pp. 107—8.
37. Birrell, 'Peasant deer poachers', pp. 77—8.
38. *Calendar of New Forest Documents*, no. 250, p. 113.
39. Parker, 'Stories of deer-stealers', p. 14.

40. Birrell, 'Peasant deer poachers', p. 76. See also *Calendar of New Forest Documents*, nos 234, 235, pp. 109–10.
41. Birrell, 'Peasant deer poachers', pp. 71–3.
42. Grant, *Royal Forests*, p. 32.
43. Crook, 'Hunting rights in Nottinghamshire', p. 106.
44. Ibid., p. 103; idem, 'Hunting rights in Derbyshire', p. 234.
45. *Documents of the Baronial Movement*, pp. 76–91, quote on pp. 80–1.
46. Crook, 'Hunting rights in Derbyshire', p. 236.
47. Keen, *Outlaws*, p. 166.

Chapter 4: Hunting Goes Tame

1. *Master of Game*, pp. 4, 11.
2. Hatcher, 'England in the aftermath', p. 3. See also Hinde, *England's Population*, pp. 39–52, esp. 44–7.
3. Hatcher, 'England in the aftermath', pp. 10–25.
4. Hinde, *England's Population*, pp. 47–50; Dyer, *Making a Living*, pp. 265–362.
5. Consider, for example, the hunting enjoyed by the Cely family in the vicinity of London in the fifteenth century. *Cely Letters*, pp. 17–18, 72, 115, 124–6, 179.
6. The key medieval hunting tracts are Twiti, *Art of Hunting*; *Master of Game*; *Boke of St Albans*, pp. 57–87; *Tretyse off Huntyng*. Literary works with a significant hunting element include *Sir Gawain and the Green Knight*; *Awntyrs off Arthure*; 'Summer Sunday'; Chaucer, 'Book of the Duchess'; idem, 'The Knight's Tale'. See also, *Devonshire Hunting Tapestries*, a unique set of fifteenth-century hunting tapestries belonging to the Dukes of Devonshire; and Claxton, 'Sign of the dog', pp. 127–81.
7. Twiti, *Art of Hunting*, p. 41.
8. *Master of Game*, pp. 4–5, 11.
9. Rooney, *Hunting in Middle English Literature*, pp. 7–8.
10. *Master of Game*, pp. 188–99.
11. *Sir Gawain*, pp. 42–3, ll. 1126–77.
12. *Master of Game*, pp. 188–99; *Sir Gawain*, p. 42, ll. 1134, 1144–5.
13. *Sir Gawain*, p. 48, ll. 1321–2.
14. *Master of Game*, pp. 130–64.
15. Ibid., p. 174.
16. Ibid., pp. 174–8; *Boke of St Albans*, pp. 76–9. The ritual dissection of the hinds killed by Bertilak and his men is described in *Sir Gawain*, pp. 48–9, ll. 1325–62. Cf. von Strassburgh's *Tristan* poem, in which Tristan had demonstrated his noble birth by showing expertise in the undoing of a hunted stag, pp. 78–82.
17. Chaucer, 'Book of the Duchess', pp. 31–2, ll. 344–86.
18. See also Sykes, 'Zooarchaeology, pp. 191–7. Her analysis of archaeological sites between the fifth and fifteenth centuries indicates a dramatic change in the composition of the deer body parts they contain before the end of the eleventh century, a pattern which she explains by the introduction of new hunting techniques, probably from Norman Sicily rather than Normandy itself, at the time of the Conquest. See also, idem, 'Introduction of fallow deer', pp. 75–83.
19. Cummins, *Art of Medieval Hunting* p. 53.
20. *Master of Game*, pp. 28–9; Twiti, *Art of Hunting*, pp. 46–7; Barnes, *Boke of Hunting*, pp. 24–6; *Boke of St Albans*, p. 58.
21. Barnes, *Boke of Hunting*, p. 26. The same point is made in *Boke of St Albans*, p. 59. See also the comprehensive word lists in ibid., pp. 83–7.
22. *Master of Game*, pp. 254–5; Barnes, *Boke of Hunting*, pp. 40–2 See also the discussion in Almond, *Medieval Hunting*, pp. 85–9.
23. *Sir Gawain*, pp. 51–3, 56–8, ll. 1414–75, 1560–1622. *Master of Game*, pp. 46–53; Barnes, *Boke of Hunting*, pp. 30–2, 66–8; *Boke of St Albans*, pp. 61, 76.

24. *Sir Gawain*, pp. 51–2, ll. 1421–37.
25. Ibid., p. 57, ll. 1583–1940.
26. Ibid., p. 58, ll. 1605–18.
27. Woolgar, *Great Household*, p. 115.
28. Twiti, *Art of Hunting*, p. 40; Barnes, *Boke of Hunting*, p. 32; see also 34, ll. 42–50; *Master of Game*, 'the hare is a good little beast, and much good sport and liking in the hunting of her, more than that of any other beast that many man knoweth', p. 12; *Boke of St Albans*, pp. 61–2, 66–9.
29. Quoted in Almond, *Medieval Hunting*, p. 101.
30. *Master of Game*, pp. 181–7, esp. 186; Barnes, *Boke of Hunting*, p. 34.
31. 'Parliament of the Three Ages', p. 133, l. 22.
32. Ibid., p. 134, ll. 38–49. See also *Early French Tristan Poems*, pp. 65–89, ll. 1279–1834 *passim*.
33. *Master of Game*, p. 74. See also his comments on men using nets, pipes and cords for hunting hare. Ibid., p. 22.
34. See Bailey, 'Rural society', p. 163.
35. Almond, *Medieval Hunting*, p. 150.
36. *Queen Mary's Psalter*, p. 162.
37. Ibid., p. 191. See also *Master of Game*, p. 74.
38. *Luttrell Psalter*, p. 32.
39. *Queen Mary's Psalter*, p. 168; *Luttrell Psalter*, p. 36.
40. Hinde, *England's Population*, p. 64; Wrigley and Schofield, *Population History*, p. 207.
41. Almond and Pollard, 'The yeomanry of Robin Hood', p. 73; Bailey, *Marginal Economy?*, pp. 245–51.
42. 13 Ric. II, stat. 1 c. 13; *English Historical Documents*, p. 1004.
43. Ibid.
44. *Anglo-Saxon Charters*, no. 56, p. 117: Darby, *Domesday England*, pp. 201–3; Liddiard, 'Deer parks of Domesday', pp. 4–23.
45. Cantor, 'Forests, chases, parks and warrens', pp. 73–82, esp. 76–7.
46. Crook, 'Clipstone Park', p. 25; Rackham, *Ancient Woodland*, p. 191.
47. Lyth, 'Deer parks', p. 14; Way, *Study of Imparkment*, pp. 16–25; Richardson, *Forest, Park and Palace*, pp. 1–7, 26–35. See also Manning, *Hunters and Poachers*, pp. 116–28.
48. Cantor, 'Forests, chases, parks and warrens', p. 81.
49. Birrell, 'Deer and deer farming', pp. 112–26.
50. Ibid., p. 116.
51. Ibid., p. 118. See also Richardson, *Forest, Park and Palace*, pp. 34–5.
52. Quoted in Cummins, *Art of Medieval Hunting*, p. 62.
53. Richardson, *Forest, Park and Palace*, p. 1.
54. Cox, *Royal Forests*, pp. 32–4. Cummins, *Art of Medieval Hunting*, pp. 132–41.
55. See above, Chapter 1.
56. Quoted Cummins, *Art of Medieval Hunting*, p. 132. Cf. *Master of Game*, p. 54.
57. [Gascoigne], *Arte of Venerie*, p. 363. This book was reprinted in 1908 and erroneously ascribed to Turberville. The 1575 edition is cited here.

Chapter 5: The Tudors

1. 'Gest of Robyn Hode', p. 94, ll. 125–8, repr. in *Robin Hood and Other Outlaw Tales*.
2. Van Cleave Alexander, *First of the Tudors*, pp. 1–28; Webster, *Wars of the Roses*.
3. Webster, *Wars of the Roses*, passim, esp. pp. 214–17.
4. Gunn, 'Courtiers of Henry VII', p. 164.
5. Grant, *Royal Forests*, pp. 181–2.
6. Manning, *Hunters and Poachers*, pp. 28–9.
7. Quoted in Williams, 'Hunting, hawking', p. 23.
8. See, for example, *Letters and Papers of the Reign of Henry VIII*, iii. pt 1, pp. 348, 350; iv. pt 2, p. 2031.

9. Ibid., iii. pt 1, p. 350.
10. *Letters of Henry VIII*, p. 57. See also pp. 33, 61.
11. Ives, 'Henry VIII: the political perspective', p. 22.
12. *Letters and Papers of the Reign of Henry VIII*, iv. pt 1, p. 1049. See also ibid., iv. pt 1, p. 983; Ibid., i. p. 26.
13. Ibid., xvi. p. 17. See also ibid., xvii. p. 668.
14. Ibid., *passim*.
15. See Pettit, *Royal Forests of Northamptonshire*, pp. 14, 44.
16. Ibid.
17. Cox, *Royal Forests*, pp. 296–7. See also Lasdun, *English Park*, pp. 24, 29–30.
18. Cole, *The Portable Queen*, p. 14.
19. Manning, *Hunters and Poachers*, p. 200. See also Thurley, 'Palaces for a nouveau riche king', pp. 10–14.
20. Quoted in Williams, 'Hunting, hawking', p. 22.
21. Ridley, *Henry VIII*, pp. 300–1.
22. Thurley, 'Sports of kings', p. 166.
23. *Letters and Papers of the Reign of Henry VIII*, xvi. p. 533. See also ibid., xxi. pt 2, p. 10 for a similar occasion.
24. Ibid., xvi. p. 533.
25. Lasdun, *English Park*, p. 24.
26. Cox, *Royal Forests*, pp. 171–2.
27. Ibid., pp. 174–5.
28. Ibid. Champion, in this context, refers to an expanse of open level country.
29. Rackham, *History of the Countryside*, pp. 39–40, 49–50.
30. See Lasdun, *English Park*, pp. 32–3. The quote is taken from Elyot, *Boke Named the Gouvernor*, i. pp. 181–2.
31. See Orme, *Childhood to Chivalry*, pp. 191–9.
32. *Lisle Letters*, iv. p. 35.
33. Boorde, *Fyrst Boke; and Dyetary of Helth*, p. 275.
34. Manning, *Hunters and Poachers*, p. 19.
35. MacCulloch, *Suffolk and the Tudors*, pp. 56–7. The accounts are reprinted in Cummins, *Art of Medieval Hunting*, pp. 260–5.
36. *Lisle Letters*: venison: i. pp. 254, 324, ii. p. 224, iv. pp. 52, 339; pheasants: i. p. 457, ii. p. 640, iii. p. 472; partridge: v. pp. 299, 308, 652, 655; geese: v. p. 312; quail: i. p. 574, ii. pp. 218, 226, iii. pp. 439, 885. For dogs, see iii. pp. 156, 173.
37. MacCulloch, *Suffolk and the Tudors*, p. 57; *Lisle Letters*, ii. p. 208. See also the excellent discussion in Whyman, *Sociability and Power*, pp. 23–33.
38. Manning, *Hunters and Poachers*, p. 10.
39. The key Tudor game acts are as follows: 1485, 1 Henry VII c. 7; 1503, 19 Henry VII c. 11; 1539, 31 Henry VIII c. 12; 1540, 32 Henry VIII c. 11; 1541, 33 Henry VIII c. 6.
40. Dyer, *Making a Living*, pp. 330–46.
41. See, for example, Lyth, 'Deer parks', p. 16.
42. *Yorkshire Star Chamber Proceedings*, no. 82a, pp. 190–3.
43. See in particular, Manning, *Hunters and Poachers*, *passim*, esp. pp. 41–56. See also Beaver, 'Great deer massacre', pp. 187–216.
44. 1494, 11 Henry VII c. 17 (pheasants and partridges); 1523, 14 & 15 Henry VIII, c. 10 (hares); 1533, 25 Henry VIII c. 11 (wildfowl); 1540, 32 Henry VIII c. 8 (pheasants and partridges).
45. Trench, *Poacher and Squire*, pp. 81–2.
46. Manning, *Village Revolts*, p. 289.
47. Manning, *Hunters and Poachers*, p. 42.
48. For the riots see Beer, *Rebellion and Riot*; Wood, *Riot, Rebellion and Popular Politics*, pp. 60–70.
49. Manning, 'Violence and social conflict', p. 33.
50. MacCulloch, *Suffolk and the Tudors*, pp. 310–11.

51. Beer, *Rebellion and Riot*, p. 149.

52. 1549, 3 & 4 Edward VI c. 7.

53. See Almond and Pollard, 'The yeomanry of Robin Hood', pp. 52–77.

54. Several fifteenth- and sixteenth-century Robin Hood ballads are reprinted in *Robin Hood and Other Outlaw Tales*, pp. 21–267. References here are taken from this edition. The literature on Robin Hood is extensive. Good introductions include: Keen, *Outlaws*; Holt, *Robin Hood*; Pollard, *Imagining Robin Hood*.

55. 'Robin Hood and the Monk', p. 47, l. 325; 'Gest of Robyn Hode', p. 94, l. 158, p. 111, l. 686, reprinted in *Robin Hood and Other Outlaw Tales*.

56. Ibid., pp. 135–40, ll. 1413–1756.

57. 'Adam Bell', p. 241, ll. 13–16, reprinted in ibid.

Chapter 6: Elizabeth and the Puritans

1. Darell, *Discourse of the Life of Servingmen*, sig. F4r.

2. Stubbes, *Anatomy of Abuses*, p. 178.

3. Hibbert, *Virgin Queen*, p. 133.

4. Nichols, *Progresses of Elizabeth*, i. p. 17.

5. [Gascoigne], *Arte of Venerie*, p. 133.

6. Nichols, *Progresses of Elizabeth*, i. p. 438.

7. *Calendar of State Papers, Domestic Series, 1547–1625*, viii. p. 451.

8. Two accounts of the queen's visits are reprinted in Nichols, *Progresses of Elizabeth*, i. pp. 426–84, 485–528.

9. Ibid., p. 436.

10. Richardson, *Forest, Park and Palace*, p. 81.

11. Wilson, *Entertainments for Elizabeth I*, pp. 88–95. The hunt is described on p. 89. See also Dorey, *An Elizabethan Progress*, p. 115: in 1578, Usher Anthony Wingfield built a standing at Kirtling Tower in Cambridgeshire at the cost of 25 shillings for the queen's visit during her progress.

12. Quoted in Berry, *Shakespeare and the Hunt*, p. 3. See also Cox, *Royal Forests*, p. 297.

13. Cox, *Royal Forests*, p. 141.

14. Trench, *Poacher and Squire*, p. 90.

15. Quoted in Manning, *Hunters and Poachers*, p. 4.

16. See Darell, *Discourse of the Life of Servingmen*; M., *Health to the Gentlemanly Profession*.

17. *Boke of St Albans*, p. xiii. For reprints, see, for example, Gryndall, *Hawking, Hunting, Fouling*; *Jewel for Gentrie*; Markham, *Gentleman's Academie*.

18. Cockaine, *Short Treatise*, sig. A3r; [Gascoigne], *Arte of Venerie*, 1575 edn.

19. Orme, 'Medieval hunting', p. 143.

20. [Gascoigne], *Arte of Venerie*, p. 53.

21. Ibid., pp. 54–9.

22. Ibid., p. 100.

23. John Lyly, *Midas* (1592), quoted in Manning, *Hunters and Poachers*, p. 57.

24. Taylor, 'Ravensdale Park', p. 37.

25. Richardson, *Forest, Park and Palace*, pp. 80–2.

26. Ibid., p. 81.

27. Roberts, *Royal Landscape*, p. 137; Taylor, 'Ravensdale Park', p. 53.

28. See Cockaine, *Short Treatise*, sigs B.4–C.1. See also Elyot, *Boke Named the Gouvernor*, i. p. 195. He thought the hunting of hares 'right good solace'.

29. [Gascoigne], *Arte of Venerie*, p. 160.

30. Ibid., p. 162.

31. Twiti, *Art of Hunting*, p. 55.

32. *Master of Game*, p. 65.

33. [Gascoigne], *Arte of Venerie*, pp. 191–2; Cockaine, *Short Treatise*, sig. B2v.

34. *Master of Game*, p. 68.
35. [Gascoigne], *Arte of Venerie*, pp. 190–1.
36. Cleland, *Institution of a Young Noble Man*, p. 223.
37. For population trends see Wrigley and Schofield, *Population History*, p. 207.
38. See Hill, *Society and Puritanism*, pp. 1–15; Eales and Durston, eds, *Culture of English Puritanism*, pp. 1–31.
39. See, however, Thomas, *Man and the Natural World*, pp. 160–5.
40. Chambers, *Elizabethan Stage*, ii. p. 450.
41. The French ambassador noted the following evening's entertainment in May 1559: 'And after dinner to bear and bull baytyng, and the Quens grace and the embassadurs stod in the galere lokying at the pastime tyll vi at nyght'. Ibid., p. 453.
42. Ibid., p. 449. See also, Dawson, 'London's bull-baiting', pp. 97–101.
43. *Records of Nottingham*, iii. p. 449.
44. Chambers, *Elizabethan Stage*, ii. p. 455; Kingsford, 'Paris Garden and the bear-baiting', pp. 155–78. See also Platter, *Platter's Travels*, p. 169.
45. Chambers, *Elizabethan Stage*, ii. p. 454. See also, Hentzner, *Journey into England*, p. 42.
46. The incident is described in Stubbes, *Anatomie of Abuses*, p. 179. See also Chambers, *Elizabethan Stage*, ii. pp. 462–5, 471.
47. Stubbes, *Anatomie of Abuses*, pp. 181–2.
48. Quoted in Thomas, *Man and the Natural World*, p. 162.
49. Assheton, *Journal*, pp. 49–50, 57–67.
50. Quoted in Heal and Holmes, *Gentry in England*, p. 292.
51. Quoted in Thomas, *Man and the Natural World*, p. 161.

Chapter 7: Two Sporting Monarchs

1. Quoted in Manning, *Hunters and Poachers*, p. 202.
2. Quoted in MacGregor, 'Household out of doors', pp. 86, 109.
3. *Stuart Proclamations*, i. p. 227. See also Nichols, *Progresses of King James*, i. p. 491. James's hunting is also discussed in Semenza, *Sport, Politics and Literature*, p. 88.
4. *Letters of King James*, pp. 245–9, quote at p. 246.
5. In a slightly different vein, he also held it therapeutic to bathe his gouty legs in the warm blood of bucks he had killed. See *Calendar of State Papers, Domestic Series, 1619–1623*, pp. 53, 56.
6. See, for example, Nichols, *Progresses of King James*, i. pp. 67–8, 521; ii. pp. 79–80; iii. p. 285.
7. Manning, *Hunters and Poachers*, p. 202.
8. MacGregor, 'Household out of doors', pp. 98–9.
9. Manning, *Hunters and Poachers*, p. 203. See also Semenza, *Sport, Politics and Literature*, p. 87.
10. Manning, *Hunters and Poachers*, p. 203.
11. Thomas, *Man and the Natural World*, p. 160; Manning, *Hunters and Poachers*, p. 202. See also *Report on the Laing Manuscripts*, i. pp. 99–100.
12. Manning, *Hunters and Poachers*, p. 196.
13. Ibid., p. 205.
14. *Stuart Proclamations*, i. pp. 227–30, 348, 590–1; ii. pp. 434–6, 444–6, 597–8.
15. Pettit, *Royal Forests of Northamptonshire*, p. 46.
16. *Letters of King James*, pp. 232–3. See also p. 227.
17. Manning, *Hunters and Poachers*, pp. 204–5.
18. Kirby, 'Stuart game prerogative', p. 241.
19. Nichols, *Progresses of King James*, iii. pp. 264–5. Bear-baiting is recorded at ibid., i. pp. 517, 528. See also Gilbey, *Sport*, pp. 16–17.
20. Ibid., i. pp. 515–16; ii. p. 88. See also Chambers, *Elizabethan Stage*, ii. p. 454.
21. Tait, 'Declaration of sports', pp. 561–8. See also the discussion in Semenza, *Sport, Politics and Literature*, pp. 85–114, esp. 93–6.

22. Lasdun, *English Park*, pp. 32–3. See also Cantor, *Changing English Countryside*, pp. 113, 116.

23. Moryson, *An Itinerary*, iv. pp. 148–9, 168.

24. Lasdun, *English Park*, p. 22.

25. Cliffe, *World of the Country House*, p. 50.

26. Manning, *Hunters and Poachers*, p. 44. See also Beaver, "'Bragging and daring words'", pp. 149–65, for further examples of feuding gentlemen.

27. Harrison, *Description of England*, pp. 254, 327.

28. Cliffe, *World of the Country House*, pp. 50–4.

29. The new qualifications were £40 in freehold land or £200 in movable property. 2 Jac. I., c. 27; 3 Jac. I, c. 13; 7 Jac. I, c. 11.

30. Quoted in Kirby, 'Stuart game prerogative', pp. 242–3.

31. Carlton, *Charles I*, pp. 3, 89, 129, 286.

32. Manning, *Hunters and Poachers*, p. 207.

33. *Calendar of State Papers ... Venice, 1632–6*, pp. 10, 17–18, 63, 220, 247, 268, 459, 466, 511; *1636–9*, pp. 14, 33, 46, 64, 269, 279, 316, 325, 433, 435–6.

34. Young, *Charles I*, pp. 72–125.

35. Grant, *Royal Forests*, pp. 187–8.

36. The best general account of Charles's forest policy is Hammersley, 'Revival of the forest laws', pp. 85–102. See also Crook, 'Records of forest eyres', p. 190.

37. Grant, *Royal Forests*, p. 193.

38. Ibid. The incident may go some way to explaining why the Earl of Warwick became a key Parliamentary figure during the 1630s, helping to lead gentry opposition to Charles I. See Hunt, *Puritan Moment*, pp. 267–8.

39. Petitt, *Royal Forests of Northamptonshire*, p. 88.

40. Grant, *Royal Forests*, pp. 191, 194.

41. Ibid., p. 191.

42. Pettit, *Royal Forests of Northamptonshire*, p. 88; Hammersley, 'Revival of forest laws', p. 96.

43. Quoted in Pettit, *Royal Forests of Northamptonshire*, p. 83.

44. 16 Car. I, c. 16. See Manning, *Hunters and Poachers*, p. 209.

Chapter 8: Civil Wars and the Decline of the Deer

1. Manning, *English People*, p. 190.

2. Gentles, 'Management of Crown lands', pp. 36–7.

3. Young, *Charles I*, pp. 126–72.

4. Hotson, 'Bear gardens and bear-baiting', p. 278.

5. *Acts and Ordinances*, i. p. 420.

6. Hotson, 'Bear gardens and bear-baiting', pp. 278–83.

7. Ibid., pp. 285–6.

8. *Writings and Speeches of Oliver Cromwell*, iii. pp. 484–5.

9. See also Parker, *English Sabbath*, p. 218; Sharpe, *Personal Rule*, p. 300.

10. See Marples, *History of Football*, pp. 24–40. See also Semenza, *Sport, Politics and Literature*, pp. 63–6.

11. Quoted in Cliffe, *World of the Country House*, p. 156.

12. Cox, *Royal Forests*, p. 299; Thomas, *Man and the Natural World*, p. 161.

13. Cliffe, *World of the Country House*, p. 156.

14. Manning, *English People*, pp. 188–90; Roberts, *Royal Landscape*, p. 118.

15. Roberts, *Royal Landscape*, p. 190.

16. Seddon, 'Application of forest law', p. 38.

17. Pettit, *Royal Forests of Northamptonshire*, p. 47; Manning, *English People*, p. 190; Gentles, 'Management of Crown lands', pp. 28–30.

18. Madge, *Domesday of Crown Lands*, pp. 107–15, 239–46. The act is reprinted in *Acts and Ordinances* ii. pp. 782–812, 946–9.

19. Petitt, *Royal Forests of Northamptonshire*, p. 70.
20. *Calendar of State Papers, Domestic Series, 1655*, p. 198; *Acts and Ordinances*, ii. pp. 116–22.
21. Cox, *Royal Forests*, pp. 142–3.
22. Manning, *English People*, pp. 191–2.
23. Cliffe, *World of the Country House*, p. 52. A private park in Gloucestershire saw a population of 700 deer reduced to about 100 during the 1640s. See Manning, *English People*, p. 192.
24. Seddon, 'Application of forest law', p. 38.
25. Manning, *English People*, pp. 192–3.
26. Ibid., p. 193.
27. Trench, *Poacher and Squire*, p. 107.
28. Rackham, *The Last Forest*, p. 104.
29. Lyth, 'Deer parks', pp. 20–3.
30. Hutton, *British Republic*, pp. 114–32.
31. Fraser, *King Charles II*, pp. 159, 292–3, 420.
32. Pepys, *Diary*, ii. p. 152.
33. Cox, *Royal Forests*, p. 79.
34. Whitehead, *Hunting and Stalking*, p. 21.
35. MacGregor, 'Household out of doors', p. 102; Roberts, *Royal Landscape*, p. 118.
36. Lasdun, *English Park*, p. 63.
37. Thompson, *Whigs and Hunters*, p. 56.
38. Cox, *Royal Forests*, pp. 130, 180.
39. MacGregor, 'Household out of doors', p. 103.
40. [Barrow], *Monarchy and the Chase*, p. 101.
41. Whitehead, *Hunting and Stalking*, pp. 22–3.
42. Ibid., p. 23; Hore, *The History of the Royal Buckhounds*, pp. 256–61.
43. [Barrow], *Monarchy and the Chase*, p. 105.
44. Ibid., pp. 110–18.
45. Hey, *Fiery Blades*, pp. 20–3.
46. Ibid.
47. Whitehead, *Hunting and Stalking*, pp. 103–22.
48. Ibid., pp. 123–33.
49. [Barrow], *Monarchy and the Chase*, pp. 113–18. See also Surtees, *Hunting Tours*, pp. 39–48, 50–61, 109–19; *Sporting Magazine*, April 1822, pp. 40–1; November 1822, pp. 88–9; Turner, *Heaven in a Rage*, pp. 84–7; *The Times*, 27 March 1807.
50. [Barrow], *Monarchy and the Chase*, p. 111. See also *Sporting Magazine*, Dec. 1797, p. 112.
51. *Sporting Magazine*, April 1793, pp. 41–4; Oct. 1793, pp. 1–5.
52. See, for example, Surtees, *Hunting Tours*, pp. 39–48; *Sporting Magazine*, Aug. 1830, pp. 292–3. Compare the decline of wild-deer hunting with Grassby's account of the failure of falconry to regain its place in upper-class culture following the Civil Wars, a development which he explains in part at least in terms of a shortage of hawks. See Grassby, 'Decline of falconry', pp. 37–62, esp. 54–62.
53. Broad, 'Whigs and deer-stealers', p. 59.
54. Gilmour, *Riot, Risings and Revolution*, pp. 193–8; Thompson, *Whigs and Hunters*, pp. 21–4. The act is reprinted in ibid., pp. 270–7; Broad, 'Whigs and deer-stealers', esp. pp. 60–7.

Chapter 9: A New Era Dawns

1. 1671, 22 & 23 Chas. II c. 25.
2. To place this figure in context, the basic qualification for the electoral franchise was £2 – as one opponent of the law commented, this qualification meant that fifty times the property was required 'to enable a man to kill a partridge, as to vote for a knight of the shire'. Blackstone, *Commentaries*, iv. p. 175.

3. Historians have estimated that no more than about 1 per cent of the population of around five million met this qualification. Munsche, *Gentlemen and Poachers*, p. 28; idem, 'Game laws in Wiltshire', p. 28.

4. 1691, 3 Wm & Mary c. 10.

5. On this point see in particular, Munsche, *Gentlemen and Poachers*, pp. 13–14.

6. Knox, *Essays Moral and Literary*, ii. p. 154.

7. Blackstone, *Commentaries*, iv. p. 409.

8. A useful summary of this legislation may be found in Munsche, *Gentlemen and Poachers*, pp. 167–86.

9. 1671, 22 & 23 Chas. II, c. 25.

10. 1707, 4 & 5 Wm & Mary c. 23. Also 1706, 5 Anne c. 14; 1710, 9 Anne c. 25.

11. 1755, 28 George II c. 12.

12. Quoted in Gilmour, *Riot, Risings and Revolution*, p. 195.

13. Knox, *Essays Moral and Literary*, ii. p. 153.

14. Taplin, *Observations on the Present State*, p. 2.

15. Blackstone, *Commentaries*, iv. p. 175.

16. Country Gentleman, *Remarks on the Laws Relating to the Game*, pp. 5–6.

17. Kirby, 'English game law system', p. 250.

18. Munsche, *Gentlemen and Poachers*, p. 28.

19. Taplin, *Observations on the Present State*, p. 5.

20. Marshall, *The Rural Economy of Norfolk*, i. pp. 172–3.

21. Ibid., pp. 173–5.

22. Ibid., p. 175.

23. *Essays on the Game Laws*, p. 5.

24. See in particular, Gilmour, *Riot, Risings and Revolution*, pp. 198–201.

25. Ibid., p. 199; Archer, *By a Flash and a Scare*, p. 224.

26. Daniel, *Rural Sports*, i. pp. 333–4.

27. Gilmour, *Riot, Risings, and Revolution*, p. 198.

28. Cox, *Gentleman's Recreation*, p. 87.

29. Gardiner, *Art and Pleasure of Hare-Hunting*, p. 4.

30. In addition to ibid., see Somervile, *The Chace*.

31. Munsche, *Gentlemen and Poachers*, p. 33.

32. *The Complete Family-Piece*, p. 311.

33. For the history of coursing see Daniel, *Rural Sports*, i. pp. 365–402; [Lawrence], *British Field Sports*, pp. 355–6; Harewood, *Dictionary of Sports*, pp. 34–5.

34. Cox, *Gentleman's Recreation*, bk 3; Jacob, *Compleat Sportsman*, pp. 18–32. Contrast this with the scale of game-shooting in France: Blanning, *Pursuit of Glory* (forthcoming), ch. 8.

35. See, for example, Cox, *Gentleman's Recreation*, bk 3, pp. 3–5.

36. *Sportsman's Dictionary*, ii. p. 158; See also Markland's poem devoted to extolling the joys of shooting flying: Markland, *Pteryplegia: or, the Art of Shooting-flying*.

37. Hastings, *English Sporting Guns*, pp. 7–10; George, *English Guns*, pp. 187–90.

38. George, *English Guns*, pp. 190–1. See also Trench, *History of Marksmanship*, pp. 126–91.

39. Edie, *Treatise on English Shooting*, p. 11; see also idem, *Art of English Shooting*.

40. In addition to the works by Edie quoted above, see Page, *The Art of Shooting Flying*; Montagu, *Sportsman's Directory*.

41. Montagu, *Sportsman's Directory*, p. 98.

42. [Lawrence], *British Field Sports*, p. 222.

43. See, for example, ibid., pp. 222–6; Taplin, *Sporting Dictionary and Rural Repository*, ii. pp. 247–89.

44. Taplin, *Sporting Dictionary*, ii. pp. 247–89; Daniel, *Rural Sports*, iii. pp. 44–51; [Lawrence], *British Field Sports*, pp. 222–6; Harewood, *Dictionary of Sports*, pp. 293–306.

45. See Hawker, *Diary of Colonel Peter Hawker*, 2 vols.

46. *Sporting Magazine*, March 1828, p. 314.

47. *Sporting Magazine*, May 1828, p. 45; April 1827, pp. 341–2. See also ibid., Nov. 1827, pp. 15–16; Dec. 1827, pp. 67, 84–5, 103; Jan. 1828, pp. 180–5, 230.

48. Daniel, *Rural Sports*, iii. pp. 61, 65.

49. Munsche, *Gentlemen and Poachers*, p. 39.

50. [Banville], *Banville Diaries*, pp. 60, 86, 101.

51. *Sporting Magazine*, Jan. 1823, p. 226. See also ibid., Jan. 1824, p. 227. On 21 November 1825, nearly 400 head had been killed at Mr Coke's Holkam estate. *Annals of Sporting*, Jan. 1826, p. 52.

52. Daniel, *Rural Sports*, iii. p. 33.

53. Ibid., iii. pp. 33–8; Harewood, *Dictionary of Sports*, pp. 241–2; [Lawrence], *Practical Treatise on Rearing Poultry*, pp. 105–12.

54. Hopkins, *Long Affray*, p. 73.

55. Munsche, *Gentlemen and Poachers*, p. 44.

56. Idem, 'Game laws in Wiltshire', p. 342.

57. Kirby, 'English game law system', pp. 244–5.

58. Quoted in Longrigg, *English Squire and his Sport*, p. 248.

59. Byng, *Torrington Diaries*, i. p. 395.

60. Munsche, *Gentlemen and Poachers*, p. 42.

Chapter 10: Hunting the Fox: 'fascinating and soul stirring sport'

1. The quote comes from Harewood, *Dictionary of Sport*, p. 140.

2. Quoted in Itzkowitz, *Peculiar Privilege*, p. 6.

3. Cook, *Observations on Foxhunting*, pp. 139–40; Willoughby de Broke, *Hunting the Fox*, pp. 86–7; Johnson, *Hunting Directory*, pp. 22–5.

4. [Gascoigne], *Arte of Venerie*, p. 192.

5. Stringer, *Experienc'd Huntsman*, p. 159. See also *Complete Family-Piece*, p. 294.

6. See for example, Nimrod, *The Chace*, pp. 28–31; Radcliffe, *Noble Science*, p. 155; Johnson, *Hunting Directory*, pp. 22–5.

7. For Meynell, see also Carr, *English Foxhunting*, pp. 38–41.

8. Stringer, *Experienc'd Huntsman*, p. 165.

9. Ibid., p. 172.

10. Gardiner, *Art and Pleasure of Hare-hunting*, p. 2.

11. Cook, *Observations on Foxhunting*, p. 151. Emphasis in original.

12. Landry, *Invention of the Countryside*, pp. 14–15.

13. Beckford, *Thoughts on Hunting*, p. 217.

14. Radcliffe, *Noble Science*, pp. 62–3, 104–26.

15. O'Keeffe, *The Fox-Chace*.

16. Barrow, *Monarchy and the Chase. Sporting Magazine*, Feb. 1793, p. 305.

17. Quoted in Carr, *English Foxhunting*, p. 41.

18. Taplin, *Sporting Dictionary*, i. p. 292.

19. Beckford, *Thoughts on Hunting*, p. 187.

20. Cook, *Observations on Foxhunting*, p. 137; 'Sir Edward Littleton's foxhunting diary', pp. 140, 142.

21. Ibid., p. 142.

22. Cook, *Observations on Foxhunting*, p. 139. See also Beckford, *Thoughts on Hunting*, p. 175; [Lawrence], *British Field Sports*, p. 397. Compare, however, Johnson, *Hunting Directory*, which in 1830 still advised that 'an early hour is most favourable to sport', p. 174.

23. Nimrod, *The Chace*, p. 30.

24. Cook, *Observations on Foxhunting*, pp. 187–92. See also, Radcliffe, *Noble Science*, pp. 283–6, esp. 285; Nimrod, *The Chace*, pp. 39–41.

25. Bray, *Sketch of a Tour*, p. 98.

26. Itzkowitz, *Peculiar Privilege*, p. 75. See also Carr, *English Foxhunting*, pp. 114–18.

27. Itzkowitz, *Peculiar Privilege*, p. 75. See also [Lawrence], *British Field Sports*, pp. 407–8.

28. See, for example, Cobbett, *Rural Rides*, i. p. 38.

29. Cook, *Observations on Foxhunting*, p. 103.

30. Byng, *Torrington Diaries*, iii. p. 163.

31. Beckford, *Thoughts on Hunting*, p. 176.

32. Quoted in Dixon, *History of the Bramham Moor Hunt*, pp. 210–11. See also Cook, *Observations on Foxhunting*, pp. 94–106; Smith, *Extracts from the Diary of a Huntsman*, pp. 70–2, 85–96.

33. See Ellis, *Leicestershire and the Quorn*, pp. 24–9; Finch, '"Grass, grass, grass"', pp. 44–6.

34. Carr, *English Foxhunting*, pp. 68–71; Bovill, *England of Nimrod and Surtees*, pp. 31–7. See also [Lawrence], *British Field Sports*, pp. 409–10.

35. Radcliffe, *Noble Science*, pp. 128–31, quote at p. 128.

36. Itzkowitz, *Peculiar Privilege*, pp. 50–66, esp. 52.

37. Surtees, *Handley Cross*, p. 11.

38. See also Carr, *English Foxhunting*, pp. 106–10. Ellis, *Leicestershire and the Quorn*, pp. 94–5.

39. Beckford, *Thoughts on Hunting*, p. 214; [Lawrence], *British Field Sports*, pp. 421–3.

40. Blaine, *Encyclopaedia of Rural Sports*, p. 503.

41. Bovill, *England of Nimrod and Surtees*, pp. 99–101.

42. See, for example, Smith, *Extracts from the Diary of a Huntsman*, pp. 117–28; Blaine, *Encyclopaedia of Rural Sports*, pp. 285–6, 480–9.

43. Bray, *Sketch of a Tour*, p. 98.

44. Nimrod, *The Chace*, p. 27.

45. Nichols, *History of Leicester*, iii. p. 101n.

46. Landry, *Invention of the Countryside*, p. 14.

47. Ibid.

48. Radcliffe, *Noble Science*, pp. 132–40, quote at p. 133. See also Surtees, *Hunting Tours*, pp. 7–8; idem, *Analysis of Hunting Field*, pp. 2–3.

49. Carr, *English Foxhunting*, p. 60.

50. Quoted in Bovill, *England of Nimrod and Surtees*, pp. 121–2. See also Itzkowitz, *Peculiar Privilege*, p. 24.

51. See, in particular, Jones, 'Meeting the costs of the hunt', pp. 36–8.

52. Itzkowitz, *Peculiar Privilege*, p. 32; Finch, '"Grass, grass, grass"', p. 48.

53. *Essays on Hunting*, p. 52.

54. Radcliffe, *Noble Science*, p. 134. See also *Sporting Magazine*, Jan. 1823, p. 210.

55. Somervile, *The Chace*, p. 20. See also Donald, *Divided Nature* (forthcoming), ch. 7.

56. Coss, *Lady in Medieval England*, p. 67; Manning, *Hunters and Poachers*, pp. 12–13.

57. Contrast with Landry, *Invention of the Countryside*, pp. 145–67.

58. Thomson, *The Seasons*, p. 35.

59. Cook, *Observations on Foxhunting*, p. 173.

60. Surtees, *Analysis of Hunting Field*, p. 293.

61. Idem, *Hunting Tours*, p. 107; idem, *Analysis of Hunting Field*, p. 294.

62. Cook, *Observations on Foxhunting*, p. 173.

63. Ellis, *Leicestershire and the Quorn*, p. 107.

64. Quoted in ibid., p. 108.

65. Itzkowitz, *Peculiar Privilege*, pp. 48–9.

66. *Sporting Magazine*, March 1795. See also ibid., June 1830, pp. 98–109.

67. Ibid., Jan. 1836, pp. 258–61.

68. Harrison, *Description of England*, pp. 325–6.

69. Carr, *English Foxhunting*, p. 110.

70. For the planting of coverts see in particular, Finch, '"Grass, grass, grass"', pp. 46–7; Ellis, *Leicestershire and the Quorn*, pp. 60–4. See also Cook, *Observations on Foxhunting*, pp. 42–54, 66–70; Blaine, *Encyclopaedia of Rural Sports*, pp. 450–1.

71. See, for instance, [Lawrence], *British Field Sports*, pp. 428–9.

72. Surtees, *Hunting Tours*, p. 86.

73. Daniel, *Rural Sports*, i. p. 211.
74. *Sporting Magazine*, April 1827, pp. 340–1.
75. Cook, *Observations on Foxhunting*, p. 49.
76. *Sporting Magazine*, July 1828, p. 241.
77. Ibid., April 1828, pp. 393–5.
78. Daniel, *Rural Sports*, i. pp. 211–12.
79. Beckford, *Thoughts on Hunting*, pp. 325–7.
80. Surtees, *Mr Sponge's Sporting Tour*, p. 73. See also *Sporting Magazine*, Jan. 1823, p. 210; April 1823, p. 18; Dec. 1827, pp. 102–3.
81. See Bovill, *England of Nimrod and Surtees*, pp. 45–52.
82. *Sporting Magazine*, April 1828, p. 394; July 1828, p. 239.
83. Ibid., March 1824, p. 294.
84. Ibid., April 1826, pp. 363–4.
85. Bovill, *England of Nimrod and Surtees*, p. 50.
86. Surtees, *Hunting Tours*, pp. 95–6.
87. *Sporting Magazine*, April 1826, p. 263. See also ibid., Jan. 1823, p. 210; April 1828, p. 394.
88. See, for example, Gillard, *Operations of the Quorn*, p. 15.
89. Blaine, *Encyclopaedia of Rural Sports*, p. 502.
90. Bovill, *England of Nimrod and Surtees*, p. 48. For more on Russell and his hunting see Noon, *Parson Jack Russell*, pp. 47–54, 74–87, 100–17.
91. *Sporting Magazine*, April 1826, p. 367; Oct. 1826, p. 428; May 1828, p. 23. Surtees, *Hunting Tours*, pp. 317–18.
92. Thomas, *Fifty Years of my Life*, p. 342.
93. Grose, *The Grumbler*, pp. 14–15.
94. The expression is from Somervile, *Chace*, p. 48.
95. Carr, *English Foxhunting*, p. 215.
96. Ibid., pp. 216–17. See also Itzkowitz, *Peculiar Privilege*, pp. 67–70.
97. Osbaldiston, *British Sportsman*, p. 527.

Chapter 11: 'A busy and anxious disposition to legislate'

1. *Hansard's Parliamentary Debates*, 3rd series, xxix (1835), cols 537–8.
2. Any number of sources might be used to illustrate this sentiment. See, for example: Granger, *Apology for the Brute Creation*, pp. 6, 15; Barry, *Bull-baiting!*, p. 3. See also Tucker, *Affectionate Address*, p. 8; *The Country Clergyman's Shrovetide Gift*, p. 5; Jenyns, *Disquisitions*, p. 18; Stockdale, *Remonstrance against Inhumanity*, p. 4; Primatt, *Duty of Mercy*, p. 7; Smith, *Lessons for Youth*, p. 2; *Gentleman's Magazine*, Jan. 1750, pp. 18–19, May 1761, pp. 201–2.
3. Richmond, *Sermon*, p. 8.
4. Macaulay, *Essay on Cruelty*, p. 10.
5. Moore, *Sin and Folly of Cruelty*, p. 4.
6. Bentham, *Principles of Morals and Legislation*, p. 412n.
7. See, for example, *Spectator*, 18 July 1711; *Guardian*, 21 May 1713; *London Magazine*, Dec. 1747; *Universal Magazine*, Oct. 1758, p. 166; *Familiar Essays*, p. 154. Montaigne had argued that there was a 'certain Respect, and a general Duty of Humanity, that ties us not only to Beasts that have Life, and Sense, but even to Trees and Plants. We owe Justice to Men, and Grace and Benignity to other Creatures that are capable of it.' Bentham, *Montaigne, Essays of Montaigne*, ii. p. 173. See also the discussion in Thomas, *Man and the Natural World*, pp. 143–65; Ryder, *Animal Revolution*, pp. 59–80.
8. *European Magazine*, July 1800, p. 27. See also ibid., Jan. 1752, p. 51: 'we are bound to animals by the general duties of humanity'. On preventing unnecessary suffering, see also, *Adventurer*, 13 March 1753, p. 218; *World*, 19 Aug. 1756, p. 150.
9. Griffin, *England's Revelry*, p. 116. See also Donald, *Divided Nature* (forthcoming), ch. 8.
10. Griffin, *England's Revelry*, pp. 119–22.

11. *Bury and Norwich Post*, 7 Nov. 1792; *Lincoln, Rutland and Stamford Mercury*, 8 Nov. 1811.

12. *Sporting Magazine*, Dec. 101, p. 133.

13. *York Courant*, 21 Oct. 1790.

14. *Lincoln Mercury*, 12 Nov. 1819.

15. *Sporting Magazine*, Dec. 1801, pp. 132–3. Other writers reported on a 'poor innocent bull', and a 'poor animal' they had watched being baited. See *Stamford Mercury*, 10 Nov. 1802; *Sporting Magazine*, Dec. 1801, p. 133.

16. *Sporting Magzaine*, Dec. 1802, p. 132.

17. *Aris's Birmingham Gazette*, 7 Oct. 1792.

18. Platter, *Platter's Travels*, p. 169.

19. Von Uffenbach, *Travels of Uffenbach*, p. 59.

20. Rathgeb, 'Narrative of excursion', p. 46.

21. Houghton, *Collection for Husbandry*, p. 290. See also, Hentzner, *Journey into England*, p. 42 (bull-baiting was 'not without great risque to the dogs'); Misson, *Memoirs*, pp. 24–7.

22. See, for instance, the case of the crowd in Bury St Edmunds cutting off a bull's hooves in order to enrage him, reported in *Monthly Magazine*, Dec. 1801, p. 464.

23. Lawrence, *Philosophical Treatise on Horses*, i. p. 125.

24. Ibid., pp. 125, 127.

25. Turner, *Reckoning with the Beast*, p. 15.

26. *Parliamentary History*, xxxv (1800), col. 202.

27. Ibid., col. 203.

28. *The Times*, 25 April 1800.

29. Barry, *Bull Baiting!*; Stockdale, *Remonstrance against Inhumanity*.

30. Turner, *Reckoning with the Beast*, p. 15.

31. Ryder, *Animal Revolution*, p. 834.

32. *Hansard's Parliamentary Debates*, xiv (1809), col. 1036.

33. Turner, *Reckoning with the Beast*, p. 16.

34. Ryder, *Animal Revolution*, pp. 84–6.

35. 1822, 3 Geo. IV c. 126.

36. Turner, *Reckoning with the Beast*, pp. 39–40; Ritvo, *Animal Estate*, p. 127.

37. 1835, 5 & 6 Wm. IV c. 59.

38. Harrison, 'Animals and the state', pp. 788–9; 1849, 12 & 13 Vic. c. 92.

39. The suppression of bull-baiting in the west midlands is described in Griffin, *England's Revelry*, pp. 235–49.

40. *Bury and Norwich Post*, 10 Nov. 1841, p. 2; 10 Nov. 1842, p. 3; 23 Nov. 1842, p. 45; *East Anglian Miscellany*, pp. 37–8.

41. Turner, *Reckoning with the Beast*, pp. 40–5; Turner, *Heaven in a Rage*, pp. 129–30, 146–7; Ryder, *Animal Revolution*, pp. 89–92.

42. Harrison, 'Animals and the state', pp. 789, 794.

43. Taplin, *Sporting Dictionary*, pp. 44, 93–6. Likewise, when Pierce Egan's fictional hero Tom went to the Westminster pit to watch a monkey-baiting he found 'a motley group ... all in rude contact, jostling and pushing against each other'. Egan, *Life in London*, p. 259.

44. See also Ritvo, *Animal Estate*, pp. 126–57.

45. *Parliamentary History*, xxxvi (1802), col. 848. For the full debates see ibid., cols 829–54.

46. *Parliamentary History*, n.s. x (1824), col. 133.

47. Quoted in Malcolmson, *Popular Recreations*, pp. 154–5.

48. Turner, *Heaven in a Rage*, pp. 129–30, 141–60.

49. Sydney Smith, 'Society for the suppression of vice', *Edinburgh Review*, 13 (Jan. 1809), p. 340.

Chapter 12: Game Laws in the Nineteenth Century

1. Kingsley, *Yeast*, p. 115.

2. Arch, *Ploughtail to Parliament*, p. 157.

3. See, for example, *Norfolk Chronicle and Norwich Gazette*, 15 Jan. 1820; 26 Feb. 1820.

4. Hopkins, *Long Affray*, p. 41.

5. Arch, *Ploughtail to Parliament*, p. 29.

6. 1831, 1–2 Wm. IV. c. 32.

7. Archer, *By a Flash and a Scare*, p. 234.

8. Arch, *Ploughtail to Parliament*, pp. 159–61.

9. Hawker, *Instructions to Young Sportsmen*, pp. 51–65; Hastings, *English Sporting Guns*, pp. 12–13; George, *English Guns*, pp. 245–52.

10. George, *English Guns*, pp. 303–28.

11. Ibid., pp. 246–9.

12. [Cresswell], *Eighteen Years on Sandringham Estate*, p. 70.

13. Hopkins, *Long Affray*, p. 74.

14. *The Times*, 2 Nov. 1836.

15. Ibid., 4 Feb. 1845.

16. Martelli, *Elveden Enterprise*, p. 42.

17. *The Times*, 4 Feb. 1845.

18. Thomas, *Fifty Years of my Life*, ii. p. 240.

19. Hopkins, *Long Affray*, pp. 213–14.

20. *The Times*, 17 Jan. 1845. See also Ruffer, *Big Shots*, pp. 19–24, 26–36, 54–60.

21. *The Times*, 4 Feb. 1845.

22. Ibid.

23. Hopkins, *Long Affray*, p. 208.

24. Kirby, 'Attack on the English game laws', p. 29.

25. *The Times*, 4 Feb. 1845.

26. *Report of Select Committee on Operation of the Game Laws*, xxiv (1845); ix pt 1 and pt 2 (1846).

27. Jefferies, *Amateur Poacher*, p. 261.

28. Hawker, *James Hawker's Journal*, p. 20.

29. Arch, *Ploughtail to Parliament*, p. 154.

30. Hopkins, *Long Affray*, pp. 246–7.

31. Richardson, *Complete Foxhunter*, pp. 26–50.

32. 1880, 43 & 44 Vic. c. 47.

33. The act is discussed in Fisher, 'Property rights in pheasants', pp. 165–80, esp. 173–6.

34. Ibid., p. 177.

35. Martelli, *Elveden Enterprise*, pp. 50–1. For some record bags at Elveden, see also Turner, *Memoirs of a Gamekeeper*, pp. 51–8, 142–5. For pheasant-rearing see pp. 24–5, 129–32.

36. Jefferies, *Amateur Poacher*, pp. 259–60.

37. Hawker, *James Hawker's Journal*, p. 56.

38. Ibid., p. 55.

39. Ibid., p. 54.

40. *I Walked by Night*, pp. 124, 156.

Chapter 13: Hunting Attacked

1. Freeman, 'Morality of field sports', p. 354.

2. Trollope, 'Mr Freeman on the morality of hunting', p. 625.

3. Freeman, 'Morality of field sports', pp. 370, 378.

4. Lawrence, *Philosophical Treatise on Horses*, ii. p. 13.

5. *Hansard's Parliamentary Debates*, n.s. x (1824), p. 488.

6. Trollope had already laid out his support for hunting in his *Hunting Sketches* published in 1865.

7. Trollope, 'Mr Freeman on the morality of field sports', p. 619.

8. Ibid., p. 623.

9. See also the discussions in Carr, *English Foxhunting*, pp. 204–5; Itzkowitz, *Peculiar Privilege*, pp. 143–5.

10. See the discussion in the *Daily Telegraph*, 18 Dec. 1869, 21 Dec. 1869, 29 Dec. 1869, 4 Jan. 1870, 14 Jan. 1870; Helen Taylor, 'A few words', pp. 63–8.

11. Beaufort, *Hunting*, pp. 322–33.

12. Carr, *English Foxhunting*, pp. 181–4. See also Finch, '"Grass, grass, grass"', p. 48; Ellis, *Leicestershire and the Quorn*, pp. 133–48.

13. Thompson, *History of the Fernie Hunt*, p. 93.

14. Whyte-Melville, *Riding Recollections*, p. 215.

15. Race, *Seventy Years a Master*, p. 164.

16. Trollope, *Hunting Sketches*, p. 30.

17. Ibid., pp. 29–41, quote at p. 31.

18. Idem, *Duke's Children*, pp. 445–9.

19. Idem, *Eustace Diamonds*, esp. pp. 296–318.

20. See also O'Donoghue, *Ladies on Horseback*, esp. pp. 81–130; Richardson, *Complete Foxhunter*, pp. 98–108.

21. The quote is taken from Elmhirst, *Best Season on Record*, p. 191. Correct female riding attire in the 1860s is described in Clarke, *Habit and Horse*, pp. 19–20, 30–2.

22. Ellis, *Leicestershire and the Quorn*, p. 113.

23. Fane, *Chit-Chat*, p. 136.

24. Ridley, *Fox Hunting*, pp. 81–2.

25. Elmhirst, *Cream of Leicestershire*, pp. 234–5.

26. Thompson, *History of the Fernie Hunt*, pp. 131, 133.

27. Lovell, *Hunting Pageant*, p. 148.

28. Buxton, *Ladies of the Chase*, pp. 94–5, 104–24.

29. *Hunting Diary and Guide, 1913–1914*, pp. 157–60.

30. See, for example, Richardson, *Compete Foxhunter*. This chapter on 'Hunting nowadays' contains sections on bag foxes and shortages of supply. Ibid., pp. 25–51.

31. Carr, *English Foxhunting*, pp. 223–7; Itzkowitz, *Peculiar Privilege*, p. 148.

32. *Baily's Hunting Directory*, 1901, p. 26.

33. Ibid., 1905, pp. 1–18.

34. Fisher, 'Victorian vulpicide', p. 124.

35. Ibid.

36. Ibid.

37. Winsten, *Salt and his Circle*, pp. 45–50. Ryder, *Animal Revolution*, p. 126.

38. Ryder, *Animal Revolution*, p. 127.

39. Taylor, '"Pig-sticking princes"', p. 36.

40. Weinbren, 'Against *all* cruelty: the Humanitarian League', p. 97.

41. Fairholme, *Century of Work*, p. 100.

42. Turner, *Heaven in a Rage*, p. 240.

43. Ibid., p. 242.

44. Thomas, *Politics of Hunting*, p. 47.

45. Taylor, '"Pig-sticking princes"', p. 35.

46. Quoted in ibid., p. 47. In the 1930s, one hunter labelled the opponents of hunting 'Communists, Pacifists, Shavians, and other vegetarians'. See Watson, *Hunting Pie*, p. 20.

47. Quoted in Weinbren, 'Against *all* cruelty: the Humanitarian League', p. 94.

48. *The Times*, 16 April 1902, p. 11.

49. Ibid.

50. Ibid., 23 Jan. 1903, p. 7. See also ibid., 21 Nov. 1903, p. 11; 24 Nov. 1903, p. 12; 21 March 1910, p. 21.

51. Thomas, *Politics of Hunting*, p. 216.

52. Turner, *Heaven in a Rage*, p. 242.

53. McKenzie, 'British Field Sports Society', pp. 178–9.

54. Ibid.

55. 1911, 1 & 2 Geo. 5 c. 27.

56. Thomas, *Politics of Hunting*, pp. 214–15.
57. Salt, *Animals' Rights*, p. 68.
58. Idem, ed., *Killing for Sport*, pp. v–viii.
59. Ibid., p. 59.
60. Ibid., p. xx.
61. Turner, *Heaven in a Rage*, p. 283.
62. Ridley, *Fox Hunting*, p. 148.
63. Lovell, *Hunting Pageant*, p. 137.
64. H. W. Selby Lowndes, quoted in Ridley, *Fox Hunting*, p. 146.
65. Willoughby de Broke, *Hunting the Fox*, p. 1.
66. Ibid., p. 5.
67. Ridley, *Fox Hunting*, pp. 153–4.
68. Isaacson, *Wild Host*, p. 138.
69. Watson, *Hunting Pie*, pp. 89–90.
70. Ibid., p. 86; *More Foxhunting*, p. 97.
71. Summerhays, *Elements of Hunting*, p. 19.
72. Churchward, *Master of Hounds Speaks*, pp. 15, 5.
73. Ridley, *Fox Hunting*, p. 147.
74. Lovell, *Hunting Pageant*, p. 143.
75. Buxton, *Ladies of the Chase*, pp. 125–44.
76. Elmhirst, *Best Season on Record*, p. 191.
77. *The Times*, 8 Nov. 1905, p. 9. See also Buxton, *Ladies of the Chase*, pp. 91–2.
78. *The Times*, 8 Nov. 1905, p. 9.
79. Menzies, *Women in the Hunting Field*, pp. 35, 45.
80. Buxton, *Ladies of the Chase*, p. 106. The wearing of a white collar was (and still is) a highly prized privilege awarded to hunters who have excelled in the field.
81. Menzies, *Women in the Hunting Field*, pp. 38–9, 42–4.
82. Buxton, *Ladies of the Chase*, pp. 132–3.
83. *More Foxhunting*, p. 49.
84. Churchward, *Master of Hounds Speaks*, p. 21.
85. 1921, 11 & 12 Geo. V c. 14. See also Thomas, *Politics of Hunting*, p. 215 and the table summarising anti-hunting legislation on p. 217.
86. Ryder, *Animal Revolution*, pp. 135–6.
87. *The Times*, 9 March 1929, p. 1; 3 March 1926, p. 1.
88. Ibid., 5 March 1927, p. 7; 8 Aug. 1928, p. 14; 7 Aug. 1929, p. 12.
89. Ibid., 8 Aug. 1928, p. 14.
90. Thomas, *Politics of Hunting*, p. 67.
91. Ibid., p. 68.
92. Ibid., p. 67; George, *Rural Uprising*, p. 20.
93. George, *Rural Uprising*, p. 20.
94. Ryder, *Animal Revolution*, p. 135.
95. McKenzie, 'British Field Sports Society', pp. 181–2. See also *The Times*, 28 March 1929; 20 May 1919; 5 Dec. 1930.
96. *Baily's Hunting Directory*, 1938, p. 49.
97. See, for example, *The Times*, 19 March 1901, p. 11; 2 May 1901, p. 6.

Chapter 14: A New Jerusalem?

1. For example, a new scarlet riding coat required eighteen clothing coupons in 1947. A new top hat was virtually unobtainable. See Ridley, *Foxhunting*, p. 172.
2. Smith, *Magic of the Quorn*, pp. 33–42, quote p. 34.
3. Chapman, '1949 Committee', in Moore, ed., *Against Hunting*, p. 139.
4. *Report of the Committee on Cruelty to Wild Animals*, p. 5.

5. Ibid.
6. Ibid., p. 110.
7. Quoted in Thomas, *Politics of Hunting*, p. 120.
8. Chapman, '1949 Committee' in Moore, ed., *Against Hunting*, p. 140.
9. Ibid.
10. Isaacson, *Wild Host*, pp. 145–6.
11. Clayton, *The Chase*, pp. 6–10.
12. Beaufort, *Fox-hunting*.
13. Clayton, *The Chase*, p. 14.
14. Ibid., p. 10.
15. Smith, *Magic of the Quorn*, p. 93.
16. Ridley, *Foxhunting*, pp. 167–9, 175.
17. Buxton, *Ladies of the Chase*, pp. 145–6.
18. Lovell, *Hunting Pageant*, p. 157.
19. *The Times*, 17 April 1976, p. 12.
20. Ibid., 9 Nov. 1974, p. 16.
21. Pye-Smith, *Fox-Hunting*, p. 5.
22. Ridley, *Foxhunting*, p. 131.
23. *Baily's Hunting Directory*, 1908, pp. 3–6.
24. Watson, *Hunting Pie*, p. 79.
25. Ibid., pp. 80–1.
26. *Baily's Hunting Directory*, 1928, pp. 36–7.
27. *Field Hunting Year Book, 1936–7*, p. xx.
28. Summerhays, *Elements of Hunting*, p. vii.
29. Clayton, *Foxhunting in Paradise*, p. 161.
30. Ibid., p. 85.
31. Guest and Jackson, *Hunting Year*, p. 27.
32. Thomas, *Politics of Hunting*, pp. 190, 221.
33. Ibid., p. 191.
34. Ibid., p. 193.
35. *Report of the Committee on Cruelty to Wild Animals*, p. 45.
36. Thomas, *Politics of Hunting*, p. 75.
37. *The Times*, 3 Feb. 1976, p. 1.
38. Thomas, *Politics of Hunting*, p. 94.
39. *The Times*, 20 Nov. 1972, p. 1; 14 Dec. 1972, p. 1; 16 Dec. 1972, p. 13; 28 Dec. 1972, p. 2.
40. Ibid., 8 Dec. 1972, p. 16.
41. Ibid., 2 April 1976, p. 3.
42. Thomas, *Politics of Hunting*, p. 220.
43. Ibid., p. 221.
44. Ibid., p. 193.
45. Ibid., p. 225.
46. Ibid., p. 235.
47. Ibid., p. 226.
48. Ibid., p. 225.
49. *The Times*, 16 May 1975, p. 6.
50. Ibid., 20 April 1968, p. 2.
51. Ibid., 24 Dec. 1970, p. 10; 27 Dec. 1974, p. 3.
52. Ibid., 6 March 1978, p. 3.
53. Ibid., 20 April 1977, p. 2.
54. Ibid., 29 July 1977, p. 2.
55. Ibid., 20 March 1980, p. 4. Another case is reported in ibid., 6 Feb. 1981, p. 5. For the very different treatment meted out to those accused of assaulting the hunters, see ibid., 9 April 1980, p. 4; 3 June 1980, p. 2.

56. Ibid., 8 March 1978, p. 2; 13 June 1978, p. 1; 29 June 1978, p. 1; 11 July 1978, p. 2

Chapter 15: A Last Reprieve

1. Politicians' responses to John McFall's Wild Mammals (Protection) Bill designed to prohibit hunting with hounds. *The Times*, 4 March 1995.
2. George, *Rural Uprising*, p. 40.
3. Thomas, *Politics of Hunting*, p. 99. See also idem, 'Hunting as a political issue', pp. 19–30.
4. Thomas, 'Hunting as a political issue'.
5. *The Times*, 18 May 1982, p. 3.
6. Ibid., 14 Feb. 1982, p. 3; 31 May 1982, p. 4.
7. Ibid., 9 Dec. 1982, p. 19.
8. Ibid., 16 Sept. 1980, p. 2.
9. Ibid., 12 May 1982, p. 2; 13 May 1982, p. 5.
10. Ibid., 7 May 1982, p. 3.
11. Ibid.
12. Thomas, *Politics of Hunting*, pp. 100–2.
13. George, *Rural Uprising*, p. 41.
14. Or as one hunt saboteur put it, 'if we can punch them in the guts on their own ground, it will be the end of foxhunting'. *The Times*, 31 March 1982, p. 3.
15. Ibid., 26 March 1982, p. 3; 1 April 1982, p. 3; 9 Dec. 1982, p. 19.
16. Ibid., 13 May 1982, p. 2.
17. Ibid., 17 May 1982, p. 3; 19 May 1982, p. 1.
18. George, *Rural Uprising*, p. 43.
19. *The Times*, 26 May 1982, p. 3; 9 Dec. 1982, p. 19.
20. Ibid., 13 May 1983, p. 4. See also Thomas, *Politics of Hunting*, chapter 9.
21. *The Times*, 24 May 1982, p. 3; 17 June 1982, p. 2.
22. Ibid., 2 Aug. 1982, p. 3.
23. Ibid., 29 July 1983, p. 4.
24. *Guardian*, 10 Feb. 1986.
25. George, *Rural Uprising*, p. 43.
26. Ibid., p. 45.
27. *Guardian*, 21 Jan. 1988; 27 Jan. 1988.
28. Ibid., 14 March 1978, p. 3; Clayton, *Foxhunting in Paradise*, pp. 132–4.
29. Clayton, *The Chase*, p. 7; *Daily Mail*, 27 Oct. 1994, p. 3.
30. Ibid., pp. 7, 56–7.
31. Ibid., pp. 13, 33.
32. Ibid., pp. 101, 106.
33. Carroll, *Diary of a Foxhunting Man*, p. 170; *Sunday Times*, 19 Nov. 1989.
34. Clayton, *The Chase*, p. 33.
35. Ibid., p. 106.
36. Carroll, *Diary of a Foxhunting Man*, pp. 170–1.
37. Ibid., p. 171.
38. Pye-Smith, *Fox-Hunting*, p. 5.
39. Carroll, *Diary of a Foxhunting Man*, p. 23.
40. See, for example, Thompson, *History of the Fernie Hunt*, pp. 159–62.
41. Clayton, *The Chase*, pp. 109–12; Carroll, *Diary of a Foxhunting Man*, pp. 108–15.
42. Blackwood, *In the Pink*, p. 104.
43. Carroll, *Diary of a Foxhunting Man*, p. 118.
44. See the account in Blackwood, *In the Pink*, pp. 100–7, 124–36. See also Carroll, *Diary of a Foxhunting Man*, pp. 130–9.
45. *Committee of Inquiry into Hunting with Dogs*. Central Committee of Fell Packs, 2.1.
46. Wadsworth *et al.*, *Vive la Chasse*, pp. 51–2.

47. Ibid.
48. Ibid.
49. *Committee of Inquiry into Hunting with Dogs*. Central Committee of Fell Packs, 4.5, 5.5, 6.3, 7.3, 8.4, 9.4.
50. Pye-Smith, *Fox-Hunting*, p. 6.
51. *The Times*, 20 July 1937, p. 8.
52. *Guardian*, 21 Oct. 1988. See also *The Times*, 27 Aug. 1988.
53. *Sunday Times*, 30 Oct. 1988.
54. Membership fell by 7,000 (from 37,000 to 30,000) between 1977 and 1984. Figures quoted in *The Times*, 27 Dec. 1985, p. 3.
55. Ibid.
56. Ibid., 19 March 1982, p. 9.
57. Ibid., 27 Dec. 1986; *Guardian*, 19 Dec. 1988.
58. *The Times*, 27 Dec. 1986.
59. *Guardian*, 28 Dec. 1987.
60. *The Times*, 27 Dec. 1988.
61. Ibid., 19 Nov. 1984.
62. Ibid., 28 Dec. 1984.
63. Ibid., 27 Dec. 1984.
64. Ibid.
65. Ibid., 28 Dec. 1984, p. 2.
66. *Guardian*, 27 Dec. 1984.
67. *Sunday Times*, 12 Sept. 1993.
68. *Independent*, 27 Dec. 1994.
69. *Guardian*, 29 July, 1994; *Daily Mail*, 29 July 1994.
70. *Independent*, 27 Dec. 1994; 1 Nov. 1995.
71. Ibid.
72. Ibid.
73. Cowley and Stace, 'Wild Mammals Bill', pp. 339–55.
74. *Evening Standard*, 14 Feb. 1992.
75. *Guardian*, 28 April 1993.
76. Ibid., 13 Feb. 1995.
77. *Daily Mail*, 4 March 1995. Most of the votes had been cast by Labour and Liberal MPs, but nearly thirty Tories had also supported the bill.
78. Ibid.
79. *Guardian*, 11 July 1995.
80. *The Times*, 3 March 1995.
81. Ibid., 4 March 1995; *Independent*, 4 March 1995.
82. *The Times*, 5 Aug. 1993.
83. *Guardian*, 30 Sept. 1993.
84. Ibid., 28 Dec. 1993.
85. *The Times*, 14 Dec. 1990.
86. *Sunday Times*, 9 July 1989; *Daily Mail*, 6 Oct. 1993.
87. The full list is printed in *The Times*, 22 May 1982, p. 10.
88. *The Times*, 27 Nov. 1982, p. 9.
89. Ibid., 1 Nov. 1990. By way of contrast, historians have estimated that around 50,000 people rode to hounds during the 1880s. See Jones, 'Meeting the costs of the hunt', pp. 36–8.

Chapter 16: The End of the Road

1. *Morning Star*, 24 Nov. 2004.
2. *Independent*, 5 Aug. 2006.

3. A brief summary of Labour's position on hunting is contained in Garner, *Political Animals*, pp. 111–21.
4. *The Times*, 23 May 1997, 12 June 1997; *Independent*, 12 June 1997; *The Times*, 17 June 1997.
5. *The Times*, 17 June 1997.
6. Ibid., 11 July 1997.
7. *Independent*, 11 July 1997.
8. *The Times*, 29 Nov. 1997.
9. *Independent*, 29 Nov. 1997; *Daily Mail*, 29 Nov. 1997.
10. *Independent*, 29 Nov. 1997.
11. Mori Poll (71% 10 July 1997). BBC1's viewer telephone vote, *Daily Mail*, 10 July 1997.
12. *Guardian*, 21 Feb. 1998.
13. *The Times*, 2 March 1988.
14. *Guardian*, 2 March 1988.
15. *The Times*, 2 March 1998.
16. *Sunday Times*, 1 March 1998.
17. *Observer*, 1 March 1998; *Independent*, 21 Sept. 1997.
18. *Independent*, 16 Nov. 1995.
19. Ibid., 12 Nov. 1995; *The Times*, 2 March 1998.
20. *Independent*, 21 Sept. 1997; *Guardian*, 22 Sept. 1997.
21. *Guardian*, 15 Nov. 1995.
22. *Independent*, 12 Nov., 1995.
23. *The Times*, 3 Feb. 1997.
24. *Independent*, 2 March 1988.
25. *Guardian*, 28 Feb. 1998.
26. *Independent*, 4 April 1998; *The Times*, 26 Dec. 1998.
27. *Report of the Committee into Hunting with Dogs*, p. 1; *Independent*, 12 Nov. 1999.
28. *The Times*, 15 Dec. 1999.
29. Ibid., 8 April 2000.
30. *Report of the Committee into Hunting with Dogs*, p. 1.
31. See for example, *Independent*, 13 June 2000; *The Times*, 13 June 2000.
32. *Telegraph*, 21 Dec. 2000; 18 Jan. 2001.
33. *The Times*, 27 March 2001.
34. Ibid.
35. *Guardian*, 9 May 2001.
36. Ibid., 11 May 2001.
37. *The Times*, 18 Nov. 2004, p. 21.
38. Hunting Act, 2004, c. 37.
39. *The Times*, 29 Jan. 2005, p. 4; 17 Feb. 2005, p. 2.
40. Ibid., 14 Oct. 2005, p. 33.
41. *Guardian*, 18 Nov. 2004.
42. *Report of the Committee into Hunting with Dogs*, pp. 7, 83.
43. As the *Independent* observed, 'There are one or two known facts about fox-hunting: foxes are not classed as significant pests and hunts probably kill only 2–3 per cent of the population in a season. But as the debate overheats it is unlikely these will get much of a hearing.' *Independent*, 11 Feb. 1992.
44. *Telegraph*, 9 Dec. 2000.
45. *Horse and Hound*, 23 Sept. 2004.
46. *Guardian*, 3 March 1995.

Chapter 17: Conclusion

1. The poor soils of Exmoor form a notable exception, and explain why deer-hunting continued here well into the twentieth century.

Bibliography

Primary Sources

Parliamentary Papers

Parliamentary History of England, xxxv (1800), pp. 202–14.
Parliamentary History of England, xxxvi (1802), pp. 829–54.
Hansard's Parliamentary Debates, xiv (1809), pp. 804–8, 851–3, 989–90, 1029–*1032.
Hansard's Parliamentary Debates, n.s. x (1824), pp. 130–4, 368–9, 486–96.
Hansard's Parliamentary Debates, 3rd series, xxix (1835).
Report of Select Committee on Operation of the Game Laws, xxiv (1845); ix pt 1 and pt 2 (1846).
Select Committee on Amendment of Game Laws. Minutes of Evidence, xiii (1873).
Hansard's Parliamentary Debates, 3rd series, cclxxvi (1883).
Report of the Committee on Cruelty to Wild Animals. London, 1951.
Committee of Inquiry into Hunting with Dogs in England and Wales. CD Rom. London, 2000.
Report of the Committee of Inquiry into Hunting with Dogs in England & Wales. London, 2000.

Printed Primary Sources

Acts and Ordinances of the Interregnum, 1642–1660, i–ii. Ed. C. H. Firth and R. S. Rait. London, 1911.
Alken, Henry, *The National Sports of Great Britain*. London, 1821.
Anglo-Saxon Charters. Ed. with translation and notes by A. J. Robertson. Cambridge, 1939.
Anglo-Saxon Chronicle. A Revised Translation. Ed. Dorothy Whitelock. London, 1961.
Arch, Joseph, *From Ploughtail to Parliament. An Autobiography*. Ed. Norman Willis and Alun Howkins. London, 1986.
The Art of English Shooting. London, 1777.
Assheton, Nicholas, *The Journal of Nicholas Assheton of Downham*. Ed. F. R. Raines. Chetham Soc., 14, Manchester, 1848.
The Awntyrs off Arthure at the Terne Wathelyne. Ed. Robert J. Gates. Philadelphia, PA, 1969.
[Banville, Larry], *The Banville Diaries: Journals of a Norfolk Gamekeeper, 1822–44*. Ed. Norma Virgoe and Susan Yaxley. London, 1986.
Barnes, Juliana, *Boke of Hunting*. Ed. and trans. Gunnar Tilander. Cynegetica, xi. Karlshamn, 1964.
Barry, Edward, *Bull-Baiting! A Sermon on Barbarity to God's Dumb Creation*. Reading, 1802.
Bayeux Tapestry. A Comprehensive Survey. Ed. Frank Stenton *et al.* London, 1957.

Beaufort, Henry Charles Somerset, *Hunting, by His Grace the Duke of Beaufort*. London, 2nd edn, 1886.

Beckford, Peter, *Thoughts on Hunting*. London, 1782.

Bentham, Jeremy, *A Fragment on Government, and, An Introduction to the Principles of Morals and Legislation*. Ed. Wilfrid Harrison. Oxford, 1948.

'Beroul's *Tristran*', in *Early French Tristan Poems*, i. pp. 11–199. Ed. Norris J. Lacy. Cambridge, 1998.

Blackstone, Sir William, *Commentaries on the Laws of England*, iv. Oxford, 1769.

Blaine, Delabere, *Encyclopaedia of Rural Sports*. London, 1870.

Blome, Richard, *The Gentleman's Recreation*. London, 1686.

Blundell, Nicholas, *The Great Diurnal of Nicholas Blundell of Little Crosby, Lancashire, 1702–1728*, 3 vols. Ed. Frank Tyrer, Record Society of Lancashire and Cheshire, 110–14 (1968–72).

Boke of St Albans, in Rachel Hands, *English Hawking and Hunting in the 'Boke of St Albans': A Facsimile Edition of sigs. a2-f8 of the 'Boke of St Albans' (1486)*. London, 1975.

Boorde, Andrew, *Fyrst Boke of the Introduction of Knowledge; and A Dyetary of Helth*. Ed. F. J. Furnivall. Early English Text Society, London, 1870.

Brathwaite, Richard, *The English Gentleman*. London, 1660.

Bray, William, *Sketch of a Tour into Derbyshire and Yorkshire*. London, 1783.

Brown, R. Allen, *The Norman Conquest. Documents of Medieval History*. London, 1984.

Byng, John Viscount Torrington, *The Torrington Diaries*, 4 vols. Ed. C. B. Andrews. London, 1934–8.

Caius, John, *Of English Dogges, London, 1576*, in Andrew Lang, ed., *An English Garner*, pp. 1–44. London, 1903.

A Calendar of New Forest Documents, 1244–1334. Ed. D. J. Stagg. Hampshire Record Series, iii, Winchester, 1979.

Calendar of State Papers, Domestic Series, of the Commonwealth, 1655. Ed. Mary Anne Everett Green. London, 1881.

Calendar of State Papers, Domestic Series, of the Reign of James I. 1619–1623. Ed. Mary Anne Everett Green. London, 1858.

Calendar of State Papers, Domestic Series, of the Reigns of Edward VI, Mary, Elizabeth [and James I] 1547–1625, 12 vols. Ed. Robert Lemon. London, 1856–72.

Calendar of State Papers and Manuscripts … in the Archives and Collections of Venice, xxiv–xxv. Ed. Rawdon Brown. London, 1864.

The Cely Letters, 1472–1488. Ed. Alison Hanham. London, 1975.

Chaucer, Geoffrey, 'The Knight's Tale', in Nevill Coghill, ed., *The Canterbury Tales*, pp. 42–102. London, 1951.

—— 'The Book of the Duchess', in Brian Stone, ed., *Love Visions: The Book of the Duchess, The House of Fame, The Parliament of Birds, The Legend of Good Women*, pp. 22–57. Harmondsworth, 1983.

The Chronicle of Battle Abbey. Ed. and trans. Eleanor Searle. Oxford, 1980.

Chronicle of the Third Crusade. A Translation of Itinerarium Peregrinorum et Gesta Regis Ricardi. Helen Nicholson. Aldershot, 1997.

Churchward, Robert, *A Master of Hounds Speaks*. London, [1960].

Clarke, Mrs J. Stirling, *The Habit and the Horse*. London, 1860.

Cleland, James, *The Institution of a Young Noble Man*. Oxford, 1607.

Cobbett, William, *Rural Rides*, 2 vols. London, 1853.

Cockaine, Sir Thomas, *A Short Treatise of Hunting, 1591, by Sir Thomas Cockaine*. Ed. with an introduction by W. R. Halliday. Oxford, 1932.

The Complete Family-Piece: and, Country Gentleman, and Farmer's, Best Guide. London, 2nd edn, 1737.

Cook, Colonel John, *Observations on Foxhunting*. London, 1826.

The Country Clergyman's Shrovetide Gift to His Parishioners. Sherborne, n.d.

Country Gentleman, *Remarks on the Laws Relating to the Game, and the Association set on Foot for the Preservation of it*. London, 1753.

Cox, Nicholas, *The Gentleman's Recreation*. London, 5th edn, 1706.

[Cresswell, Louise,] *Eighteen Years on Sandringham Estate, by 'the Lady Farmer'*. London, 1887.

Crosfield, Thomas, *The Diary of Thomas Crosfield*. Ed. Frederick S. Boas. London, 1935.

Cynegetica or Essays on Sporting Consisting of Observations on Hare Hunting. London, 1788.

Daniel, Revd William Barker, *Rural Sports*, 3 vols. London, 1812.

Darell, W., *A Short Discourse of the Life of Servingmen. Hereunto is also annexed a Treatise Concerning Manners and Behaviours*. London, 1578.

Delme Radcliffe, F. P., *Noble Science*. London, 1839.

The Devonshire Hunting Tapestries. Ed. George Wingfield Digby and Wendy Hefford. London, 1971.

Dialogus de Scaccario and the Constitutio Domus Regis. Ed. E. Amt and S. D. Church. Oxford, forthcoming.

Dixon, W. Scarth, *History of the Bramham Moor Hunt*. Leeds, 1898.

A Documentary History of England, 1066–1540. Ed. J. J. Bagley and P. B. Rowley. Harmondsworth, 1966.

Documents of the Baronial Movement of Reform and Rebellion, 1258–1267. Ed. R. F. Treharne and I. J. Sanders. Oxford, 1973.

Early French Tristan Poems, i. Ed. Norris J. Lacy. Cambridge, 1998.

East Anglian Miscellany, Reprinted from the East Anglian Daily Times, 1901. Ipswich, 1965.

Edie, George, *A Treatise on English Shooting; with Necessary Observations for the Young Sportsman*. London, 1772.

—— *The Art of English Shooting*. London. 1777

Egan, Pierce, *Life in London, of the Day and Night Scenes of Jerry Hawthorn, esq. and his Elegant Friend Corinthian Tom*. London, 1822; repr. 1859.

Elmhirst, Edward Pennell, *The Cream of Leicestershire*. London, 1883.

—— *The Best Season on Record: Selected and Republished from 'The Field'*. London, 1884.

Elyot, Sir Thomas, *The Boke Named the Gouvernor*, 2 vols. Ed. H. H. S. Croft. London, 1883.

English Historical Documents, 1327–1485, iv. Ed. A. R. Myers. London, 1969.

Essays on the Game Laws, now Existing in Great Britain; and Remarks on their Principal Defects. London, 1770.

Essays on Hunting. Containing Philosophical Enquiry into the Nature and Properties of the Scent. Southampton, [1782?].

Evelyn, John, *The Diary of John Evelyn, 1647–1676*, ii. Ed. Austin Dobson. London, 1906.

Familiar Essays on Interesting Subjects. London, 1787.

Fane, Lady Augusta, *Chit-Chat*. London, 1926.

The Field Hunting Year Book and Point-to-Point Record. London, 1936.

Freeman, E. A. 'The morality of field sports', *Fortnightly Review*, 6:34 (Oct. 1869), pp. 353–85.

—— 'The controversy on field sports', *Fortnightly Review*, 8:48 (Dec. 1870), pp. 674–91.

Gaimar, *Lestorie des Engles solum la Translacion Maistre Geffrei Gaimar*, ii. Ed. Thomas Duffus Hardy and Charles Trice Martin. London, 1889.

Gardiner, John Smallman, *The Art and Pleasure of Hare-Hunting*. London, 1750.

[Gascoigne, George], *The Noble Arte of Venerie or Hunting*. London, 1575.

Gerald of Wales, *The Historical Works of Giraldus Cambrensis*. Ed. Thomas Wright. London, 1863.

Gesta Stephani. The Deeds of Stephen. Ed. and trans. K. R. Potter. London, 1955.

Gillard, Frank, *The Operations of the Quorn Hounds, 1869–70*. Ed. Squire de Lisle. Wymondham, 1972.

Granger, James, *An Apology for the Brute Creation: or Abuse of Animals Censured*. London, 1772.

Grose, Francis, *The Grumbler: Containing Sixteen Essays, by the late Francis Grose*. London, 1791.

Gryndall, William, *Hawking, Hunting, Fouling and Fishing, 1596*. Facsimile repr. Amsterdam, 1972.

Harewood, Harry, *A Dictionary of Sports*. London, 1835.

Harrison, William, *The Description of England, 1587*. Ed. George Edelen. Ithaca, New York, 1968.

Hawker, James, *James Hawker's Journal: a Victorian Poacher*. Ed. Garth Christian. Oxford, 1961.

Hawker, Col. Peter, *Instructions to Young Sportsmen in all that Relates to Guns and Shooting*. Philadelphia, 1846 (1st American, from the 9th London edn).

——— *The Diary of Colonel Peter Hawker, 1802–1853*. Intro. Ralph Payne-Gallwey, 2 vols. London, 1893.

Hentzner, Paul, *A Journey into England, in the Year 1598*. Trans. Richard Bentley. Strawberry-Hill, 1757.

Homer, *The Odyssey*. Trans. Robert Fagles, intro. and notes Bernard Knox. London, 2001.

Hore, J. P., *The History of the Royal Buckhounds*. London, 1893.

Houghton, John, *A Collection for the Improvement of Husbandry and Trade*. London, 1727.

Howitt, Samuel, *Orme's Collection of British Field Sports*. Guildford, [1955].

Hunting Diary and Guide for 1913–1914. London, 1913.

I Walked by Night: Being the Life and History of the King of the Norfolk Poachers, Written by Himself. Ed. Lilias Rider Haggard. London, 1935.

Jacob, Giles, *The Compleat Sportsman*. [London], 1718.

Jefferies, Richard, *The Gamekeeper at Home & The Amateur Poacher*. Ed. David Ascoli. Oxford, 1948.

Jenyns, Soame, 'On cruelty to animals', in his *Disquisitions on Several Subjects*. London, 1782.

A Jewel for Gentrie, 1614. Facsimile repr. Amsterdam, 1977.

John of Salisbury, *Policraticus. Frivolities of Courtiers and Footprints of Philosophers: being a translation of the first, second, and third books and selections from the seventh and eighth books of the Policraticus of John of Salisbury*. Ed. Joseph B. Pike. Minneapolis, 1938.

John of Worcester, *Chronic Chronicarum. The Chronicle of John of Worcester*, iii. Ed. and trans. P. McGurk. Oxford, 1998.

Johnson, T. B., *The Hunting Directory; Containing a Compendious View of the Ancient and Modern Systems of the Chase*. London, 1830.

Kingsley, Charles, *Yeast*. London, 1897.

Knox, Vicesimus, *Essays Moral and Literary, by Vicesimus Knox*, 2 vols. Dublin, 1783.

[Lawrence, John], *A Philosophical and Practical Treatise on Horses, and on the Moral Duties of Man towards the Brute Creation*, 2 vols. London, 1796–8.

——— *British Field Sports by William Henry Scott*. London, 1818.

——— *A Practical Treatise on Breeding, Rearing, and Fattening, all Kinds of Domestic Poultry. By Bonington Moubray*. London, 5th edn, 1824.

Laws of Plato. Ed. and trans. Thomas L. Pangle. Chicago, 1980.

Letters and Papers, Foreign and Domestic, of the Reign of Henry VIII: Preserved in the Public Record Office, The British Museum and elsewhere in England, 21 vols. London, 1880–91.

Letters of Henry VIII. Extracts from the Calendar of State Papers of Henry VIII. London, 2001.

The Letters of King James VI and I. Ed. G. P. V. Akrigg. Berkeley, 1984.

Life of King Edward. Ed. F. Barlow. Oxford, 1992.

The Lisle Letters, 6 vols. Ed. Muriel St Clare Byrne. Chicago, 1981.

The Luttrell Psalter: Two Plates in Colour and One hundred and eighty-three in Monochrome from the Additional Manuscript 42130 in the British Museum. Ed. Eric George Millar. London, 1932.

M., I., *A Health to the Gentlemanly Profession of Serving Men, 1598*. Ed. A. V. Judges. Oxford, 1931.

Macaulay, James, *Essay on Cruelty to Animals*. Edinburgh, 1839.

Magna Carta. Ed. J. C. Holt. Cambridge, 1965.

Manwood, John, *A Treatise of the Laws of the Forest*. London, 1665.

Markham, Gervase, *The Gentleman's Academie. Or the Boke of St Albans. Reduced into a Better Method*. London, 1595.

Markland, George, *Pteryplegia: or, the Art of Shooting-flying. A Poem*. [Dublin], 1727.

Marshall, William, *The Rural Economy of Norfolk*, 2 vols. London, 1787.

The Master of Game, by Edward, Second Duke of York: The Oldest English Book on Hunting. Ed. W. A. Baillie-Grohman and F. Baillie-Grohman. London, 1909.

Matthew Paris, *Matthew Paris's English History*, 2 vols. Ed. J. A. Giles. London, 1852.

Medieval England, 1000–1500: a Reader. Ed. Emilie Amt. Peterborough, 2001.

The Medieval Life of King Alfred the Great. A Translation and Commentary on the Text attributed to Asser. Alfred P. Smyth. Basingstoke, 2002.

Menzies, Mrs Stuart, *Women in the Hunting Field*. London, 1913.

Mildmay, Humphrey, *Humphey Mildmay, Royalist Gentleman. Glimpses of the English Scene*. Ed. Philip Lee Ralph. New Brunswick, 1945.

Misson, Henri M., *Misson's Memoirs and Observations in his Travels over England, 1627*. Ed. John Ozell. London, 1719.

Montagu, George. *The Sportsman's Directory: or, Tractate on Gunpowder*. London, 1792.

Montaigne, Michel de, *Essays of Montaigne, Rendered into English by Charles Cotton*, 3 vols. London, 1685.

Moore, Patrick, ed., *Against Hunting: a Symposium*. London, 1965.

Moore, Thomas, *The Sin and Folly of Cruelty to Brute Animals. A Sermon*. Birmingham, 1810.

More Foxhunting by the Correspondent of the Times. London, 1937.

Moryson, F. *An Itinerary: Containing his Ten Years Travell through Twelve Dominions, 1676*, iv. Glasgow, 1908.

Neville, Sylas, *The Diary of Sylas Neville, 1767–88*. Ed. Basil Cozens-Hardy. Oxford, 1850.

Nichols, John, *The Progresses and Public Processions of Queen Elizabeth, from Original Manuscripts*, 3 vols. London, 1823.

—— *The Progresses, Processions and Magnificent Festivities of King James, from Original Manuscripts*, 4 vols. London, 1828.

—— *The History and Antiquities of the County of Leicester*, 4 vols. London, 1795–1815.

Nimrod [Charles James Apperley], *The Chace, the Road, and the Turf*. London, 1898.

—— *Life of John Mytton*. London, 1915.

O'Donoghue, Nannie Power, *Ladies on Horseback*. London, 1881.

O'Keeffe, John, *The Fox-Chace. A Favourite Hunting Song, Sung at the Grand Hunts of England*. [London?], [1790?].

Ordericus Vitalis, *The Ecclesiastical History of Orderic Vitalis*, 6 vols. Ed. and trans. Marjorie Chibnall. Oxford, 1969–80.

Osbaldiston, William, A., *The British Sportsman, or, Nobleman, Gentleman, and Farmer's Dictionary, of Recreation and Amusement*. London, [1792–96?].

Page, T., *The Art of Shooting Flying: Familiarly Explain'd by Way of Dialogue*. Norwich, 1766.

'The Parliament of the Three Ages', in John Gardner, *Alliterative Morte Arthure, The Owl and the Nightingale, and Five Other Middle English Poems in a Modernized Version with Comments on the Poems and Notes*, pp. 133–51. Carbondale, IL, 1973.

Pepys, Samuel, *The Diary of Samuel Pepys: a New and Complete Transcription*, 11 vols. Ed. Robert Latham and William Matthews. London, 1970–83.

Platter, Thomas, *Thomas Platter's Travels in England, 1599*. Trans. and ed. Clare Williams. London, 1932.

'Pleas of the Forest', ed. G. Wrottesley, in *Collections for a History of Staffordshire*, v. London, 1884.

Primatt, Humphry, *A Dissertation on the Duty of Mercy and Sin of Cruelty to Brute Animals*. London, 1791.

Queen Mary's Psalter: Miniatures and Drawings by an English Artist of the Fourteenth Century, Reproduced from Royal Ms.2B.VII in the British Museum. Ed. George Warner. London, 1912.

Race, George, *Seventy Years a Master: a Huntsman's Reminiscences*. London, [1911].

Radcliffe, Delmé, *The Noble Science*. London, 1839.

Rathgeb, Jacob, 'A True and faithful narrative of the bathing excursion, which his serene highness, Frederick, Duke of Wirtemberg … made a few years ago in the far-famed Kingdom of England, 1592', in *England as Seen by Foreigners*, ed. William B. Rye. London, 1865.

Records of the Borough of Nottingham, 1485–1547, iii. Nottingham, 1885.

Report on the Laing Manuscripts preserved in the University of Edinburgh, i. London, 1914.

Richard fitz Nigel, *Dialogus de Scaccario: The Course of the Exchequer, and Constitutio Domus Regus: the King's Household*. Ed. and trans. Charles Johnson. London, 1950.

Richardson, Charles, *The Complete Foxhunter*. London, 1908.

Richmond, Legh, *A Sermon on the Sin of Cruelty toward the Brute Creation*. Bath, 1802.

Robin Hood and Other Outlaw Tales. Ed. Stephen Knight and Thomas Ohlgren. Kalamazoo, 2000.

Roger of Howden, *The Annals of Roger de Hoveden*, 2 vols. Ed. Henry T. Riley. London, 1853.

Roger of Wendover, *Flowers of History; comprising the History of England from the Descent of the Saxons to A.D. 1235, formerly ascribed to Matthew Paris. Translated from the Latin by J. A. Giles*, 2 vols. London, 1849.

'Romance of Horn', in Judith Weiss, ed., *The Birth of Romance; An Anthology*. London, 1992.

Salt, Henry S., *Animals' Rights, considered in Relation to Social Progress*. Ed. Peter Singer. London, 1980.

—— (ed.), *Killing for Sport. Essays by Various Writers*. London, 1915.

Sassoon, Siegfried, *Memoirs of a Foxhunting Man*. Intro. by Alan Lascelles. London, 1971.

Select Pleas of the Forest. Ed. G. J. Turner. Selden Society, 13. London, 1899.

'Sir Edward Littleton's foxhunting diary, 1774–89'. Ed. M. W. Farr. *Essays in Stafford History; presented to S. A. H. Burne*. 1970.

Sir Gawain and the Green Knight. Trans. Keith Harrison; ed. Helen Cooper. Oxford, 1998.

Smith, Abraham, *Easy Lessons for Youth, Designed to Inspire the Minds of the Rising Generation with Love for God's Word, and Kindness to the Animal Creation*. London, 1838.

[Smith, Sydney], 'Proceedings of the Society for the Suppression of Vice', *Edinburgh Review*, 13 (Jan. 1809), pp. 333–43.

Smith, Thomas, *Extracts from the Diary of a Huntsman*. London, 1841.

Somervile, William, *The Chace. A Poem*. Glasgow, 1755.

The Sporting Dictionary and Rural Repository, 2 vols. London, 1803.

The Sportsman's Dictionary: Or the Country Gentleman's Companion to all Rural Recreations, 2 vols. London, 1735.

The Statutes at Large, 42 vols. Ed. Danby Pickering. Cambridge, 1762–1807.

Stockdale, Percival, *A Remonstrance against Inhumanity to Animals; and Particularly against the Savage Practice of Bull-baiting*. Alnwick, 1802.

Strabo, *The Geography of Strabo*, 8 vols. Trans. Horace L. Jones. London, 1917–32.

Stratton, Revd J., *Royal Sport. Some Facts concerning the Royal Buckhounds*. London, 1891.

Stringer, Arthur. *The Experienc'd Huntsman, or, a Collection of Observations upon the Nature and Chace of the Stagg, Buck, Hare, Fox, Martern and Otter*. Belfast, 1714.

Stuart Proclamations, 2 vols. Ed. James F. Larkin and Paul L. Hughes. Oxford, 1973–83.

Stubbes, Philip, *Anatomy of Abuses in England*. Ed. Frederick J. Furnivall. London, 1877–82.

'Summer Sunday', in John Gardner, *Alliterative Morte Arthure, The Owl and the Nightingale, and Five Other Middle English Poems in a Modernized Version with Comments on the Poems and Notes*, pp. 155–8. Carbondale, IL, 1973.

Summerhays, Reginald Sherriff, *Elements of Hunting*. London, 1938.

Surtees, Robert Smith, *Handley Cross*. London, [19??].

—— *Analysis of the Hunting Field*. London, 1846.

—— *Mr Sponge's Sporting Tour*. London, 1911.

—— *The Hunting Tours of Surtees*. Ed. with introduction by E. D. Cuming. London, 1927.

Taplin, William, *Observations on the Present State of the Game in England, in which the late Methods of Preservation are clearly Refuted and Condemned*. London, 1772.

—— *The Sporting Dictionary and Rural Repository of General Information upon Every Subject Appertaining to the Sports of the Field*, 2 vols. London, 1803.

Taylor, Helen, 'A few words on Mr. Trollope's defence of foxhunting', *Fortnightly Review*, 7/31 (Jan. 1870), pp. 63–8.

Thomas, George, Earl of Albemarle, *Fifty Years of my Life*, 2 vols. London, 1876.

Thomas, Sir William Beach, *Hunting England*. London, 1936.

Thomson, James, *The Seasons*. London, 1730.

The Tretyse off Huntyng. Ed. Anne Rooney. Brussels, 1987.

Trollope, Anthony, *Hunting Sketches*. London, 1865.

—— 'Mr. Freeman on the morality of hunting', *Fortnightly Review*, 6/36, Dec. 1869, pp. 616–25.

—— The Eustace Diamonds. Introduction by P. D. James. London, 1990.

—— The Duke's Children. Introduction by Roy Jenkins. London, 1991.

Tucker, Josiah, An Earnest and Affectionate Address to the Common People of England, concerning their Usual Recreations on Shrove Tuesday. London, n.d.

Turner, T. W., Memoirs of a Gamekeeper: Elveden, 1868–1953. London, 1954.

Twiti, William, The Art of Hunting: 1327. Ed. Bror Danielsson. Stockholm Studies in English, 37, Cynegetica. Stockholm, 1977.

von Strassburgh, Gottfried, Tristan; with the 'Tristan' of Thomas. Ed. A. T. Hatto. London, 1960, pp. 78–82.

von Uffenbach, Zacharias Conrad, London in 1710. From the Travels of Zacharias Conrad von Uffenbach. Trans. and ed. W. H. Quarrel and Margaret Mare. London, 1934.

Walter Map, De Nugis Curialium: Courtiers' Trifles. Ed. and trans. M. R. James; revised by C. N. L. Brooke and R. A. B. Mynors. Oxford, 1983.

Watson, Frederick, Hunting Pie; or the Whole Art and Craft of Foxhunting. London, [1931].

Whyte-Melville, G. J., Riding Recollections. London, 1875 (repr. 1985).

William of Malmesbury, William of Malmesbury. Gesta Regum. The History of the English Kings, i. Ed. R. A. B. Mynors, R. M. Thomson and M. Winterbottom. Oxford, 1998.

William of Newburgh, The History of William of Newburgh. Trans. Joseph Stevenson. Felinfach, 1996.

Willoughby de Broke, Richard Greville Verney, Hunting the Fox. London, 1920.

The Writings and Speeches of Oliver Cromwell: The Protectorate, 1653–55, iii. ed Wilbur Cortez Abbott. Oxford, 1988.

Yorkshire Star Chamber Proceedings, vol. 3. Ed. William Brown. Yorkshire Archaeology Society, li (1913).

Secondary Sources

Almond, Richard, 'Medieval hunting: ruling classes and the community', Medieval History, 3 (1993), 147–55.

—— Medieval Hunting. Stroud, 2003.

—— and A. J. Pollard, 'The yeomanry of Robin Hood and social terminology in fifteenth-century England', Past and Present, 170 (2001), pp. 52–77.

Amt, Emilie, Accession of Henry II in England. Woodbridge, 1993.

Anderson, K., Hunting in the Ancient World. Berkeley, 1985.

Archer, John, By a Flash and a Scare: Incendiarism, Animal Maiming, and Poaching in East Anglia, 1815–1870. Oxford, 1990.

Austin, David, 'The castle and the landscape: annual lecture to the Society for Landscape Studies', Landscape History, 6 (1984).

Bailey, Mark, A Marginal Economy? East Anglian Breckland in the Later Middle Ages. Cambridge, 1989.

—— 'Rural society', in Rosemary Horrox, ed., Fifteenth-century Attitudes. Perceptions of Society in Late Medieval England. Cambridge, 1994.

Baring, F. H., 'The making of the New Forest', English Historical Review, 27:107 (1912), pp. 513–15.

Barlow, Frank, William I and the Conquest. London, 1965.

—— The Norman Conquest and Beyond. London, 1983.

—— William Rufus. London, 1983.

Barnard, A., Hunters and Herders of Southern Africa. A Comparative Ethnography of the Khoisan Peoples. Cambridge, 1992.

Barnett, R. D., Sculptures from the North Palace of Ashurbanipal at Nineveh, 668–627 B.C. London, 1976.

[Barrow, Albert], Monarchy and the Chase. London, 1948.

Bazeley, Margaret Ley, 'The Forest of Dean in its relations with the Crown during the twelfth and thirteenth centuries', *Transactions of the Bristol and Gloucestershire Archaeological Society*, 33 (1910), pp. 153–286.

—— 'The extent of the forest in the thirteenth century', *Transactions of the Royal Historical Society*, 4th ser., 4 (1921), pp. 140–72

Beaufort, Henry Somerset, Duke of, *Fox-Hunting*. Newton Abbot, 1980.

Beaver, Dan, 'The great deer massacre: animals, honour and communication in early modern England', *Journal of British Studies*, 38:2 (1998), pp. 187–216.

—— '"Bragging and daring words": honour, property and the symbolism of the hunt in Stowe, 1590–1642', in Michael J. Braddick and John Walter, eds, *Negotiating Power in Early Modern Society: Order, Hierarchy and Subordination in Britain and Ireland*. Cambridge, 2001, pp. 149–65, 278–86.

Beer, B., *Rebellion and Riot: Popular Disorder in England during the Reign of Edward VI*. Kent, OH, 1982.

Berry, Edward, *Shakespeare and the Hunt: a Cultural and Social Study*. Cambridge, 2001.

Bevan, Elinor, *Representations of Animals in Sanctuaries of Artemis and Other Olympian Deities*, 2 vols. Oxford, 1986.

Birrell, Jean, 'Who poached the king's deer? A study in thirteenth-century crime', *Midland History*, 7 (1982), pp. 9–25.

—— 'Deer and deer farming in medieval England'. *Agricultural History Review*, 40 (1992), pp. 112–26.

—— 'A great thirteenth-century hunter: John Giffard of Brimpsfield', *Medieval Prosopography*, 15 (1994), pp. 37–66.

—— 'Peasant deer poachers in the medieval forest', in Richard Britnell and John Hatcher, eds, *Progress and Problems in Medieval England*. Cambridge, 1996, pp. 68–88.

Blackwood, Caroline, *In the Pink*. London, 1987.

Blanning, Tim, *The Pursuit of Glory: Europe 1648–1815*. London, forthcoming.

Bovill, E. W., *The England of Nimrod and Surtees, 1815–1854*. Oxford, 1959.

Broad, John, 'Whigs and deer-stealers in other guises: a return to the origins of the Black Acts', *Past and Present*, 119 (1988), pp. 56–72.

Buxton, Meriel, *Ladies of the Chase*. London, 1987.

Cantor, Leonard, 'Forests, chases, parks and warrens', in L. M. Cantor, ed., *The English Medieval Landscape*. London, 1982.

—— *The Changing English Countryside, 1400–1700*. London, 1987.

Carlton, Charles, *Charles I: the Personal Monarch*. London, 1983.

Carpenter, David, *The Minority of Henry III*. London, 1990.

Carr, Raymond, *English Foxhunting: a History*. London, 1976.

Carroll, Terence, *Diary of a Foxhunting Man*. London, 1984.

Carter, Michael J., *Peasants and Poachers: a Study in Rural Disorder in Norfolk*. Woodbridge, 1980.

Chambers, E. K., *The Elizabethan Stage*, 4 vols. Oxford, 1903–23.

Church, S. D., 'Some aspects of the royal itinerary in the twelfth century', *Thirteenth-Century England*, xi, forthcoming.

Churchward, Robert, *A Master of Hounds Speaks*. London, [1960].

Claxton, Ann, 'The sign of the dog: an examination of the Devonshire hunting tapestries', *Journal of Medieval History*, 14: 2 (1988), pp. 127–81.

Clayton, Michael, *The Chase. A Modern Guide to Foxhunting*. London, 1987.

—— *Foxhunting in Paradise*. London, 1993.

Cliffe, J. T., *The World of the Country House in Seventeenth-Century England*. New Haven, 1999.

Cole, Mary Hill, *The Portable Queen: Elizabeth and the Politics of Ceremony*. Amherst, 1999.

Contenau, Georges, *Everyday Life in Babylon and Assyria*. London, 1954.

Coss, Peter, *The Lady in Medieval England, 1000–1500*. Stroud, 1998.

Cowley, P. and N. Stace, 'The Wild Mammals (Protection) Bill: a parliamentary white elephant', *Journal of Legislative Studies*, 2 (1996), pp. 339–55.

Cox, J. Charles, *The Royal Forests of England*. London, 1905.

Cronne, H. A., 'The royal forest in the reign of Henry I', in H. A. Cronne *et al.*, eds, *Essays in British and Irish History in Honour of James Eadie Todd*. London, 1949.
—— *The Reign of Stephen, 1135–54. Anarchy in England*. London, 1970.
Crook, David, 'Clipstone Park and "Peel"', *Transactions of the Thoroton Society*, 80 (1976), pp. 35–46.
—— 'The struggle over forest boundaries in Nottinghamshire, 1218–1227', *Transactions of the Thoroton Society*, 83 (1979), pp. 35–45.
—— 'The records of forest eyres in the Public Record Office, 1179–1670', *Journal of the Society of Archivists*, 17 (1996), pp. 183–93.
—— 'The development of private hunting rights in Nottinghamshire, c. 1100–1258', *Transactions of the Thoroton Society*, 105 (2001), pp. 101–9.
—— 'The development of private hunting rights in Derbyshire, 1189–1258', *Derbyshire Archaeological Journal*, 121 (2001), pp. 232–43.
Crouch, David, *The Reign of King Stephen, 1135–1154*. London, 2000.
Cummins, John, *The Hound and the Hawk. The Art of Medieval Hunting*. London, 1988.
Daniell, Christopher, *From Norman Conquest to Magna Carta. England, 1066–1215*. London, 2003.
Darby, H. C., *Domesday England*. Cambridge, 1977.
Dawson, Giles E., 'London's bull-baiting and bear-baiting arena in 1562', *Shakespeare Quarterly*, 15: 1 (1964), pp. 97–101.
Donald, Diana, *Divided Nature: The Representation of Animals in Britain, c. 1750–1850*. New Haven and London, forthcoming.
Dorey, Zillah, *An Elizabethan Progress. The Queen's Journey into East Anglia, 1578*. Stroud, 1996.
Dyer, Christopher, *Making a Living in the Middle Ages. The People of Britain, 850–1520*. London, 2003.
Eales, J. and C. Durston, eds, *Culture of English Puritanism, 1560–1700*. Basingstoke, 1996.
Ellis, Colin D. B., *Leicestershire and the Quorn Hunt*. Leicester, 1951.
Erickson, Carolly, *The First Elizabeth*. New York, 1983.
Fairholme, Edward G., *A Century of Work for Animals. A History of the RSPCA, 1824–1924*. London, 1924.
Finch, Jonathan, '"Grass, grass, grass": foxhunting and the creation of the modern landscape', *Landscapes*, 2 (2004), pp. 41–52.
Fisher, John, 'Property rights in pheasants: landlords, farmers and the game laws, 1860–80', *Rural History*, 11: 2 (2000), pp. 165–80.
—— 'Victorian vulpicide: a hunting and shooting dispute in south Nottinghamshire', *Transactions of the Thoroton Society*, 105 (2001), pp. 123–36.
Fisher, W. R., *The Forest of Essex: Its History, Laws, Administration and Ancient Customs and the Wild Deer which Lived in it*. London, 1887.
Fowkes, D. V., 'Nottinghamshire parks in the eighteenth and nineteenth centuries', *Transactions of the Thoroton Society*, 71 (1967), pp. 72–89.
Fraser, Antonia, *King Charles II*. London, 1979.
Garner, Robert, *Political Animals: Animal Protection Politics in Britain and the United States*. Basingstoke, 1998.
Gentles, Ian, 'The management of the Crown lands, 1649–60', *Agricultural History Review*, 19 (1971), pp. 25–41.
George, Janet, *Rural Uprising: The Battle to Save Hunting with Hounds*. London, 1999.
George, J. N., *English Guns and Rifles*. Harrisburg, PA, 1947.
Gilbey, Sir Walter, *Sport in the Olden Time*. Liss, Hants, 1975.
Gillingham, John, *Richard I*. New Haven and London, 1999.
Gilmour, Ian, *Riots, Risings and Revolution: Governance and Violence in Eighteenth-century England*. London, 1992.
Grant, R., *The Royal Forests of England*. Stroud, 1990.
Grassby, Richard, 'The decline of falconry in early modern England', *Past and Present*, 157 (1997), pp. 37–62.

Greswell, W. H. P., *Forests and Deer Parks in the County of Somerset*. Taunton, 1905.

Griffin, Emma, *England's Revelry: A History of Popular Sports and Pastimes, 1660–1830*. Oxford, 2005.

Guest, Alison and Tony Jackson, *The Hunting Year*. London, 1978.

Gunn, Steven, 'Courtiers of Henry VII', in John Guy, ed., *The Tudor Monarchy*. London, 1997, pp. 163–89.

Hammersley, George, 'The revival of the forest laws under Charles I', *History*, 45 (1960), pp. 85–102.

Harrison, Brian, 'Animals and the state in nineteenth-century England', *English Historical Review*, 88 (1973), pp. 786–820.

Harwood, Dix, *Love for Animals and How it Developed in Great Britain*. New York, 1928.

Hastings, Macdonald, *English Sporting Guns and Accessories*. London, 1969.

Hatcher, John, 'England in the aftermath of the Black Death', *Past and Present*, 144 (1994), pp. 3–35.

Hay, Douglas, 'Poaching and the game laws in Cannock Chase', in Hay *et al.*, *Albion's Fatal Tree. Crime and Society in Eighteenth-Century England*. London, 1975.

Heal, Felicity and Clive Holmes, *The Gentry in England and Wales, 1500–1700*. Basingstoke, 1994.

Hey, David, *The Fiery Blades of Hallamshire: Sheffield and its Neighbourhood, 1660–1740*. Leicester, 1991.

Hibbert, Christopher, *The Virgin Queen. The Personal History of Elizabeth I*. Harmondsworth, 1990.

Hill, Christopher, *Society and Puritanism in Pre-Revolutionary England*. London, 1964 (1994 edn).

Hinde, Andrew, *England's Population. A History since the Domesday Survey*. London, 2003.

Hingston, Frederick, *Deer Parks and Deer of Great Britain*. Buckingham, 1988.

Hoffman, Michael, *Egypt before the Pharaohs. The Prehistoric Foundations of Egyptian Civilisation*. Austin, TX, 1991.

Hollister, C. Warren, 'The strange death of William Rufus', *Speculum*, 48 (1973), pp. 637–53.

Holt, J. C., *Robin Hood*. London, 1982.

Hooke, D., 'Pre-Conquest woodland: its distribution and usage', *Agricultural History Review*, 37 (1989), pp. 113–29.

Hopkins, Harry, *The Long Affray: The Poaching Wars, 1970–1914*. London, 1985.

Hotson, J. Leslie, 'Bear gardens and bear-baiting during the Commonwealth', *Publications of the Modern Language Association*, 40 (1925), pp. 276–88.

Howe, J., 'Fox hunting as ritual', *American Ethnologist*, 2 (1981), pp. 278–300.

Hull, Denison Bingham, *Hounds and Hunting in Ancient Greece*. Chicago, 1964.

Hunt, W., *The Puritan Moment. The Coming of Revolution in an English County*. Cambridge, MA, 1983.

Hutton, Ronald, *The British Republic, 1649–1660*. Basingstoke, 1990.

Isaacson, Rupert, *The Wild Host. The History and Meaning of the Hunt*. London, 2001.

Isenberg, Andrew, *The Destruction of the Bison: An Environmental History, 1750–1920*. Cambridge, 2000.

Itzkowitz, David, *Peculiar Privilege: a Social History of English Foxhunting, 1753–1885*. London, 1977.

Ives, Eric, 'Henry VIII: the political perspective', in Diarmaid MacCulloch, ed., *Reign of Henry VIII: Politics, Policy and Piety*. Basingstoke, 1995.

Jones, D. J. V., 'The poacher: a study in Victorian crime and protest', *Historical Journal*, 22: 4 (1979), pp. 825–60.

Jones, Kyle, 'Meeting the costs of the hunt', *History Today*, 53: 9 (2003), pp. 36–8.

Kean, Hilda, *Animal Rights. Political and Social Change in Britain since 1800*. London, 1998.

Keen, M. H. *The Outlaws of Medieval Legend*. London, 1961.

Kingsford, Charles Lethbridge, 'Paris Garden and the bear-baiting', *Archaeologia*, 70 (1920), pp. 155–78.

Kirby, Chester, 'The attack on the English game laws in the Forties', *Journal of Modern History*, 4 (1932), pp. 18–37.

—— 'The English game law system', *American Historical Review*, 38 (1933), pp. 240–62.

—— and Ethyn Kirby, 'The Stuart game prerogative', *English Historical Review*, 46 (1931), pp. 239–54.

Landry, Donna, *The Invention of the Countryside: Hunting, Walking, and Ecology in English Literature, 1671–1831*. Basingstoke, 2001.

Lasdun, Susan, *The English Park: Royal, Private and Public*. London, 1991.

Lee, R. B., *The !Kung San: Men, Women and Work in a Foraging Society*. Cambridge, 1979.

—— and De Vore, I., *Kalahari Hunter-Gatherers: Studies of the !Kung San and their Neighbours*. Cambridge, MA, 1976.

Lewis, Henry, ed., *Angles and Britons. O'Donnell Lectures*. Cardiff, 1963.

Liddiard, Rob, 'The deer parks of Domesday Book', *Landscapes*, 4: 1 (2003), pp. 4–23.

Longrigg, Roger, *English Squire and his Sport*. London, 1977.

Lovell, Mary S., *A Hunting Pageant*. Hindhead, Surrey, 1985.

Lyth, P., 'The deer parks of the Archbishop of York at Southwell', *Transactions of the Thoroton Society*, 90 (1986), pp. 14–29.

MacCulloch, D., *Suffolk and the Tudors*. Oxford, 1986.

MacGregor, Arthur, 'The household out of doors: the Stuart court and the animal kingdom', in Eveline Cruickshanks, ed., *The Stuart Courts*. Stroud, 2000, pp. 86–117.

McKenzie, Callum C., 'The origin of the British Field Sports Society', *International Journal of the History of Sport*, 13: 2 (1996), pp. 177–91

Madge, S. J., *The Domesday of Crown Lands: A Study of the Legislation, Surveys, and Sales of Royal Estates under the Commonwealth*. London, 1938.

Malcolmson, Robert W., *Popular Recreations in English Society, 1700–1850*. Cambridge, 1973.

Manning, Brian, *The English People and the English Revolution, 1640–1649*. London, 1976.

Manning, Roger Burrow, 'Violence and social conflict in mid-Tudor rebellions', *Journal of British Studies*, 16: 2 (1977), pp. 18–40.

——*Village Revolts: Social Protest and Popular Disturbances in England, 1509–1640*. Oxford, 1988.

——*Hunters and Poachers. A Cultural and Social History of Unlawful Hunting in England, 1485–1640*. Oxford, 1993.

Marples, Morris, *A History of Football*. London, 1954.

Martelli, George, *The Elveden Enterprise: A Story of the Second Agricultural Revolution*. London, 1952.

Mew, Karin. 'The dynamics of lordship and landscape as revealed in a Domesday study of the *Nova Foresta*', *Anglo-Norman Studies*, 23 (2000), pp. 155–66.

Munnings, Sir Alfred, *The Second Burst*. London, 1951.

Munsche, P. B., 'The game laws in Wiltshire 1750–1800', in J. S. Cockburn, ed., *Crime in England, 1550–1800*. London, 1977, pp. 210–28.

——*Gentlemen and Poachers. The English Game Laws, 1671–1831*. Cambridge, 1981.

Nelson, Janet, *Charles the Bald*. London, 1992.

Noon, Charles, *Parson Jack Russell: the Hunting Legend, 1795–1883*. Tiverton, 2000.

Oggins, Robin S., *The Kings and their Hawks: Falconry in Medieval England*. New Haven and London, 2004.

Olmstead, A. T., *History of Assyria*. Chicago, 1975.

Orme, Nicholas, *From Childhood to Chivalry. The Education of the English Kings and Aristocracy, 1100–1530*. London, 1984.

—— 'Medieval hunting: fact and fancy', in Barbara Hanawalt, ed., *Chaucer's England: Literature in Historical Context*. Minneapolis, 1992.

Parker, F. H. M., 'Some stories of deer-stealers', *Transactions of the Cumberland and Westmorland Archaeological and Antiquarian Society*, n.s. 7 (1907), pp. 1–30.

—— 'The forest of Cumberland', *Journal of the British Archaeological Association*, n.s. 15 (1909), pp. 15–20.

—— 'The forest laws and the death of William Rufus', *English Historical Review*, 27: 105 (1912), pp. 26–38.

Parker, Kenneth L., *The English Sabbath. A Study of Doctrine and Discipline from the Reformation to the Civil War*. Cambridge, 1988.

Peck, Russell A., 'The Careful Hunter in *The Parlement of the Thre Ages*', *English Literary History*, 39 (1972), pp. 333–41.

Pettit, P. A. J., *The Royal Forests of Northamptonshire: a Study in their Economy, 1558–1714*, Northamptonshire Record Soc., 23 (1968).

Pollard, Anthony James, *Imagining Robin Hood: the Late Medieval Stories in Historical Context*. London, 2004.

Pye-Smith, Charles, *Fox-Hunting. Beyond the Propaganda*. Oakham, 1997.

Rackham, Oliver, *Ancient Woodland: its History, Vegetation and Uses in England*. London, 1980.

—— *The History of the Countryside*. London, 1986.

—— *The Last Forest. The Story of Hatfield Forest*. London, 1989.

Richardson, Amanda, *The Forest, Park and Palace of Clarendon, c.1200–c.1650. Reconstructing an Actual, Conceptual and Documented Wiltshire Landscape*. Oxford, 2005.

Ridley, Jane, *Foxhunting*. London, 1990.

Ridley, Jasper, *Henry VIII*. London, 1984.

Ritvo, Harriet, *The Animal Estate: the English and Other Creatures in the Victorian Age*. Cambridge, MA, 1987.

Roberts, J., *Royal Landscape. The Gardens and Parks of Windsor*. New Haven, 1997.

Rooney, Anne, *Hunting in Middle English Literature*. Cambridge, 1993.

Ruck, Carl A. P. and Danny Staples, *The World of Classical Myth*. Durham, NC, 1994.

Ruffer, Jonathon Garnier, *The Big Shots. Edwardian Shooting Parties*. Tisbury, Wilts, 1977.

Ryder, Richard, *Animal Revolution. Changing Attitudes towards Speciesism*. Oxford, 1989.

Savage, H. L. 'Hunting in the middle ages', *Speculum*, 8 (1933), pp. 30–41.

Seddon, P. R., 'The application of forest law in Sherwood Forest, *c.* 1630–1680', *Transactions of the Thoroton Society*, 82 (1978), pp. 37–44.

Semenza, Gregory M. Colon, *Sport, Politics and Literature in the English Renaissance*. London, 2003.

Sharpe, Kevin, *Personal Rule of Charles I*. New Haven and London, 1992.

Shaw, Ian, ed., *Oxford History of Ancient Egypt*. Oxford, 2000.

Smith, Ulrica Murray, *The Magic of the Quorn*. London, 1980.

Sykes, N. J., 'The introduction of fallow deer to Britain: a zooarchaeological perspective', *Environmental Archaeology*, 9 (2004), pp. 75–83.

—— 'The Zooarchaeology of the Norman Conquest', *Anglo-Norman Studies*, 27 (2005), pp. 185–97.

Tait, James, 'The declaration of sports for Lancashire', *English Historical Review*, 32 (1917), pp. 561–8.

Taylor, Antony, '"Pig-sticking princes": royal hunting, moral outrage, and the republican opposition to animal abuse in nineteenth- and early twentieth-century Britain', *History*, 89: 293 (2004), pp. 30–48.

Taylor, Chris, 'Ravensdale Park, Derbyshire, and medieval deer coursing', *Landscape History*, 26 (2004), pp. 37–57.

Thomas, Keith, *Man and the Natural World: Changing Attitudes in England, 1500–1800*. Harmondsworth, 1984.

Thomas, Richard H., *Politics of Hunting*. Aldershot, 1983.

—— 'Hunting as a political issue', *Parliamentary Affairs*, 39 (1986), pp. 19–30.

Thompson, E. P., *Whigs and Hunters. The Origins of the Black Act*. New York, 1975.

Thompson, George, *History of the Fernie Hunt*. Leicester, 1988.

Thurley, S., 'The sports of kings', in D. Starkey, ed., *Henry VIII: a European Court in England*. London, 1991.

—— 'Palaces for a nouveau riche king', *History Today*, 41: 6 (1991), pp. 10–14.

Trench, Charles Chenevix, *The Poacher and the Squire: A History of Poaching and Game Preservation in England*. London, 1967.

—— *A History of Marksmanship*. Chicago, 1972.

Turner, E. S., *All Heaven in a Rage*. London, 1964.

Turner, James, *Reckoning with the Beast. Animals, Pain and Humanity in the Victorian Mind*. Baltimore, 1980.

Turner, Ralph V., *King John*. London, 1994.

Turville-Petre, Thorlac, '"Summer Sunday", "De tribus regibus mortuis" and "The Awntyrs off Arthur": three poems in the thirteen-line stanza', *Review of English Studies*, 25: 97 (1974), pp. 1–14.

Van Cleave Alexander, Michael, *The First of the Tudors. A Study of Henry VII and his Reign*. London, 1981.

Vincent, Nicholas. 'New charters of King Stephen with some reflections upon the royal forests during the anarchy', *English Historical Review*, 114 (1999), pp. 899–928.

Wadsworth, Waddy, *et al.*, *Vive La Chasse. A Celebration of British Field Sports Past and Present*. Brookland, Kent, 1989.

Walker, David, *The Normans in Britain*. Oxford, 1995.

Warren, W. L., *King John*. London, 1961.

—— *The Governance of Norman and Angevin England, 1086–1272*. Stanford, 1988.

Way, Twigs, *A Study of the Impact of Imparkment on the Social Landscape of Cambridgeshire and Huntingdonshire from c. 1080 to 1760*. BAR, British ser., 258. Oxford, 1997.

Webster, Bruce, *The Wars of the Roses*. London, 1998.

Weinbren, Dan. 'Against *all* cruelty: the Humanitarian League, 1891–1919', *History Workshop Journal*, 38 (1994), pp. 86–105.

White, G. H., 'The *Constitutio Domus Regis* and the king's sport', *Antiquaries Journal*, 30 (1950), pp. 52–63.

Whitehead, G. K., *Hunting and Stalking Deer in Britain through the Ages*. London, 1980.

Whyman, Susan E., *Sociability and Power in late-Stuart England: the Cultural Worlds of the Verneys, 1660–1720*. Oxford, 1999.

Wickham, Chris, 'European forests in the early middle ages: landscape of land clearance', *Settimane di Studio del Centro Italiano di Studi sull'Alto Medioevo*, 37 (1990), pp. 479–548.

Williams, James, 'Hunting, hawking and the early Tudor gentleman', *History Today*, 53: 8 (2003), pp. 21–7.

Wilson, Jean, *Entertainments for Elizabeth I*. Woodbridge, 1980.

Winsten, Stephen, *Salt and his Circle, with a Preface by Bernard Shaw*. London, 1951.

Wood, Andy, *Riot, Rebellion and Popular Politics in Early Modern England*. Basingstoke, 2002.

Woolgar, Christopher M., *The Great Household in Late Medieval England*. New Haven, 1999.

Wright, Elizabeth Cox, 'Common law in the thirteenth-century English royal forests', *Speculum*, 3: 2 (1928), pp. 166–91.

Wrigley and R. S. Schofield, *The Population History of England, 1541–1871: A Reconstruction*. London, 1981.

Young, Charles R., 'English royal forests under the Angevin kings', *Journal of British Studies*, 12: 1 (1972), pp. 1–14.

—— *The Royal Forests of Medieval England*. Leicester, 1979.

Young, Michael B., *Charles I*. Basingstoke, 1997.

Index

Acts of Parliament
    Game Law (1389), 62
    Act for Disafforestation (1653), 101
    Game Act (1671), 110–16, 153
    Black Act (1723), 108
    Prevention of Cruelty to Horses and
        Cattle (1822), 147–51
    Prohibition of Spring Guns (1827), 153
    Game Act (1831), 153–4, 158
    Protection of Animals (1835), 147, 163
    Cruelty to Animals (1849), 147
    Ground Game Act (1880), 159
    Protection of Animals (1911), 174, 175,
        205
    Protection of Animals Amendment,
        (1921), 180
    Hunting with Dogs Act (2004), 148, 222,
        228–30, 232, 233
    see also bills (parliamentary)
Albert, prince, 157, 159
Alfred, king (871–99), 12
Alken, Henry, 132
America, 3
Amos, Henry, 180
Ancient Greece, 6–7
Anglo-Saxon Chronicle, 11, 15
animal extremists, 213–14
animals, see under individual animals
Anne, princess, 193–4, 206
Anne, queen (1702–14), 105, 133
Anne Boleyn, 2, 68–9, 77
anti-hunting legislation, 173, 180, 182,
        194–6, 199, 201, 215–16, 217, 219–30
Apperley, Charles James, see 'Nimrod'

Arch, Joseph, 152, 153, 154, 159
Artemis, 6
Ashdown Forest, Sussex, 101
Ashfield, Derbyshire, 184
Association of Masters of Foxhounds, 165,
        169
Atherstone Hunt, 198
Audley End, Essex, 122
Aylesbury, Buckinghamshire, 158

badgers, 12, 59, 80, 83–4, 124
    badger-baiting, 148
Badsworth Hunt, 207
Bagshot Park, Surrey, 157
Banks, Tony, MP, 215–16, 228
Bankside, London, 98
Banwen Miners Hunt, 207
Battle, Sussex, 27
battue shooting, 119–21, 155–6
Bayeux Tapestry, 12, 14, 54, 60
beagling, 173, 187
Bear Garden, 86, 91, 97
bears, 12, 91
    bear-baiting, 85–7, 91, 98–9, 144, 146,
        147, 151, 220
Beaufort Hunt, 168–9, 177, 213
Becket, Thomas, Archbishop of Canterbury,
        28
Beckford, Peter, 127, 128, 128, 131, 137
Bedfordshire, 20, 33, 91
Bell, Ernest, 180
Belvoir Hunt, 124, 169–70, 206
Benn, Tony, MP, 200, 201
Bentham, Jeremy, 142

Berkshire, 81, 95, 173, 100, 104, 105, 157, 173, 214
Bicester and Warden Hill Hunt, 186
bills (parliamentary)
    Preventing the Practice of Bull-baiting Bill (1800), 146
    Prevention of Bull-baiting (1802), 146–7, 150
    To Prevent Malicious Cruelty to Animals (1809), 147
    Cruelty to Wild Animals (1900), 173, 176
    Protection of British Wild Animals from Cruelty (1947), 184–6
    Wild Mammals (Protection) Bill (1992), 215
    Wild Mammals (Protection) Bill (1995), 216
    Wild Mammals Hunting with Dogs (1997), 219–23, 225–6, 230
Black Acts, 108–9
Black Death, 49–50, 61, 63, 106
Blackmore Vale, Dorset, 41
Blaine, Delebere, 131, 138
Blair, Tony, 221, 230, 233
Blenheim Palace, Oxfordshire, 123
boars, 3, 7, 12, 13, 14, 20, 33, 44, 50, 56–7, 68, 80, 84, 124, 135
Boke of St Albans, 50, 79
Book of Sports, 91
bow and stable, 51–2, 55, 58
Bramham Moor Hunt, 181
Bright, John, 157–8
Bristol, 49, 168
British Field Sports Society, 181, 185, 193, 195–6, 204, 217, 218, 220, 223
Buckinghamshire, 27, 140, 157, 158, 160
buffalo, 3
bull-baiting, 86, 91, 98, 143–51 passim, 152, 164, 175, 231, 232, 233
Burns Committee, 226–7, 231
Bury St Edmunds, Suffolk, 144
Bushbridge, Surrey, 93

Cambridge, 170
Cambridgeshire, 100, 170, 204
Cambridgeshire Hunt, 165–6
Campana Forest, Derbyshire, 39
Cannock Chase Hunt, 128
Cannock Forest, Staffordshire, 43
Canterbury, Kent, 27
car followers, 4–5, 183, 188–90, 209–11, 213, 218

carted deer-hunting, 105–7, 171–2, 174, 180–1, 184, 202
cats, 46, 149
cattle, 70, 149
Charlemagne, Carolingian empire, 17
Charles, prince, 2, 206, 207
Charles I, king (1625–49), 9, 93–6, 97, 99
Charles II, king (1660–85), 102, 103–5
chase, grants of, 19–20
    see also Malvern Chase; Needwood Chase
Chaucer, Geoffrey, 53
Cheshire, 131, 137
Chiddingfold, Leconfield and Cowdray Hunt, 214
Chiddingford, Surrey, 72
Chigwell, Essex, 95
Churchward, Robert, 179–80
Civil War (1642–51), 3, 96, 97–104, 106, 109, 110, 112
Clarendon Park, Wiltshire, 65, 75, 79, 81
Clark, Alan, MP, 215
Clipstone Park, Nottinghamshire, 63
close season
    deer, 56, 83, 84
    foxes, 83
Cockaine, Thomas, 82, 83, 125
cockfighting, 85, 98–9, 142, 143, 147–50, 152, 175, 220
cockpit, 91
Cocks, Seymour, MP, 184–5, 215
Compton Verney, Warwickshire, 176
Conservative Party, 194–5, 200, 203–5, 215–17
Co-operative Party, 202–3
Cornwall, 31, 33, 207
Cottesmore Hunt, 206
Countryside Alliance, 219, 221–26, 229
Countryside March, 1 March 1988, 1, 2, 221–3, 225–6
coursing, 117–18, 123, 141, 142, 149, 171–4, 180, 184–5, 194–6, 201–2, 204, 205, 213
    see also deer-coursing
Coventry, Warwickshire, 102
Cowdray, Sussex, 79
Cox, Nicholas, 117, 118
crane, 44
Crawley and Horsham Hounds, 197
Cromwell, Oliver, 98, 101, 102, 103
Cumbria, 45, 92

Dartmoor, Devon, 71, 106
deer, 3, 4, 7, 8, 12–96 passim, 99–109, 110,

116, 121, 124, 126, 130–1, 141, 153, 162, 171, 191, 204–5, 212, 236–8
deer-coursing, 81, 162
Derbyshire, 27, 38–9, 46, 65, 81, 92, 184, 203
Devon, 33, 71, 106, 138, 196, 3, 106, 180, 202
Devon and Somerset Staghounds, 196–7
Dialogues of Aelfric, 12–15, 44, 54
dissolution of monasteries, 69, 73
dog-fighting, 147, 148, 220
dogs, lawing of, 62, 95
Domesday Book, 18, 63
Dorset, 41, 204, 207
drive hunt, 14, 23, 51–2, 55, 58
drive shoot, 155–7, 162
ducks, 93, 105

Edgar, king (957–75)
Edward the Confessor, king (1042–66), 12
Edward I, king (1272–1307), 39
Edward II, king (1307–27), 39, 50, 80, 236
Edward VI, king (1547–53), 75, 77
Edward VII, king (1901–10), 159, 160, 171–2
Edward VIII, king (1936), 177, 181
Edward, Duke of York, 50, 52, 53, 55, 57, 59
Egham, Surrey, 100
Egypt, 6–7
Elizabeth I, queen (1558–1603), 77–9, 81, 86–7, 90, 133
Elveden, Norfolk, 156, 160
Enfield Chase Hunt, 187
Essex v. Capel (1809), 140
Essex, 20, 27, 33, 95, 97, 100, 101, 104, 105, 114, 122, 137, 205
'Establishment of the King's Household', 21–2
Eton, Berkshire, 173
Exmoor, Devon, 3, 106, 180, 202

Farnham, Surrey, 102
Feckenham Forest, Worcestershire, 45, 68
fell packs, 187, 210–11
Fernie Hunt, 165, 167, 189
ferrets, 59, 83, 93, 112
fishing, 150–1, 174, 175, 185
Flintshire, 156
foot followers, 187–90, 209–11, 213, 218
football, 99
Forest Charter, 36–48 passim, 61–3, 68, 236
forest eyre, 27–8, 33, 34, 38–9, 68, 92, 94–6, 102

forest law, 15–19, 32, 33, 34, 36–7, 61, 76, 79, 90, 94–6, 112, 236, 239
Forest of Dean, Gloucestershire, 15, 27, 95–6, 105
Forest of Epping, Essex, 105
Forest of Huntingdon, Huntingdonshire, 40, 41
Forest of Pickering, Yorkshire, 42
Forest of Salcey, Northamptonshire, 95–6
Forest of the High Peak, 70
Forest of Windsor, Berkshire, 95
forests, *see under individual forests*
foxes, 12, 19, 46, 50, 65, 80, 83, 117, 124–40 passim, 211, 212, 238
    preservation of, 168, 179–80, 238
    shortage of, 135–9, 164, 168–9, 174, 179–80, 186
    trade in, 4, 137, 146, 168–9, 179, 238
foxhunting, 4, 8, 105, 113, 124–40 passim, 141, 150–1, 164, 174
    cost, 128–9, 133, 165, 177, 187–8, 206–8, 211, 217
foxhunts, *see under individual foxhunts*
Foster, Michael, MP, 219–20
    see also bills (parliamentary): Wild Mammals Hunting with Dogs (1997)
Framlingham, Suffolk, 72
France, 4, 12, 17, 33, 37, 49, 122, 135, 137, 142, 238
Freeman, E. A., 163–5, 175

Galtres Forest, Yorkshire, 94
game laws, 62, 71, 73–6, 93, 108, 110–16, 122, 123, 152–4 157–9, 236–8, 239
game preservation, 132, 136
gamekeepers, 71, 72, 73, 93, 111, 116, 152–3, 157–9, 161, 211
Gascoigne, George, 125
Gaston Phoebus, 50
George, Janet, 224, 225
George I, king (1714–27), 105
George II, king (1727–60), 105
George III, king (1760–1820), 105–6
George IV, king (1820–30), 106, 127, 132, 172
George V, king (1910–36), 160, 172
Germany, 104, 137
Glamorgan Hunt, 203
Gloucestershire, 15, 27, 43, 72, 81, 95–6, 101, 105, 168–9, 186
goats, 13, 15
Grantham, Leicestershire, 201, 213

Green Park, London, 105
Greenwood, George, MP, 170, 174, 175
Grey, Lady Jane, 77
greyhounds, 117–18
guns, 118–19, 121, 122, 154–6, 162, 238

Hampshire, 2, 17, 18–19, 20, 22, 27, 33, 45,
    72, 94, 156, 214, 33
Hampton Court, London, 69, 70, 105
hares, 12, 19, 44, 46, 47, 50, 56–7, 62,
    72, 80, 82–3, 87, 93, 110–13, 115,
    117–18, 123, 124, 126, 127, 133, 154,
    157–61, 171, 173, 184, 185, 187, 204,
    212, 237–8
Harold, king (1066), 11–12
Harrogate, Yorkshire, 181
Hartwell Park, Northamptonshire, 69
Hatfield, Hertfordshire, 70, 77
Hatfield Forest, Hertfordshire, 103
Hatfield Hunt, 134
Hawker, James, 159, 161
hawking, 70, 79, 87, 99–101
Heffer, Eric, MP, 194
Henry I, king (1100–35), 20, 23, 26, 27, 29,
    33, 65
Henry II, king (1154–89), 27–9, 32, 34,
    36–7, 39
Henry III, king (1216–72), 35, 36–9, 41, 44,
    46–7, 236
Henry V, king (1413–22), 50
Henry VI, king (1422–61), 67
Henry VII, king (1485–1509), 67–8, 74
Henry VIII, king (1509–47), 2, 68–71, 73,
    74, 77, 90
hens, 44
Heracles, 6
Hereford, 33–4
Herefordshire, 33–4, 42, 44, 102
Heseltine, Michael, MP, 214, 215
Heythrop Hunt, 186
Holkham, Norfolk, 156
Holland, 4, 137
Homer, 6
hounds, 21, 22, 29–30, 55, 83, 125–7, 129
    lawing of, 18, 36, 37
Howard, Michael, MP 214, 215
Humanitarian League, 170–6, 180, 194
Humberside, 203
Hunt Retribution Squad, 213–14
hunt saboteurs, 196–9, 212–14, 216, 221, 229
hunt servants, 44, 46, 55
hunt supporters' clubs, 189, 209

hunting
    books, manuals, treatises, 50–3, 55–6,
        57, 58, 59, 78–84, 121, 162
    dress, 131–2, 133, 165, 177, 183, 188,
        207, 208, 211, 238
    hunting horn, music, 31–2, 50–5, 57, 80,
        82, 238
    literature, 53–4, 55, 57
    ritual dissection of carcass, 53, 55, 57, 58,
        78, 80, 82, 84, 130–1
    techniques, see bow and stable; drive
        hunt; par-force hunting
    terminology, 55–6, 80, 131, 238
Huntingdonshire, 37, 40, 41, 93

Inglewood Forest, Cumbria, 45
Isabella, queen consort, 40
Isleham, Cambridgeshire, 100

James I, king (1603–25), 2, 78, 88–92, 93,
    94, 96, 111, 113
James II, king (1685–88), 105
Jefferies, Richard, 159, 161
John, king (1199–1216), 29, 30–5, 36, 96
John of Salisbury, 25, 31, 32
Justice Department, 214

Kenilworth, Leicestershire, 78–9
Kent, 27, 44, 97, 204
King, Tom, MP, 214, 215
Kingsley, Charles, 152
Kingswood Forest, Gloucestershire, 101

Labour party, 9, 184–6, 194, 195, 199–200,
    203–5, 215–16, 218, 219–30, 233, 239
Lake District, 205, 210
Lancashire, 72, 75, 91, 105, 217
Lavenham, Suffolk, 147–8
League Against Cruel Sports, 180, 193–4,
    196, 201, 202, 205, 212, 213–14, 207
Leicestershire, 20, 27, 37, 125, 130, 131, 135,
    137, 165, 177, 189, 203, 206–7, 217,
    218
Liberal Party, 204
Lincoln, 144, 204
Lincolnshire, 59, 144, 204
lions, 91
Liverpool, 213
Livingstone, Ken, MP, 227
London, 91, 137, 187, 203
Longleat, Wiltshire, 122
Loughborough, Leicestershire, 189, 218
Luttrell Psalter, 59–60

McFall, John, MP, 216
McNamara, Kevin, MP, 205, 215, 216
Magna Carta, 9, 34–5, 36
Malvern Chase, Worcestershire, 68
Manchester, 181
mantraps, 116
martens, 12, 124
Martin, Richard, MP, 147, 150
Master of Game, 50, 83
Masters of Foxhounds Association, 208, 210, 213
Melchet Forest, Wiltshire, 94
Melton Mowbray, Leicestershire, 131, 135, 177
Merstham Hunt, 135–6
Meynell, Hugo, 125–8, 131, 135
Middlesex, 148
Mid-Glamorgan, 203
Milton Keynes, 184
mink, 212
monkeys, 86
Montaigne, Michel de, 142
moorfowl, 110
motorways, 4–5, 186
Munnings, Alfred, 172

National Society for the Abolition of Cruel Sports, 196, 211
National Trust, 207, 211–12
Needwood Chase, Staffordshire, 64
Needwood Forest, Staffordshire, 79, 101–2
New Forest, Hampshire, 2, 17, 18–19, 20, 22, 27, 45
New Forest Hunt, 176, 178
'Nimrod', 128, 131, 132
Nonsuch Palace, Surrey, 69
Norfolk, 118, 121, 123, 137, 146, 154, 155, 156, 158, 160, 161, 172, 205
Norman Conquest, 3, 7–9, 11–23 passim, 55, 61, 63, 64, 111
Normandy, 33, 34
North Mimms, Hertfordshire, 74–5
North Warwickshire Hunt, 186
Northamptonshire, 42, 69, 90, 93, 95–6, 99, 101, 102, 130 137, 165
Northumbria, 40, 88, 92
Norwich, Norfolk, 146
Nottingham, 28, 86
Nottinghamshire, 27, 28, 37, 45, 46, 45, 63, 71, 86, 88, 92, 100, 101, 102, 103, 165

Odiham Park, Hampshire, 72
Odysseus, 6

Old Berkeley Hunt, 140
Old Berkshire Hunt, 186
otters, 12, 80, 83, 124
Oxford, 20, 137, 224
Oxford Parliament, 47
Oxfordshire, 20–1, 29, 27, 123, 137, 204, 224

Pamber Forest, Hampshire, 94
par-force hunting, 7–9, 52–8, 80, 146, 238
Paris, Matthew, 38, 47
parks, 3, 33–4, 47, 62, 63–6, 69, 71–2, 73, 75, 79, 81, 87, 91–2, 97, 102–3, 104–5, 106, 108, 236–7
'Parlement of the Thre Ages', 58–9
parks, *see under individual parks*
partridge, 44, 46, 59, 60, 72, 93, 110, 113, 115, 118–21, 122, 124, 140, 160, 237–8
peafowl, 44
Peasants' Revolt (1381), 47
Pengwern, Flintshire, 156
Pennine Foxhounds, 211
Petition of Barons, 47
pheasants, 19, 44, 46, 59, 72, 93, 110, 113, 115, 118–21, 122, 124, 140, 152–62 passim, 237–8
pheasantry, 122
pigs, 44, 103
Plato, 6–7
poaching, 9, 18, 43, 58–9, 73–6, 87, 100–1, 108, 110, 116, 133, 152–4, 157, 158–9, 161–2
polecat, 83
Portman Hunt, 207
Portsmouth, Hampshire, 33
poultry, 83, 149
Price, William, MP, 193
Puritans, 9, 85–7, 90–1, 99, 104, 141–2, 175
Pytchley Hunt, 129–30, 137, 178, 190, 204

Queen Mary's Psalter, 59–61
Quorn Hunt, 125–6, 131, 137, 167, 177, 183, 189, 204, 206, 218

rabbits, 12, 19, 44, 59, 62, 72, 82–3, 154, 158–61, 173, 184
railways, 4, 130, 168
Redale, Yorkshire, 74
Restoration (1660), 3, 103–5, 106, 108, 109
Richard I, king (1189–99), 29, 32–3
Richard II, king (1377–99), 62, 236
Richard III, king (1483–5), 67–8, 86

Richard fitz Nigel, 25, 29
Richmond Park, London, 105
riots, 75, 97, 100–1
Robin Hood, 67, 76, 87, 237
'Romance of Horn', 31
Royal Buckhounds, 105, 171–2, 173, 175,
　　182
royal forest, 15–21, 25–31, 33–5, 36–41,
　　65, 68–71, 75, 76, 79, 90–1, 94–6,
　　100–2, 105–6, 133, 236–7
royal progress, 69, 70, 78, 88–9, 91
RSPCA, 148, 150–1, 170, 172–3, 180, 181,
　　191–3, 212
Rushbrooke, Suffolk, 116
Rutland, 37, 93, 130
Ryder, Richard, 193

St James's Park, London, 91
Salisbury, Wiltshire, 156
Salisbury, Marchioness of, 134–5
salmon, 44, 72
Salt, Henry Stephens, 170–1, 173, 174–5,
　　180
Sandringham, Norfolk, 155, 160, 172
Scotland, 3, 39, 88, 96, 137, 217
Scott Henderson Report, 184–6, 190, 192,
　　194
Shaw, George Bernard, 170, 175
sheep, 15, 70–1, 103, 115, 149
Sherwood Forest, Nottinghamshire, 45, 63,
　　71, 92, 100, 101, 102
shooting, 132, 136, 141, 150, 152–62 passim,
　　180
shooting flying, 118–19, 162, 238
Shropshire, 33, 37, 205
Shropshire Hunt, 185
Sir Gawain and the Green Knight, 51–2, 56–7
Snelston, Derbyshire, 92
Somerset, 204, 205
South Glamorgan, 203
South Shropshire Hunt, 179
Southwark, London, 86
Southwell Deer Park, Nottinghamshire, 103
Sporting Magazine, 128, 134, 136, 137, 138,
　　179
spring guns, 116, 153
squirrels, 12, 46, 59, 124
Staffordshire, 33, 43, 64, 79, 101–2, 128
Stapleford, Leicestershire, 92
Star Chamber, 73–5, 92
Steel, David MP, 204–5, 224, 232
Stephen, king (1135–54), 26–7
Stowe, Buckinghamshire, 157

Strabo, 7
Stringer, Arthur, 125–6
Stubbes, Philip, 77, 87
Suffolk, 72, 121, 127–8, 116, 144, 147–8
Surrey, 33, 37, 72, 93, 100, 102, 157
Surtees, Robert, 130, 134, 137
Sussex, 27, 33, 37, 79, 101, 132, 156, 197,
　　214
Swaffham, Norfolk, 118
swans, 44

Talybont Hunt, 207
Taporley Hunt, 131, 137
Taunton, Somerset, 180
Thatcher, Margaret, 200–2, 205, 212, 223
Theobalds Park, Hertfordshire, 90
Thomson, James, poet, 134
traps, snares, nets etc., 14, 18, 32, 41, 44,
　　59–60, 62, 73, 74, 83, 93, 118, 131,
　　137, 184, 237
Trent, 207
Tristan, 31
Trollope, Anthony, 163–5, 166

Vale of Aylesbury Hunt, 186
Vale of White Horse Hunt, 186
venison, 43–5, 47, 64, 71, 72, 75, 76, 102,
　　106, 237
Victoria, queen (1837–1901), 148, 157, 171–2
vulpicide, 138–9, 169–70

Wales, 97, 127, 156, 207, 210
Waltham Forest, Essex, 100, 104
warren, grants of, 19–20, 46–7, 62
Warwickshire, 102, 176
Warwickshire Hunt, 220
Waters, Valerie, 198–9
West Glamorgan, 207
West Kent Foxhounds, 185
West Norfolk Hunt, 172
Whaddon Chase Hunt, 186
Wherstead, Suffolk, 121
White Hart Forest, see Blackmore Vale
Whittlewood Forest, Northamptonshire, 42
Widdecombe, Ann, MP, 215
Widdrington Castle, Northumbria, 88
wildcats, 12, 19, 46, 59, 83, 124
William I, king (1066–87), 2, 11–23 passim,
　　35, 41, 109, 236
William II, king (1087–1100), 19–20, 22, 26
William III, king (1689–1702), 105
William Twiti, 50, 57, 80
Wilton, Wiltshire, 122

Wiltshire, 65, 75, 79, 81, 94, 122, 125, 156, 186, 204, 205
Windham, William MP, 146–7, 164, 232
Windsor, Berkshire, 173, 214
Windsor Forest, Berkshire, 100, 104, 105
Windsor Great Park, Berkshire, 100, 105, 157
Windsor Little Park, Berkshire, 81
wolves, 3, 12, 21, 46, 65, 80, 135
women, 59, 61, 64, 77–9, 81, 86–7, 92, 133–5, 166–8, 176, 178–9, 182, 187, 191, 194, 208
hunting dress, 134, 166–7, 178
side saddle, 134, 166–7, 178–9
Woodstock Park, Oxfordshire, 20–1, 29
Worcestershire, 14, 33, 44, 45, 68
Worksop, Nottinghamshire, 88

Yorkshire, 20, 33, 42, 73–4, 92, 94, 105, 181, 204, 207, 210, 211